12 $\frac{50}{a}$

D1271925

GEORGE III, LORD NORTH,
AND THE PEOPLE
1779-80

GEORGE III
LORD NORTH
AND THE PEOPLE
1779-80

BY

H. BUTTERFIELD, M.A.

Professor of Modern History
in the University of Cambridge

NEW YORK / RUSSELL & RUSSELL

FIRST PUBLISHED IN 1949
REISSUED, 1968, BY RUSSELL & RUSSELL
A DIVISION OF ATHENEUM HOUSE, INC.
BY ARRANGEMENT WITH HERBERT BUTTERFIELD
L. C. CATALOG CARD NO: 68-10907
PRINTED IN THE UNITED STATES OF AMERICA

TO

G. M. TREVELYAN, O.M.

PREFACE

THE last few months of the year 1779 and the early part of 1780 saw such a heightening of political conflict in this country that the period has an unusual importance not merely in the reign of George III but in the whole panorama of English history. The drama as a whole had reached a state of tension in which many issues seemed to be rising to their crisis at the same time; and the issues themselves had become so enlarged that each of them individually had come to appear momentous. Towards the close of 1779 the ministry of Lord North sank into a state of chaos and misery almost unparalleled in modern centuries, almost unthinkable save in the special conditions of George III's general system and of North's own personal predicament. It is at this point that we see the critical moment in the development—we see the emergence into effective politics—of three movements which are of considerable importance in our general history. They are so curiously inter-connected that it is desirable to envisage the story of these particular years in one survey, and to see it as a single whole.

First there was the semi-revolutionary crisis in Ireland in the autumn of 1779, connected with the rise of the Volunteers and leading in the following April to Grattan's declaration of legislative independence. Secondly, in the closing months of 1779 we see the beginning of the most remarkable movement of extra-parliamentary opinion in the history of eighteenth-century England: namely, the Yorkshire Association, which, apart from its immediate threat to the ministry, represented the effective cradling of the programme of parliamentary reform—the first presentation of this issue on a genuinely national scale. Thirdly—and more closely connected with the Yorkshire movement than students of history have generally realized—there occurred in the early months of 1780 one of the most dramatic epochs in British parliamentary history. A remarkable opposition campaign, based initially on Burke's plan of "Economical Reform", culminated on 6 April in the passage of Dunning's famous resolution that "the influence of the crown has increased, is increasing, and ought to be diminished."

It happens to be the case that every part of the story of these three movements incessantly draws our attention to a significant issue: namely, the question of the mode in which extra-parliamentary opinion could operate upon what we often call the "unreformed house of commons". In the absence of proper channels for the operation of this factor—channels of the kind which we possess to-day—the problem became so acute that not only in Ireland but in England the situation must be described as quasi-revolutionary to a degree which the world has since forgotten. As an additional illustration of the difficulties and dangers involved in the current attempts to find ways of exerting pressure upon the proceedings of parliament, the Gordon riots were to come in June 1780 to round off the story. In one of their aspects at least they are merely a further example of what we must regard as one of the main themes of the present study.

Because the ministry of Lord North did in fact surmount the crisis of 1779–80 we to-day are tempted to underestimate the significance of the dangers which it had to meet in this period. Because the enemies of Lord North both inside parliament and in the country at large were working for an immediate result there was a sense in which they failed—they themselves realized only too vividly by the middle of 1780 that they had missed their real objectives. But, though North's ministry fell in 1782, in some respects it was rather at this earlier date that the conflict came to its climax and the system of George III was most in jeopardy. The fact that the King surmounted the dangers of this earlier period might well be regarded as more significant in the long run—a more momentous piece of history—than the fact that Lord North was compelled to resign office and leave the field for a brief interval to the hated Rockinghamites and their collaborators two years later. It would even be perhaps not too far-fetched if we were to say that the real "revolutionary moment" in this whole period of English history is the moment at which catastrophe loomed threatening, but was circumvented—was escaped by a fairly narrow margin. Our "French Revolution" is in fact that of 1780—the revolution that we escaped.

While working upon the career of Charles James Fox I have found over a long period that on the one hand the accident of repeatedly meeting new evidence and on the other hand the teasing nature of some of the problems involved have constantly drawn my attention back to the events of the years 1779–80. The sources for the life of Fox himself fail to give all the precision which a biographer must desire to attain in this period, but they are sufficient to show the very great importance of this chapter of English history in his political growth as well as in the larger story of the development of whiggism as a whole. As a result of many little re-focusings at one point and another over the range of this historical landscape, it has seemed to me that the picture has come to be set more squarely, and the things which were blurred and muddy have at last emerged more steady and clear. Without pretending to have read everything—which is no simple matter— therefore, I have attempted to re-tell what is already a famous story, hoping that the narrative will at least throw fresh light on the genesis of parliamentary reform, the emergence of the problem of Ireland, the failure of Burke and Dunning in 1780, and the whole character of the North ministry; hoping also that perhaps it will give a closer picture of England as a whole at a remarkable period of transition, a period when some extraordinary events marked what were really the growing-pains of a new world and a new era.

After reading of Lord North and indeed of George III himself so largely through the medium of a tradition that had descended from their whig enemies, I have tried not only to look at that unfortunate ministry from the inside, but also to see how the Rockingham and Shelburne whigs appeared in the eyes of the administration and the closet. Without neglecting the noble picture that seems to emerge when we read of the Rockingham- ites in the speeches of Burke and Fox, I have paid attention not only to the figure which they presented to George III, but to the way in which they appeared to Christopher Wyvill and the other more radical leaders. In all cases it is necessary to put the evidence of enemies together with the evidence of friends, though for a long time the result is liable to be blurred and needs considerable industry to bring to a proper focus. Everything is easy to the person who judges the Protestants in the ideal (or on their own evidence) and compares them with the Roman Catholics as they are in actuality (or as they appear on the evidence of their enemies); and many conjuring-tricks are possible if we interpret one political party in terms of vested interests while construing the other in terms of its higher theoretical ends. The truth is that in politics the two are entangled—on both sides we are likely to find the play of vested interests, the sheer struggle for places, profits, and power, while on both sides there will be honest men, and some justification in terms of higher purpose. To see all these things together is perhaps a more difficult kind of history both to write and to read than many people realize; but it is this kind of history which—if we can get the combination into proper focus—will give us something like the stereoscopic picture, the landscape in proper relief.

When this is achieved it will appear to some of us, perhaps, that the politics of George III's reign are more "Balkan" in character—more raggedly mixed with private and vested interests on all sides—than our traditional story assumes, though on all sides again there will shoot into the picture a streak of something which we may recognize as noble even while we disagree with it. It is not a clear case of the righteous fighting the wicked—and even the Rockinghamites (though we may love their cause), have their egotisms, their vested interests, their pettinesses and their wilful ways. At the same time even George III will be seen to have had his impressive qualities.

Sections of the following work have already been treated—though upon evidence which has been further supplemented since—in the *Cambridge Historical Journal* for 1937 and in an article in the *Transactions of the Royal Historical Society* for 1947, which I am grateful to be allowed to reproduce in part. Besides my gratitude for special kindnesses from the authorities in the Cambridge University Library, the Bodleian Library, the Manuscripts Room of the British Museum, and the Public Record Office, I must express my thanks to the King's Librarian for permission to consult the correspondence of George III at Windsor Castle; to the

Master of Trinity College, Cambridge, for much inspiration and for the loan of the papers of Charles James Fox; to the Librarian of the York City Library, for permission to see the papers in that Library relating to the Yorkshire movement, and for procuring copies of the York newspapers of the period; to the Rt. Hon. Earl Stanhope, K.G., P.C., etc. for permission to study the papers of his predecessor—Lord Mahon, in 1780—at Chevening; to His Majesty's Treasury Solicitor for permission to consult at the Record Office the minute book of the Society for Constitutional Information, as well as other documents relating to that body; to the Marquess of Abergavenny for permission to study the political papers of John Robinson when these were deposited at the British Museum some years ago; and to the Librarian of the Wiltshire Archaeological Society for the loan of *Copies of the Proceedings of the General Meetings of the County of Wiltshire*. I owe most grateful thanks also to my wife for help in the correction of proofs, and to Mrs Bogle for great assistance in the proofs and the preparation of the Index.

CONTENTS

Part I

THE VICISSITUDES OF LORD NORTH, 1779

Chapter I

INTRODUCTION

§I. GEORGE III

AMONGST the private papers of George III at Windsor Castle—and lying in the neighbourhood of such of these as belong to the year 1772—is an undated document which begins as follows:

It has been my lot to change so frequently Administrations & those out of place have ever laid the blame on Me, that I owe it to myself to write an exact narrative of the principal transactions of my Reign without making any Reflection on them . . . I mean them chiefly for the instruction of my son.

Only a little over a page of this autobiographical fragment exists, and its last sentence is a note on George's policy at the very opening of his reign:

The only difference of conduct I adopted was to put an end to those unhappy distinctions of party called Whigs and Torys, by declaring I would countenance every Man that supported my Administration and concurred in that form of Government which had been so wisely established by the Revolution.[1]

The title of "whig" could still be taken—and indeed often was taken—to denote the men who swore by the revolution of 1688 and favoured the importation of the Hanoverian dynasty into England. On this view both George III and Lord North could legitimately take pride in the fact that they themselves belonged to the whig tradition. George, when he came to the throne in 1760, could regard the "Glorious" revolution and the Hanoverian succession as closed issues—no longer the peculiar fighting-creed of those whig connections which had so long profited from them, no longer the symbols of the achievement or the victory of a mere party. Both

[1] Windsor Castle Mss. George III, Private I, 1755–82, f. 15, 672.

had become the heritage of the British people everywhere, and he accepted them fully, as a monarch of his dynasty was bound to do in any case. Great alterations in the manner of governing the country, however—great changes in the distribution of power—had been taking place in the generation before his accession; and these had occurred not by virtue of anything in the Bill of Rights or the Act of Settlement, for example, but partly as a result of the fact that the whig connections had made the revolution their own property —had established a monopoly in the Hanoverian régime. So it came about that George III found it necessary to combat what both he and his grandfather regarded as the unauthorized political and constitutional developments which had been allowed to occur in Great Britain since 1714. Neither he nor the great body of his subjects was yet prepared to accept as recognized "conventions of the constitution" those political practices, those anomalies and usurpations, by means of which under the first two Georges a combination of whig aristocrats had been able to engross political power. George III might well feel himself the champion of a popular purpose and a public cause when he set out to break the power of these whig oligarchs and to recapture for the crown that authority which had been enjoyed by William III. He hoped to rid the country of a division which had now become meaningless and abolish party-names, which had been allowed to continue too long merely to provide the excuse for a policy of proscription. Coming to the throne at the age of twenty-two, and thinking perhaps too much in terms of the ideas of a previous generation, he counted on being the benevolent father of his country, the pattern of a "Patriot King".

The whig aristocrats—besides the tremendous patronage which they enjoyed as territorial magnates—had captured for their use that rich fund of offices, sinecures, pensions, and the like, which constituted the patronage and the bounty of the crown. It was to be a question whether a bishop who in fact had been promoted by the Duke of Newcastle would ever be brought to remember that the real source of the favour he enjoyed—the real fountain of honour in the state—was still the monarch himself. Combining the two sources of "influence"—the aristocratic and the governmental— the whig leaders had made themselves formidable, and had been able to stand as an independent power in the face of the king. It was this usurpation that George III attacked, as he was bound to do if he was to keep to his initial intention, that is to say, if he was to prevent office and favour from being confined to the adherents of a single party. Furthermore, George, who would have found his opinion echoed by many independent people in the country, objected to the way in which this natural system of patronage had been screwed up and made taut—and turned into too direct a mode of control over parties and votes—in the course of the century. He knew that if he could command the system he could destroy its evils—he was the only person who could rid the country of corruption. Then, as he once wrote to Bute, "our memories" would be "respected and esteemed to the end of time".

Never was a youthful dream so turned to ashes. Never was a noble purpose so twisted and torn as it began to move and assert itself in the world of concrete things—began to struggle in a universe of tricks and chances. When we study the reign of George III it is always necessary to remember that this is not what he intended it to be—what we see is not what he wanted to happen, and what he himself did is not at all what he set out to do. We imagine too often that a single man's purposes can make history, and the righteous are often deceived because they think that a good intent gives an individual a claim to exercise a certain kind of sovereignty over the affairs of human beings. It is easy to forget that in the world one human will must mix and mingle with countless other wills; and the result—the piece of tapestry actually produced by the processes of history—is a compounding and a composition between these; like the music of an orchestra, it is a complicated result that depends on inter-actions and harmonies. At the same time, those who are obstinately well-intentioned—the men like George III—are too prone to overlook the fact that other individuals, equally valid, equally self-acting, equally well-intentioned, have their own view of what is "the good", or what is the next turn that ought to be given to human history. He who sets out to achieve a good purpose regardless of these other people—and *coûte qui coûte*—must take care of his soul, for he sins by self-righteousness. He must be prepared to find that, even if only in the conflict with other people's good intentions, he may do more harm than any of the abuses he has had it in mind to remove.

From the earliest years of the reign, George's policy had the effect of multiplying and enlarging the very evils which it had been his dream to see annihilated. Precisely because he was so conscious of his rectitude he could not bear to be beaten, and he was willing, when it came to the point, even to fight corruption with more corruption. Having embarked upon this course, he was bound perhaps to remain a prisoner of the system so long as the whig oligarchy remained in a position to challenge his policy and his régime. Henceforward, in any case, we see George III not as he meant to rule, not as he had set out to be; and the system which he came to personify would never even have presented itself in his mind to be chosen as the next-best-thing. What we have to observe is the plan of government to which he was compelled to resort in order to fight the whig oligarchy—a poor, make-shift interim system, a necessary evil, to be borne until the whig magnates had decided to abandon the struggle. It was hardly even a plan of government, but rather a plan of campaign—a chain of emergency-measures and desperation-policies on the part of a king who could not have what he wanted and had to clutch at anything within reach if he was to keep head above water at all. The dice were loaded in his favour for the purpose of the particular game that he had to play against the main body of the whigs, because he controlled his own patronage now, and because the men who were politically effective in the country were biassed in favour of order and government in any case. Fortunately for the King the course of events during the century since 1660 had brought additional weight to monarchical authority, and had even helped to undo some of the effects of the revolution of 1688, by adding to that "influence" of the crown which was now said to be more dangerous than the ancient "prerogative". The growth of commerce and industry and the spread of empire had multiplied the exchequer officials, the custom-house officers, the colonial places, the government contracts, so that the patronage at the disposal of a ministry had expanded more than the whigs of 1688 would ever have dreamed to be possible. These reasons, rather than any particular viciousness in George III, explain the increasing significance of the problem of corruption during his reign.

Henceforward, also, George was so hemmed in by the opponents of his system—reduced to such desperate straits by the clamour of parties and by the coalition of his enemies—that time after time, though he was able to form ministries and keep his head above water, he found it impossible to establish the multi-party government he had hoped for, or to put into office the trusted first minister he so desired to have. No one needed advice and hungered for counsel so much as George III—no one so cast about to find at each moment the person who would tell him what to do, or confirm his own judgment, or at least hold his hand in the darkness. No king was prepared to do more and to suffer more—as we shall see—provided it was for a first minister in whose loyalty he could really have confidence; and at the beginning of his reign nothing could have been more pathetic than his childish faith in Bute. It was perhaps not an unreasonable claim that he made in these days when kings were not at all supposed to be mere figureheads—the claim that the chief minister should be a man in whom he could trust, a man who would be faithful to him personally. As it was, he might defeat his enemies on particular issues, but he could not choose his first minister where he wanted—could not select a government freely in the free air. He had to take anybody who was willing to fight the hostile whig combination, and once for a moment, in 1765–66, he had to allow his enemies—now under the leadership of Rockingham—to establish themselves in office. From the time of George Grenville in 1763 the first minister might have to be a man not of the first rank in ability, even a man not at all after George III's heart. This being the case, George, still needing counsel—still needing to be told how he must handle even his first minister—would resort to one man here or another one there, seeking the advice on which he could rely, privately consulting people who were not constitutionally responsible for the suggestions they made. On occasion he would even be in the position of conspiring to thwart or to overthrow his own chief minister. So, to the acknowledged abuses of the time, there was added the evil of "closet-influence" and "unconstitutional advice". Now, therefore, his whig enemies had a further article upon which they were able to indict his government.

In this conflict between the King and the main body of the whigs, the supporters of the royal authority thought that they were saving the country from enslavement to a proscriptive aristocratic clique, a Venetian oligarchy. The opponents of George III felt sure that a royal victory at this time would mean, now or later, the establishment of a permanent despotic system. We to-day know that either of these alternatives might have been evil, but, when we resurrect such old quarrels, we ourselves are under a limitation, for we cannot empty our minds of the knowledge that we possess of after-events. We may well be sceptical—may well feel that each party to the struggle was guilty of over-dramatizing the issue to a certain degree. The politician sees contemporary events as too cataclysmic—he thinks that all the future depends on *this* fight; and sometimes he does not discern the deeper kind of history-making that is to transform the whole situation in any case. To see more than George III could see in the minds of his opponents—to know more than politicians consent to learn of the thinking of their political enemies—and to discern those deeper movements which the actors in the story fail to take account of, but which come like the beat of an ocean-wave to deflect and over-ride their purposes—these are the reasons why we study history.

In the reign of George III even the battle between the King and the aristocracy is only the surface-drama, and if we mark it as the ruling theme we do so only at the first level of analysis. It is one of the ironies of the story that in this battle neither of the contestants really defeated the other—neither the King nor the aristocracy was to have the victory—and, though each thought that the whole of the future hung upon his success in this conflict, liberty was saved rather because they fought one another, and because neither of them won, so that a third party could rise and run away with the spoil. Below this surface-drama is a movement long, slow, and deep, and to see something of its progress—to hear its rumbling—is one of the primary objects of the present study. We must conceive it not as a conflict but as a tide—one which throughout the century is bringing wider classes of Englishmen to intellectual awareness and a realization of the part they might play in politics. John Wesley, John Wilkes, and Lord George Gordon are only the most famous examples of those who led this movement, or used it for their purposes, and thereby added to its power. Behind them all the progress in society—all the advance in education, the spread of literature, and the growth of towns—was changing the character of the world itself. Greater masses of people were being brought by various means to a consciousness of their importance, a sense of their public rights, a habit of local self-help and an interest in the destiny of their nation.

In 1768 John Wilkes returned from France, though an outlaw. He knew that for offences committed years before he would in fact have to go to gaol. He was in great need of money and he had determined to retrieve his fortunes by a sensational intervention in English politics. The government of the day—the government of the Duke of Grafton—knew that it was dangerous to lay hands on him, and they had determined not to touch him lest they should assist him in his project of becoming a martyr. He not only secured election to parliament by the freeholders of Middlesex, however— he determined that the government should not be allowed to wash their hands of him, and he provoked them more and more extravagantly, until he compelled them to take notice, and indeed to proceed against him. He was expelled from the house of commons but he was repeatedly re-elected, in spite of the fact that the house had declared that the sentence of expulsion had made him ineligible for any parliamentary seat, at least for the time being. On the argument that votes polled for a man who was not qualified to stand could be treated merely as spoiled votes, his rival, Colonel Luttrell—though his poll had been inferior to that of Wilkes—was finally adjudged the properly-elected candidate. It could be argued that the government had interfered with an election and that the corrupt majority which it possessed in the house of commons had appointed its own nominee as member for Middlesex, in disregard of the duly-recorded wishes of the electors. Petitions rained upon the King from town and county, since by the offence to the electors of Middlesex a blow had been struck at the rights of freeholders everywhere. That new factor, extra-parliamentary opinion, made itself

felt as never before in the country, and began to throw up new
leaders, to whom the existing aristocratic methods in politics and
the aristocratic form of the government seemed packed with
anachronisms and abuses. With the clamour of the people behind
them, the various factions of the opposition united on the issue of
the Middlesex election, and inside parliament itself a formidable
combination now confronted the ministry. This is the period, also,
when the famous *Letters of Junius* scandalized the world and regis-
tered the intensity of the political situation. Here indeed was one of
the great crises of the reign of George III, and in the uproar of
1769-70 the government was in danger for a period. The first
minister, Grafton, broke before the storm and resigned, though
George III's system survived, as Lord North took over the leadership. By North's skilful debating-tactics the situation was rectified
inside parliament. Outside, in the country at large, the agitation
soon died down.

North was a man in whose loyalty George III could trust. We
might imagine—as the King himself did—that here at last was one
who could genuinely play the part of "confidential minister". After
his experience in 1770, however, George had one misgiving. Grafton had deserted him precisely when he needed him most, precisely
in that dangerous crisis which only the firmest determination could
surmount. He felt it as a betrayal. Over and over again the misgiving
seems to return to his mind. Lord North must never desert him at a
crisis as the Duke of Grafton had done.

§II. PARTY IN THE EIGHTEENTH CENTURY

The political world with which we are confronted in the eighteenth
century is already visible in the reign of Charles II. There is a
re-distribution of forces and a new setting of the stage from this
time, and the eighteenth-century situations, problems, idioms and
patterns are already visible. To take merely a single example, the
old conflict against "prerogative" is already in process of transformation and is turning into the fight against royal "influence".
Ages of history, however, overlap, and curious throw-backs occur,

or it will happen that, as the world changes, men are slow in making their mental adjustments. In a sense the revolution of 1688 and the Hanoverian succession have reference to the older state of things; they rule off the earlier story of the direct fight against the prerogative. The old issues between whig and tory ceased to have relevance in the succeeding age, and if in certain localities the tory and high-church squire might continue his antique prejudices for a long time even now—if rival families would maintain the labels of whiggism and toryism to cover their factiousness or their local rivalries—still it could not be said that Jacobitism went on being an authentic issue of parliamentary politics. There was no important religious conflict to sharpen the edge of the older type of high-church toryism; Bolingbroke, for example, emphatically denied that he was at issue with Walpole on ecclesiastical questions. And if the whigs succeeded in placing their enemies under proscription in the early Hanoverian days, it was the tories who tended to become anti-government and even anti-king—tended, like Bolingbroke himself, to attack the tyranny of the executive.

In reality there was an anarchy of party, a problem that exercised the minds of many politicians and theorists. If we remember that nothing is simple—remember still that the old age overlaps into the new one, that old prejudices linger, and that contemporaries can never see themselves in perspective or clear up their own situation as the later historian is sometimes able to do—we may say that the real "party" in the Hanoverian period, the real structure of politics, was based on the principle of "connection". At its simplest the unit is a magnate with his relations, dependents, agents and friends, or possibly there is an alliance of a number of such magnates and their dynastic systems. Most people would seem to have been born into the particular connection to which they belonged, or at least the matter was rarely one of serious choice; for men would drift into one set or another by reason of friendships at school, or the attractions of a certain social circle, or marriage alliances, or the idea that here was a good prospect of promotion. Admiration for a certain politician—for the elder Pitt at one time, for Fox at another—might draw some people into a connection, creating within it a circle held together by a personal attachment. The various groups might make alliances for longer or shorter periods; or a particular two might be distinguished by an extraordinary hatred of one another. One of these connections might split up into various parts —the Temple faction was once divided into three, each under a separate leader, and each going its own way, but all combining again for a time at a later date. On the other hand a particular circle might be attached more or less loosely to one of the great connections, as happened with the friends of Charles James Fox, skirmishing somewhat freely at first at the side of the Rockingham whigs. A curious illustration of the mixtures and confusions of the eighteenth century is the fact that George III, as we have already seen, in his attack on "party", said that he proposed to abolish the distinctions of "whig and tory". Yet, in his mind, his chief concern in opposing the principle of "party" was rather to break the old "connections"; and this adds point to the determination of the Rockinghamites to come to power all together or not at all.

The co-existence of a number of these connections gave eighteenth-century politics some of the features of the French group-system. The government at a given moment was likely to contain a combination of various groups; and we do not expect normally to see the dismissal of a whole ministry and its replacement by a party of men who have previously been in opposition. A change of ministry—the fall of Walpole for example in 1742—was likely to produce a re-shuffling of the various groups; and the new government was likely for the most part to contain a repetition of the personnel of the preceding one. A government was weak if the parties composing it were at friction with one another, straining and chafing under an uneasy alliance. The kind of blow that the head of a ministry feared was the secession of one of the factions upon whose support he depended in parliament—a secession which would tend to come if he had failed to attach a group to his administration by giving it sufficient vested interests, an adequate number of promotions and pensions. And cabinets tended to be destroyed chiefly as a result of the cleavages within themselves; for an adverse parliamentary vote tended to be the effect rather than a cause of the disintegration of a ministry. Much, therefore, was bound to depend upon the negotiations that took place between the various groups, or within the alliances.

Further than this, we must be careful not to assume that the "connections" of the eighteenth century represented varying policies or diverging principles, though occasionally it would happen that a given group would identify itself with some particular object. It would even be the case sometimes that the divergences within a single group were greater than any that divided the groups from one another. Chatham and his brother-in-law, Grenville, were poles apart on the subject of the American colonies. Burke and Fox differed more greatly at a later date (on the subject of parliamentary reform for example) than either of them differed in general from the younger Pitt. The transition from parties based on traditional connection to the modern form of parties based on differences of principle was much more subtle and difficult than many people imagine. It was made still more difficult because—like one film super-imposed upon the pattern of another—there still survived till it was almost anachronistic, or a mere handle for political abuse, a vague cross-division based on old ideas of whig and tory. The transition to the modern conception of party has itself been more slow than many people have realized, and still the old age has tended to survive into the new. As long as there remained families traditionally tory, as long as it was true that a child was actually born a little liberal or a little conservative, there existed even in modern "party" something of a paradox—namely, a cohesive principle derived from old "connection".

This whole pattern of eighteenth-century politics—which we must not imagine as discoverable in its absolute purity, or as inconsistent with the co-existence of independent gentry who would make a virtue of the fact that they had no "party"—would hardly have become so marked if there had been a great and authentic political issue to divide the nation after 1714. The reason for opposition to government under this system, was—to a degree which is often not appreciated—a private one, a matter of vested interest. It was rancour against a minister who had proscribed a certain group or had disappointed the expectations of a particular set of supporters. And rarely was it an initial difference in principle or policy that caused a man to withdraw his support from a government. Indeed, if it were known that you were attached to a particular point of principle, you might be permitted to vote, say, against a government bill, for the simple reason that it was so clear to everybody that you were not to be construed as voting for the overthrow of the ministry. Once in opposition, however, you would never be at a loss for principles and policies to adopt, and for issues on which to attack the men who happened to hold office at the moment. What existed in fact was something that we can almost call a stock opposition programme changing little throughout the reigns of the three Georges, a set of criticisms that could be directed against any ministry that happened to be in power, whether the men out of office were of a connection that could be called "whig" or were the survival of the tory party of Queen Anne's reign. Bolingbroke could claim that he rather than Walpole was the real heir of the principles of the seventeenth-century whigs. His works provided material for the radical leaders of 1780,[1] and his arguments against the government of Walpole were repeated by the enemies of George III. Bolingbroke organized the system and party of opposition in Hanoverian England, and much of the programme that he codified on principles taken from Davenant passed into the whiggism of Charles James Fox.

If you were out of office you could always cry out against "corruption", though, as Bolingbroke himself had discovered, you would use this form of influence, and perhaps you could not exist without it, once you had come into power. Similarly, if you were out of office you complained of the subservience of the house of commons to the ministers, and you attacked everything that could be regarded as an encroachment on the part of the executive government. You tiraded against standing armies or fortifications, which you could regard as a threat to liberty. Bills to prevent placemen from sitting in the house of commons, attacks on rotten boroughs, the insistence on the right of constituents to send instruc-

---

[1] In the *London Courant*, 6 Jan. 1780, for example, Metullus writes of Bolingbroke as "The ablest defender of our liberties and the noblest asserter of the excellence of our constitution as it was established at the Revolution." Cf. my *Statecraft of Machiavelli*, 1940, IV, "Machiavelli and Bolingbroke".

tions to members of parliament, protests against the Septennial Act, were part of your stock-in-trade. You did not spare the king himself, but attacked the expenses of his civil list, or the undue subservience of British foreign policy to Hanoverian interests. Because in these days the king was identified with the government, and a partner of the men in power—not yet a mere umpire between the parties—it was still true that opposition to the government meant opposition to the king. It often happened, therefore, that under all the three Georges the opposition—or part of it—would attach itself to the Prince of Wales and support him in his quarrels with his father or speculate on the chance of his early succession. For this and for other reasons we must hold the view that opposition was not yet regularized or assimilated into the constitution. The men in opposition would attack the very things they themselves would have to do if ever they came to power. When you were out of office you tended indeed to advocate policies which at that date would have made executive government impossible.

Even when Burke stated the case for "party" in 1769, in his *Thoughts on the Cause of the Present Discontents,* it was urged against him that he had no "programme" in the modern sense of the word, no end save to see the Rockinghamites in power, nothing to put before his connection save the overthrow of George III's system. His arguments in favour of the party of the Duke of Newcastle were "long possession of government; vast property; obligations of favour given and received; connection of office; ties of blood, of alliance, of friendship; and the name of whig, dear to the majority of the people". Even at the end of his career and in the days of the French Revolution he declared that his attachment to the Rockinghamite party had been based on the principle of aristocratic government as such. He is definitely of the eighteenth century, therefore, and his political theory does not by any means replace old connection by modern party. Yet he contributed to the education of the Rockinghamites, and weaned them from mere wilfulness of opposition. He taught them what by their history and their situation they were in a better position to learn than other opposition factions: namely to assume a responsible attitude; to behave as people who had a right to govern the country and who would soon be governing it again; to avoid therefore those policies in opposition which tended to undermine the system of aristocratic government itself. He taught them to beware of such things as "instructions from constituents", annual parliaments, etc., which it was easy for men out of office, mere seekers of popularity, to demand.

George III's attempt to break the power of the main body of the whigs, who acted first under the Duke of Newcastle and then under the Marquess of Rockingham, was bound to produce its effects on the character of that party. He presented them with an issue which involved the whole question of the rôle of the monarch in the constitution—one, therefore, which raised fundamental problems concerning the nature of the state itself. The war with the American colonies brought a more tangible issue for party-conflict; for though the Americans claimed to be revolting against the legislative authority of the parliament in Westminster, the whigs insisted that George III was the essential enemy. George himself took this issue as a "test" and made the war peculiarly his own—nobody could serve him in office or pretend to be on his side who opposed the attempt to reduce the American colonies to obedience. And because a success overseas would have contributed to his victory at home, the domestic issue and the colonial one were kneaded into the same single lump of dough, and all the traditional doctrines of liberty were mixed and moulded into the compound. So long as the American war continued the country was divided on a great issue, therefore; and the Rockinghamites, because they were out of office, were put into a position to resume more genuine contact with the doctrines of seventeenth-century whiggism. They did not like the policy of imposing "tests" on candidates for election to parliament, however—did not like the idea of making an election depend upon the commitments to support a certain programme instead of commitments to act with a certain body of men.

On the other hand, Wilkes, after his return to politics in 1768, and his successes in Middlesex, had founded something which was a party in a different sense. His followers lacked all that Burke had prized—traditional experience in government, vast property, ties of blood, the power of patronage, high connections, and even the name of whig. They lacked the things which gave influence and a "respectable" appearance in the England of the eighteenth century; and precisely because they were disinherited in a sense, they might even run to wildness, lacking the responsibilities that helped in those days to keep men sober and reliable. This party, representing the rise of a new kind of world, had no principle of cohesion save an engagement to support certain articles in a programme. It demanded "tests" for candidates in parliamentary elections, instructions from constituents, place-bills, shorter parliaments, and a reform in the representative system. Both by its own character and through the social changes of which it was the symptom it was calculated to raise, in a more authentic manner than the factious opposition parties earlier in the century, the issue of the relations between members of parliament and the constituencies. It had the raggedness which many movements have in their early stages; but it was the herald of a new age.

§III. LORD NORTH

Just after the middle of September 1777, when North had already on many occasions complained "that he found his Health much impaired, his abilities Fail, and his Mind inervated, and that he was unable to bear the Anxieties and Distress", it was brought to the King's attention that his depressions and his drooping spirit were partly to be accounted for by the situation of his private affairs. George wrote to him:

I ... must insist You will now state to me whether 12, or £15,000. will not set Your affairs in order if it will, nay if £20,000. is necessary I am resolved You shall have no other person concerned in freeing them but myself ... You know me very ill if you do not think that of all the letters I have ever wrote to You this one gives me the most pleasure, and I want no other return but Your being convinced that I love You as well as a Man of Worth as I esteem You as a Minister; Your conduct at a critical minute I never can forget.[1]

[1] [Sir John Fortescue, The] Corr[espondence of King] George III (1927–28), III, 474–80. (By kind permission of the King's Librarian I have checked these with the originals at Windsor Castle) Cf. H[istorical] M[anuscripts] C[ommission, 10th Report, Appendix, Part VI] Abergavenny Mss., No. 146; and [British Museum] Add. Mss. 37,833, J. Robinson to George III, Sept. 1777.

It is not to be suggested that, in the subsequent transaction which relieved North of his burden of debt, anything took place between the King and the minister that would be dishonourable to either. In spite of the controversies that have taken place on the subject, however, it must be regarded as beyond doubt that North at this time not only made an important private resolution, but committed himself to the King by a promise that was later to give him some embarrassment. Only a few weeks after the opening of the negotiation which led to the payment of his debts North revealed the situation to Thurlow in a letter which he asked to be kept "a profound secret". In this letter he made an overture to Thurlow, and the most important point that he had to communicate to him was the promise that he should be granted "the first Chief Justice's place that shall be vacant". North then addressed himself to the problem that might well come uppermost in the mind of the lawyer to whom he was writing—the question whether the ministry would endure, whether a promise for the future was a thing upon which it would be safe to place any reliance. North wrote:

Perhaps you may think it of some consequence to your determination that I should say something of my own intention; I certainly always have wished and do still wish to quit my present situation and will take the first fair and honourable opportunity of doing it; but I am under such obligations to the King that I can never leave his service while he desires me to remain in it and thinks I can be of any use to him; which he possibly may as long as I continue in the House of Commons.

If North, who so often complained of the burdens of office, felt committed to staying at the head of the ministry, if necessary until the death of his father removed him to the house of lords, this was more than an ordinary effect of a natural gratitude—it was a matter that had been talked over with the King. That there was an actual promise and that it was regarded as having a long-term validity, however, is proved by another letter to Thurlow, of two years later, 8 November 1779—a letter which does not seem to have been brought into the discussion of this question, though in fact it completes the chain of argument. North asks through Thurlow, now Lord Chancellor, that the King shall interpret in a certain way "My resolution of not deserting him".[1] It cannot be doubted, however, that a "resolution" which has been communicated to the King in this way, and which is presented as a matter to be "interpreted" in some mode or another, is more than a resolution—it is a promise and commitment. North may often have undertaken that he would not "desert" in the way the Duke of Grafton had done; but, on this occasion, the same promise, if even in the same form of words, had assumed a more binding character. He was to remain at the service of the King until he was virtually granted a release.

He might have broken even such a promise as this, but in moments of terrible humiliation and bitter anguish, it was the one thing he did not do. The tragic nature of his position was emphasized by the fact that only a few weeks later came the news of the capitulation of Saratoga and his authentic sorrow, his genuine martyrdom, now began. On the other hand, he mooned and whimpered and declared that he was "tied to the stake", and some men wondered why in the circumstances he endured the misery. It was notorious—it was a matter of taunt even in parliamentary debate—that he declared his unwillingness to hold the office of first minister, his desire to be relieved of the burden, his sense of his own incapacity. We read even in the newspapers that he was anxious to resign but that "a certain Great Person would not permit him." To the King he would write, not resigning from office, but repeatedly asking for release, persuading him, beseeching him, and wearying him with his importunity. In his capacity as the King's responsible adviser he would give it as his official opinion that his own continuance in office would only be a disaster for the country and the crown. On his own private behalf he would complain of illness, depression of mind, loss of memory and general unfitness for the post that he held. Men near to the King were surprised that he remained in office, after his pathetic cries for release, and even conjectured that his griefs and appeals and importunities were but the

[1] British Museum, Egerton Mss. 2,232 (transcripts) f.17.

cover for a secret determination to cling to power. In his fidelity to the King, indeed, he endured distress and humiliation under conditions which no other ministry in England ever suffered and survived.

In desiring North to remain in office in this way the King was moved, as he would confess on occasion, by the man's utility and success in the house of commons. Here, more than anywhere else, North seems to have enjoyed his duties, and here it was known that his work did not suffer, as so often it did in other fields, from his inability to fix his attention upon it. Here, also, he kept his good humour and his patience, very seldom losing his temper, and showing a whimsical, attractive disposition. He was disarming in his self-depreciation, unexpectedly frank in some of his confessions, courteous and complimentary to his enemies; and he could goad the opposition by his air of imperturbability while refusing to be goaded as a rule himself. He could turn off the edge of an attack with much humour and was most brilliant and tantalizing and charming in his tricks of evasive action, when he accepted all the arguments of the other side, and merely showed that they were inapplicable to him and to the present case. It is often said that all the debating-talent was on the side of the opposition during this reign, but the assertion is unfair while North conducts the campaign on behalf of the government. It is not even true that the opposition always had the best of the argument, or that they consistently produced the cleverest debating-points. The King was wise in realizing the importance of having a North to defend the policy of the government, and it would be a mistake to think that corrupt influence pulled over to the side of the administration men who consistently closed their ears to the best speeches and the cleverest arguments. North's talent was the greater in that an opposition can even afford to be unreasonable, to use arguments which are barred to men in the possession of responsibility—opposition could make those criticisms which are always obvious and easy, those demands which, if conceded, would make the conduct of government impossible. North was particularly skilful in putting his finger on the concealed fallacies, in stating that case which is always so much more difficult to argue—the case for the compromises, the half-measures and the concessions to practicability which responsible ministers always have to make.

There were clever lawyers in the house who would be willing to support the government of George III, and in any case a king in his position would always be possessed of the means by which to bribe them over. It is to the credit of George III that he saw through them, and realized that all their debating-skill would not make them a substitute for North; and sometimes, though he made use of their services, he showed that he despised them for their mercenary character. In any case these lawyers tended to be ambitious, they were bent on promotion in their profession, and the reward they required for their support was such as would take them quickly to the house of lords. For long-term purposes in the house of commons, therefore, they were almost certain to be unreliable.

For the sake of North's fidelity and his skill in debate, however, George III had to suffer much; for, though capable of being a good Chancellor of the Exchequer, the man was often in a poor state for the conduct of business, and he had many shortcomings as the head of a ministry. He shirked responsibility and even in the house of commons would say that he was answerable for his own department, the Treasury, while he repudiated the idea that he was a "prime minister". Concerning various matters, including the American war and the legislation connected with it, he said that he only accepted such responsibility as he shared with every other member of the house of commons. In 1766 Chatham had formed his Broad-Bottomed Administration, collecting young men from all parties, and turning them into a ministry so miscellaneous in character that only he could form its bond of union—all was bound to be anarchy without the influence of his directing mind. So that he should be "First Minister" indeed (reserving himself for the superintending duties of that office) he was even freed from the burdens and the leadership of the house of commons; and if the Duke of Grafton was made First Lord of the Treasury, he for his part accepted only the departmental functions of that commission, specifically refusing to admit any of the obligations that a first minister would be expected to fulfil. The illness and incapacity of Chatham, and the unwillingness of Grafton to exercise an effective directing authority in the ministry, made cohesion impossible and reduced the government to a series of independent departments. North, out of sheer indolence and by his dislike of responsibility, perpetuated that lack of system, and even defended himself against his dissatisfied colleagues on one occasion by saying "I never have interfered in any of their departments." George III himself would remind North of the special position he had as chief confidential minister. It was North's colleagues and friends who repeatedly complained that he spent his time in office-work that others should have been doing, and neglected the "superintending duties". His evasiveness and his indolence in this respect contributed more than anything else to the rise of the idea that George III wished it to be so, wished to rule himself and keep all the threads in his hands, determined to act as his own prime minister.

In fact, though the state of things undoubtedly multiplied the occasions on which the King had to intervene, it is rather true to say that what North neglected nobody else undertook, and the efficiency of the administration greatly suffered from this lack of a directing mind. The complaints of North's colleagues were numberless, and they reveal the fact that the need for a superintending leader was recognized even then, and was one of the things taken for granted in English politics, especially for a time of war. Too many matters were referred to the cabinet for decision, it was said, because North was unwilling to accept responsibility save such as he recognized for his own department. When the cabinet met, too often the business had not been prepared beforehand, it would be sprung upon the meeting without notice, previous informal discussions had not been held, nothing had been done to save time or forestall difficulties, and North himself would refuse to give a lead. Decisions would be postponed, even though the business was urgent; or they were not properly committed to paper and there would be difficulties concerning the question of what had actually been decided. And North, who, in periods of depression, could be difficult himself—moody and incommunicative—did not know how to oil the wheels of administration, how to improve personal relationships and ensure smoothness and amity in the cabinet. I. parliament were due to meet there would have been too little preliminary discussion again; and when government legislation was brought up there would have been too little concert and communication between the ministers who had to speak in support of it in debate. The country gentlemen, whose votes were so important, would not have been nursed and coaxed and coached; and when they had supported the administration they would too often be left without thanks or encouragement. North himself would suffer from long periods of inactivity and in his moods of depression would be reduced for a time to what seems to have been something like a state of paralysis. When there were difficulties he would be tormented by indecision, and even a King who was prepared to support him in what he decided can be seen sometimes waiting in anxiety for months until he made up his mind. At moments of great crisis there would be a fever in the ranks of the ministers and their supporters, as the word went round that North was still waiting and nothing was done.

One member of the government complained that he trusted too much to direct corruption, and did not see the importance of some "seasoning"—of the more imponderable things that ease human relationships. A comparatively junior supporter urged him to give dinners and tried to make him realize the importance of what we should call the personal touch. When he was over-anxious and depressed he would be warped and soured, unable to communicate what was in him, and lacking in frankness in the royal closet. His own friends talked about his "weak mind", and he was easily frightened, too prone to submit to bullying from those who claimed that they had received less than their due reward. He was absent-minded and would make commitments for the future, would neglect to mention these to a soul, and then would forget them, granting the promised reward to another claimant altogether. On one occasion he declared himself so entangled by the multiplicity of his promises that there was nothing left for the King to do but to dismiss him so that all the commitments would fall to the ground. In general it was said of him that he would give way to the danger that was immediate, failing to realize the greater perils and difficulties which such a mode of conduct might store up for the future. His oppressed mind was continually so anxious concerning his

majority in the house of commons—so obsessed with the idea that
this was about to dissolve away—that, as he himself once suggested,
it was absurd to suppose that all the corruption alleged against his
government was enough to give a feeling of security. To all these
disadvantages which George III endured with such admirable
patience, such amazing sympathy, must be added the fact that
North would make clear to the King himself—as well as to the
world outside—that he for his part did not believe in the war against
the American colonies.

The whole story of the domestic politics of Britain in this period
must be regarded as taking place in the shadow of the American
War of Independence—a war which in 1778 had brought the country also into conflict with France. As the story proceeds the hardships of a time of war are already beginning to make a perceptible
impression even on that very considerable proportion of the people
which had once been eager for the struggle with the recalcitrant
colonies. Events were beginning to close in on a nation which had
too long neglected the cultivation of its ties with other states, and
which now realized that it was almost too late to remedy the diplomatic isolation, too late to appease the malice of those governments
that had envied the success and hated the aggrandisement or resented the selfishness of this country fifteen years before. The hardships
which in 1779 were becoming palpable to all classes, and the growing impression that both the war in America and the diplomacy in
Europe were being badly managed, put a great strain on the loyalty
of those who out of love for George III or out of hatred for the
Rockinghamite alternative had been willing to tolerate the admitted defects of Lord North and his ministerial colleagues. We must
not be surprised if many men supported North in the house of commons but complained bitterly of their disappointments when they
were outside the walls of parliament. On this, as on so many other
occasions, it was clear that the support given to government would
be misconstrued if it were not interpreted as the choice of what
seemed the least among a number of possible evils.

George III's views of the limitations of North are made apparent
in a letter which he wrote to the Secretary of the Treasury on 6
November 1778, just before our story opens:

But to deal frankly He must cast off His indecision and bear up or no plan can succeed; He must be more exact in answering letters or let others do it for him, and He must let measures be thoroughly canvassd before undertaken and when adopted must not quit them.[1]

[1] Add. Mss. 37,834, f. 39; *ibid*, 37,835, f. 164, George III to J. Robinson, 14 Sept. 1780: "I hope Mr. Robinson will as much as he can decently attend to Lord North's sending in due time answers to the letters he receives."

Chapter II

THE GENESIS OF THE CRISIS OF 1779

§1. THE PROBLEM OF THE MISSING SECRETARY OF STATE

THE condition of the ministry of Lord North had already come to appear sufficiently critical before the close of the year 1778. We, looking down upon the landscape from a distant peak, can realize that at that date the thunders had hardly begun to growl; but contemporaries were already feeling that the storm must be near its climax—to some men it seemed scarcely possible that the government should survive. Even before our story begins, North himself, in the middle of November 1778, had been appealing once again to be allowed to lay down the burdens of office. His application had provoked the King to one of those sallies which add colour to the narrative of these years, one of those swift interventions which make it seem as if a human finger was interpolating itself in the clockwork and imparting to the wheels a movement or a bias of its own. Without prejudice to any judgment that might be made upon his final political ends or his larger purposes as the ruler of a country, one can hardly fail to be impressed by the varied streaks of character that keep appearing, one can hardly fail to admire the way in which, when everything around him is tottering, the King enheartens others by his resolution and seems alone sometimes to have the spirit that rides the storm. Sometimes when he intervenes he almost disarms our hostility as he comes out with some piece of intimate self-revelation; and this happened in November 1778 when he thought that he detected in North something of that mood in which on occasion this minister would complain of a withholding of confidence. For North, in his request for permission to resign, had alleged his own lack of "authority" as well as his lack of ability amongst the reasons for his unhappiness in his office. He seemed to be hinting that he was without that degree of royal support which was necessary to give him weight and a commanding position at the head of a ministry. George III's reaction was instantaneous, and we must regard his answer as honest and faithful, though we may feel that he was no better than most men in his capacity for self-examination. He wrote:

> The word *authority* puzzles me, for from the hour of Lord North's so handsomely devoting himself on the retreat of the D. of Grafton, I have never had a political thought which I have not communicated unto him, have accepted of persons highly disagreable to me, because he thought they would be of advantage to his conducting public Affairs, and have yielded to measures my own opinion did not quite approve; therefore I must desire to have an explanation in writing on what is meant to be conveyed by that word.

North answered that his complaint had had a different innuendo —that the authority which he had lacked had been "that authority of character, that ascendancy which must procure weight and deference to his opinions". He took the opportunity to remind the King however, that, in accepting office in the first place, and in consenting to remain in service since that time, he had only acted in obedience to the royal command.[1]

After this date—after the close of 1778—however, the condition of the ministry became so much worse, that the historian, seeing the whole story of this period, may well pick up the threads at this point and say that only now did the real sorrows of North begin. From this moment the government of Britain presents a spectacle rarely, if ever, equalled in the course of centuries. We should weaken the story if we told it from the evidence of the opposition—the wretchedness and inefficiency can only be measured if we study the correspondence of those who belonged, so to speak, to the inner circle. The bitterest critics of the North ministry were amongst its members and supporters, for they alone were in a position to know the worst. While the old problems were still unsolved—America unbeaten, France a menace, the executive offices inefficient and the ministry weak—the new ones which were emerging in the year 1779 were themselves more directly the result of the inactivity, the incompetence or the disunion which characterized the government. We shall watch them growing with incredible swiftness and

[1] *Corr. George III*, IV, 219–22.

complicating themselves with the old to produce such a degree of entanglement that the hand cannot catch up with the unravelling. The attempt to rectify the mischief in one area seems to multiply the embarrassment elsewhere, and when one evil has been exorcized there are always seven devils to take the place of the first. So a comparatively minor intrigue at the opening of the year 1779 becomes involved in everything else, and enables us to traverse the whole question of the condition of the ministry. And the story of this intrigue will lead us directly to the crisis of autumn 1779, and will help us to set the stage for the movements of the following year.

Before the opening of the year 1779 North had begun to be haunted by what was to be the standing problem—the unremitting crisis from this time—namely, the question of the composition of his ministry. The attacks of the opposition were already concentrated upon the three men who were chiefly responsible for the conduct of the American war—North himself, Lord Sandwich who was at the head of the Admiralty, and Lord George Germain who had been appointed the "Third" or "American" Secretary. And more serious than the attacks of the parliamentary opposition was the fact that supporters of the government, and even members of the ministry, had come to regard these men—Sandwich and Germain in particular—as unsatisfactory, and as a source of weakness to the administration as a whole. Sandwich's position had been further undermined as a result of the factions in the navy, and it was now still more closely threatened by his mismanagement of a conflict with Admiral Keppel, which had recently broken out as a result of one of the many naval fiascos of the war. The King himself decided that it would be necessary to part with Sandwich, and a little later he was to confess also that Lord George Germain "has not been of use in his department"—that indeed, in view of his previous career, the government could not afford to risk its credit by retaining him.[1] Yet these two were men in the fidelity of whom George III for a long time had had special confidence.

[1] *Corr. George III*, IV, 356–57; cf. *ibid.* 258, where the King on 10 Jan. asks Lord North "to weigh the inconveniences that may arise if there is no alteration made in the Head of the Admiralty Commission," though on 1 Mar. he writes, *ibid.* iv, 293–94, "I am clear Lord Sandwich fills the Admiralty much better than any other Man in the Kingdom would."

Early in 1779 attempts were made through various channels to negotiate with such members of the opposition as did not share the exclusive principles of the Rockinghamites. A reconstruction of the ministry seemed all the more necessary since the Earl of Suffolk had declared his intention of resigning very soon from the office of secretary of state. This whole transaction, which envisaged the accession of men like the Duke of Grafton, Lord Camden, the sons of George Grenville, and Charles James Fox (who at this moment thought Rockingham too uncompromising),[1] led to further uneasiness in the ministry and in the closet itself, since the negotiators might work for their private ends, or even intrigue to secure the overthrow of North. George III at one moment stated that he was willing to negotiate on the basis of the retirement of North, but would insist in such an event that Lord Weymouth should be the new head of the Treasury.

A new field of disturbance, however, had been opened when at the close of 1778 Lord Carlisle and William Eden had arrived back in England after an unsuccessful mission to America. The demand for the strengthening of the administration, and particularly the dismissal of Sandwich and Germain, was now to be pressed by the tactics of the blackmailer and the champing of the persistent bully. Together with Alexander Wedderburn (the Attorney General), Eden was attached to the Earl of Suffolk, who had carried his faction to the side of the ministry after the death of its former leader, George Grenville. Suffolk, as we have seen, had decided to retire from the secretaryship of state, and all his party were uncomfortable and discontented. They were to feel still more unhappy when in March Suffolk died after a painful illness, and they found themselves without the support of their powerful protector. From the beginning of the year Eden entered upon a series of activities which were to bring the miseries of North and the difficulties of the ministry to a higher degree of intensity in 1779 than had ever been known before. On 7 January we can see him opening his campaign with what is immediately recognizable as a course of incipient sabre-rattling, as he writes to Lord North in the following terms:

[1] Albemarle, *Memoirs of . . . Rockingham*, II, 371–74.

Though my Disposition & worldly situation led me to wish for Office under a compact and active Government, I could not help foreseeing under the present System a Series of Disgraces and distresses, which I had rather lament in narrow Circumstances and Retirement than blush at in Affluence and Office.[1]

At first Eden affected to be prepared to give a detached and gloomy kind of support to the government, as one who was willing to concur in it from a private station. He soon made it clear, however, that he had no intention of adhering to such a line of conduct; and he carried his threatening policy further by putting out the hint that, in order to justify the part he himself had played in the recent American Commission, he might wish to see some of the relevant papers produced before the house of commons—a move which he knew would be serious for the ministry. Also he now pretended to be troubled by the question: "Am I to encourage Others to concurr in supporting Ministers, who I know will fail in their Undertakings?" On 17 January he poured out his soul to his friend, the Attorney General, and affected not to be able to make up his mind what a man in his position ought to do. The American conflict had only become formidable, he said, "by the Waverings and Delays of this Side". The continued misfortunes of the ministry had "shaken the confidence of its best friends and of the Nation in general". The cabinet "as at present constituted" was "totally unequal to the Undertaking". Sandwich was unpopular amongst the naval men, Germain amongst the military. The times required unparalleled "Spirit, Invention, Enterprise", of which "I see neither the existence nor the possibility."

Wedderburn took all this as a hint, forwarded the letter to North, attached to it some further private complaints of his own, and added the menacing declaration that the question of his own future conduct was one which could only be answered by North himself. North had failed to take him into his confidence on the subject of both men and measures especially in the last six weeks, he said. The Earl of Carlisle was induced to join in the intrigue against the ministry. Towards the end of January and in the early days of February

[1] Add. Mss. 34,416, f. 242 (transcribed by Eden in letter of 17 Jan.).

an intensified attempt to enlarge the ministry proved unsuccessful, so that Eden renewed his pressing communications which came like incessant drum-taps intended to drive Lord North out of his mind. In a letter of 4 February he harped once again on the "melancholy and dead suspense which prevails through every Department and Plan of Government". Less than a week later he seemed to be carrying out his threat, for he informed the minister of his intention to move immediately in the house of commons for the production of the papers relating to the recent American Commission. North replied in dismay, pointing out that "ill-intentioned men" might make a harmful use of the documents, and saying:

Consider this matter well and if you think us sinking, direct your measure against us personally without taking any step which threatens such mischief to the public.

When he informed the King of the movements that were being made against him North added the gloomy comment: "This disposition of quitting administration . . . increases every day."[1]

It happened that at this time the Secretary of the Treasury was John Robinson, a trusted servant of North, and a man intimately connected with the jobbery that accompanied the conduct of administration in the eighteenth century. Standing at North's right hand, courted as his private mentor, and quoted as his recognized interpreter, he was well acquainted with his moods and with the difficulties of the government; and on occasion, in his uneasiness, he would write concerning these direct to the King. It was he who in 1777 had informed George III that North was depressed because his private financial situation had been preying on his mind. At the same time, at the side of George III himself, was Charles Jenkinson, whom Horace Walpole once described as the "sole confidant of the King", and who seemed to stand almost as an archangel amongst "the King's Friends". The mantle of Bute was supposed to have

[1] For the above narrative and correspondence, see Add. Mss. 34, 416, ff. 233-34, 241-69; *Corr. George III:* iv, 272; H.M.C. *Carlisle Mss.* 419.

fallen upon his shoulders. Indeed, his initial rise to favour had been largely owing to the influence of Bute. Jenkinson was now Secretary at War and not even a member of the cabinet, but he would send letters to the closet informing the King of the underhand movements that were taking place or advising him how to deal with North or the other ministers. The connection between the ministry and the royal closet was all the more close since Robinson would write confidential letters to Jenkinson concerning the manœuvres that were taking place or the difficulties that beset him—letters which revealed to the closet some of the innermost secrets of the ministry. Early in March a formal recognition was given to this correspondence and the King authorized Robinson to hold "free and unreserved communication" with Jenkinson on everything relating to his affairs—everything which he did not chose to send direct to the closet. In this way the circle was completed and the ministry was caught up in a round of continual whispering and tale-telling, a net-work of anxious manœuvre, reminiscent of a system of double diplomacy. The whole procedure was meant to serve the interests of North or at least of his ministry. It was intended to be concealed from him, however. It could not be entirely concealed; and at moments it aroused his jealousy.

Robinson and Jenkinson were full of solicitude for North, yet apprehensive of his weaknesses, and greatly concerned to rescue him from the machinations of Eden and Wedderburn.[1] On 21 February Jenkinson called the King's attention to the "Spirit of Intrigue and Negotiation which prevails among the Inferiour Instruments of your Majesty's Government". Four days later Robinson was writing that Eden was "alarming Lord North's fears, knowing well how that operates to carry any job he wants". Robinson made it part of his function to keep watch on Lord North so

[1] For the following narrative see, under the appropriate dates, Add. Mss. 38,210-11 [letters from Robinson to Jenkinson]; Add. Mss. 37,834 [correspondence between Robinson and George III]; Mss. of the Marquess of Abergavenny, partly summarized in H.M.C. Abergavenny Mss. [correspondence of Robinson]; Corr. George III, which needs to be checked with the Windsor Castle Mss. [letters beteen George III and Jenkinson, and between George III and North]; Add. Mss. 34,416 [letters between Eden, Wedderburn, Carlisle, and North].

that he should not "engage a step ... even the most trivial", save with the approbation of George III.[1] When it transpired that Eden —if he was to give his support to a ministry in which he had no confidence—desired amongst other things £600 a year in the form of a pension for his wife, Robinson at the Treasury surveyed the course of this transaction with a jealous eye. On seeing that the pension was being given for life he took care that the news should reach the closet in order that the scandal should be checked. Even after this he still had to report that in his view the grant was virtually being made for life, and was only "cooking up in a different way in words".[2]

When all this had been done Eden would not waive his demand for changes in the ministry and complained on 19 February that Lord North, instead of entering upon this major question, always short-circuited the problem "by asking me in earnest terms what I wished to have done for myself". The difficulty lay in the fact that, as Jenkinson wrote to North, "you cannot negotiate in the present moment but to great disadvantage. The claims of all mankind will be exorbitant." Eden was well aware of this. He established contacts with the friends of Lord Shelburne and with Sandwich's arch-enemy, Admiral Keppel; but he must have been aware that the closet would regard such overtures with the greatest suspicion.

At this point a new and more serious difficulty arose, however, and the early days of March produced a problem and a dilemma that multiplied the misfortunes of the government for a considerable period. In this conjuncture it soon became clear that the suspicions of Robinson and Jenkinson had been justified—that Eden and Wedderburn were in fact distressing the ministry for private political ends. In eighteenth-century England there were normally two secretaries of state, and in the hands of a strong man the office might be of the greatest importance since it carried with it the power to issue orders in the name of the king. It was in the capacity

[1] Add. Mss. 38,210; ff. 293-97. Robinson remarked, "There is something more behind that is [not?] yet ready to be brought out."
[2] See also my article, "Lord North and Mr. Robinson, 1779," in the *Cambridge Historical Journal*, 1937, p. 260 and note 16.

of secretary of state that the elder Pitt had conducted the Seven Years' War, sending his commands even, for example, to the Lords of the Admiralty, and even direct to ships at sea without the intervention of the Admiralty Board. If Lord Sandwich and Lord George Germain were responsible for the weakness of the executive departments, some compensation might have been found in the appointment of one or two efficient secretaries of state; and, even if the functions of the office were construed within the narrowest limits, its importance was real at a time when English diplomacy had reached one of the unhappiest moments in its history, when our diplomatic isolation seemed to be becoming complete, and when the problem of Ireland was developing in a sensational manner. The continued intrigues of Eden and Wedderburn, however, prevented the appointment of a successor to Lord Suffolk until the following October. This is the situation to which Burke alluded in the following year in his famous speech on "Œconomical Reform":

Lord Suffolk, dead to the state, long before he was dead to nature, at last paid his tribute to the common treasury to which we must all be taxed. But so little want was found even of his intentional industry, that the office, vacant in reality to its duties long before, continued vacant in nomination and appointment for a year after his death. The whole of the laborious and arduous correspondence of this empire, rested solely upon the activity and energy of Lord Weymouth.

If we examine the resulting situation and enquire to what degree the virtues of Lord Weymouth in reality supplied compensation for the absence of a second secretary of state, we discover that the condition of the ministry has become still more paradoxical in precisely the period that we are studying. In the early months of the year Weymouth was being carefully watched, because it was thought that he and his friends were too anxious to make terms with members of the opposition. On 31 March we learn that Lord North "complains bitterly of Lord Weymouth's Coldness and not drawing cordially with Them." On 11 May John Robinson remarked to North that people "attribute[d] Lord Weymouth's coldness, his inattention to business and silence in the House of Lords (except in communication with Lord Rockingham and members in opposition) ... to be a settled design to leave you." On 27 May the Duke of Richmond declared in the house of lords:

It was a matter of amazement that their lordships were so seldom indulged with a sight of the only Secretary of State who had a seat in that House.

Finally, we shall find that, while a serious crisis was arising in Ireland, the Lord Lieutenant, Lord Buckinghamshire, repeatedly complained of the incommunicativeness of Weymouth and the lack of instructions from London. When to the weaknesses of North, the wilfulness of Wedderburn, and the admitted deficiencies of Sandwich and Germain, we add the lukewarm character of Weymouth's services and the spectacular defects in the whole department of the secretary of state, it is difficult to see what was left for the making of a ministry—difficult to know how such a ramshackle administration can have remained in existence at such a critical time.

A new secretary of state was clearly needed then, in March 1779, and at the end of the month Lord North declared his intention of proposing the Earl of Hillsborough for the office that had been vacated by the death of Suffolk. Jenkinson reported to the King that Lord North was "very earnest to make this arrangement". Not till the middle of April, however, did North in fact communicate his desire to the King, who immediately agreed but declared it necessary to avoid giving any offence to Lord Carlisle at this moment.[1] Carlisle's name had been mentioned amongst others for the post. He had recently returned with Eden from America; he was anxious for some sort of office; and he was important owing to his connection with Lord Gower, the leader of the Bedford whigs. Two days later, however, the blow came from another quarter; for Wedderburn and Eden, who had cried out so loudly for ministerial arrangements, now seemed determined to make them impossible.

[1] *Corr. George III*, iv, 325 [printed as 6 April 10 m. pt. N, but is 16 April 10 m. pt. M. in the Mss.—apparently, therefore, in the early moments of 17 April].

On 18 April Robinson wrote to Jenkinson that Eden wished "to get & keep an hold of the secretary of state's office", to "carry another job" and even "to overturn the King's Government" in order to have "a chance of rising out of troubled waters".

Lord North seems to see it, but has not resolution to resist—It is a Misfortune his Temper is so good; . . . he is therefore worked upon and misled even altho' he sees their designs.[1]

Jenkinson forwarded this letter to the King with the comment:

It is clear that the Attorney as well as Mr. Eden want something and that Lord North is not to be allow'd to do anything till that something is obtained.

Jenkinson suggested that Lord North should be ordered "to fill up this office *instantly* with Lord Hillsborough or some one else". Two days later the King, after learning directly from North himself about "the present ill humour of the Attorney General", wrote a reply thanking him for his confidence—"it had the appearance of unbosoming to a friend"—but urging him to beware of the intrigues of Wedderburn and Eden, and to rely rather on the assistance of two other lawyers—the Lord Chancellor, Thurlow, and the Lord Advocate, Dundas. A week later, on 28 April, however, the King was informed that the whole issue of the new appointment was in suspense again. Everything had been done by George III and by the unofficial advisers of both the King and Lord North. But the sabre-rattling was too much for North's weak spirit. He was giving way once more.

Alexander Wedderburn contrived to present to the world a semblance of cupidity and meanness which, if we were dealing with fiction, would be condemned as the intrusion of unconvincing melodrama. He was forty-six years of age at this time, and in the year 1770 he had distinguished himself by the extravagance of his opposition to the ministry of North. It was thought that he was battering violently at that time because he was bidding high for office, and when he became Attorney General in the ministry in

[1] Add. Mss. 38,210, ff. 22-25, [misdated 1778, instead of 1779, in the Ms.].

the following year his sudden reversal gained notoriety—it has been described as "one of the most flagrant cases of *ratting* recorded in our party annals". To the more naked kind of cupidity which characterized some of the upstart lawyers of George III's reign he added a quality that rendered it more ugly and mean—a cringing fear, which would make him sometimes feel that he was about to be cheated by Fortune, so that he would whine at one moment, and then, at another, seize that goddess by the throat. It would appear that in 1779 Wedderburn was afraid lest the ministry of North should be defeated and disbanded before he had been given the Chief Justiceship, the promise of which had hitherto kept him faithful. Either he wished to force the hands of North and secure it instantly; or he desired compensation for the risk he was running; or he was taking up a position which would enable him to leave the sinking ship and join a new one. He had the power to strike terror at this moment into the heart of North, who felt a desperate need for the support of his debating-talents in the house of commons.

In spite of the fact that earlier in the year George III had tried to console Lord North by saying that "this Country will never regain a proper tone unless Ministers as in the reign of King William will not mind being now and then in a Minority," it became clear by 11 May that some unhappy debates, an incidental defeat in the house of commons and the intrigues amongst his own supporters were combining to depress the spirit of the minister and paralyse his will.[1] On that day the King found it necessary to write to the Secretary of the Treasury, "Mr Robinson must today attempt his irksome part of rouzing Lord North to act as he ought." Robinson in fact had anticipated his instructions, but had approached Lord North by letter, hoping that "at a leisure Moment" the man would "cooly peruse what it is very difficult to get him to converse calmly upon". It may be interesting to observe the method this Secretary of the Treasury adopted in his attempt to stiffen the courage and harden the will of the man who was the head of the government.

[1] *Corr. George III*, IV, 334–35; *Parliamentary History*, XX, 726–50; Mss. of Marquis of Abergavenny, No. 212, abridged in H.M.C. *Abergavenny Mss.* p. 25, H.M.C. *Lothian Mss.* 351.

I am confident however there is nothing can more contribute to [your success] than your standing forward & keeping your old ground as much as may be. My mind is also so strongly impressed with ideas that everything which can shew your firmness will contribute to the strength of Government & the present administration that I beg you will allow me to again urge you the appointment of the Secretary of State . . . There ought to be something ostensibly yours to be done & held out to the public; nothing I think can do this better than the appointment of Lord Hillsborough. You have your sovereign's approbation; you have his wishes repeated to you for it, & why then not do it immediately. You will have the goodness to excuse me my dear Lord for being so pressing in this but it is the sincerest opinion of my heart & therefore I express myself strongly.

That very evening Wedderburn himself had a talk with Robinson and at last brought out what he had in his mind, though it could give little comfort to the ministry. He asserted that the death of his patron, the Earl of Suffolk, had robbed him of the witness of North's earlier promises to him—the ally whose political weight would have enabled him to give effect to his claims. He complained that he had not been in North's confidence during the whole parliamentary session; and took the view that the Lord Chancellor and Lord Advocate had been receiving much better treatment than he had. He added that if Sandwich and Germain had been removed, as he had advised at the beginning of winter, the administration would have been saved the great troubles it was now having in parliament. He "was violent"—Robinson reported—when he discussed the suggestion that Lord Hillsborough should be made secretary of state. He demanded the fulfilment of an ancient promise—that he should be made Chief Justice of the Common Pleas and given a peerage. In any case he would refuse to continue any longer in the office of Attorney General.[1]

North admitted the promise to Wedderburn but declared that if either of the objects were conceded at this moment he would be unable to continue at the head of the ministry. Robinson asked the Attorney General whether he would be willing to discuss the

[1] Add. Mss. 37,834, ff. 74-5.

possibility of an alternative form of compensation. "He admits the promise but declines the performance" wrote the latter in a bitter communication to Eden. George III declared that the Attorney General could hardly demand anything so unpopular as the retirement of the Chief Justice of the Common Pleas merely to satisfy his ambition. If Lord North agreed to the law arrangement, said the King, "it will certainly give disgust in many quarters." If the peerage were to be granted in addition to this, "I will not answer for the number of Enemies Lord North may create by that Step." Robinson was ordered not to leave the minister until the latter had realized the policy which the good of the country required, the policy which he would know how to follow if he had any regard for "the interest of his Family". No wonder Robinson wrote to North: "I apprehend consequences . . . that would be ruinous to Your Lordship & I fear prejudice to hurt you in the Closet."[1] Finally, on 15 May Jenkinson advised the King to state his terms "in a firm Tone" to Lord North—namely, that Wedderburn should have a great law office, when one fell vacant, "provided he continues to serve Your Majesty *till then*".

Mr. Robinson thinks that Lord North's opinion is really the same as your Majestys, & that His weak Mind only wants *Support* which your Majesty may give it.[2]

The King took the advice and said that he did it in the conviction that such firmness would "prevent Lord North being teazed every two or three months". He pressed the minister to put his confidence in other lawyers, and steps were now taken to make sure of the fidelity of one of these, namely Dundas, the Lord Advocate.[3] Very soon the quarrel with Wedderburn had broken out afresh, however; and the latter was saying "that it was impossible for him to go near Lord North again". "I should think if Lord North were

---

[1] Add. Mss. 37, 834 f. 77; Mss. of the Marquess of Abergavenny, No. 216, not printed in H.M.C. *Abergavenny Mss.* p. 25.

[2] *Corr. George III*, IV, 342–43; Wedderburn was also to become Chancellor of the Duchy of Lancaster. Lord North, however, was to accede to these conditions, "*not at once*, but only by degrees".

[3] At the end of March Dundas himself had decided to raise his price if he was to go on supporting the government: Matheson, *Life of Dundas*, 54–57.

rid of him it would be advantageous," wrote George III when he heard the news.[1]

Here, then, is the first of the misfortunes that went to the máking of the autumn crisis—not merely the failure to create a second secretary of state but an almost complete paralysis on the admittedly urgent question of the further rearrangements in the ministry. North stands helpless precisely at that point where it might have been imagined that he would find his opportunity, namely, at the moment when he has places to distribute and important appointments to make. If he makes a move he seems to "disoblige" more people than he reconciles, so he is afraid to do anything, afraid to put his foot upon the serpent-coils. It was a situation always calculated to produce a paralysis in him, and when he was in such a dilemma neither he nor anybody else could be sure what was due to weakness or infirmity, and what to the tactics of deliberate delay. George III wrote in connection with this episode:

Intriguers should never approach a man of Lord North's cast who with many good qualities too much tends to the difficulties of the moment and to procrastination, and Lord North from wanting to get out of the evil of the day but too often falls into what may prove ruin in futurity; I owne my mind always inclines to meet difficulties as they arise, and I would much rather have them soon fall on my head if not to be avoided than to know that in future that must inevitably happen. Public Men ought always to act on system not from the occasion of the minute, 'tis that alone has given advantage to Franklin, 'tis by uniformly attending to that, we may yet retrieve our affairs.[2]

Lord North's dilemma continued, however, and he did not dare to bring the issue to a head by appointing to the secretaryship of state the man whose name had provoked the recent crisis. Throughout June the question dragged on, though on the 15th George III had written: "Lord North will apprize the Cabinet that on Thursday Lord Hillsborough will receive the seals." In August Robinson still writes of Lord North: "the appointment of Lord Hillsborough

[1] Add. Mss. 37,834, ff. 92-93; Corr. George III, IV, 349, 6 June.
[2] Add. Mss. 37,834, f. 93.

worries him to death almost." By this time Eden, who had been so involved in the responsibility for the deadlock, was making the delay an additional item in his list of reproaches against the minister.

§II. THE GOVERNMENT AND THE SPANISH DECLARATION

In the first half of June the spirit of George III still rose in a sovereign manner above the tumult of opposition, the murmurs of discontent, the pressure of circumstances and the chances of war. To all who had sympathy with the end for which he was fighting, his obstinacy in this period must have seemed the noblest kind of resolution. And indeed he erred not by malice or evil design or lust for despotic power, but rather by an unimaginative self-righteousness—conscious always of heavy responsibility but too immoveable in the service of an object not originally unworthy. He accepted the blows of Providence with a patient spirit; yet he trusted Providence and still thought—perhaps too surely—that he was its special servant. In one sense he was like Dante's monarch, outside the play of faction, above the clamour of vested interests; for not Rockingham or North or Fox or Grafton served England so faithfully, so nearly without a glance at private purposes or party aggrandisement. And if Chatham was his equal in this devotion and service, he was much more prone to do injury by excessive egotism and vanity. In politics, however, the effects of many private virtues may be rendered nugatory if one lacks the imagination to enter into the views of others. And though even the stubborn heart of George III was brought to self-questioning in 1779, his mind failed to break through the circle of his customary ideas.

On 11 June Sir William Meredith was to move in the house of commons an address in favour of peace with the American colonies —an address which declared that no nation had "ever sent fleets and armies of such strength and magnitude on so remote a service as those which Great Britain has poured into America". That very morning George III, fearing what he regarded as the weakness of the chief minister on this subject, wrote a letter to him declaring "I have heard Lord North frequently drop that the advantages to be

gained by this contest could never repay the expence"; and depre-
cating the tendency to weigh events in "the Scale of a Tradesman
behind his Counter".

Whether the laying a Tax was deserving all the Evils that have
arisen from it, I should suppose no man could alledge that without
being thought more fit for Bedlam than a Seat in the Senate; but
step by step the demands of America have risen—independence is
their object. . . Should America succeed in that, the West Indies
must follow them. . . Ireland would soon follow the same plan.

Jenkinson reported to the King after the debate that Lord North had
held "much firmer language with respect to America than I have
known Him . . . so that the Cause of Government wore a better
Face than it has done for some time." He added the significant comment: "It is clear that what your Majesty thought proper to write
and say, had its Effect."[1]

A few days later, on 16 June, the Spanish ambassador in London
transmitted to the secretary of state a manifesto which amounted
to a declaration of war. In the previous October George III
had declared that he expected this to happen in the spring; when
"I trust the British Navy will be in a State to cope with both
Nations." By 23 May 1779 intelligence from France had given
George III to understand that an expedition known to be associated with "M. le Fayette" was being prepared "not for North
America but [for] an insult on our Coast or that of Ireland".[2]
George had ordered that "some intimation should be given to Lord
Sandwich"; but it was not yet known in England that after a long
period of diplomatic activity France and Spain, by a convention of
12 April, had agreed to make the operation a joint one. When the
full extent of the danger came to be realized in the middle of June,
the Duke of Richmond declared in the house of lords that the crisis
was the "most awful this country had ever experienced". The Earl
of Shelburne "entered into a minute account of the internal state
of this country, when it was threatened by the Spanish Armada",
and recalled the time after the battle off Beachy Head in 1690

[1] Corr. George III, IV, 350–51, 354–55; Add. Mss. 37,834, f. 96.
[2] Add. Mss. 37,834, f. 85.

"when the fleet of France rode for full two months triumphant in our channel".

Less than a week after this there occurred one of the most remarkable of the King's personal interventions in the government of the country at this period. North, after further appeals for release, had consented on the 19th to "serve in office till his Majesty can replace him without inconvenience". On the 20th the King had written him a further letter, in which he had stated that such conduct "will ever Secure You my warmest Support". At one o'clock on the 21st George III presided over a meeting of the ministers which he had arranged to be held at the Queen's House—a meeting to which, we are informed, "all the members of the Cabinet were summoned by a message in the King's own handwriting." Lord North had previously asked him what was the reason for this unusual course of action, but had been told that he would learn the reason when the meeting actually took place. George "sat down at the head of his library table, and desired, for the first time since he became King, all ministers to sit down". It appears that for a moment Lord George Germain entertained the conjecture that the ministry were about to be dismissed.

The King spoke for half an hour or more and it is apparent that he had been moved to take action by the urgency of the external crisis, the dismantled state of the ministry, the indolence in some of the departments, the depression of North, and the inefficiency that resulted from internal intrigues. He "recapitulated the whole progress of our difficulties ever since the repeal of the Stamp Act"; said that the establishment of the Rockingham ministry and the repeal of that piece of legislation had been the great mistake of his life; "declared to God he had never harboured a thought of injuring the constitution or abridging his people's liberties"; and expressed both his gratitude to Lord North for taking office after Grafton had "deserted", and his thanks to Lord Sandwich for the "respectable" state of the navy, which "had been let down too low after the Peace of 1748 and not sufficiently provided for after the last". Finally he said that he was "willing to enlarge the bottom of his administration"—he had never allowed personal "prejudice" to set him against the appointment of a man whose principles he "approved".

In any event he "expected firmness and support from his ministers", for "it was [his] resolution to part with his life rather than suffer his dominions to be dismembered."

For an hour and a half the cabinet then discussed "the mode of increasing our strength by sea and land". The Lord Chancellor suggested the advisability of a union with some members of the opposition, and though there was no response to this—since he seemed to have no particular alliance in mind—the idea created a flutter in the closet, especially as the Lord Chancellor was one of the Bedford whigs, a party somewhat under suspicion at the moment. Later in the day the King wrote to Sandwich:

I wish to hear whether, in the kind of stupor of some departments, my idea of speaking out hath not given some degree of confidence. If others will not be active, I must drive.

The same night he wrote to Lord North asking that no delay should be permitted—if it were met with in any quarter he would "instantly be ready to assist in removing it". Talking to Lord George Germain a day or two later on the subject of his meeting with the cabinet he said that if any minister "wished to go out he thought he had better go". Concerning Lord North he added:

Although he is not entirely to my mind, and there are many things about him I wish were changed, I don't know any who would do so well, and I have a great regard for him and a very good opinion of him.[1]

In the meantime North's spirit seemed to be breaking, as private misfortune was added to the public ones, and a bill for doubling the militia provoked in the house of commons a remarkable opposition attack that ranged over the whole period of his ministry. On 21 June, after the cabinet meeting at the Queen's House, he was brought to his feet more than once by melodramatic charges relating to the corruption and treachery which were alleged to have

[1] *Corr. George III:* iv, 361, 366–70, 378; Navy Records Society, *The Private Papers of John, Earl of Sandwich, 1771–82,* III, 25–6; *Various Mss.* VI, Knox Mss. 260–61, where it is stated that the King spoke for nearly an hour.

existed in the counsels of the King. Two days earlier he had lost his fourth son, a child of two—"a favourite child, whom he loved with a fondness which only you can conceive", wrote the Earl of Carlisle to George Selwyn—and he appears to have been more than usually sensitive in the course of the debate to attacks which on other occasions he would have cleverly turned aside. In a vein somewhat pathetic he recounted how "he had been in a most laborious and very expensive office for twelve years, without asking for a single emolument, either for himself or his family." He had accepted the Wardenship of the Cinque ports at the lower salary of former days—about £1,000, he thought—as well as a reversionship of a similar amount on the lives of his two younger sons, which his predecessor, Pelham, had similarly enjoyed. There was a further £500 a year, so insignificant "that several of his predecessors in office had thought it beneath the acceptance of any part of their family". He had always been ready to resign the Cinque Ports, and when he went out of office "the whole he was in possession of was 1,500 a year for his children ... and his was a pretty numerous family." At these words "his lordship struck his breast, and burst out into a flood of tears, probably from the casual recollection that one of his sons lay dead at that moment."

The house, touched at the circumstance, called for the question, but his lordship, recovering himself desired leave to go on.

Still on 21 June William Eden, undeterred by the proximity of sorrow, un-awed by the very majesty of death, continued his sapping operations, reproaching North for the fact that even if spirited measures were resolved upon in the cabinet they would be "procrastinated in the execution or frittered away in the War Office" so that they only added to "the Consumption of Blood and Treasure".[1] On the following day, the minister went to the house of commons "under a remarkable dejection of spirits", having had to spend two hours attempting to console Lady North, who had been "so much afflicted since the death of her son that she had alternately fainted and been seized with violent convulsions". Even now Fox

[1] Add. Mss. 34,416, f. 367.

renewed the cry of treachery; said that North "must certainly have sold his opinion" or "he could never have acted in the manner he had done"; and denied that men of honour could make alliance with a set of ministers who "had led us on from one degree of wretchedness to another", prostituting the public strength and public fortune. Wedderburn, in the very act of defending the ministry, managed to breathe hints of menace against North; and Dundas, on the day after this, publicly "called on the minister to exert himself". While the waters thundered over the head of North, George III in a letter of 22 June rose to what in other circumstances might have been regarded as almost Churchillian grandeur:

> Before I will even hear of any Man's readiness to come into Office I will expect to see it signed under his hand that He is resolved to keep the Empire entire.

Jenkinson reported on 25 June that Lord North was "in good spirits and determined to go on"; so that the world breathed freely again as if to say "All is well; now we can get on with the war." Since Weymouth and Gower in the cabinet, however, declared that the bill for doubling the militia would lead to upheaval, while North replied "that he could not put his disgrace against Tumults and Insurrections and ... take all the measure on himself", that bill, after the great struggle in the commons, was amended in the lords, the Bedford whigs working with the assistance of Sandwich. Only the raising of the volunteer companies was now authorized, and Jenkinson held that these were "no better than the common militia, and yet interfere more than any other with the recruiting of the Army". The dissension in the cabinet was revealed to all the world, and those who had borne the brunt of the battle in the commons regarded themselves as betrayed. After a conversation between Wedderburn and North, Robinson reported that the mind of the latter became "quite unhinged" and that the administration was in danger "if his Majesty from His Firmness and Good Sense cannot save it".[1] The King brought Wedderburn to heel however[2]; and

[1] Add. Mss. 38,211, ff. 171–74, 175.
[2] *Corr. George III*, IV, 384, 386; Add. Mss. 37,834 ff. 90, 103, 105.

the prorogation of parliament assured the ministry of another breathing-space.

If the decks seemed to have been cleared at last, however, it was only to leave the vision unhindered and the mind undistracted in the face of what might best be described as the Great Apprehension. It came looming like a mighty thing at sea—a thing long dreaded and at last taking shape—but unexpectedly murky and drab, curiously inglorious and unheroic, now that it had actually materialized. M. Lacour-Gayet, in his study of French maritime power at this time, makes the note that "Never, at any period of history—not even in the days of [Napoleon's] camp at Boulogne—did the French navy see itself so near to the objective it had so often meditated, the achievement of a landing in England." The test had come at the worst of all possible times for Englishmen; and it is curious, though it is not incomprehensible, that the occasion should not have been more widely publicized, more generally celebrated in our history. The country made what men might well regard as a hair's-breadth escape. There was no place for songs and Te Deums, however. And there was no splendour of victory.

It was not only in the extravagant complaints of the opposition that the danger in the summer of 1779 was regarded as acute. A few days after the Spaniards had declared themselves, the Lord Chancellor reminded the First Lord of the Admiralty that here was "a crisis more alarming than this country had ever known before". North himself wrote to Sandwich on 22 June: "For God's sake make haste with your pressing [of sailors] for the national safety essentially depends upon it." At the same time, the enemies of the government did not allow any of the aggravating features of the crisis to escape their discernment and criticism. Already on 16 June, the day of the Spanish declaration, the Duke of Richmond called attention to the fact that "28 ships of the line sailed from Brest on the 3rd instant, and were at that minute, if they chose, masters of the British Channel." Sandwich had made a mistake which his successors in the Revolutionary and Napoleonic period were to take care not to repeat; he had taken no measures to prevent the French from putting out to sea; and he had allowed the event to happen while the British Channel fleet was still unready.[1] Richmond added the statement: "he understood that the fleet of Spain was in a formidable state of forwardness." The situation would be serious, he said; for he conjectured that the Bourbon fleets, if they combined, would have sixty ships, while the British would have to meet them with only half that number.

It was noted with great resentment that the challenge of the Bourbon enemies, now that it had come, found the maritime power of England dispersed, and the country distracted by despairing commitments at the other end of the world. In the period of peace the British had neglected their navy, and in the last four or five years they had failed duly to appreciate the considerable revival that had been taking place in the maritime power of France. In 1778 Admiral Keppel had found the fleet insufficient for coping with a single Bourbon power; and the fiasco in the Channel during the first year's campaign against France had led to a renewal of faction in the navy, a foolish trial of Keppel by court-martial, and a bitter parliamentary attack upon the First Lord of the Admiralty in the early months of 1779. Henceforward Lord Sandwich was never allowed to forget how he had once declared that head of the Admiralty to be worthy of execution who should fail to maintain a navy capable of meeting the combined forces of France and Spain.

Sandwich for all his faults was enthusiastically devoted to the maritime interests of the country. He had long ago pressed for more ships, and it was not without justice that he had defended himself earlier in the year, by diverting the responsibility for Britain's unpreparedness to the rest of the cabinet.[2] From the time when he had become First Lord he had been faced with peculiar difficulties in his endeavour to restore the navy—firstly "Combinations amongst the Timber Growers and Timber Merchants to keep up the Price of their Commodities"; secondly the "vast and unnecessary profusion of shipbuilding" carried on by the East India Company; thirdly, peculiar difficulties in regard to labour—"Nothing

---

[1] On 21 May, however, Sandwich had written to Hardy, who was in command of the Channel fleet, "all mankind begin to be extremely anxious about getting you to sea." He had expressed the hope that the fleet would at least be ready by the end of May. It sailed 16 June. *Sandwich Papers*, III, 13–14, 19.

[2] *Parliamentary History*: XX, 443–4; *Sandwich Papers*: II, 258–79, Notes for a Speech on 23 April 1779.

but the increase of working shipwrights both in the King's and Merchants' Yards can increase our ship-building." Great mistakes had been made in the earlier period of peace, and, as was pointed out in a paper drawn up in Sandwich's defence not long before the fall of the North ministry, once the emergency had actually arisen there was a limit to what could be achieved—"a line beyond which the Exertions of every [any] Country cannot go". During the 1770's practically the whole of the fleet was protected by the device of coppered bottoms, however—"one that all other nations are imitating as fast as their means of procuring the materials will allow them".[1] George III was not undiscriminating when he repeatedly noted that Sandwich had a claim on his gratitude for the work he had done in restoring the navy, and Sandwich himself was ready to take pride in the fact that the fleet was bigger than it had ever been "since Great Britain was a kingdom". It would have been better if he could have said that for purposes of a major war we had sufficient ships to cope with the combined fleets of the Bourbon powers.

Though there was much corruption under the administration of Sandwich there is evidence from an authoritative naval source which suggests that the situation was not appreciably different after the Rockingham whigs had come to power and Sandwich had been succeeded at the Admiralty by his old enemy, Keppel. On the other hand, the régime of Sandwich had produced bitter faction in the navy; the courts-martial and the parliamentary debates in the early months of 1779 had led to the aggravation of these[2]; and it was a misfortune that a number of whig sailors, like Keppel himself, had announced their refusal to serve under him any more.[3] The trial of Keppel had confirmed the dangerous impression that the ministry—and particularly Sandwich—would be ready to charge the responsibility for misfortune upon the service-officer concerned, especially if he belonged to a hostile political party. Before there had been any news of the intervention of the Spaniards, Sir

[1] Add. Mss. 38,344, ff. 284 et seqq.
[2] H.M.C. Dartmouth Mss. I, 441, George III to Dartmouth, 6 Feb. 1779: "Undoubtedly the unfortunate court martial is big with mischief, and as I owne I foresaw will end in nothing but creating that degree of faction in the Fleet which perhaps may never again be eradicated."
[3] See e.g. H.M.C. Appendix to 9th Report: Part II Pembroke Mss. 380.

Charles Hardy—"pulled from a well-earned retirement of fourteen years at Greenwich Hospital"—had been appointed to the command of the main fleet, partly because others had refused to serve and partly because his seniority seemed to guarantee that he would be able to rally the discontented officers and surmount the factions. Hardy was sixty-four, and we are told that he was "old for his age". Indeed, he died almost exactly a year after his appointment. He put to sea too late to prevent the French from coming out of Brest, as we have already seen, but too early to have heard of the Spanish manifesto which appeared on the day of his departure. He did not know that the country was at war with Spain until the beginning of July.

Though there were a few more ships almost ready to be sent to Hardy, it transpired that now there was a further hitch, and this time it was because the necessary seamen were lacking. The emergency was such that it was decided to press into the royal service— from merchant-ships, fishing-boats, coastal and river transports— various classes of men who were explicitly exempted by law from such impressment. When Sandwich hesitated before the illegality —crippled by the knowledge that the opposition had already marked him out for special attack and were ready to pounce upon every indiscretion that he committed—even North became importunate and imperative. The Lord Chancellor wrote to explain to Sandwich the things which might be done, the things which ought to be done—in confidence of future indemnification—when the state is in genuine danger.[1] Immediately after the passage of the bill for doubling the militia, a further bill was in fact introduced in the house of commons to give legality to the new impressment.

Across the Channel, at Le Havre and Saint Malo, 40,000 men— including Dumouriez, the future Revolutionary leader, and, a few days later, La Fayette, now back home from America—were fretting and chafing, as they waited for news of the French and Spanish fleets. On 10 June the French commander, d'Orvilliers, had arrived in the neighbourhood of Corunna, where the Spaniards were to join him; and it was not the British Admiralty which could now prevent the combination of the Bourbon forces. We now know

[1] *Sandwich Papers*, III, 24–29; *Corr. George III*, IV, 362–63, 367–70.

that the project of an invasion of Ireland had been shelved in Paris, and that a landing was intended at Gosport, near Portsmouth, or, failing that, upon the Isle of Wight. We know also that in the face of this menace the advice of British naval men was not unanimous; and that North leaned to the more timid counsels, and Sandwich was prepared to acquiesce, so that the instructions sent to Hardy were sometimes over-cautious. George III was ever the same, and there would be a strong case for saying that the event proved him right, though more than once he gracefully submitted to the more prudent decisions of his ministers. He said he would "not be satisfied if persons count what number of ships are brought against us". He resented the growing tendency—whether amongst his servants or in the ranks of the opposition—to judge that the fleet should not risk an action where the enemy had the superiority in numbers. So we find him writing:

It was the vigour of mind shown by Queen Elizabeth and her subjects, added to the assistance of Divine Providence, that saved this island when attacked by the Spaniards.[1]

Yet two days later than this, on 19 June, instructions were sent to Hardy to the effect that if the French and Spanish fleets had combined and he considered their superiority "so decided" as to "make it improper to risk the event" of a battle, he was to go to Spithead or Torbay and await further orders there.

Now it was the case that some men, like Mulgrave, a Lord of the Admiralty who was in service under Hardy, regarded such caution and timidity as unnecessary. Mulgrave claimed that "Thirty sail is as great a number as . . . can be brought properly to action in a line." It was his view that the combined Bourbon force would be unwieldy, that the British ships were superior in quality, and that the Spaniards would be lacking in discipline "till they have been a considerable time at sea". Others, however, such as the Comptroller of the Navy, Captain Charles Middleton, believed that time was on the side of the British provided they refused to risk themselves by an early action. "France and Spain cannot get on now so

[1] *Sandwich Papers*, III, 20.

fast as we can; and unless we meet a defeat by hazarding too much, we shall in two months be superior to them in the Channel." George III, for his part, was impatient and when he wrote to the First Lord of the Admiralty he would say: "I sigh for an action."[1] It was not his fault that the country did not meet the threat of what was called the Bourbon confederacy in heroic and jubilant eagerness. And since the country escaped disaster, perhaps the chief effect of the cautious counsels and the lack of confidence was in the communication of an unheroic and complaining mood even to the services themselves; also the prevalence of an impression that the government did not rise to the challenge at this moment, but rather felt the disgrace.

For in the wars of the past it has often proved that victory went, not to superb efficiency, but to the somewhat less inefficient of two untidy, ramshackle, conflicting systems. And those were right who in the summer of 1779 refused to take their cue from the dismal bleatings of the opposition, and who reckoned that, bad as our condition was, we could afford to count on imperfections in the enemy, provided the spirit in our own fleet was high. If Sir Charles Hardy was old, the French commander, d'Orvilliers, was older still. He had started out from Brest in gloom, and nearly every despatch that he wrote was full of misery and complaining. He, too, has been reproached for thinking too much of the disgrace that would come from a possible defeat, instead of filling his sails with a foretaste of the pride that would come from victory. He arrived near Corunna, as we have seen, on 10 June, but he had to wait more than six weeks for the arrival of the Spanish vessels that were due to come from Cadiz. While he waited, his ships were ravaged by disease, which took off his only son, and when the Spaniards arrived it was found that nothing had been done to prepare a system of signalling that would be comprehensible to the men of both nations. Those Englishmen who said that the combined fleet would be too big to manoeuvre are confirmed by an early statement to the same effect in a letter of d'Orvilliers himself, who clearly thought the task beyond his capacity. The Spanish commander made matters more difficult by disputes over etiquette, and d'Orvilliers found it neces-

[1] *Sandwich Papers*, III, 41-2, 8 July.

sary to humour him. Finally d'Orvilliers was quickly able to confirm what Mulgrave had stated in a letter to Sandwich—the Spaniards were unskilful in the management of their ships.

§III. THE INVASION-THREAT

From the latter part of June England presented the spectacle of a country preparing for invasion—seriously apprehending for two months an actual landing on the coast. Towards the end of the month instructions were given for "the putting out the lights of the lighthouses and pulling up the buoys on the approach of the enemy." On 9 July a proclamation ordered that in the event of an enemy landing the cattle and supplies in the neighbourhood of the coast should be removed into the interior of the country. The younger Pitt, then in Cambridge, wrote that "in this Inland County our Oxen and Horses continue to Graze in Security, and the Gentlemen of the University seem scarcely more affected than the Brute Creation." The proclamation concerning the movement of cattle, however, "produces many Speculative Discussions between Meeke and Villiers and some verbal Criticisms on the Terms in which it is couched".[1]

The country was indeed astir and on 9 July Charles Jenkinson at the War Office was suggesting the ways in which the patriotic fervour could best be used for the strengthening of the forces available for defence. He stressed the importance of directing the efforts of London and the counties so that they should contribute to the primary purpose of bringing existing regiments to their full complement. Subscriptions were raised and here a locality offered five guineas, there a committee was appointed to distribute six guineas, as an addition to the ordinary bounty granted to recruits. Jenkinson further pressed for the recruiting of troops in Ireland—a policy

---

[1] H.M.C. *Westmorland Mss.* 25-26, W. Pitt to Lord Westmorland, 13 July. See also the Memorandum dated "August 1779" in *Sandwich Papers* III, 52-54, on the subject of the defence of the coast, and beginning, "Not a moment should be lost in taking every step that may possibly be of use on the supposition of our fleet's being defeated."

which had been neglected in late years, he said, because though there was no shortage of men it had proved a costly matter to transport them to England.[1] George III put his views on this whole question on to paper, and desired the gentlemen of the different counties

> To enter into an Association for each Gentleman to mount himself and a Servant properly armed with a Broad Sword and Pistols to serve if an invasion should take place; when such Association is made to send a deputation to the Lord Lieutenant offering their Service and empowering him to lay this before me.[2]

Noblemen and gentlemen had already begun to come forward offering to raise regular regiments at their own expense; and "within two months", says Fortescue, "thirteen regiments of infantry for general service, three regiments of Fencible Infantry, a twenty-second regiment of Light Dragoons and yet another small corps of cavalry were raising without cost to the country." The correspondence of Lord Amherst at the War Office for July 1779 records the resolutions of meetings at which one locality and another had decided to form volunteer companies. In Dover they set out to raise six companies of sixty men each for the defence of the town, the captains and lieutenants to be commissioned by the King. In Westminster it was hoped to raise twenty-four companies with at least sixty privates in each—the government to furnish arms but otherwise to be at no expense and the officers to be commissioned by the King. Even the smugglers were "anxious to make their peace with offended Government by forming themselves into a Corps to serve his Majesty at this Juncture", and it was reported on their behalf that they had subscribed £1,500. The War Office was reminded that "His Majesty under the Stanary Laws has the power to embody a part of the Tinners", who, since many of them were out of employment, could very conveniently be called upon to play their part in the defence of the country. It transpired furthermore that "Thomas Fasbrook . . . has got a list of subscribers, and their places of residence, who are willing to lend a Thousand

---

[1] Public Record Office, W.O. 34/116, ff. 10–13.
[2] Add. Mss. 37,834, f. 117; to J. Robinson, 11 July.

Horses on the Shortest Notice." At a later date we find John Wesley commending "to all our Brethren whom it may concern" a plan drawn up by Captain Webb to embody and train a number of Methodists, whose officers were to be commissioned by the King, though chosen by the men of their company, the voting to be by ballot.[1] Middlesex and Devon are reported as each producing twenty-four companies of volunteers, while Sussex produced seventeen. In provincial towns there was corresponding activity. "Before the end of 1779 there were close upon one hundred and fifty companies, each with a strength of at least fifty men."[2]

Lord Amherst in the meantime would be receiving reports on the state of the defences in Sunderland and Tynemouth, in Whitehaven and East Anglia, in Plymouth, Portsmouth and the Isle of Wight. "The Capital indeed is covered, but the dockyards are naked," the Earl of Pembroke complained in the summer; "the enemy may easily land 150 miles from a single soldier." In July Amherst learned that in Swansea "we have not a Musquet & Bayonet in the Town." From Swansea, in fact, the report had come that "we have this week had fourteen of our Vessels taken almost at our Door," and that fifty or sixty men could make a landing and either raise "what contribution they pleased or set the Town on Fire".[3] The Duke of Richmond was to remind the house of lords at a later time of the way in which the opposition for eighteen months had been trying to warn the government about Plymouth in particular; for Plymouth was the "land and marine key of the kingdom . . . the second naval arsenal . . . where, probably one third of our naval stores, and the materials from which future navies were to be built were deposited". Lord North repeatedly said that he expected the chief attack to be directed against Plymouth, and told Lord Amherst that the garrison "appears to me too small and not well composed". Even when he heard that there was to be an additional threat against Sussex, a plan to push forward thence to London, "to burn and destroy every thing that falls into their power"—even though he expected this to be attempted by

[1] H.M.C. 9th Report, Appendix III, Stopford Sackville Mss. p. 132, 24 Oct.
[2] For this paragraph see W.O. 34/116, ff. 1, 20–21, 43, 162–63.
[3] W.O. 34/116, f. 183.

the enemy while the fleets were away to the west, and instructed Lord Amherst to watch the Sussex coast every single hour—he still regarded the main threat as likely to come in the region of Plymouth. Amherst, on the other hand, complained of the lack of troops, and insisted on reserving the available forces for the purpose of intercepting a march on the capital.

The military governor of Plymouth, Sir David Lindsay, had arrived there at the beginning of June. He had soon complained of the Admiralty's refusal to spare for military exercises the shipwrights who were supposed to be doing two days' work in one to prepare ships for Hardy's fleet. He protested against the neighbourhood of French prisoners, who (since nine of them escaped in one day) were likely to prove an embarrassment to the defence of the locality. On both 23 and 29 July, he announced to the War Office that there was nobody to man the big guns, and nothing to prevent an enemy landing—therefore he would not be "responsible for any consequences that may happen". Before the enemy fleet had made its appearance the War Office had begun to treat him as a querulous man who did not like his post.[1] In the critical county of Sussex, the Lord Lieutenant was the Duke of Richmond who proved recalcitrant when he received instructions concerning the possible movement of cattle. He called a county meeting which resolved that letters from military officers "cannot be looked upon as Commands" which a Lord Lieutenant was "bound to obey", and demanded a distribution of weapons by the government. The Duke himself declined to confer officially with Lieutenant-General Pierson, but announced his willingness to visit him "as an individual".[2]

Woefully unprepared, then, the country awaited the coming

---

[1] For this and the preceding paragraph, see W.O. 34/116, ff. 84-85, 87-88, 101, 110, 112-16, 142, 195-96, 218-78. Lindsay's successor (after the danger had passed) and the local ordnance officers and engineers denied the alleged defects in the defences of Plymouth, W.O. 34/116, ff. 265-79; but cf. p. 265 below and see *Parliamentary History*, 1068-85 and xxi, 459-91, (with further reports in *York Courant*, 2 May and *York Chronicle*, 5 May 1780). See also notes on the Parliamentary debates in *Sandwich Papers*, III, 313-19; and H.M.C. *Rutland Mss. IV*, 238-39, where Robert Thoroton writes from Plymouth (2 Sept. 1779): "The conduct of the Ministry in regard to this place is such as if they intended to deliver it into the hands of the enemy."

[2] W.O. 34/116, ff. 214-16.

ordeal, and from the end of June the question of the invasion seemed to be in everybody's mind. "As to me", wrote George III on 28 June,

I thank Heaven my Resolution rises with difficulties, and I put the strongest reliance in the protection of the Almighty, the justice of my Cause and the purity of my own intentions, these are such props that nothing can shake and I am resolved to shew I can save my Country.[1]

At the very start, however, there occurred an event which was disappointing to him more even than to anybody else; for on 5 July —almost immediately after the news of the Spanish declaration had reached him—Sir Charles Hardy, commanding the Channel fleet, had to report that he had allowed a westerly gale to force him into Torbay. It is clear that the government, though prepared to accept his version of the facts, heard the news with a considerable degree of misgiving. Apart from the official instructions which were now sent to him, the King induced Sandwich to write him a private letter, showing the importance that was attached to his immediate return to sea, and the royal expectation that there would be an action at the earliest opportunity. "There is every reason imaginable to expect that the combined fleets will attempt something against England or Ireland," wrote Sandwich, "and the more time is given to them the greater their strength will be."[2] Even now, however, Sandwich was cautious enough to remind the Admiral that in the event of mistake he could not build any plea on the rigid and inescapable tenour of his instructions—the responsibility for the decision must be his own.

Even the confident eagerness of George III seems to turn into delirium and infatuation when we learn what was being said of Sir Charles Hardy by the captains of his own fleet, particularly Kempenfelt, who, apparently in response to the demands of the service, had in May been appointed first captain or chief of staff. Kempen-

[1] Add. Mss. 37,834, f. 99.
[2] For Admiralty correspondence in this section see the Navy Records Society publications, especially *Sandwich Papers*, III, 40–98, supplemented by Sandwich correspondence in *Corr. George III*, IV.

felt was a student of tactics and was crying out during this year for
the translation of French text-books, which had shown a significant
development in the art of manœuvre. He wrote on 2 July, from
his ship, the *Victory*, which was then with the Channel fleet:

> My situation is extremely disagreeable; I would give all the little
> I am worth to be out of it. Does the people at home think the nation
> is in no danger? Where is Lord Howe at this alarming period... All
> seems to depend upon the abilities with which this fleet is conducted
> —let that be well considered.

He was no more oppressed than George III by the mere superiority of numbers that the enemy fleet might be favoured with. On the
contrary he thought that "twenty-five sail of the line, coppered,
would be sufficient to hazard and tease this great, unwieldy, combined Armada." But before the Franco-Spanish fleet had appeared
he was asking if the ministry "think that ships are sufficient of themselves, without wisdom to direct and order their operations". He
was saying of the appointment of Hardy, "So much indifference at
so dangerous a crisis is astonishing and alarming." Again he wrote
to the Comptroller of the Navy:

> In confidence I must inform you the confused conduct here is
> such that I tremble for the event... An odd obstinacy... makes all
> advice useless. There is a fund of good nature in the man, but not
> one grain of the commander-in-chief.

He drew a portrait of Hardy which, in fact, might well have been
a Dickensian caricature of a commander-in-chief. "I hear it often
said the salvation of Britain depends upon this fleet," he added. "I
never hear the expression but I turn pale and sink. My God, what
have your great people done by such an appointment." Later again
he wrote: "How you can remedy the evil of this injudicious
appointment I can't say."

The culmination of the story in August—when, as the opposition
exultingly agreed, the country was saved "by Providence"—was
unfortunate for the ministry, since it was spectacular, yet was calculated to conceal the virtues of administration, to advertise its errors

and weaknesses, and to multiply all the appearances of disgrace. After disastrous delays off the coast of Galicia, the Franco-Spanish fleets steered north on 30 July, and sighted Plymouth on 16 August, being themselves in a pathetic condition—while Hardy had been told to stand well to the west. New instructions had been sent to the Channel fleet on the 14th, however, for by this time the Admiralty had learned something of the state of the enemy, having received "reports of sickness and of ships disabled in the bad weather". Hardy was now told that, if his information confirmed the view that they were weak and desirous of avoiding action, he should not confine himself to any station which would hinder him from doing his utmost to give the enemy battle. George III rejoiced in these instructions and prayed for a west wind to "bring Sir Charles Hardy into the Channel, when I trust that Divine Providence will permit these faithless foes to receive that chastisement which so infamous a conduct deserves".

In the meantime the atmosphere in England had become intense, especially as it now became known that the French and Spaniards had also begun the blockade of Gibraltar. On 31 July Lord Mahon thought it would be a friendly act to give Lord Shelburne the tip that "there is beginning to be a considerable shyness in *our* Part of the Town, to the changing even of the smallest Bank Notes." A few days after this, North himself was spreading the news that he expected the French within a week. Horace Walpole was reporting in his letters the enemy boast that the English capital would be burned to the ground. As the Franco-Spanish fleet was approaching one of the supporters of the government talked of "half the admin-istration making hay in the country and nobody left in Town to oppose the designs of Europe, Asia, Africa and America but Lord Weymouth and Jack Douglas". Another writer declared: "In the midst of all these dangers the Ministry are fast asleep, or diverting themselves as if nothing had happened."[1]

[1] Add. Mss. 34,416, f. 380; Jesse, *George Selwyn and his Contemporaries*, IV, 236. Cf. *A Short History of the Administration during the Summer Recess of Parlia-ment* (1779), p. 74: "The President of the Council has been but once at the Board in course of the summer recess. . . The ministers have fled to their country-seats and delivered over the management to clerks in offices and the interior cabinet."

In the centre of the ministerial disorder—and the unhappy victim of the sorry tragedy—stands the figure of Lord North, who in his suffering almost persuades us to think of him as a dumb animal. As the distresses multiply, as the difficulties rise around him, they only appear to reduce him to a paralysis more complete than before; or he seems to burrow himself more deeply in the purely routine business of the Treasury, where he seems to find at times a submergence and a self-forgetting, or at least a servitude far more congenial than his ministerial one.

"I will do all I can to push him on," the King had written on 4 July, "but find by experience on paper I can some times succeed but conversation never does anything with Him."[1] John Robinson, who had written to North in May, "Hold yourself up as the minister with spirit," reported on 23 July:

I don't perceive any Sympton of Vigour and Exertions to meet the difficulties or distresses or any probability of the Mind being brought to it.

On 11 August, only a few days before the Franco-Spanish fleet appeared in the English Channel, Robinson illustrated in a letter to Jenkinson the results of the general lack of leadership:

Indeed I see combustibles heaping up on every side, and a small spark will fire them, and I shall not be surprised if the whole Administration blows up even before the Meeting of Parliament—It can't last after that, for in the manner of going on it is impossible—Nothing done, or attempting to be done, no Attention to the necessary arrangements at Home, none to Ireland, nothing to India, and very little I fear to foreign Affairs, a Cabinet totally disjointed, *hating* I may say, but I am sure not loving, each other, never acting with Union even when they meet, looking forward with Anxiety to the Moment of their parting, can never do, can never direct the great Affairs of this Kingdom, scarce at any time, much less at this critical Moment—Indeed my Dear Sir it must blow up. If it does what must follow—very great Confusion indeed. To see it and apprehend the Consequences of it daily works me almost to distraction... I know you and I differ in Opinion about Lord North,

[1] Add. Mss. 37,834, f. 90, to J. Robinson.

indeed he is the most altered Man I ever saw in my Life. He has not Spirits to set to anything, they are quite gone as to Business though well and full as to the Table and Amusements and his Judgment still good when you can fix his Attention but that is most difficult to do—He writes me from Kent that "nothing can be more miserable than I am" are his Words... All is Confusion and each department blaming another.

While the combined fleet was at hand, Eden was bombarding North with more of his long letters, attacking "the enervated system", "the notorious Insufficiency of the executive offices", the "nervelessness" of the government departments. At a time when "the uninterrupted vigilance of a great superintending minister" was needed, he reproached North for engaging "at least two-thirds of your attention in the discussion of Contractors' Jobbs and Custom House scruples and in the memorials of Individuals respecting pounds, shillings and pence".

If you cannot rouse the powers of your own mind you ought to quit as immediately as is consistent with the urgent circumstances in which we find ourselves.[1]

Meanwhile the insolent enemy rode with impunity in the Channel, while the British fleet was away to the west. For two and a half weeks the vessels of d'Orvilliers were never twelve hours sail from Plymouth, and an attack was expected every day. Before the crisis was over the military governor of Plymouth, Sir David Lindsay, stated to the Admiralty that,

on the 17th when nineteen sail of the French fleet after taking the *Ardent* stood into the Sound having a leading gale ... if they had risked an attack ... the dockyard would have been in their possession in less than six hours.

In another report, a little earlier than this, and dated 26 August, he claimed that, without special assistance from the navy and the dockyard, it would have been "impossible for us to fire ten shots at an enemy if they came here". Ourry, the commissioner of the

[1] Add. Mss. 34,416 f. 391-92, 25 Aug.; f. 393.

dockyard, made a similar confession on 20 August. "I did not think . . . that I should be Master of the Dockyard in ten hours longer," he said.

For some days past I put the question to myself, Shall I, Paul Ourry, or you, Jack Dorvilliers [the enemy commander] set fire to the dockyards.

In these circumstances it is easy to see the anxiety which prevailed at Plymouth during those August days when the enemy fleet was at hand and nobody imagined that they would make their departure without attempting any serious enterprise. It was officially reported that many of the inhabitants of the region "deserted their homes and professions and retired into the country"; though it is true that other men in the neighbourhood flocked to the point of danger where many of them were provided with arms. Hundreds of Cornish miners were brought into the locality to assist in the extemporary defensive work. While all this was proceeding, the government was not entirely free from apprehension concerning other parts of the English coast. Vice-Admiral Sir Hugh Palliser, for example, wrote to the Admiralty:

The wind being easterly and our fleet far to the westward, may it not be apprehended that the enemy will make their embarkation in all their ports pass over unmolested and land under protection of their fleet?

Above all, the problem of the emergency measures to be taken at Plymouth revealed in some places inefficiency, exposed in others panic, and provoked in the services themselves new quarrels and factions. The undue alarm and the administrative disorder were exactly calculated to produce irritation and dispute. The governor, Lindsay, had informed the commander-in-chief (as he now reminded him) that "from the deficiency of artillerymen, a defence at the entrance of the harbour became impracticable." He secured three hundred men from the navy and two hundred from the dockyard to relieve the situation, but the Admiralty cancelled these measures, claiming that the men were more important on the ships and in the yard. Yet later, when in parliamentary debate the government was reproached for having had no men to man the guns, both Sandwich and Admiral Schuldam (the naval commander-in-chief at Plymouth) made virtue of that transfer of naval personnel which the Admiralty had both rebuked and reversed. The government had no defence to make, except that these men would have been available; yet when the threat had seemed imminent their services had been refused. In a similar manner, the governor of Plymouth and the commissioner of the dockyard—possibly seized with panic, but not less virtuous for taking energetic measures without waiting for instructions from the government—began the construction of a boom across the entrance to the harbour. Sandwich, who knew something of the state of the enemy fleet, and in any case was far away in the capital, may be credited with more coolness and confidence in the crisis; for he explained more than once: "I own I can never be brought to believe that the enemy will in any case attempt to force their way into Hamoaze by shipping until they are in possession of the shore." Sandwich sent Le Cras, a commissioner of the navy, to Plymouth to check the activities of the men on the spot—sent "a kind of spy", said the Duke of Richmond with some malice during the later debate in the house of lords; "for . . . there was spy upon spy, for that was the system of government." The boom was countermanded by the Admiralty, and if this decision was not without justification, it seems to have been made on the mistaken notion that such a device would have prevented the British ships from moving out of the harbour.[1] The result of these interferences was a sullen rebelliousness on the part of the governor of Plymouth, and his removal before the crisis was at an end. Here was a further scandal to be aired before the world when the new session of parliament began. Here was another military commander let loose to give evidence against the ministry.

There was still a further misfortune, which confirmed the impression that there had been a fiasco, and this was one which produced consternation within the ministry itself. On 2 September Sandwich was writing to Sir Charles Hardy:

[1] On the boom, see *Sandwich Papers*, III, 64–83.

I think a battle is inevitable . . . your fleet will now be considerably augmented. . . I need not tell you that the eyes of all the world are upon you.

The world was truly expectant, yet on 3 September Hardy brought his fleet to Spithead, and neither George III nor the country in general could hear the news in peace of mind. A hostile account of what had happened was given by the Duke of Richmond at a later date, when the whole episode was under discussion in the house of lords. Sir Charles Hardy, he said:

fled before a pursuing enemy, by gradual progresses, from the very mouth of the Channel, to Falmouth, Plymouth, Portland, to St. Helen's; and as if an universal panic had seized the whole fleet, he did not look upon himself safe, till by the aid of the next tide he found himself safely moored at Spithead.

Mulgrave, the lord of the Admiralty who was serving under Hardy, declared at the time his "astonishment" at the withdrawal to Spithead, and begged Sandwich to come in person to deal with the situation. The King, when informed of this, wrote to the First Lord of the Admiralty, "I trust on Your not losing one moment in proceeding with the utmost despatch to Portsmouth." Palliser said that if Hardy was at Spithead he was liable to be "attacked at anchor", while Mulgrave expressed the opinion that he was in danger of being "blocked up". Sir Charles Douglas, another of Hardy's captains, seems to give the show away, for he wrote a letter which spoke of "the fleet having made good its retreat". He expressed great anxiety, and, like Kempenfelt, cried out for the leadership of Lord Howe. Kempenfelt wrote: "When so much depends upon the fleet, 'tis matter of great astonishment so little care was taken in the choice of the conductor." He noted also:

There is none of that ardour remains now that upon extraordinary occasions urged everyone to try to have his ship the first ready; but there is a supine languor and indifference reigns *now*.

Walsingham, the captain of the *Thunderer*, wrote as though he assumed that Hardy would have to be superseded. "All Party now

I hope is laid aside," he said; "give us a man to command us that we have confidence in . . . and we will ensure you success." According to Major Floyd "the seamen hung their hammocks before the *Victory's* head, that she might not see such days."[1]

Part of the irony of the situation lay in the fact that it was politically impossible for the government to throw any blame on the commander-in-chief at this time, or to admit that in their choice of him they had been restricted, or to confess that the appointment had been unwise. They had attempted too often to shift the responsibility for failure on to the shoulders of the serving officers. It was the cry of the opposition that the refusal of the ablest men in the navy to serve under Sandwich had left the Admiralty without commanders adequate to the needs of the service in time of war. At the same time, when the matter came to be debated in the house of lords on 25 November, Sandwich was unable entirely to repudiate the damaging account which Richmond had given of the withdrawal to Spithead. He supported the commander-in-chief, however, and concerning the whole campaign he said: "It was true that Sir Charles Hardy, discovering the vast apparent superiority of the enemy did not seek an engagement, nor would it have been prudent for him if he had." He gave as his reason that "no less, perhaps, than the very fate of the country would be depending, in a great measure, on the issue." It was curious that before the end of his speech he was able to deny, however, that the numerical superiority of the enemy implied a superiority in "efficient strength". And it was hardly possible for him to say, what he must have felt, namely, that, with a man like Hardy in command, it was perhaps fortunate that a major action did not take place.

After the withdrawal to Spithead George III, who had lost none of his spirit, wrote: "the enemy must not quit the Channel without having received hard blows."

---

[1] Wedderburn, writing to Eden at this time, [Add. Mss. 34,416, f. 514,] talks of the "officers out of humour with the Admiral". Keppel wrote, [*H.M.C. Rutland Mss.* III, 20], "What would our departed friend Lord Chatham have said?" Cf. *Corr. George III*, IV, 429, which shows that the idea was entertained of appointing Lord Howe or Keppel at this time.

It is the fashion to term the arrival of the fleet a retreat from the enemy, consequently before the meeting of Parliament an engagement must be not only hazarded, but forced if possible.[1]

The ministry was in doubt and confusion, and North himself, still taking the timid view, wrote on 7 September: "I confess I am not one of those who think that Sir Charles Hardy should engage them *at all events*."[2] The question was ultimately resolved for the government by D'Orvilliers; for the combined enemy fleets, harassed by disease and in a state of great dejection, themselves called off the adventure, and returned to Brest before the middle of the month. It is not often that the irony of fate or the mercy of Providence provides the historian with a campaign which both of the combatants can only look back upon with a gloom almost without alleviation. Perhaps the French have reason to be—as indeed they are—the more depressing in their recollection of this enterprise.[3] They had expended great sums, and had been at high tension with their hopes and anticipations, and they had achieved virtually nothing at all. North afterwards confessed that if the dejected and sickly state of the French fleet had been properly realized in this country, Hardy "would have wished and earnestly sought an engagement", and he himself "would not have felt the least anxiety or alarm for the event of such a conflict".

It is difficult to see how the country's escape from the danger of an enemy landing could have been combined with a more definite appearance of failure, or a more spectacular disgrace for the North administration. George III went far beyond anything that was usual in his severity towards ministers in the middle of September 1779, when it became clear that there had been an excess of timidity in the conduct of the recent campaign. He confessed: "No one can deny that the House of Bourbon have brought their united Navy to a degree of strength that no Englishman can see with ease." Sandwich pointed out that "England till this time was never en-

---

[1] *Sandwich Papers, III*, 93, 96.

[2] *Ibid.* III, 97; cf. *Corr. George III:* IV, 419–30.

[3] In H.M.C. *14th Report, Appendix IX*, Round Mss., p. 309, a writer from Oxford says of the Franco-Spanish fleet: "So many sailors were flung into the sea as made the Inhabitants eat no fish for a month."

gaged in a sea war with the House of Bourbon thoroughly united, their naval force unbroken, and having no other war or object to draw off their attention and resources." But the King declared: "We must be ruined if every idea of Offensive War is to lye dormant until this Island is thought in a situation to defy attacks." He reiterated the argument: "If we alone attend to home Security ... every valuable possession will be lost before any effort is made to any other tendency but making the country secure against foreign Invasion." George III in fact expressed the view that Englishmen must if necessary repel an invader after he had landed in the country, "though not a Ship remained for its defence".[1]

Now it happened that at this very moment Admiral Barrington had returned from the West Indies with a further tale of gloom. The French had taken the offensive there in the previous year and had captured Dominica in September though they had lost St. Lucia three months later. In June 1779 they possessed the superiority in those waters and captured the island of St. Vincent. Three weeks later our fleet was badly handled by them and they captured Granada, "our richest sugar island after Jamaica". General Grant, who had been sent from New York to defend the West India islands, came into conflict with Lord George Germain, whose instructions he despised as impracticable. Admiral Barrington, who commanded the fleet in the West Indies, belonged to the whig opposition and could claim that the government at home had failed to furnish him with adequate forces. Before the middle of September he was in London, asserting "that every one of the Possessions in that material part of the World if attacked by either France or Spain must inevitably fall." Sandwich had to confess on 14 September that an attempt to "throw in a supply of Stores & provisions" to Gibraltar would meet with "great if not insurmountable" obstacles; and that very soon "whatever Ships are sent by us to Gibraltar ... will inevitably fall into the hands of the enemy who are between them & England with a superior force." He added: "The State of our fleet in the Leeward Islands is, it is to be feared very deplorable." He then said, "I come next to Jamaica upon which I own I speak with trembling, for I see the danger with

[1] *Corr. George III*, IV, 434–35, 441.

which that Island is surrounded without being able to suggest any effectual means of giving it relief." Finally, he said, that the "stock" of ships at home "should not be drawn so low, as to leave us unable to resist the united efforts of the house of Bourbon in these seas." Once again it was George III who was prepared for a bold decision—unwilling to keep a great many ships in the Channel while our overseas possessions were being captured one by one.[1]

Since we have seen how General Grant and Admiral Barrington were so critical of the government at home we may note in conclusion the attitude of General Clinton who had charge of the operations on the American continent. He had written in May 1779 to Lord George Germain: "For God's sake, my lord, if you wish to do anything, leave me to myself and let me adapt my efforts to the hourly change of circumstances." In the very period when the enemy fleets were in the neighbourhood of Plymouth, Clinton was asking for the second time to be relieved of his command.

On 13 August, just before the arrival of the combined fleets—and at a moment when Lord North seemed to be driving everybody to despair—George III, writing to the Secretary of the Treasury, produced a comment on his chief minister which was at the same time a curious piece of self-revelation.

On the whole Lord North if he will take a decided part is sure of my Support and consequently may easily bring things into tone, but I fear his irresolution is only to be equalled by a certain vanity of wanting to ape the Prime Minister without any of the requisite qualities. If he will take a clear line and get as vacancies arise the proper Men the Circumstances permit and content himself with being acquainted with whatever is going forward and confine himself chiefly to the Finance branch, he may still be a very useful Minister and may gain much reputation, but He must fill up the Vacant Offices and get the Irish Affairs into some train.[2]

[1] *Corr. George III*, IV, 436–42; cf. *Sandwich Papers: III*: 154–71. Concerning Barrington see H.M.C. *Various Mss.* VI, Knox Mss. p. 162, Lord George Germain to Knox, 20 Sept. 1779: "Admiral Barrington's whole information is so desponding that I flatter myself he is only diverting our attention from enquiring into the reasons of his quitting his post."
[2] Add. Mss. 37,834, f. 133.

Since the King was disposed to be amenable to cabinet decisions, and the cabinet in the middle of August was in the distracted state which has already been described, we may say that this letter leaves out of account one of the aspects of leadership most essential in this period—the "superintending" duties which Eden and others so often described. To add to the misfortunes of the country at the beginning of September, it was suddenly realized that North had still done nothing about the ministerial rearrangements—or about the missing secretary of state—which had been the subject of discussion throughout the course of the year.

On 4 September therefore, Charles Jenkinson gave the following description of the general state of things:

> I believe this country was never in so perillous a situation as it is at present, and the Events of the next fortnight will probably be as important, as ever were known in History.[1]

Only after this, did Lord North, under pressure from the King and from some of his associates, begin to take in hand that question of ministerial rearrangements which had been now under discussion and now in a state of suspension since the beginning of the year. We find him writing on 10 September that "for these last three months the threatened invasion of this kingdom" had prevented him from giving his attention to the matter.[2] In order to secure the wavering fidelity of the Bedford whigs he proposed that the Earl of Carlisle (the son-in-law of the leader of that party, Lord Gower) should be given the Presidency of the Board of Trade, an office which had recently been attached to the third secretaryship of state, so that Lord George Germain, the "American Secretary", had to be approached for his consent. Earlier in the summer George III had declared that Germain would never agree to it; but he showed himself amenable though he said that he regarded the arrangement as "degrading" for him. Having offended this man, however, North now stood paralysed and postponed the matter, as though determined to reap the disadvantages without the

---

[1] Add. Mss. 38,307, ff. 27–28, to Lord Gower.
[2] H.M.C. *Appendix to 9th Report, Pt. III*, Stopford Sackville Mss. pp. 97–98.

advantages of this policy. He neglected to communicate the offer of the post to Carlisle himself. And he shrank from informing Lord Stormont that he was designed for the vacant secretaryship of state.

But the admirable firmness of George III can be seen on 13 September 1779 when he wrote to the Earl of Sandwich a letter all the more significant in that it rules off the story of the invasion threat which had at that moment passed away. It shows how a certain moral strength that he possessed helped to prolong the ministry of North and the agonies of this part of the reign. It ended:

If Ministers will take a firm decided part and risk something to Save the Empire I am ready to be the foremost on the Occasion, as my Stake is the deepest; but if nothing but measures of caution are pursued and further Sacrifices are made from a Want of boldness which alone can preserve a state when hard pressed I shall certainly not think myself obliged after a conduct shall have been held so contrary to my opinion, to screen them from the Violence of an enraged Nation.

Sandwich replied that he would "never be found backward in taking his share" in the decisions that were necessary.

But the rest of your Ministers should take their part allso, and the advice to be given to your Majesty from the meetings should (as was usual before) be reduced into writing, and when a question is agitated there it ought to be decided one way or the other, and not put off as now most frequently happens, without any determination.

Lord Sandwich has, in this Situation of things thought it adviseable to write very seriously to Lord North to recommend firmness & decision to him, & to shew him how necessary it is that he should take the lead at our councils, and act with the spirit that becomes the principal person who has the honour of your Majesty's confidence as a Minister.[1]

---

[1] *Corr. George III*, IV, 433–35.

Chapter III

THE GENESIS OF THE IRISH MOVEMENT

§I. RETROSPECT: 1778

ARTHUR YOUNG had studied the condition of things in Ireland during his tours of 1776–78. He reconsidered his views at the end of 1779 and drew up his general conclusions in the light of the events of that year. It was his verdict that:

> Ireland has been absolutely new built within these twenty years, and in a manner far superior to any thing that was seen in it before; it is a fact universal over the whole Kingdom; cities, towns, and country seats; but the present is the æra for this improvement, there being now far more elegant seats rising than ever were known before.[1]

He rolled the idea into various shapes, and from one angle and another tried to drive the moral home, so that on this theme his writing became pressing and reiterate. "The towns of Ireland have very much increased in the last twenty years . . . and it is a strong mark of rising prosperity." "The rents of land have at least doubled in twenty-five years, which is a most unerring proof of a great prosperity." Finally: "The whole tenour of the preceding minutes proves that Ireland has flourished for these last thirty years to an uncommon degree, I believe more than any country in Europe." There is evidence of the fact that certain sections of the Roman Catholic population had been having their share in the benefits of the general economic advance to which he was referring. And the whole rising tide seemed to come with wider sweep and in higher waves after the achievement of legislative independence in 1783. The latter half of the eighteenth century was clearly a most important period, therefore, in the history of Ireland.

It was important in a still larger sense, and in realms far transcending the sphere of purely economic activities. A still wider and more

[1] Arthur Young, *A Tour in Ireland* (1892), II, 253; cf. 270–73.

imposing framework for our narrative—a still more interesting attempt to estimate the place where Ireland stood at this time in the whole stream of history—had already been made by Edmund Burke. Writing to the Speaker of the Irish house of commons after the relaxation of the penal laws had given the Roman Catholics a greater degree of security in their property, he had said:

You are now beginning to have a country; and I trust you will complete the design. You have laid the firm, honest, homely rus- tick of property; and the rest of the building will rise in due har- mony and proportion. I am persuaded that when that thing called a Country is once formed in Ireland, quite other things will be done than were done whilst the zeal of men was turned to the safety of a party. . . . Your people will begin to lift up their heads and wait and think like men.[1]

Though the depth of its influence and the width of its occurrence may easily be exaggerated—especially in the period before 1778— a certain political consciousness had been developing, and various factors had been contributing to its rise. The growing security had made the Protestant ascendancy less preoccupied with the need of having English assistance for the purpose of keeping the Catholics down. In Charles Lucas Ireland had already had its Wilkes, and in some fields—for example, in the use of the privileges of the city of Dublin for purposes of conflict with the house of commons—he had been in operation earlier than his opposite number in Middle- sex. A great change had occurred through the Octennial Act of 1768, which had restricted to eight years the life of a parliament that had hitherto continued in existence until the death of the king. And the fact that the Lord Lieutenant had begun to reside continu- ously in the country was both a symptom and a cause of changes that were taking place in political life. The multiple contacts be- tween English and Irish politicians, the influence of parties in West- minster and the solicitude of absentee landlords at this side of the water for their rights and their property at the other side, helped to hasten the course of this development. Then had come the War of American Independence, raising in a vivid form (and

[1] H.M.C. *Appendix to 8th Report, Pt. I*, Emly Mss. p. 199, 12 Aug. 1778.

upon an imposing scale) the whole issue of the relations between Great Britain and her "dependencies". One pamphleteer in our period said that there had long been a Protestant interest, a Popish interest, and an English interest; but "till the year 1778, I never heard of an *Irish* interest in Ireland since the reign of queen Elizabeth."[1]

Finally, it was to prove important that at the end of 1776 there came to Ireland a Lord Lieutenant who represented a change in policy and adopted a new attitude. He firmly believed that an improvement in the condition of Ireland itself was necessary in order to make that country more serviceable to Britain—even more immediately serviceable for the purpose of the struggle with the American colonies. Before he had been in office a year he thought it prudent to guard himself in advance against the possible accusation that he was "ambitioning the character of an Irish patriot."[2]

He was the Earl of Buckinghamshire—though he would sign his letters "Buckingham"—and the favour of Lord George Germain was supposed to have assisted his appointment in 1776. Lord North had desired that Lord Hillsborough should become Lord Lieutenant, but the King—in spite of a curious protest made by Robinson in view of North's unhappiness—had refused to accept a man who "has no property but in Ireland". The precedent seemed to him to be too dangerous. Lord Buckingham on the other hand had been "knocking at every door", he said; and in deference to Robinson's arguments he promised not to appoint this man "because he would not appear as recommended by Lord North". He asked Robinson "to recommend any decent peer to Lord North", and the idea was entertained of prolonging the tenure of the existing Lord Lieutenant, Lord Harcourt. Finally, the chief minister had to confess that he had made an engagement to appoint Buckingham if his previous recommendations came to nothing—which may explain why the rejection of Hillsborough had seemed to distress him so unduly. Buckingham became Lord Lieutenant after all therefore; and in view of this man's relations with Hillsborough,

[1] *The First Lines of Ireland's Interest in the Year* 1780 (1779), p. 40.
[2] H.M.C. *Stopford Sackville Mss.* I, 247.

Robinson, and North in the subsequent course of the story, the whole transaction is not without its significance.[1]

Buckingham had not been in the country very long before he made the announcement that "Government cannot long be conducted upon the system which for some years has prevailed." Faced with great financial arrears, and unsympathetic towards the régime that he found in existence in Ireland, he sought to form his administration on a basis less expensive—less directly corrupt— than that of his predecessors, Lord Townshend and Lord Harcourt. He had family and political relations with certain men in Ireland, like Conolly and the Duke of Leinster, who—as some alleged— tended to draw him away from the connections upon which the previous Lords Lieutenant had relied. If we are to search into all possible private motives for his conduct we must note that at a later date—at the time of his retirement—he disclosed the resentment he had had against successive administrations in England (as well as against one of his predecessors, Townshend) because of the treatment he had so long had to suffer from them at home, in his county of Norfolk. Ministers had shown a "uniform determination," he said "to depress my family and exalt the Townshends and Walpoles."[2] These facts are not the explanation of his conduct as Lord Lieutenant; but they may have operated in his mind to remove some inhibitions and hindrances. After he had been in office for over eighteen months it was not from the ministry in England that he met with difficulty, however, and he said that Lord North's conduct had been "uniformly honourable and liberal". In Ireland "the immediate friends of the late Administration are disgusted at my not placing an implicite confidence in them"; and there was "secret dissatisfaction against that oeconomy" which he said he had first adopted on principle, but which by now had become a matter of necessity. But Lord North, Lord George Germain and a number of men in England who condemned his conduct at a later date were

---

[1] Add. Mss. 37,833, ff. 84–85, 89–90, 91; H.M.C. *Appendix to 5th Report, Pt. I,* Sutherland Mss. 209, Lord North to Lord Gower, 20 Nov. 1776 (after an application had been made on behalf of the Earl of Carlisle); *ibid. Various Mss.* VI, Knox Mss. 263–65; *ibid. Abergavenny Mss.* p. 15, No. 118.

[2] H.M.C. *Lothian Mss.* p. 373.

ready in this earlier period to applaud his work as Lord Lieutenant. He was congratulated on his success in his first parliamentary session. It was he who pointed out at that very moment that "my present ground in Ireland . . . is a little tender."[1]

As a further feature in that general background which we have to assemble around our narrative, we must note the fact that the ministry of North attempted to treat the Irish in a generous manner. North at least had the wish to be liberal, and if he could not break through the limitations of the traditional British attitude, he seems to have been more generous in his desires than many of the politicians in Westminster. In any case, even if no friendly or generous disposition had existed, the revolt of the American colonies— and the fear of a parallel upheaval nearer home—would have tended to encourage an accommodating attitude on the part of the British ministry. The intervention of the French on the side of the colonists, and the fear that a French attempt at invasion might bring out a mutinous spirit in Ireland, induced the government to relax the penal laws (as they had carried the Quebec Act in Canada), in order to secure the affection of the Roman Catholics. At a later date North could say on this whole question of his policy towards Ireland:

If they [the Irish] will look back to the transactions of this century, they will find more attention paid to the interests of Irish individuals and of the kingdom in general, within these last ten years than in all the rest of it. Both the Legislative and Executive powers have been disposed to favour Ireland.[2]

All these features of the situation, then, were in favour of Ireland in this period, and would give reason for the supposition that if things had taken their natural course—if all had proceeded without clash and without cataclysm—the age would in any case have seen a

[1] H.M.C. *Stopford Sackville Mss. I*, 251–52; *ibid. Lothian Mss.* 326–27, where Hillsborough praises his management of "the longest and most difficult Session of Parliament I ever remember in Ireland."

[2] H.M.C. *Appendix to 8th Report, Pt. I*, Emly Mss. pp. 201–02; cf. *Parliamentary History*, XX, 662 and 1229–30, and *Thoughts on the Present Alarming Crisis of Affairs* (Dublin 1779) pp. 7–12.

remarkable development in that country. The same features would appear to confirm the accepted view that a revolutionary spirit arises when things are beginning generally to improve; the view also that the discontented find their opportunity at the moment when a government is trying to be kind. In spite of these signs of a profound form of progress that was taking place, great distresses did exist, and these are the things that made the most noise in 1779, precisely because they were on the surface. Men in any case are prone to see grievances—and to make much of them—and it requires an effort to induce them to be still for a moment and to count their blessings. Whatever Arthur Young might say, an Irish pamphleteer could go back to the reign of James I, and complain that Ireland had progressed so little since that time compared with the American colonies.

Ireland was a country in which the social situation was so defective that, if economic advance was taking place, its more palpable benefits might be confined to comparatively few people whether in town or in country-side. The great mass of the inhabitants seemed to exist on a somewhat precarious footing—almost, one might say, at the mercy of any local change of wind. The British policy of trade-restriction put a serious curb upon the economic development of the country and hardly the fringe of it was touched (until the close of 1779) by Lord North's attempts to be generous. The subjection of the Roman Catholic part of the population was so serious in its economic effects that Arthur Young—like some other people—regarded them as a greater check upon the prosperity of the country than all the other causes put together.[1] The tremendous drainage of money to Britain for the payment of pensioners and absentee landlords put a further strain upon the resources of the country; and, as the Irish commissioners of revenue pointed out later, required "an uncommon Balance of Trade in our Favour, to enable Us even to exist as a Commercial Nation". So the Irish could make for themselves a rosy picture of what their progress would have been like in the last generation but for these harassments and hindrances. The Lord Chancellor of Ireland, writing in

[1] A. Young, op. cit. II, 271-72, where Young gives a list of the things which have impeded Irish prosperity.

September 1779, could describe the Kingdom as "kept . . . on the very margin of distress", and could claim that it needed assistance "to lift it above the power of little accidents to bring it into such difficulties as it is now in."[1]

The "accident" which in any case proved too much for the system to bear was the War of American Independence, the subsequent conflict with France, and, over a year later still, the added hostility of Spain. In a way which official statistics would hardly reveal, the war destroyed an important clandestine trade with America—a trade in woollens in particular—as well as the commerce with France. In spite of the signs of progress which Arthur Young claimed to have seen, neither the Lord Lieutenant, nor his advisers, nor the commissioners of the revenue in Dublin—neither North, nor the other ministers in England, nor even the Anglophile enemies of the Lord Lieutenant—denied the reality of the distresses in Ireland in our period. These showed themselves in the failures of manufacturers, merchants and banking families; in landlords complaining of rents unpaid; and in the sinister starving crowds that were seen in the Dublin streets. Even a sceptic who did "not think the manufacturers so extremely distressed as some represent them", was willing to admit that "two banks and nineteen merchants breaking in ten days" was to be regarded as a serious matter. And if he was right in saying that the failure of a scoundrel, Mr Birch, "first began the train of bankruptcy" (after which "the run on banks and merchants became general"), he did not deny that things were too near the margin in any case—and indeed he insisted that something would have to be done for Ireland very soon. Even he wrote: "whenever peace shall be restored between us and America, emigrations will desolate this nation and men of rank and fortune will join them."[2] The distress was palpable—far beyond anything which the War of American Independence had so far produced in Great Britain. The Lord Chancellor of Ireland wrote:

When I look back to the State of this Country only ten or eleven years ago and compare it with the present State of Things I see a

[1] See below, p. 97.
[2] H.M.C. Dartmouth Mss. III, 240–41; cf. 242.

mighty difference. The Treasury was in Credit and every Thing was well paid. The Trade and Manufactures were such as to afford my Eye an appearance of Ease and Prosperity, and there was not as I recollect any Thing of that Public and Private Distress that is now felt.

The English themselves could point to scenes of distress at home, and could invite the Irish to envisage their misfortunes—in the way they themselves had found it natural to do—that is to say, as the unhappy incidents of a state of war. The Irish, however, did not blame the mischances of war, or their defective social system, or the operation of the penal laws or even the totality of the compound situation. Out of all the varied factors that were combining to produce distress they picked out the single one which seemed amenable to human volition and capable of remedy, the one which, so long as it was unremedied, must clearly be held responsible. They took the usual course, which is to blame whatever enemy is handy, whatever enemy is vulnerable—particularly if it is a government— and most of all if it is a government not quite one's own. For distresses which from 1776 were apparently unavoidable in the transition to a state of war, and which were connected with the dearth and high price of provisions, they blamed for a long time the embargo placed by the English ministry on the export of provisions from Ireland—a measure regarded as necessary for the purpose of preventing supplies from reaching the enemy.[1] This was gradually taken off in due course but the general policy of trade-restriction still remained and it was this, they said, which tipped the balance and made Ireland so sensitive to the accident of a war. There was logic in the argument and the historian would be unfair if he merely demonstrated academically that the distresses were due to the conflict with the American colonies.

On the question of trade restrictions Lord North, at a comparatively early stage in the story, allowed himself to be committed by his very sympathies for Ireland, so that henceforward his rear was entirely exposed. The one thing we can say is that, at these higher levels, Britain, even at this early date, was ready to be generous in

[1] Theresa M. O'Connor, "The Embargo on the Export of Irish Provisions 1776-9," in *Irish Historical Studies*, II (1941), pp. 3 *et seqq*.

the matter of commerce. As a result of North's influence the British house of commons on 8 April 1778 were induced to carry almost unanimously five significant resolutions, which announced what the Irish regarded as remarkably generous principles of commercial policy. The wave of protest from vested interests in England and Scotland, however, was too formidable for a government only too conscious of its weakness; and the concessions had to be reduced to something almost derisory. It was not for the sake of Britain in general, therefore, not for the benefit of the British Empire as a whole, but palpably to please particular interests in England and Scotland that the Irish were deprived of their objective at this period. Yet the fact that the resolutions in favour of Irish trade had been carried at all in the British house of commons, had a significance which could not be mistaken. The English had confessed their sins; the parliament at Westminster had admitted its duty to Ireland—who that was an Irishman at all could now deny that his country had a case? From this date the question of the commercial restrictions ceased to be a mere banner for factious enemies of the ministry in Ireland. As the distresses increased and feeling was intensified it became the burning issue. The principle of "free trade" from this moment was turned into something like a national cause.

The same period—April and May 1778—also saw the rise of an issue perhaps even more momentous, the question of the formation of companies of Volunteers. France had just entered the war and there was a general fear on both sides of the Channel that Ireland was about to be invaded. In any case there was danger from privateers, who were able to roam with impunity off the British and Irish coasts. The army in Ireland had been greatly depleted for service across the Atlantic; such of it as existed on paper was deceptive, for it was known that many of the men who had been left in the country could be of little service in actual battle.[1] It was admitted that the numbers were barely sufficient even for garrison duty in any case. And nobody denied the fact that the country was virtually without defence.

It would be difficult to charge the Lord Lieutenant with an excess of anxiety at this crisis, for the messages from London only

[1] H.M.C. *Lothian Mss.* pp. 335-36.

justified his alarm and increased his fears. A militia bill was passed by the parliament in Dublin, but it was a question whether the country could bear the expense, and in any case there were reasons why the expedient of a militia would hardly answer to the needs of the situation. It was in parliament and in the circle around the Lord Lieutenant that the question of forming Volunteer companies was aired and debated in March and April 1778. It was by the house of commons, the privy council and the Lord Lieutenant himself that the expedient was proposed to the British government as the only one which was really appropriate to the crisis. When the militia bill came to the privy council, "by much the greater number of lords were of opinion that it would not answer the good purposes for which it was formed." In the south "the number of Protestants is so inconsiderable that it would be difficult to form a militia"; and the regular troops would be stationed there in any case. In the north a militia was intended for "the preservation of the peace and good order amongst the lower ranks of the people", since it was feared that in the absence of the regular troops there would be a recurrence of "that opposition to the payment of rents, tithes and assessments which prevailed so strongly in some of the northern counties some years ago". In this region, however, the militia "would be composed of that body of the people which may be suspected of being inclined to enter such riots". For this reason it would be particularly unreliable as an instrument for the repression of disorder.

The British government was therefore urged to adopt officially the policy of "raising in such particular counties as shall be thought fitting a certain number of independent companies". The crown would commission the officers; it was to be presumed that the government would be able to control the movement; and Buckingham was prepared to budget for forty companies or 4,520 men, though he imagined that the number would not need to be carried so high as this. The Irish house of commons had had it in mind to submit legislation on this matter, and, for example, had actually been inclined at one moment to introduce a clause on the subject into the militia bill. If it had finally decided to hold its hand and carry the militia bill without such a clause, this had not been out of any preference for a militia, "but on a suggestion of its being improper" to attempt to legislate on that further topic. The view had been put forward "that His Majesty might by his prerogative in times of danger, raise independent companies without any enabling authority from Parliament". No effort was spared to induce the English ministry to recommend this course of action to George III. It was argued that the Irish militia would be unsatisfactory in other ways—"that discipline could not be kept up by the mode of fining prescribed in the Bill". The Speaker of the Irish house of commons, Edmond Pery, was sent to London to press the case, and he was not to be put off even if it transpired that there was doubt concerning the legality of raising independent companies by royal prerogative. In such an event he was to be introduced to the Attorney General and Solicitor General in London, and Buckingham evidently still nursed the hope that the "difficulty" would be "removed". The majority of the Irish privy council recommended this policy. Buckingham declared his own preference for it, and pressed it—even describing it as a "matter of the greatest consequence". Everything seemed ready for such a scheme, and he wrote:

Several gentlemen of considerable property declared in the House of Commons that they would, if authorised, raise without loss of time independent companies formed out of their respective tenantries, of men upon whom they could depend . . . men much better to be relied on than a militia.[1]

Indeed the raising of such companies on a limited scale or as a purely local affair was not unprecedented in Irish history. In 1760 they had been organized under Lord Charlemont for the defence of Belfast after the French had landed at Carrickfergus. During the Whiteboy troubles they had been raised in various parts for the protection of life and property. Since Ireland had been so largely denuded of regular troops they were necessary if some of the ordinary actions of executive government were to be made effective in certain localities.

[1] H. Grattan, *Memoirs of . . . the Rt. Hon. Henry Grattan*, I, 301–02.

While the whole matter was being discussed in the spring of 1778 such companies were already being formed in Ireland, at Wexford, for example, and then in Belfast, where, though the inhabitants had been warned of imminent danger, Buckingham had had to announce that "government could not immediately afford a greater force for their protection than sixty troopers."[1] One writer said later that "the independent companies are so necessary, that they seem to owe their existence to an instinctive consent, operating on all minds at the same moment".[2]

The whole issue was presented to the British government at the very moment when the crisis on the question of the commercial restrictions had become serious—when the resolutions of the house of commons in Westminster on 8 April had precipitated a fury on the one side of the water and a fever on the other. The ministry refused to give the authorization which the Lord Lieutenant had desired, but the latter took his revenge in a manner that fitted their mood as well as answering to his own diagnosis of the needs of the situation; for, having already allowed the movement to begin, he merely went on doing nothing. He refused to authorize the companies or to distribute arms to them, and took refuge in a policy of *laissez-faire*.

By December 1778 he felt it necessary to give the British government some explanation of his conduct in regard to the Volunteers. By this time indeed he had to report a further development: "I now find that these associations are spreading into the internal parts of the Kingdom." In regard to this new stage of the movement he declared later:

In the interior and remote parts of Ireland, where Magistrates are scarce, and those few act with reluctance and timidity, the mode of suppressing them would have been difficult and delicate.

[1] H. Grattan, *Memoirs of . . . the Rt. Hon. Henry Grattan*, 1, 347–49; cf. H.M.C. *Lothian Mss.* p. 330, where in reply to a request for naval defence against a privateer, the First Lord of the Admiralty says: "It is not want of inclination but want of means of doing it that prevents our having a larger number of ships stationed for the purpose"; and suggests that the Irish might supply seamen.

[2] *A Letter to the People of Ireland on the Expediency and Necessity of the Present Associations* (Dublin, 1779), p. 16.

In February 1779 he reported:

The numbers of the associated companies greatly exceed my expectations, they have grown up insensibly, but none of the servants of the Crown seem to think them dangerous.

In the same month, however, as there was "some solicitude in England respecting the Independent Companies", he asked various people who were in his confidence to procure "nearly a correct account of the number of men under that description in the parts of Ireland where you stand most intimately connected, and how they are commanded". In the following May he informed the English secretary of state that he put the number in the region of 8,000.[1]

§II. THE CRISIS IN ANGLO-IRISH RELATIONS

From spring 1779 the situation in Ireland began to give promise of a crisis more serious in both its scale and its character than anything which had previously been envisaged. The British ministry had made only minor niggling attempts to give any satisfaction to the country; though on 19 March, for example, it had proposed in the house of commons that "the whole charge of regiments on the Irish establishment, now serving out of that kingdom", that is to say, employed in the American War, should be taken over by Great Britain. Irish petitions concerning "the stagnation of commerce and the failure of public and private credit" began from this time to be succeeded by a series of non-importation agreements. Local associations were formed and mutual engagements were made for the purpose of encouraging industry at home and stopping the introduction into the country of British manufactures in particular. The British secretary of state agreed with the Lord Lieutenant that "in this moment of heat, any interference might have pernicious effects." The movement was regarded, however,

[1] *Grattan Memoirs*, I, 347–49; H.M.C. *Lothian Mss.* p. 345; *ibid. Appendix to 8th Report: Pt. I, Emly Mss.* p. 200.

as a dangerous one; and Buckingham was urged to try to prevent further developments.[1]

It was a strong argument against the whole policy of trade-restriction that Ireland had been one of England's best customers for a long time. Her significance in this respect had become greater than ever now that the American colonies seemed to be making good their claim to independence. The value of her imports was assessed at two millions pounds a year, and this sum was regarded as capable of considerable expansion if she could only be permitted to increase her purchasing-power. On the contrary, however, Ireland's capacity to import the produce of Great Britain had lately been reduced. The new associations quickly became the fashion, and a considerable publicistic campaign had the effect of raising them to the dignity of a patriotic cause. They could claim to pay a dividend, for news was received that a palpable effect had been produced on British towns—indeed on the very ones which had so recently prevented the emancipation of Irish trade. It was calculated that in any case these associations were in a position to prevent a million pounds a year from leaving the country; and it was even argued that Ireland could not do better than this if the British government were to make the commercial concessions that had so long been desired.

Sinister though they were, the non-importation agreements, however, were not the principal agency in the developments that took place in 1779. They operated perhaps somewhat as a hindrance of hindrances, by the mere fact that they struck directly at the obstinacy of the vested interests in Great Britain. They were a restricted and dubious instrument of policy, ragged in their consequences, and limited in their staying-power. The attempt was made on occasion to publish the names of dealers, who infringed the non-importation policy, so that these might become subject to popular resentment. Goods imported in defiance of the patriotic movement might even be destroyed by an indignant mob. In 1780 an association was to be formed in Dublin against thieves who operated on the pretext of enquiring into the stocks of imported foreign goods.

[1] [Public Record Office] S[tate] P[apers], 63/464 ff. 314-15, 330 (printed in *Grattan Memoirs*, I, 345-47); also f. 344.

The whole movement was open to the reproach at a later period that it "brought on its own dissolution"; since within Ireland it gave opportunity to the unscrupulous and the unworthy. It provided scope for further forms of exploitation—"extravagant prices and base workmanship of every manufacture".

The effects of the movement of Irish resistance were considerably enlarged before the end of May 1779 by the emergence of developments still more sinister and the revelation of potentialities still more vast in the Volunteer companies. These companies now began both to show a serious increase in number and to assume a different character. The Lord Lieutenant had only lately been assured that "the spirit of the Independent Companies would subside." He wrote on 23 May, however, that:

within these few days intelligence has reached me, that additional companies are forming; and it has been asserted that this arises from the insinuations which are daily circulated in the public prints, that the idea of their numbers may conduce to the attainment of political advantages to their country.

It is from this point that the state of the question begins to be transformed and the real intensity of the crisis of 1779 takes its start. And it gives us no surprise to find the British secretary of state replying to the Lord Lieutenant that "the reasons" which had been given to account for the spread of the Volunteer associations in this period "must be considered as alarming".

It requires the utmost vigilance of Government that no injury should arise to the State, by the means that have been used by well-designing subjects for the defence of the country, and the support of the civil magistracy.[1]

The Lord Lieutenant, who had already considered that any attempt to interfere with the non-importation associations would be dangerous, was advised in Dublin that it would be similarly unwise to attempt to stop the recruiting of the Volunteer associations. He convinced the secretary of state that it would be imprudent to allow these bodies even to imagine that they were feared or

[1] *Grattan Memoirs*, I, 347–49, 358–60; cf. S. P. 63/464, f. 360.

suspected by the administration. Buckingham had been hampered all the time by his sympathy with the grievances of Ireland; by his view that the independent companies were essential both for the purpose of defence and for the maintenance of order in the localities; by the knowledge that he himself lacked the force which was necessary to make executive government effective; and by the casual manner in which he was being treated by the ministers in Westminster. Up to a comparatively late date it was held that the French invasion-threat of 1779 would be directed against Ireland,[1] and in any case this latter country was not in a position to feel itself secure throughout the summer. If it may be argued that Buckingham ought to have met the Volunteer crisis with a stronger policy, it is doubtful whether even for this purpose he would have received much assistance from the ministry in London at this date. We must beware of one of the perpetual optical illusions of historical study— the impression that all would have been well if men had only done "the other thing."

If the despatches of the Lord Lieutenant reveal a considerable extension of the crisis—and an increase in his anxieties—during the closing days of the month of May, it is interesting to note that now, for the second time in the course of this narrative, the intensification of the pressure in Ireland was connected with events that had recently taken place in the British parliament. His sympathies with Ireland did not prevent the Lord Lieutenant from putting forward the view that the champions of that country in the house of commons had aggravated the state of Irish opinion. Months later he still repeated that the Volunteers never became a formidable problem "till Lord Beauchamp and others mentioned them in the English Parliament as a reason for awing the Legislature into concessions". The Irish press had quickly taken the hint. Henceforward the development of the Volunteer movement was to be a subject of genuine anxiety.[2]

From the beginning of the year there had been motions in the British parliament on behalf of what were called the "famishing"

[1] See e.g., *Corr. George III*, IV, 370.
[2] S. P. 63/468, Buckingham to Hillsborough, Secret, 2 Jan. 1780; cf. H.M.C. *Stopford Sackville Mss.* I, 255; *Grattan Memoirs*, I, 347.

Irish. On 11 May, however, the Marquess of Rockingham opened in the house of lords a debate which was of a very different order; in more respects than one it will be seen that it was the starting-point of that chapter—the real opening of that stage of the story—upon which we are now entering. Before putting his motion, Rockingham spoke to the King, saying that "he had always made it his practice to inform his Majesty of his intentions before he moved anything in Parliament"—which surprised George III who declared that he had not seen him in his closet since he went out of office in 1766. George saw that he had come prepared to make "a long set speech", so at a convenient moment (when Rockingham was explaining that "he was not impelled by personal consideration for his estate" in Ireland, where "he was so happily circumstanced that he always received his rents") he decided that "this was a good opportunity to make him shorten" his speech, by "diverting" him from the plan he had prepared. George "asked him how he managed so well"—why he was so successful with his Irish property—and afterwards gave the following account of the interview:

This made him talk a little about his own affairs and took him out of his speech; and when he came to resume it again, he could not take it up in form but huddled the substance together.

Rockingham desired Ireland to have the liberty of sending grain into England, and the right to export the coarser kind of woollen cloth. But, said the King afterwards.

I could not help observing how people are affected by their particular interest; for I was talking of what Lord Rockingham proposed to Lord Hertford and he said the exportation of woollens will do nothing for Ireland; advantages in the linen were the things wanting.

According to his own account George replied to Rockingham that he had opened the discussion in the wrong place; "for it was the House of Commons that was principally concern'd in these sorts of questions".[1]

[1] H.M.C. *Various Mss.* VI, Knox Papers, pp. 261-62.

The King might play a cat-and-mouse game with him in the closet, but Rockingham had his revenge and seemed determined to play with fire when he made his motion on 11 May in the house of lords. He may have realized that Ireland was already moving in the direction of revolution. He was ready in any event to let it be known that if she resorted to drastic policies she would have the support of the opposition in England. He did not shrink from pointing out in a series of parallelisms the curious sympathy and correspondence between the American and the Irish movements of resistance. He put the case that "the American war commenced in addresses and petitions; that when those were turned a deaf ear to, they were followed with non-importation agreements"; and that Ireland "was precisely in that situation which, if not speedily remedied, would, in the opinion of many, justify resistance." Repeatedly he drew attention to the Volunteer associations. If they had been formed to guard the country against a French invader, he said, they might also be used for the purpose of resisting the oppressions of the British government.[1]

Rockingham carried his main object, which was an address desiring information concerning the trade of Great Britain and Ireland. His ultimate purpose was to procure an inquiry into the measures that would be most suitable for promoting the prosperity of the two countries. Lord Gower, a government spokesman, accepted the essential features of this motion, and made statements which, both at the time and by his own admission at various subsequent dates, were interpreted as implying a promise that something should be done for Ireland.[2] The total result was that the Irish could be sure of having the powerful opposition parties in England behind them if they sought in any way to make their resistance more effectual. In any case their hopes had been definitely raised, and the

---

[1] *Parliamentary History*: xx, 635–42 cf. e.g., H.M.C. *Stopford Sackville Mss.*, I, 255.

[2] The commitment was so clear that Shelburne in a later debate of 2 June [*Parliamentary History*, xx, 664], appealed to the house to remember whether he himself "had not on that day [11 May] been the single peer to cry out *doucement*; whether he had not stood up alone and said, 'Gently, take care what you do, don't promise too much, for fear you should not be able to perform all that you say you'll do'."

disappointment would be the more bitter if disillusionment were to follow, as indeed it was almost bound to do.

The revision of Anglo-Irish trading relations was necessarily a difficult matter. It would have to be the subject of serious inquiry and grave transaction before it could be embodied in the statute-book. It was stated on behalf of the ministry that in any case there would have to be some negotiation with British interests before anything of significance could be achieved. Rockingham in London, however, was impatient, and was well aware of what was to be expected from the administration of Lord North. On 26 May, only just over a fortnight after his original motion, he raised the question again, announcing that "with infinite astonishment he saw that no one step had been taken in that important business." As the demand for information had been punctually transmitted to Dublin, and the Lord Lieutenant there had welcomed the opening and had immediately set to work upon the matter, Rockingham was behaving perhaps in a somewhat incendiary manner when he declared at this early stage in the proceedings:

This fresh instance of duplicity or total neglect would exasperate the oppressed people of Ireland and work them up into such successive paroxysms of resentment, phrenzy and despair as might at length terminate in a civil convulsion which would shake the government of these Kingdoms to its foundations.

"Ministers," he said, "have determined to intercept the gracious dispositions of the crown and the good intentions of parliament." Earl Gower, who again made the most significant statement on behalf of the government in this debate, confirmed the impression which he had previously given, and showed that he regarded the motion of 11 May as a "security" that something was to be done for the Irish in the near future. At the same time he made it clear that in the opinion of the ministers the new legislation could not be prepared before the prorogation of parliament. In any case, he said, it was not a proper thing to be submitted to thinly-attended houses at the close of the existing session.

Up to this point the action of the government had been slow, and ministers had hardly seemed to realize the seriousness of the approaching crisis. The conduct of the administration had not been inexplicable, however, especially if it is remembered that vested interests in England had already taken alarm; that the members for Lancashire (solicitous for the cotton trade) had been making more protests in the house of commons, and had referred to the distresses of this country, which, they said, were as serious as those of Ireland; that finally Lord North was reduced to paralysis by a host of other anxieties and by the memory of the storm which the proposed concessions to Irish trade had provoked in the previous year. North—feeling himself in a tragic position, unable to move either to the right or to the left—chose this very moment, however, to put the government in the wrong. He made it clear that in spite of the previous statement by Gower in the house of lords he, for his part, had no intention of taking any serious action in regard to the problem of Irish trade. On 26 May he declared in the house of commons that he still regarded the Irish complaints as unfair and ill-timed; that more had been done in the last three or four years for Ireland than had been attempted in previous decades; and that he knew of no method of satisfying the Irish demands at this period which would not be detrimental to the commercial interests of Britain herself.[1] The whole problem of Irish trade, the whole issue of Anglo-Irish relations was to be embittered during the course of the summer by this discrepancy in the statements that were made on behalf of the ministry.

At the begining of June, Lord Shelburne in the house of lords called attention to the harmful effects that North's speech was bound to have, especially in view of the hope that had been raised by the repeated assertions and promises of Lord Gower.

What could the noble lord [North] mean Did he wish for a new war to mis-conduct? . . . [Lord Shelburne] desired the house to recollect that the American war had commenced upon less provocation than this country had given Ireland.

---

[1] *Parliamentary History*, xx, 661–63; cf. *ibid.* 271, where North says, 12 March, that he had a design of offering Ireland "a plan infinitely more to her advantage than allowing her to import her sugars immediately from the West India islands." It is not clear whether this project was that of a union, which emerged a few months later. Cf. pp. 160 *et seqq.* below.

He did not miss the opportunity of "stating the several instances of neglect, inattention and designed delay, which ministers had been guilty of respecting Ireland". It was Shelburne's chief purpose, however, to take up the argument where Lord Gower had left it in the previous debate—that is to say, where the point had emerged that no action was intended during the existing session of parliament. "It would be absurdity in the extreme," he argued, "to let the Irish remain unsatisfied for seven or eight months longer." He desired the King to lay before the house "an account of such steps that have been taken in consequence of the Address of this House of the 11th May." He also moved that the King should be asked:

if his royal prerogative . . . be not adequate to the relief of . . . Ireland, that he would be pleased to continue the parliament of this kingdom as now assembled, and give immediate orders for calling forthwith his parliament of Ireland.

Camden put the opposition argument in a nutshell: "Something had been promised; nothing had been done." The call was definitely made to the government, and a challenge was issued in the following terms: "Give us some one instance to show that you are sincere and in earnest." On 25 June Lord Gower reiterated his assurance in the house of lords and declared "that he understood the Irish were perfectly satisfied with the parliamentary pledge." The English parliament was to be prorogued then, for the summer, while the whole problem of restrictions on Irish trade was left in this indeterminate condition.

The speeches of the English opposition had conveyed to the Irish every hint that the prolongation of their distresses had been due to the actual duplicity of the North administration. They had given provocation to Irish resistance, incitement to the Volunteers, and a promise that a party in England was prepared to support that country even in desperate measures. It is not surprising, then, that in the latter half of May the situation in Ireland began more definitely to deteriorate, as we have seen, and the despatches of the Lord Lieutenant revealed new anxieties at the other side of the water. At the same time the British ministers before the end of the month had begun to learn from the Lord Lieutenant the more menacing aspects of the Irish situation, and the possible political importance of the Volunteers. They, too, had reason to know from this moment that the opposition in England would aid and abet the Irish in every possible way. They made a serious mistake, therefore, in proroguing the British parliament before something had been done, or some more definite assurance had been given, on the subject of Irish trade. In the face of such blindness the most respectable opposition might well feel justified in taking desperate courses.

That part of the opposition at least were bent on what might be called mischief-making, is a fact which can hardly be doubted, however, when we take a glance at the subsequent proceedings. The next turn of the screw was the work of Charles James Fox, who in this period so often added the final stroke to the arguments of his friends and put the crown upon their extravagances, as though determined to drive the whole logic of the situation to a further extreme—to go one note higher than the top note on the piano. If we are to judge by the analogy of parallel situations in this very year we may say that he spoke with a semi-revolutionary intent— he almost desired to make the problem more acute and the situation more dangerous. Little of what he said is reported, but on a motion to ask the King to defer prorogation, he made in the house of commons an allusion which, as offered at that particular moment, we can only regard as incendiary. He called attention to what he described as a "most weighty and able" pamphlet entitled *Observations respecting the extent of the power of the British Parliament, principally in relation to Ireland in a letter to Sir William Blackstone*. This pamphlet laid stress on those natural rights of man which it was claimed that no parliamentary statute could ever take away. It emphasised the radical principle that "a branch at least of the legislative power should reside in the whole body of the people." It declared that "if one branch of the legislature becomes subservient to another [a corrupt house of commons to a king, for example], the people are at liberty to constitute themselves a new legislature." Above all, it stated "that every act of power exercized by [the] legislature over the people of another community is an usurpation of the fourth natural right of mankind". Here Fox, as a man who has just made a new discovery, affects at least to give his approval to those more radical political theories with which he was certainly to be associated in the movement of 1780. He calls the attention of ministers to the doctrine that the British parliament has no *locus standi* in Ireland—no right to interfere in that country at all. These doctrines would perhaps be unexceptionable even to the great majority of Englishmen in the twentieth century. In July 1779, and in the mouth of Fox, there can be no doubt that the whole suggestion was spiced with malice.[1]

Some of the members of the English opposition, then, were not unwilling to plunge the country into a controversy which was to be more momentous than the purely commercial one. They were not slow to give respectability and recognition to a set of ideas more radical than those which were immediately in dispute. The problem of Irish trade was to be transcended and superseded by an issue that went to the roots of the body politic—the whole question of the constitutional relationship between the one country and the other. That question, now thrown upon the floor of parliament, was to become a matter of growing importance in the subsequent period.

Now it had happened that up to this point the British secretary of state, Lord Weymouth—whatever his later sins might be—had not been quite so indolent as the opposition lords had been ready to assume. He had written to Dublin on the subject of Lord Rockingham's resolution of 11 May, and by the 18th he was saying: "This Matter is under the consideration of His Majesty's Servants, and I trust I shall soon be enabled to write to you fully on the subject." It was almost in parenthesis that he had added, with reference to Rockingham's demand for information:

In the mean time I cannot doubt that Your Excellency will direct your most serious thought to this important matter, that you will transmit me Your Opinion, together with such information and materials as may lead to the forming of a proper Judgment on a

---

[1] *Parliamentary History*, xx, 875–76; cf. *ibid.* xx, 883, where Fox's uncle, the Duke of Richmond, speaking on the subject of the same pamphlet a few days later in the house of lords, affected to believe that its principles were actually held by "every person of property and common sense in Ireland". In various ways he spoke of Ireland as being "on the eve of vindicating . . . her natural and political rights".

point of such serious concern as the Welfare of the Kingdom of Ireland.

The further, and more specific, statement which Weymouth had promised never materialized. The conduct of the government even in regard to the imposing materials which the Lord Lieutenant was to send from Dublin turned out to be so remarkable that it is one of the strangest chapters in the whole story. It is not irrelevant, therefore, to note that from the first the Lord Lieutenant was only too eager to respond to the demand for information. On 28 May, he replied to Weymouth:

> Be assured that my best endeavours shall be used to obtain the fullest information upon the important matters therein mentioned, together with such materials as may lead to a proper judgment on a point of such concern.

Four days later he reported that he had communicated the Address of the British house of lords "to several persons of the first rank and consequence in Ireland and to the Commissioners of the Revenue". The latter, "from whom the fullest and most authentic information is to be expected", declared that they needed time for the conduct of their investigations; but they can hardly be blamed for the subsequent delays—it had already been announced in the British house of lords that nothing could be done before the prorogation of parliament. On 8 June, Buckingham reported again that his information would "be delayed and when given stated very cautiously except by the gentlemen who will probably recommend universal indulgence to the Commerce of Ireland". He added a hint concerning the expectations of the Irish at this date:

> Upon the whole my private opinion is that nothing short of permission to export coarse woollen goods will in any degree give general satisfaction. To this however it is necessary for me to add that no encouragement to expectations of that tendency has ever been held out by me.

From that time, for a period of over a month, Buckingham was transmitting to London the opinions of various people in Ireland and the information which was supplied to him by the Treasury in Dublin. When these had been despatched he wrote in conclusion on 12 July:

I have repeatedly mentioned how very necessary it was to give some satisfaction to this Kingdom upon Commercial points. The sentiments of the gentlemen who have been consulted upon that important consideration and the Letter from the Commissioners of the Revenue, will so fully enable H.M.'s Cabinet to form a judgment upon the whole that my entering into the subject would be trespassing upon their patience.[1]

The Lord Lieutenant, for his part, had warned the government that in view of disappointments recently suffered and indulgences recently refused—and more particularly in view of the hope and expectations raised by the recent transactions in the English parliament—a prorogation in England "without some actual Favor" would be followed by "disagreeable consequences" in Ireland. He had made it clear that he sympathized with the Irish people and he had defended them against the charge that they might be moved by mere factious hostility to England. He had warned the government against any resort to a repressive policy, and had put the case for concessions to Ireland, though doing this doubtfully sometimes, as one who thought he must deprecate his own suggestions, or rather as one who knew in advance that his hints would be unwelcome to the ministry to which he was sending them. He had kept his Chief Secretary, Sir Richard Heron, at the side of the British ministers in London, to press the Irish case, as long as the parliament had continued its session in Westminster. He even warned the ministry in London not to trust to corruption to save its face in the Irish house of commons; for on 12 June we find him writing:

It concerns me to have but too much reason to apprehend that the concessions proposed by the Gentlemen applied to in consequence of Your Lordship's dispatches of the 18 May and 1st inst. will be very extensive even from those who are conscious of their inadmissibility. The occasional favour of government cannot induce men to incur the odium of their country at a crisis which they deem critical for the attainment of her objects.

[1] S.P. 63/464, f. 342; S.P. 63/465, ff. 3-5, 99, 366; H.M.C. *Stopford Sackville Mss. I*, 255-56.

Since he was to be charged with remissness at a later time, and in particular was to be reproached for failing to send in his own views and diagnoses, we may note that as early as 28 May he had given his own analysis of the causes of the distress in Ireland. He mentioned the rise in rents, the increase in the interest on mortgages and on the national debt, the "enormous" pensions and salaries, the lack of the capacity for industry, and "the almost entire failure of paper credit". And if at one moment he made it clear that nothing less than the removal of some of the restrictions on the wool trade would satisfy the Irish, he now raised the question also of the establishment of a National Bank. On 1 July he wrote to Lord George Germain:

The same public spirit in no degree prevails in this Kingdom, which so generally pervades England, that of contributing uncompelled to the exigencys of the State. Yet candor should allow that this possibly may proceed from a circumstance which influences disagreeably in many instances, that excess of expense which in Ireland distresses every order of men.

He took the opportunity to put in a word at this point against the class of absentee landlords which comprised so many of the lords of the opposition in the British parliament, and so many of those who in general had been clamouring for concessions to Ireland. They did not deserve the benefit of the plea he had just put forward in favour of the rest of the Irish. Indeed, he said,

I understand, [they] are alarmed at the rumour of my having submitted to the Cabinet an idea of taxing them. Their not offering at this moment in some shape or other to assist a country where they possess such valuable stakes is certainly impolitick.[1]

Most important of all, however, was the collection of opinions which Buckingham induced a number of prominent Irishmen— Lord Lifford, Hely-Hutchinson, Hussey Burgh, Pery, Foster, etc.— to write, and which were despatched to London to meet the demands of Lord Rockingham, as expressed in the house of lords'

[1] *Grattan Memoirs*, I, 349–51; H.M.C. *Lothian Mss*. pp. 352–53.

Address of 11 May. Froude read them and said that they formed "the best exposition which exists of the poisonous forces which had so long been working in this country". Lecky said: "It is impossible to read them without being struck by their great ability." They were published by Professor George O'Brien in the *English Historical Review*, 1923-24. The Irish Lord Chancellor, Lord Lifford, summed up the purport of them a little later in the year and pointed out that there was complete agreement between the writers concerning the reality of the distress and the necessity of doing something to diminish it. No single person was prepared to look upon the misfortunes as the normal consequence of a state of war, and there was a tendency to point to a decline that had set in even before the outbreak of the conflict with America. The Lord Chancellor himself, when he gave his original opinion in June, talked of that "seeming Decay and Waste which like a disease has for a number of years been wearing down and weakening this Country". And his further opinion, that Ireland was too much at the mercy of "little accidents", should be put beside that of Pery, the Speaker of the Irish house of commons, who wrote:

The situation of a Nation which depends upon one single Manufacture is precarious, it must sensibly feel every revolution and uncertainty, to which every particular Manufacture is exposed.

The commissioners of the revenue pointed out that if French Protestants had not been driven to Ireland by a policy of religious persecution "we should not have preserved our linen manufacture". They said that the present distresses would have been even more severely felt if a number of artisans had not enlisted in the army, and if considerable relief had not been afforded by charitable contributions. Pery thought that the misery would have been even greater if the non-importation agreements had not "set those at work who were before unemployed".

Complaints concerning the drain of money to Britain by absentee landlords and pensioners were traced back to 1682, but the commissioners of revenue noted that the evil had greatly increased since the last peace, namely since 1763. The wealth which had then poured into England, and the fact that the interest-rates in that

country were very low, had induced many people to purchase
estates in Ireland ; while the Irish themselves for the same reason
tended to look across St George's Channel when money was
needed.

The Rents of the old Estates of Absentees have from the same
Period risen exceedingly upon the new setting of Leases except
where some Landlords have followed the Practice of taking heavy
Fines. . . . Subscriptions [to our Public Loans] have, from the
Poverty of the country, been mostly filled from Great Britain and
Foreign Parts.

The Lord Chancellor noted, however, that in earlier and better
days the country had been able to bear the payments to pensioners,
absentees, etc., and at the same time, till 1773-74, send £300,000 a
year out of the country for corn; whereas since that date corn had
been bringing money into the country. The opinions which were
transmitted to London were not merely facile and stereotyped.
And the Lord Chancellor came to an interesting conclusion concerning the economic difficulties of Ireland: "I am afraid there may
be some radical cause not yet sufficiently noticed or understood."
Many causes were discovered, many expedients suggested in
these papers. Here it was pointed out that the Irish government had
been defective in its own policies and regulations. There it was
noted that the interest-rate was too high and the country needed
capital, so that it was necessary to consider the question of forming
a National Bank. Elsewhere it would be admitted that the Irish
were idle or lacked "settled habits of industry'" and the "knack of
manufacture"—a weakness that their champions were ready to
explain by the absence of encouragement and security under the
existing system. Some men suggested the expedient of a tax on
absentees. Some pointed out that there were heavy duties (on ex-
ports, for example) which bore hardly on infant industries. Behind
all this, however, there was a general agreement that the restrictive
commercial policy of the British government ought to be relaxed;
that possibly nothing less than its total abolition would either meet
the economic situation or quieten the discontent; that at any rate
the Irish attributed their misfortunes to this system; and that its

abandonment could bring no danger to Britain, since Ireland was in no position to compete with her, and by the very nature of things her own wealth would always be drawn into England. At least the export of woollens should be allowed, for here the restrictions were "the most oppressive", and there ought to be permission to import goods directly from the West Indies, instead of through Britain (which policy had virtually resulted in the confinement of the Irish ports and the bulk of the population to the eastern side of the country). Also a small preference should be given in the English market for Irish corn, since the encouragement of an increased production of corn would "make this Country one of the greatest granaries of Europe". Sir Lucius O'Brien gave almost a foretaste of a later stage of the argument—a forewarning of what was to be a future complication in the story—when he added that such a degree of "free trade" would not be sufficient in itself to cure the ills of Ireland. The concessions, he said,

would neither remove the Distresses nor (in my Apprehension) the Discontents of this Country without a great variety of operative Regulations in this Kingdom, many of which should by no means be postponed till the Meeting of our Parliament.

Lord Newhaven, writing on 14 July, was under the impression that this collection of written opinions from Dublin had been put into the hands of George III. "When they have had his perusal", he remarked, "they will remain with ministers to be garbled just as may suit their purposes." Lord Newhaven need not have feared even this, for the prejudice or the malice of ministers was not so great as their inefficiency. The precious papers might as well have been consigned to the tender mercies of the Liffey or left to seek a destination amid the heavings and tumults of the Irish Sea.

§III. MINISTERIAL NEGLECT AND POPULAR UPHEAVAL

From the very moment when the Lord Lieutenant had collected and transmitted the most powerful persuasions that he could gather together, to break the resistance of the British ministry, further evidence began to be received to the effect that the situation in Ireland was rapidly deteriorating. Amongst the many letters which were sent from that country for the purpose of rousing the British government, was a remarkable communication from Pery, the Speaker of the Irish house of commons, addressed to Lord North, and described as "intended only for your private eye". It was dated 14 July and it opened in the following manner:

> It is my duty, though it is not in my department, to inform your Lordship of the desperate state to which this kingdom is reduced.
>
> If it is attacked in its present state, it will certainly be lost, perhaps without a blow. . . . The Treasury is exhausted, as was long foreseen and foretold. There is no money to enable the army to take the field. . . .[1]

The situation was pathetic. From the end of May when he was ordered to prepare the army for taking the field, the Lord Lieutenant struggled to convince the ministers in London that he did not possess the money either to procure the hay, flour, and horses which he was expected to acquire, or to increase the military staff. When on 24 June he was instructed to encamp the army he replied that unless money came from England the encampment would have to be "suspended within a fortnight". Lord North declared that he must regard the appropriations made by parliament as "sacred", so he declined to send financial help and Buckingham was recommended to summon his parliament immediately. At two meetings which were held at the Castle, however, it was decided that in view of the dangerous state of feeling it was impossible to risk such a measure at the moment.[2]

The reasons for this decision were given in another remarkable letter written by John Beresford, one of the commissioners of the revenue in Ireland, to John Robinson on 2 August. Beresford re-

---

[1] H.M.C. *Appendix to 8th Report, Pt. I*, Emly Mss. p. 201.

[2] On this protracted and distressing struggle between Buckingham and the British ministry, see S.P. 63/464, f. 352; S.P. 63/465, ff. 34, 74–75, 141, 143, 180, 182, 366; *Grattan Memoirs*, I, 374–77; II, 394–95; H.M.C. *Lothian Mss.* pp. 352–53; *ibid. Appendix to 8th Report, Pt. I*, Emly Mss. pp. 201–02; *Corr. George III*, IV, 376.

ported that one of the chief factors was the certainty that the summoning of parliament would bring to a head the national indignation and precipitate an upheaval on the question of "indulgences" to Irish trade. It would be difficult "to bring some people into any degree of moderation on this subject", he wrote. Nothing less than free trade would be demanded, and the cry would be backed by the formation of "general associations . . . against the consumption of British goods". Beresford continued:

When Parliament shall meet you are to expect great violence, and unless something shall be settled beforehand, I fear it will be too late to enter into the subject at such a time, and with men labouring under strong prejudice, and that guided in many instances by the various influences of a popular assembly. The country is arming from one end to the other; county meetings are now publicly advertised for the purpose of raising independent companies . . . I tell you fairly, as I have done from the beginning, that unless your Administration will turn your most serious attention to the country, in its present and alarming situation, that the consequences will go further than you may possibly imagine.[1]

Up to this date the papers from Dublin on the subject of Irish commerce had been lying in London virtually unexamined, though Robinson at the Treasury had written to Charles Jenkinson on 23 July: "As far as I can form a judgment, I fear much confusion will arise from Ireland". On 11 August he wrote:

Things are again getting very awkward, and I wished much to talk to you. Ireland is getting very bad; and indeed I fear much confusion everywhere.

Five days later he found the correspondence from Dublin so alarming that he submitted Beresford's letters to the King who sent the following reply:

I had again this day pressed Lord North to have the papers from Ireland digested and such Papers as may be necessary on the part of this Country to be drawn up; ten days ago he thought no man so

---

[1] W. Beresford, *Correspondence of the Rt. Hon. John Beresford* . . . I, 43–46.

fit to be employed in this business as Mr. Jenkinson, last Friday he was quite hurt when pressed and said it had originated in the House of Lords and that he would not take any part in it; today he wants to employ the Attorney General; to be explicit I am greatly vexed at his frequent change of opinion which stops all business.

This was the period in mid-August when the enemy fleet was daily expected, and, as we have already seen, North was driving his collaborators to despair. On 16 August Robinson determined to rouse him, and showed him Beresford's letter of the 2nd, whereupon

he expressed great uneasiness and much anxiety to have something immediately done, said that he had not time to arrange the papers and to chalk out a plan, that it was impossible for him to do it, that Lord Weymouth had got the papers from Ireland but threw it upon him [North] to do.

It was decided that Jenkinson should be asked to take charge of the matter, and Robinson offered to make a digest of the papers from Ireland, if Lord North would give him an outline of his views to serve as a guide. North, however, complained that he had no time for considering the affair—that

He was kept so employed in Treasury matters which might be done by other Lords but that he had no Lord to sit with him or for him and in short no one would do anything and then [he] fell into one of his distressing fits.[1]

Jenkinson consented to take up the question of Irish trade, though he said "I have never a moment of leisure", and he made the complaint: "I own I was surprized to hear from the Attorney and others that my industry was to be made use of on this occasion long before I heard a word concerning it from Lord North." He made it a condition that he should not be known to be engaged in the work on the Irish question; but within twenty-four hours he wrote: "I was told by my own Deputy that I was to have this Busy-

[1] Add. Mss. 38, 212, ff. 31–32, 56, 61–62; Add. Mss. 37,834, f. 133.

ness added to my other Labour and I found it had been mentiond at my office." Since the condition had been broken, he instantly declared his refusal to have any further share in the matter, especially as he felt sure that already several letters would have gone to Ireland carrying news of the part he had consented to play. In any case—just as North had been recently doing—he declared that he had had nothing to do with the engagement which had been given on behalf of the administration in the house of lords in the previous May.[1]

Even the special intervention of Robinson failed, therefore, in mid-August, and for a period of over a month again, it would appear that the papers from Ireland were left untouched. It is almost incredible that the whole matter should still have been allowed to sleep, for on 20 August the Chief Secretary of Ireland, Sir Richard Heron, wrote to Robinson, "whether you give or refuse, do it immediately upon the meeting of parliament; for be assured that delay will tend to confusion". Even when the very summit of crisis was at hand—when the floods were about to be released—and on 16 September the Lord Lieutenant was sending urgent demands for instructions ("very particular instructions" so far as the commercial question was concerned) to fix the terms of his speech at the opening of the Irish parliament, the papers from Dublin were still left unexamined. Even now the course of the story might have been different if the British ministry had studied the commercial problem and had confronted Ireland with a policy.

At last on 27 September, we find that Robinson had taken up the matter again, and was writing to Jenkinson that the Irish question and further East India business were keeping him at work "nearly 18 hours every day". He reported that he had "made an abstract of all the Irish papers transmitted to Lord North from Lord Weymouth's office", because "I could not get Ld. North to read them in their present bulky state".

In the abstract he will read them more easy and I trust will have the full purport and fair opinion of each gentleman who has been consulted.

[1] Add. Mss. 38,307, f. 19, C. Jenkinson to J. Robinson, 17 Aug.

Three days later, however, when the work had been completed, it transpired that Lord North could not be induced even to examine the "abstract".

I can't ever get even Attention paid to anything of the kind from our friend, which is really discouraging to have them only considered as Waste paper, although what is of much more consequence I can't rouse him to an Attention to Ireland and indeed, and most truly that is a most serious Business, and before the next Month if there is not Instruction sent to the Lord Lieutenant how to conduct himself on the meeting of parliament in certain events and propositions by opposition, he will be overturned himself, the country will be in confusion, English government disgraced if not ruined and he will overturn with him perhaps the King's Government here.

So far as the original problem of the trade-restrictions was concerned, then, the British ministry ran into the crisis of October almost totally unprepared.[1]

In one sense it may be said that opinion in British governing circles was becoming somewhat clarified during August 1779; though the fact only renders still more strange and unjustifiable the general failure to attend to the problem of Ireland in this period. On 21 August Lord Lucan reported from London to the Speaker of the Irish house of commons:

If Administration has time and leisure this next session of Parliament, I understand from the best authority that an union between England and Ireland is to be agitated and settled if possible and that the first step for this purpose to be taken is the naming of deputies by each House of Parliament to consider of such a union or *incorporation* which is the word now made use of.

Lucan was betraying the design to a man who, as the letter goes on to show, was known in advance to be highly jealous of such a proposal; and his information was well-grounded for on the very day before he wrote his letter the Lord Lieutenant was acknowledging the receipt of a private communication on the subject from

[1] Add. Mss. 38,212, ff. 115–16, 126–27.

Lord George Germain, who had evidently requested him to test the reactions of people in Ireland to this question. It would appear that Lord Hillsborough, Lord George Germain, and William Knox were in communication with one another and stood at the centre of the discussions in England on this subject. According to Lord Lucan there was a conviction amongst the British ministers in August 1779 that, so far as any project of this kind was concerned, it was a case of now or never; "for once trade restrictions were removed, Britain would have nothing left to offer to the Irish" as a *quid pro quo*, nothing with which to bargain in order to attain a treaty. William Knox gives the impression that the idea was entertained of having a "complete and entire union or incorporation, with the single exception of Ireland's retaining a local subordinate legislature, similar in authority to that of the Isle of Man".[1]

At this date the suggestion was not so unfriendly to the interests of Ireland as it was to appear on future occasions, when the growth of the "separatist" movement had changed the aspect of the question. Many friends of Ireland were in favour of it, and Arthur Young pressed its advantages; while the Lord Lieutenant at the very start described it as "the only measure which can produce permanent tranquillity, substantial opulence and diffuse civilization in this kingdom". Buckingham may have been tempted to speak the language of compliment when writing to one of the promoters of the plan. Already on 20 August he was in fact nervous when he saw that such a thing was being mooted, and wrote: "So many prejudices and local and individual interests must be surmounted as will render it an arduous undertaking." In 1759 the mere rumour that a union was in contemplation had been sufficient to produce a riot in Dublin. Arthur Young during his tour of 1776 "was informed that nothing was so unpopular in Ireland as such an idea". The project had been in the air in 1778, and during the August of that year Buckingham had written that the question of the opening of the

[1] H.M.C. *Appendix to 8th Report, Pt. I*, Emly Mss. p. 202; *ibid. Stopford Sackville Mss.* I, 256–57; *ibid. Various Mss.* VI, Knox Mss. 163–64, 237–38; Cf. *ibid. Appendix to 9th Report: Pt. II*: p. 382; *The Alarm or the Irish Spy* (1779), p. 16 (June); *Parliamentary History*: XX, 249; *Terms of Conciliation or Considerations on a Free Trade in Ireland* (London, 1779), pp. 54–62. See also note 1, p. 90 above.

poṛts of Ireland had become associated in the minds of some people with the plan of a constitutional union. He had then felt the question to be so delicate that he had ordered his Chief Secretary "not to risque any opinion on so nice a subject".

It was important that all the interests of the city of Dublin—which were a weighty matter in the balance of Irish opinion—were hostile to a scheme which would have seriously endangered their own importance. It was represented that the effect of a union would be an addition to Ireland's financial burdens; and though Arthur Young held the view that this would be more than counter-balanced by the advantages of a full participation in the commercial privileges of Great Britain, that argument would have only limited force with people who were hoping to secure these latter advantages in any case. More particularly it had come to be felt that a union with England would result in the extension of the land-tax to Ireland, which had hitherto been free of it, and this is why William Knox, later in the year—when the project of a union had evidently not been formally abandoned—set out to show the wisdom of beginning the whole process of change with a tax on absentees. If such a tax were imposed, those who were subject to it would be the more inclined to favour a union between the two countries, the more ready to fall in with a policy that would destroy the very conception of absenteeism, and embrace everybody in a general land-tax.[1] One pamphleteer wrote: "No union which England now has it in her power to offer can equal that which she formerly gave to Scotland." Considering the part played by Scottish members of the house of commons in British politics, as well as the conduct of the Irish absentees, he thought it questionable whether the Irish representatives sent to Westminster "might not be useless to one country and pernicious to the other". Arthur Young found it the general view that these representatives would settle in England and become absentees themselves, and then the same thing would only happen again when new ones were elected to the British parliament in their place. So it was argued:

[1] H.M.C. *Various*, VI, Knox Mss. pp. 237-38; a list of absentees and their incomes is given in Arthur Young, *op. cit.* Vol. II, 114-16. Cf. *ibid.* Vol. II, 249-52 for Young's proposed alternative to a full union.

Upon the ruins of national consequence and public sentiment, we should have a few individuals, insignificant in England, engrossing the powers of Ireland, jobbing away her interest, never residing.

It was even pointed out that any bargain made with Great Britain after a negotiation for a union would be precarious, whatever guarantees might be offered to the Irish; for Blackstone had questioned whether the guarantees in the case of the union between England and Scotland were not illusory—whether it was in fact true that the treaty of union would be dissolved if the British parliament infringed its terms—since by the union a new body politic had been created and nothing could prevent it from having sovereign power. The united parliament, it was feared, would hold the final authority, even the power to over-ride any treaty; and in this parliament the Irish like the Scots would easily be outvoted.[1]

Over a month after he had received the communication from Lord George Germain, the Lord Lieutenant—his nervousness on this subject still increasing—continued to be too shy to broach a question which was only too likely to produce an uproar. Opinion in Ireland, so far as he had observed it, gave little promise of success, he said. All that could be achieved by the best abilities in the world at that moment was a mitigation of the more immediate evils. "The effectual cure must wait for those settled times which will admit of full deliberation and uninterrupted attention." By 30 September he had discovered what the letter of Lord Lucan will have already prepared us to expect—namely, that hints of the contemplated scheme had been coming to Dublin in private correspondence. What he observed as the effects of these leakages convinced him that it was necessary to take trenchant action—a thing of which he was capable on occasion—and stamp his foot on the whole affair. A serious situation would be produced, he said, if it even became known that he had attempted to sound opinions on this question.

[1] *Letter to the People of Ireland on the Expediency and Necessity of the present Associations* (1779), pp. 62–69; *First Lines of Ireland's Interest in the Year 1780* (1779), pp. 56–60; *The People of Ireland not a parcel of lazy incorrigible Scoundrels* (1779), p. 37.

My duty to his Majesty's service therefore renders it incumbent upon me to waive any further investigation and earnestly to recommend that at this time no measures of that tendency may be agitated. I cannot, however, but be of opinion that some of the ablest men in the kingdom see the propriety of a similar arrangement, but the circumstance which the most convinces me of the immediate inexpediency is their sentiments with regard to the pressing it now.[1]

In the meantime, the developments which had been taking place in Ireland, were rendering that country less amenable than ever before to the policies or the persuasions of England. Whether we regard them as the machinery of propaganda or as an instrument of power, the independent companies grew to considerable importance in the summer of 1779. It was from the month of May that they began to make their extraordinarily rapid increase; but even in June, the Lord Lieutenant—anxious no doubt to present the ministry in London with every possible reason for a policy of *laissez-faire*, had written, "Temporising is, in my opinion, called for".

Expenses, fatigues, avocation and business, and subordination will, by rendering their situation irksome, thin their ranks, and a peace will soon put a period to their existence.

It was only during August, however, that Lord Charlemont wrote concerning his own county: "The spirit of forming independent companies is spreading itself through the county of Armagh."[2] His follower, William Brownlow, made a similar report at almost the same time: "Independent companies are increasing fast in all parts of the kingdom." Apart from these mere reports, the correspondence conducted by Lord Charlemont as a patron of the movement in the north of Ireland is direct evidence of the imposing character of the developments which were taking place in this period. And, as we have seen already, it was in August that John Beresford sent his sensational letter to Robinson and wrote: "This country is arming from one end to the other."[3] If the

[1] H.M.C. *Stopford Sackville Mss.* I, 256–58.

[2] For Armagh see also *Ulster Journal of Archæology*, 3rd Ser., Vols. IV–VII.

[3] *Beresford Correspondence*, I, 43–46. Heron also wrote, 20 August, "It is also certain that many persons are arming here." [*Ibid.* pp. 46–51.]

Lord Lieutenant was correct in estimating the number of volunteers at 8,000 in the month of May (over a year after the origin of the movement), this general view is confirmed, for by October 1779 they were numbering their tens of thousands. The writer of the *Alarm* in June spoke of the companies in the neighbourhood of Londonderry—"scarcely a town here without its quota of volunteers, men well armed, accoutred and equipped"—and described the spirit there as worthy of the descendants of the Cromwellians, a spirit favourable to republicanism and independence. Another writer says later, "Under a pretence of preparing to repell an invasion on this island, all sorts of Protestants, but dissenters most warmly, have taken up arms."

It would appear that at a certain stage in the story the prospect of receiving arms distributed by the government became something of a stimulus to the movement. The Lord Lieutenant had for a long time refused the demands, since such a compliance would have given the independent companies the blessing of an authoritative recognition. But, as he said, he had 25,000 muskets at his disposal; Ireland was in sore danger; and we can gather that he was longing to transfer weapons into the hands of the Volunteers. Even when he writes to say that he is closing his ears to the appeals which are made to him, it is possible for us to see that in fact he is already making up his mind to give way to them. On 2 June he wrote: "Offers of service from the independent companies and requisitions for arms are pressing upon me from all parts of the Kingdom and the mode of declining the one and refusing the other without offence is delicate and embarrassing." The appearance of Paul Jones off the Irish coast during the same month had the effect of increasing the importunity of the inhabitants. "Applications are hourly made for arms in consequence of the late alarms", Buckingham wrote again on the 12th. Still he was asserting that the requests should "in every instance be civilly refused". On 25 June, however, after the Spanish declaration had become known, he wrote:

Upon such an emergency as at present threatens, I submit, whether it might not be justifiable and proper to lodge a number of these under the commanding officers in some of the principal towns in the Southern parts of Ireland.

Three days later he received a private letter from the Secretary of State informing him that, according to the intelligence received in London, Cork was one of the objects of the invasion which the French were expected to attempt.

Not until 23 July, however, did the Irish government take action, moving now on its own account by a resolution of the privy council in Dublin. It was decided that 16,000 stand of militia arms should be distributed to the governors of the various counties, so that they should be available in the event of any local alarm. Buckingham declared in the following January that the Speaker of the Irish house of commons "almost compelled this Privy Council to recommend the issuing the Militia arms". Still the attitude of the Irish government was ambiguous, probably as a matter of deliberate policy, for Buckingham did not dare to authorize the further delegation of the same arms to the Volunteers themselves. When Charlemont, as the governor of a county, asked if he might transmit some of the arms in his possession to his friends, he was told by the Chief Secretary that "upon consideration and inquiry his excellency found it improper to give the sanction of government to the lending the militia arms for the use of independent companies". In any case the Volunteers had often procured their own arms since the early days of the movement; and the government stocks soon passed into their hands, for it transpired that the Lord Lieutenant in reality was prepared to wink at anything at this moment. He merely refused "to give the sanction of government" to the irregularities which were bound to take place. A letter written by William Brownlow in September comments on the ambiguous and oracular nature of the advice which was being issued from Dublin Castle on this question—advice which Brownlow interpreted as "sufficient" authorization for the distribution of arms. It was plain that the Lord Lieutenant was cautious because he felt it necessary to guard his own rear.[1]

[1] S.P. 63/465, ff. 139, 182, 440, 442; *Grattan Memoirs*, I, 358-60, 367; H.M.C. *Charlemont Mss.* pp. 353-56. Cf. S.P. 63/468, Buckingham to Hillsborough, 2 Jan. 1780.

The shy conduct of the administration in regard to the request of the Irish gentry for a distribution of arms was the result of the feeling that the grant of government arms might be interpreted as implying an official authorization of the Volunteer movement as a whole. It was possible, however, for the government to adopt exactly the opposite system of tactics and seek so to harness the movement—so to assimilate the Volunteer corps into the organization of the state—that the whole question of the illegality of the movement would be transcended, and, instead of a threat, the Volunteers would become a support to government. The need for this species of local self-defence was recognized in England, now that France and Spain were known to be preparing to make a combined attack, and were actually planning an invasion of one of the two countries. Lord George Germain on 15 July seemed doubtful of the success of the British navy and confessed that:

in truth the safety of [Ireland] will primarily depend upon the zeal and exertion of individuals, as the regular troops are by no means equal to the supplying of garrisons and to the duty in the field.[1]

He thought that "if the measure is wrong it has taken too deep a root to stop it in the present situation of Ireland". He desired the movement to be supported—and wished that it were entirely commanded—by "friends of the Constitution".

When the Irish Speaker, Pery, made his direct appeal to Lord North on the subject of the state of Ireland in the middle of July, he pressed for the official recognition of the Volunteers, and pointed out that a suspicious attitude on the part of the government would only provoke in them the very disaffection which was feared. It happened that at this very moment the War Office was discussing that identical question, and when Charles Jenkinson, as Secretary at War, produced on 9 July a memorandum on the strengthening of the British forces in view of a possible invasion, he suggested the grant of the King's commission to the officers of the independent companies in Ireland. A proposal to this effect also came from Limerick on 19 July, and appended to it is an indication

[1] H.M.C. *Appendix to 8th Report, Pt. I*, Emly Mss. p. 201.

of Lord Amherst's reply, which was to the effect that the matter was already "under the consideration of the King's Servants". Lord North replied to the letter from the Irish Speaker on 3 August, and made an emphatic declaration of the principle that every armed man should be under the authority of the crown. He indicated that the English ministry intended to regularize the situation.[1]

A little later, therefore, we find Lord Weymouth asking the Lord Lieutenant to consider the possibility of granting temporary or local commissions to the officers of the independent companies. These officers, however, were not to take rank except during the time of actual service, that is to say in the event of an invasion or an enemy attack. The Lord Lieutenant was happy to be in a position to set on foot a plan "for reducing the arm'd societies in this country into a regular and legal form". His friends, Mr Conolly and the Duke of Leinster, who had been "at first disinclined to the armed societys" but later had become fervent promoters, now expressed the desire to take His Majesty's commission as Colonel. Conolly went into north Ireland "whence he was to transmit me a list of gentlemen desirous of having inferior commissions"; and the Duke of Leinster "said he would speak to his friends". The British government had taken action too late, however, and from that moment the Duke of Leinster made no further mention of the matter, while Conolly withdrew the support which he had initially promised. Lord Shannon in the south had no greater success though he claimed that the commissions would protect the Volunteers in the event of their being captured by the enemy, and would ensure their participation in an exchange of prisoners. Buckingham had to report on 16 September that the scheme "has not yet met with the success which I hoped for, or which it deserv'd".

It was so model'd by Colonel Luttrell as in my opinion not only to obviate all objection, but to make it in every light desirable. An alarm, however, respecting it had been rapidly and successfully spread the moment it transpired that such a scheme was in agitation, and men's minds were so strongly prepossessed against the measure

[1] W.O. 34/116, ff. 10 et seqq., 119; H.M.C. *Appendix to 8th Report, Pt. I*, Emly Mss. pp. 201–02.

that it was received with every symptom of jealousy and distrust, and seem'd to be condemn'd by almost all, before it had been well explained to any.

In the following month Buckingham said:

I have been assur'd that in different parts of Ireland several have taken the oaths, and that more are inclin'd to it, but also there are some companies whose principles are determinedly republican.

The Volunteers, therefore, evaded the attempt to regularize their position and incorporate them into a governmental system.[1] They were clothed in scarlet, green, blue and orange uniforms, and it had become a matter of principle that these should be of home manufacture. They seem to have loved reviews and inspections, where they greatly over-estimated their efficiency; and it has been noted that they had frequent church-parades. At first they had consisted chiefly of the well-to-do, who purchased their uniforms and provided their own weapons, but as time went on they seem to have broadened their basis and to have become more popular in character. In September we repeatedly hear that they can provide everything save the weapons—"the expense of the musketry is really too much for them". A little later we read in one of the letters: "All are not able to bear the expense of it. Subscriptions are opened in most counties of Ireland"; and this is "to cloath" such men "as need assistance". At Newry fifty-four of "the principal gentlemen and merchants" had "provided themselves with arms and necessary accoutrements." By autumn this company was in a position to double its numbers if the government could supply arms for some tradesmen who could pay for their uniforms but for nothing more. A pamphleteer pointed out that the numbers would be greatly increased if the undertaking could be made less expensive: "No man thinks of volunteering who is not able to cloath himself, in a handsome manner, which in this poor country so few are able to do." Brownlow wrote to Charlemont at the end of August: "As it induces a good deal of expense on the parties, I think it best not to press but only to encourage."

[1] H.M.C. *Lothian Mss.* pp. 356–58; *Corr. George III*, IV, 379.

The principal inhabitants of a town would get together to form a company, or a group of neighbours in the countryside would ask one of the local landlords to undertake the work of organization. A handful of "most respectable tenants" together with "some very opulent and respectable linen drapers" might be induced to meet and to band themselves together in an association. Beresford describes how in August county meetings were being summoned to bring about the formation of companies of volunteers. One of the gentry—often in the north, for example, one of the men politically attached to Lord Charlemont who was a great patron of the movement—would be invited to take the command. The Roman Catholics complained that they were not allowed to bear arms, but they demonstrated their loyalty during the period of threatened invasion, and were ready to subscribe for the procuring of recruits for the army, or for the support of the Volunteers. Thomas Newenham described the fervour he had actually witnessed in "the few Roman Catholics who were admitted into the volunteer corps before the year 1780".[1] A rank in these companies seems to have become an object of ambition, for it gave a man prestige in society, made him a favourite among the women, and enhanced his local influence. The zeal of the volunteers would be quickened by the preaching of the clergy, many of whom seem to have had a significant rôle in the movement, and even taken part in the exercises.

They seem to have exaggerated their numbers as well as their efficiency—and they overstressed perhaps even their respectability—in this period. Historians who take their own account of themselves might be tempted to ante-date the political importance, the conscious purposefulness and even the remarkable growth of the whole movement. There is a saga of the Volunteer companies and we may wonder if we touch the fringe of it when William Brownlow says: "We shall be ready here to take the field in a fortnight," and Francis Dobbs writes that "Countrymen from being slovenly in their dress, and awkward in their manners, became . . . compara-

---

[1] *Thoughts on the present Alarming Crisis of Affairs* (1779), p. 23; Thos. Newenham, *A View of the Natural Political and Commercial Circumstances of Ireland* (1809), pp. 188–89.

tively polished and refined."[1] Dobbs is no doubt correct when he points out that in the period which we are considering they "had no fixed object, no bond of union"—they were "detached in separate companies". Each local company would choose the colour of its uniform at its own caprice, and later, when battalions and regiments were formed, might come to regret the lack of previous concert. It has been suggested that the comparative smallness of the separate units—often numbering only 40 to 80 at this time—tended to increase rather than to diminish the internal cohesion which the movement attained.

The Volunteer movement facilitated the manufacture and the communication of political ideas, and provided the machinery for the expression of these in what we to-day would call pressure-groups.[2] Opinion itself was becoming more highly inflammable throughout the summer of 1779; and the indignation which the commercial restrictions had brought to fever-heat would often find further fuel in incidental discontents. The commander-in-chief in Ireland reported the bitterness with which "the gentlemen of the Country" regarded the English recruiting which was carried on amongst the Irish, "when we have so great occasion for men to defend ourselves". He informed the Lord Lieutenant of the existence of the view that the British government "wishes to see Ireland invaded in the hope that it would prevent an invasion of England".[3] In this whole situation of things it was of the greatest significance that in Dublin there were political leaders already lying in wait for just such an opportunity. It mattered that there was Henry Grattan, now aged thirty-four, ready to take the lead in parliament, where he represented one of the boroughs in the possession of Lord Charlemont. It mattered, further, that many able Irishmen, some of them actually connected with the government—men like Burgh, Pery, Flood, and Hely-Hutchinson—were ready to make

[1] H.M.C. *Charlemont Mss.* p. 356; F. Dobbs, *A History of Irish Affairs*, 12 Oct. 1779—15 *Sept.* 1782 (1782), p. 37.

[2] *A Defence of Great Britain against a Charge of Tyranny* (1779), contains p. 23 a Letter to the Hibernian Journal from "Sarsfield" which runs: "My Countrymen are only in the infancy of association; other objects will enlarge anon. . . . association will be as dear to them as Magna Charta."

[3] H.M.C. *Lothian Mss.* pp. 355–56.

a stand against the ministry in London. In any case there were many customary supporters of the administration who were not prepared to brave the indignation of an outraged people.

At the end of September, John Robinson, watching anxiously at the British Treasury, was already aware of the skilful use which the Irish opposition intended to make of their opportunities, when, in less than a fortnight's time, the new session of parliament would open. He already knew that the opposition, while not unfriendly to the Lord Lieutenant personally—and indeed inclined rather to commend him—were proposing to make a violent attack on the administration in general, on English tyranny in Ireland, and on the government at Westminster. They had determined, he said, to move some very harsh amendments to the Address, and to continue the Additional Duties for six months only, instead of the usual two years.

All letters from Ireland agree that violent measures are to be proposed, which is in concert with the [opposition] party here, and some letters so depict the state of Ireland that what I have mentioned to be expected is but a small part of the mischief.

He also knew that some of the men in office in Ireland were refusing to promise to support the administration in the coming crisis; that Burgh, for example, "talks of acting as a sworn judge in questions that shall arise", and that the Attorney General, who was willing to work with the administration in the Irish parliament, would do it only for the sake of the English government, and not out of any love of the Lord Lieutenant.

I have wrote all this, and more to Lord North and repeatedly pressed him on the Subject and that this Day it might be brought under their Consideration for the moment is almost past. He has had for some time a curious letter from Sir Richard Heron on this business which I believe he has not carried to St. Jas's with him. Many private letters speak more strongly on this and though I am sure I am no croaker nor apt to despond yet I can't help fearing bad events if the administration there are left to their own discretion.[1]

[1] Add. Mss. 38,212, ff. 126-27.

Chapter IV

THE CRISIS

§1. THE BEDFORD CONSPIRACY

ALL that we have learned even now is but the prelude to the miseries of North. Throughout the wide field of ministerial troubles and anxieties, everything became more intense— everything was drawn to a higher degree of crisis—as the autumn brought the new session of parliament in sight, and the forces on either side began to range themselves in readiness for its opening on 25 November. At this point the separate strands of our story come together, and a serious crisis in Dublin proves to be an important factor in the débâcle which occurs at home.

Nothing but the activity and obstinacy of the closet, and the fidelity of the private advisers of the King, kept the ministry in existence in the closing months of 1779. The sole object of their endeavours at this desperate moment was to maintain Lord North in power, if necessary in spite of himself, and to hold the cabinet together, in spite of its unhappiness and dissensions. A cry of distress from Robinson, a complaint from Sandwich, a growl from the Lord Chancellor, would be sufficient to set the secret influences into motion behind the back of Lord North. The extent of the underhand activity in this period would seem to have been proportioned to the degree of North's depression—the degree to which, as a chief minister, he was somehow or other virtually incapacitated. In many cases the aim of all the wire-pulling was to rescue him from intriguers, to bring him to a decision, or to press upon him the execution of a policy that had been initially his own. Robinson would write from the Treasury that nothing but the intervention of the King could save the ministry. George III, Jenkinson, Sandwich or the Lord Chancellor, as they saw danger ahead, would order Robinson to stay at the side of Lord North until a decision had been arrived at. The "secret influence" winds its way into every part of the story, duplicating itself in Ireland, where also we shall find a private communication established with the closet. The combined forces of the whole secret system could be ineffectual for long periods, however, against the inactivity of North.

John Robinson was undoubtedly a faithful Secretary to the Treasury; and it would be difficult to deny what sometimes seems to have been almost a lap-dog affection that he had for North. More than once he would seem to have had to conquer a serious hesitation and bashfulness before he dared to break through the barriers and intercede on behalf of his leader by a direct approach to the King. It is a delicate and dangerous matter, however, when a Robinson begins to turn these emergency interventions into a normal and regular affair—when too often he thinks that he must save Lord North from himself, and too easily he says that the man's "weak Mind requires Support". Upon such an argument as this there is no limit to the attacks which can be made on a man's independence and his moral autonomy. Robinson, without being quite conscious of the fact, could become the agent of the closet, standing at the very right hand of North—pursuing his operations in a manner from within.

Already in 1777 George III—with nothing sinister in view, and clearly in a certain simplicity of mind—had shown his awareness of the fact that Robinson could be of particular use to him. What he had written had been innocuous enough. He had said:

> I have always wished [Lord North] to be quite open with Mr. Robinson, but much less so with many others that now and then do more harm than good yet who have more weight than I can well conceive they deserve.[1]

On occasion North himself would be filled with suspicion concerning Robinson's relations with the closet, as in 1780, when at one moment the King urged him to take a certain course and Robinson, by pure mischance (according to his own account) had been giving him the same advice. In more than one connection—and in relation to other men besides Robinson himself—North would suspect at times "some Trick in the Closet"; and we have

[1] Abergavenny Mss., partly printed in H.M.C. *Abergavenny Mss.* pp. 17–18, No. 146.

already seen how quickly George III at the end of 1779 imagined
that he was insinuating a complaint concerning his own lack of
a proper confidential footing there. Robinson himself complained
on a number of occasions that North would be lacking in frankness, or uncomfortable and unconfiding in the closet. He would
communicate to Jenkinson a letter or a piece of information which
he suspected that North was desirous of concealing from the King.
We even find him hastening to intercept a minister and bring him
over to the policy of the closet before North could reach the man
and collect his support for a policy of his own.

One might ask where was the pride in being a chief minister—
and where the pomp of power—when a Robinson sat like a spider
at the heart of all the intrigues, bringing this and that man together,
and suborning one member of the cabinet against another. At a
later date the suspected closet-activity drove North in one of his
morose moods to put on to paper a generalization of his grievances.
He wrote:

In short, I see every day more and more the disgraceful footing
on which I am likely to continue while [I] remain in office, which,
God knows, I have other causes enough to wish to quit.[1]

Early in October it began to be clear to those who were connected with the ministry that the storm was about to break in Ireland, and that upon this matter there had been a great neglect. At
the same time it was suddenly realized again that, after some faint
stirrings in the middle of September which had led to nothing,
North had also neglected the question of the reconstitution of the
ministry, and had failed to fill the vacant posts even in those cases
where it had seemed that the successor had been chosen. Now the
cascade was released, and upon the ramshackle ministry the
troubles came precipitate. Now began the thing North had hitherto feared most of all—the disruption of the administration itself.
From the beginning of 1779, as we have seen, Lord Sandwich and
Lord George Germain in particular had been the admitted source
of weakness in the ministry. Even the King had thought that he

[1] Abergavenny Mss., partly printed in H.M.C. *Abergavenny Mss.* p. 33, No.
285.

must part with them, and North himself had recognized the necessity of replacing them with stronger and more popular men. For his inability to arrange this, North had been persecuted by Eden and Wedderburn in the way that has been described. Now, however, it almost appears as though Sandwich and Germain have become the firmest rocks in the whole ministry. Everything else around them totters in the quicksands. Almost every other member of the administration deserts or doubts.

By about the end of the first week of October it came to be known that Lord Gower, the President of the Council, had determined to resign from the government. The particular reason for his decision was the inattention of the ministry to the problem of Ireland—the failure to fulfil the engagement he himself had given in regard to this matter on behalf of the administration in the preceding session of parliament. He stressed this aspect of the question much later when he made his explanation in a speech in the house of lords on 1 December. On this occasion he said that the charge of neglect that had been made against ministers was "strictly true, though not yet evident".

Things were not yet ripe for proof, but they would, he ventured to say, be shortly so. . . . He had presided, he said, for some years at the council-table, and had seen such things pass there of late, that no man of honour or conscience could any longer sit there.

In the conversation with North, in which he signified his intention of resigning, he said:

That he had long felt the utmost uneasiness at the manner in which [His] Majesty's affairs had been conducted & at the weakness of government. That nothing is done in the material objects of government; That, in particular, no plan is settled with respect to the affairs of Ireland in which he felt himself personally concern'd after what pass'd last year in the House of Lords. . . . That there is no discipline in the State, in the Army, or the Navy, and that inevitable ruin must be the consequence of the present system of government.

Lord North, in reporting this conversation to the King, wrote:

If [Lord Gower] carries [this resolution] into execution, there is an immediate end to the present administration. . . . I am almost certain that I shall be abandon'd in the next Session of Parliament. . . . I am forced to confess that my Spirits & my faculties fail me sensibly & grow worse every day.[1]

Gower was the leader of the Bedford faction in the ministry—Thurlow, Weymouth and Carlisle in the lords, and Rigby in the commons were his principal associates—and it was natural that the defection of the leader should produce anxiety concerning the future conduct of the rest of the party, which had been behaving in a dubious manner, especially in the early part of the year.[2] Those who were associated with the closet now found their attention focused upon the movements and the disposition of the members of this faction. The result was much whispering and caballing and proffering of non-ministerial advice—much activity on the part of Robinson, Jenkinson, and the Earl of Sandwich in particular—great anxiety to hold interviews, collect gossip and observe whether the Bedfords in office dined with the Bedfords out of office—and the despatch of the resulting observations, inferences and diagnoses to the King. Rigby, according to Sandwich, "lamented very much the indecision and weak management of Lord North to whom he attributes everything that has or may happen amiss". He said that "from North's dilatoriness and talking of arrangements which he never carried into execution he was convinced he would not meet the Parliament."

The resignation of Gower necessitated a speedy settlement of that problem of ministerial rearrangements which had been under discussion for the greater part of the year. In regard to this matter Robinson, the Secretary, held a key-position and on this occasion

[1] *Corr. George III*, IV, 442–44 [a pencil note in the Windsor Castle Mss. perhaps explains Fortescue's very doubtful conjecture that this was written as early as September] cf. *ibid.* 452–53. See also *Parliamentary History*, XX, 1175–76; and cf. Add. Mss. 38,212, f. 265.

[2] The *St. James's Chronicle* for 11–13 April 1780 also notes that "several of the friends and dependents of Lord Gower" divided against the ministry on Dunning's resolutions of 6 April 1780 though Rigby supported the ministry.

it was Sandwich who co-operated with him, goaded him, gave him his instructions, and sent reports to George III. Even now it was impossible for over a week to move Lord North to definite action. On 15 October Sandwich wrote to Robinson:

Things are now at the most critical moment, and I think that you should not be an instant from Lord North's side till something decisive is done.

On the following day the injunction was repeated with still greater force:

Surely Lord North is not gone out of town without having seen Lord Stormont, and written to Lord Carlisle. I am convinced that all will go well if you can work him up to decide and act. You have therefore more in your hands at this moment than perhaps any one in this country ever had before. You are the only person who can give good advice to the person upon whom the fate of this kingdom depends.[1]

Two days later Jenkinson was so alarmed that he wrote to the King:

Mr. Robinson called on me yesterday & gave me an account of Lord North's State of Mind, such as it is melancholy even to reflect on. I am persuaded however that He means to go on, if He can; but I am apprehensive that He will by Indecision create new Difficulties to Himself & add to the Embarrassements, to which your Majesty is at present exposed; . . . & I humbly submit to your Majesty whether You would not think it proper to call upon Lord North in the most serious manner to come to a Resolution one way or the other; & if he means to go on, to proceed without loss of time; to settle an Administration, & tell Him that He is responsible if Your Majesty's Affairs suffer any longer by His Indecision.[2]

By this time—and in view of the critical nature of the situation in the middle of October—the King had solemnly begun to think out the terms upon which he would insist if he was "obliged to

[1] H.M.C. *Abergavenny Mss.* p. 26, Nos. 228–29.
[2] *Corr. George III*, IV, 465–66.

have any step taken towards Opposition". A week earlier he had not been greatly moved by the resignation of Gower and had written, "It is not pleasant, but in reality it will unite the rest of the ministers more." Weymouth could be promoted to the Lord Presidency of the Council, he had said, and there would be an opportunity to create not one but two more active secretaries of state. All, then, might be well, "if Lord North can be persuaded to act cordially with his colleagues".[1] By the 16th, however, the King feared the breakdown of the ministry; and Jenkinson, while urging him not to negotiate with the opposition until it became absolutely necessary, said: "Such an Event is certainly nearer than one could have expected owing to the strange Conduct of some of your Majesty's present Servants and the Hatred and Dissensions that subsist between them." Since Lord Gower and his friends demanded the widening of the ministry, their party would be the one to employ for the conduct of the negotiation; and Jenkinson, who corrected the King's draft of the proposed terms, suggested that, amongst the Bedford whigs, the Lord Chancellor was the man to select, since his abilities were respected by both sides, he was attached to the King's principles, and "he will keep the Busyness from the Hands of little Agents." A preliminary approach was made therefore to Thurlow, and he was told to stand by and await more particular orders that might come in the future.[2]

At the same time, a further attempt was made to keep North in office and he was pressed once again to carry out the ministerial rearrangements that had been so long in contemplation. On 17 October he wrote to Gower:

The King not having any prospect of forming an Administration upon the plan of a coalition with parts of the Opposition, which promises in his Majesty's opinion any good to himself and the public, has ordered me to resume my former plan [of ministerial rearrangements.]

On the 19th he wrote: "The King will try no other system and we must embark and go through with it as well as we can. I have no

---

[1] Add. Mss. 37,834, f. 155.   [2] Corr. George III, IV, 457–62.

great expectation of success."[1] By this time the news of the opening of the Irish parliament had reached London. It revealed a crisis in Dublin more serious than had been expected of late.

Even now further delay took place in the appointment of Stormont to the vacant secretaryship, and he did not receive the seals until nearly the end of the month, by which time it was becoming evident that the other secretary, Lord Weymouth, was himself likely to forsake the ministry at no distant date. Weymouth, though he had not resigned with Gower after all, declared on 19 October that "he kept his place contrary to his better judgment and with a full conviction that the continuation of the present system would speedily produce the ruin of his Majesty's affairs." On 3 November came dark hints from a different direction altogether, for Wedderburn, the Attorney General, informed Jenkinson that he "had taken two Resolutions, the one was—*not to resign*; the other was *not to have any personal Intercourse with Lord North*". And Jenkinson, meditating upon the conduct of the various members of the Bedford faction, wrote on the following day:

I begin . . . to think that there is a Plot forming to get wholly rid of Lord North; How many are as yet concern'd in this, I will not presume to say; but it is probable that some of great Consideration in your Majesty's Government incline to this; & as occasions offer, they will declare themselves.

North on the other hand was writing the same day:

I am in a fever with my situation, I have been kept in it by force. If the house falls about my ears, I cannot help it. All I can do is not to quit a falling house and to use every means in my power to sustain it as long as possible.[2]

Such was the condition of things in England at the end of October; and during this period the crisis in Ireland, as we shall see, was in some respects even more alarming. It must not be imagined that the threat of invasion was as yet quite over for the year; it was not

---

[1] H.M.C. *Appendix to 5th Report, Pt. I*, p. 209; *ibid. Abergavenny Mss.* p. 27, No. 231.

[2] *Corr. George III*, IV, 471-72; Lucas, *Lord North*, II, 98.

known in this country that the French would be unwilling to
renew their attempt to make a landing. Lord Amherst wrote to
John Robinson on 29 October:

It appears out of doubt the combined fleet will sail, that their
intentions of invasion still continue, though the 29 October is a
Season that one would imagine may create some doubts of their
executing their intentions, yet we must not talk of decamping and
dispersing while our enemies are so prepared and their attempts
feasible.[1]

During the first week in November North was laid up by an
illness. At this time a further shock was suffered, though the blow
was not entirely unexpected. Weymouth himself announced his
intention of resigning from the government. An attempt to fix
his fidelity by offering him a post of honour rather than industry
failed—he declined the invitation to succeed Lord Gower as President of the Council. When George III wrote to him on the matter
he replied on 6 November: "It is not a sudden project of retiring."
As he was a member of the Bedford connection his withdrawal
from the ministry confirmed all the suspicions that had been abroad
and intensified the conviction that that party were working on a
concerted plan. It was now difficult to resist the inference that the
earlier resignation of Gower had been the prelude to the defection
of the whole group, and the signal for a general *sauve qui peut*.[2]

The month of November, therefore—and the critical period on
the eve of the meeting of Parliament—is full of the rumour of a
Bedford conspiracy against Lord North. Around the King there is
whispering and wire-pulling and anxious cabal; it is clear that men
are watching every straw that will show the way of the wind.
Attention was concentrated now upon Lord Thurlow, who, as
we have seen, was generally regarded as one of the few strong personalities in the ministry. Every word, every gesture of the Lord
Chancellor was observed and put under the microscope, and the

[1] Add. Mss. 38,212, ff. 199–200; cf. H.M.C. *Appendix to 9th Report: Pt. II:
Pembroke Mss.*, p. 382.
[2] Add. Mss. 38,212, f. 212; Add. Mss. 34,416, f. 477; *Corr. George III*, IV, 471–
75.

result of the inquiries was communicated daily to the royal closet. Jenkinson, Robinson and George III himself set out to nurse this man and to draw him into their counsels, and generally to coax him into their system. They tried to work magic by personal intercourse and a show of confidence, just the thing which Lord North was unable to do for himself. In the face of the bluntness and violence of Thurlow, however, they were discouraged, and it seemed that he was evading their overtures.

On 7 November the King again turned his mind to the possibilities of negotiation, though, he said,

> it must be coalition with my administration not the yeilding the reins of Government to Opposition, I must be sure that measures should not be changed.

He approached the Chancellor on the subject, but Thurlow could be rugged and uncouth, and he had evidently no intention of meeting the King half-way. He merely said that "a coalition with this Administration in his Opinion could not be effected." It was his view that those of the opposition who might qualify in other respects were "resolved to be no part of a system with Lord Sandwich, Ld G. Germain and Ld North". Thurlow had no consolation to offer and merely asked the King to "examine whether the present Administration would subsist any longer". George III summed up the situation by saying:

> In short He could not be brought to speak out. . . . Undoubtedly the Bedfords want to drive out Lord North, yet I do not believe they have any plan to offer . . . I therefore must get Lord North if possible to go on . . . I would much rather be beat in Parliament, than see everything ruined by an ignominious treaty with Opposition.

Jenkinson made the following comment on "the Chancellor's Coldness and Unwillingness to speak out":

> If He has any Meaning (& I am not sure that would satisfie Him) it is that your Majesty should declare that You are ready to give up

Lord North, Lord Sandwich and Lord G. Germain. . . . I have a very bad opinion of the present State of things. I doubt whether after these Defections the Administration can go on; but I highly approve of your Majesty's . . . Resolution to resist the Evil as long as you possibly can.

From all this it was clear that the fidelity of the Lord Chancellor himself was extremely dubious and the administration was in danger of losing the one personage who was admired by his colleagues and respected by the opposition. The Bedford party, in fact, were hoping to overthrow the ministry and were fighting the closet as well as North; for while they pretended to assert that a coalition was absolutely indispensable they were ready to insist at the same time that any attempt to enlarge the existing administration was doomed to failure. Lord Spencer, who claimed to be seeing much of Lord Gower after his resignation, said that the latter talked openly of his intention of turning out Lord North. Jenkinson was pessimistic on the subject of Thurlow because he was convinced that there was a "more Intimate Connection" between Gower and the Chancellor "than between any two of the Bedfords". If Thurlow insisted on a negotiation with some of the hostile peers, it could hardly be doubted that the closet would have to agree to this. In the next few days therefore Jenkinson interviewed one person after another on the question of the continuance of the government and the possibilities of an arrangement with some of the members of the opposition. An agreement was patched up between North and Thurlow on 12 November and the word went round that the ministry would continue, but within a few days the men were at feud again. It came to be felt that Thurlow was staying in the ministry in order more effectually to achieve the very end for the sake of which some of his associates had resigned. He was only seeking by different methods to promote the object of the Bedford conspiracy—to bring about the downfall of Lord North. As North always seemed to be ready to avow his own unfitness for the office that he held, it is not easy to see why the ministry should have continued in existence. To crown its difficulties North reported on 15 November that he had received a message from the Attorney General summoning him to perform his promise of recommending him to be Chief Justice of the Common Pleas, & a Peer.

On 17 November George III put into the hands of Lord Thurlow what he afterwards described as "a Paper containing a Plan on which I thought it proper to authorize you to treat." He made the declaration that since it was everybody's duty "to cast aside all private pique and animosity", he was "willing to blot from his remembrance any events that may have displeased him", and to admit any able men who would "join with part of the present ministry". He insisted that every means should be used to keep the empire entire, that the war should be prosecuted with the utmost vigour in all its branches, and that "His Majesty's past measures be treated with proper respect". That night the chief members of the Bedford party dined together—Gower, Weymouth, Thurlow and Rigby—after which the Lord Chancellor had an interview with North and asked him if it would not be a disgrace to have the King's government in a minority in the new session of parliament, and "if He thought Himself able to carry on the Government, when a rebellion in Ireland was added to our other Difficulties." Jenkinson's comment on this interview was:

I am more and more persuaded that it is the Plan of the whole of this Party to drive Lord North out of your Majesty's Service.

They could not very well threaten the King himself, but they were hoping to achieve their objective by working upon the fears and anxieties of North. Jenkinson advised George III to welcome any possible accession of strength but not to destroy the existing ministry "till you see a Certainty of forming a new one better than the present". Also, he said, Lord North ought not to be induced to resign, but should be left to decide that matter for himself.[1]

At this very point the situation itself suddenly deteriorated; North's psychological collapse became almost complete; and never

[1] On the above paragraphs see Corr. George III, IV, 475–90. In Add. Mss. 37,835, f. 30, George III writes to Robinson on 21 Nov. "I fully know the Arts using by Rigby and others to frighten Lord North out of his present situation."

before had the atmosphere seemed so heavy with thunder. From about 19 November the ministry found itself at the edge of a precipice; and the crisis was significant, for the new session of parliament was due to open in the following week. A number of unfortunate incidents at this time brought the distresses of North to an intensity which appears to have exceeded anything that we have previously observed.

At a cabinet meeting on the evening of the 19th there was a discussion concerning the attack which was certain to be made in the new session of parliament on the subject of the defence of Plymouth during the period of the recent invasion-threat. It was not doubted that there would be a demand for an inquiry especially as it was pointed out that "Opposition have been indefatigable" and that they were prepared for a great debate. John Robinson was admitted to be the great authority on such matters, and Lord Thurlow informed the rest of the ministers that Robinson regarded the motion for an inquiry as a thing which could not be resisted, but North contradicted this report of the man's views. North was wrong; he had forgotten that three weeks before Robinson had said to him that an inquiry could not be resisted—he had forgotten also how he himself had replied at the time that in such a case "there was an end of the administration." Robinson in fact was of the opinion "that to deny information and inquiry was a difficult task with us, our Country Gentlemen were always so much for it".

Lord North, therefore, when he went back to the Secretary of the Treasury to confirm his impression of the man's views, found that he had been totally in the wrong, and was treated to a long tale of woe. Robinson now said to him:

It was true they had guns but no *Gunpowder* [in Plymouth], at least very little, that the Carriages of the Guns were so bad that when the Guns came to be moved they broke down, that there were not mattrosses in any numbers proportioned to the Guns and indeed but *very few*, that there was no Matches to fire ye Guns with, that could be worked, that they were obliged to apply to Lord Shuldham for assistance and borrow match, and even he had but little . . . and could spare them little . . . that they had not spunges, rammers, Scopes etc. etc., the necessary articles for the great Guns, and were in short in want of every military store.

All this was well known, said Robinson. The militia colonels and officers in the house of commons—"our friends"—had already "committed themselves" on the subject. Dunning, Barré and the Duke of Richmond had been collecting facts for the opposition and could call on Mr Parker, the member for Devon, and other members of parliament who had been on the spot. If so, all the usual objections to inquiries in time of war would fall to the ground.

How could an Inquiry into those Facts so alledged and so declared to be true by members in their places be resisted?

North, having heard all this, wrote to the King that the matter "may be fatal to government" and that it was "one of the most alarming questions" that he ever remembered. George III replied that if Lord Amherst and the Ordnance were able to defend themselves, no evil could arise. "If they have not done their duty, it is right it should be known."[1]

To make matters worse, there had arrived in London at this very period the news of disturbances in Dublin, which, as we shall see, for the first time opened the eyes of ministers to the seriousness of the movement of Irish resistance. The information made it apparent that the affair was no mere case of recalcitrance amongst men who should have supported the government in the house of commons, but had dangerous quasi-revolutionary aspects and was a matter that affected the country at large. From this moment we read for the first time in the correspondence of Robinson that Lord North wishes to see something done in regard to the question of Irish trade and "is in a hurry about it."

There was still a further reason for the unfortunate developments which were taking place in North's state of mind, in the days before the meeting of parliament. One of the secret letters which George III so often wrote to Robinson had come into his hands,

[1] Add. Mss. 38,212, ff. 227–32. Corr. George III, IV, 491–92; cf. ibid. 494 [endorsed in Windsor Castle Mss. "21 Nov."] North retracted his original assertion in a letter of 20 Nov. to Thurlow, Brit. Mus. Egerton Mss. 2,232, f. 18.

and it contained a frank comment upon his own deficiencies. He was with Robinson when it was delivered and Robinson—as he hastened to explain to the King—felt compelled to show it to him, and to behave as though it had been meant for him to see. The King had written on 21 November in a manner which was customary during this period:

> I am willing to take my Share of labour or personal hazard to save my Country . . . but Lord North must rouze his mind and must treat his Colleagues with confidence and civility the want of which has caused much of the mischief.

The King was perturbed when he heard that North himself had seen these outspoken reflections upon his conduct, but decided to make the best of the situation and wrote to Robinson:

> Infalability nobody but the Pope pretends to, and my alledging that my Service would be benefitted by more civil Communication between the Members of my Ministry I cannot think a severe attack.

In the meantime North himself wrote a long gloomy letter to George III in which he said:

> I have been miserable for ten years in obedience to Your Majesty's commands. . . . Really it is impossible to bear misery and guilt at the same time. . . . I must look upon it as a degree of guilt to continue in office, while the Publick suffers.

This is the letter in which, speaking of his attitude to his colleagues, he said uncomprehendingly: "I have never interfered in any of their departments." George III was in a scrape, and we see the more sympathetic side of his personality in the letter by means of which— still on 21 November—he attempted to redeem the situation:

> Lord North does me great injustice if he thinks I lay any intentional evil to his charge, but I should not deal justly towards him if I did not say that little acts of civility sometimes create more good-will than any other thing, that is what I would wish him to shew his Colleagues. . . . At all events Lord North may be sure that every

hint he receives from me is actuated alone from the sincerest regard for him, and that I am ever ready to take any burthen on my Shoulders to assist him in the prosecution of public Affairs, but he must not expect that I should not say what he has so often with perfect good humour confessed that though not guilty of Sins of Commission he is not so guiltless as to Omissions in points of attention.[1]

In spite of all that had happened Lord North decided to go forward with certain ministerial arrangements, so that on 23 November the Lord Chancellor returned to the King the paper which had authorized him to make an overture to members of the opposition. On the very day after this, however, the extraordinary fiasco occurred. Lord North made a sudden decision to throw up the sponge; and this was a serious matter, for it was the day before the meeting of parliament. Because the new arrangements included the promotion of Lord Hillsborough to the office of secretary of state, Wedderburn once again announced that he was "determined to resign or worse". Lord North, therefore, early on the 24th, cancelled the arrangements for installing the new ministers in office that day, and announced that the existing system "will not last for four and twenty hours". The King declared his conduct inexplicable. Jenkinson went to see him, but found him in so jealous a mood that he thought it wiser not to mention the things he had come to discuss with him. During the course of the day North changed his mind again; and later in the morning suggested that Lord Bathurst might kiss hands as President of the Council, since Wedderburn was not opposing his appointment, and Bathurst was ready to serve "if he remains in office but a week". By evening North had entirely swung round and declared himself ready to "stand any danger . . . and carry on"—ready even to go forward with the appointment of Lord Hillsborough. The news of the cancelled arrangements had made the comedy a matter of public notoriety, however; and as George III pointed out, the incident had "undoubtedly . . . given room to many unfavourable surmises". Later the King wrote:

[1] Add. Mss. 37,835, ff. 30, 32, 35, 36, 38; *Corr. George III*, IV, 493–95.

If Lord North is resolute the Attorney will become more tract-
able, indeed if administration is not resolved to keep individuals in
order nothing but confusion can sooner or later ensue.[1]

In the meantime the closet made every endeavour to keep the
Lord Chancellor "in good humour", and he who was still the most
recalcitrant of the King's servants was the object of those assiduous
attentions which were to win him over to the position of "King's
Friend". He had come to hold the strategic place in the ministry,
which could hardly have survived on any terms if he had followed
the example of Gower and Weymouth, his Bedford associates, and
decided to go out of office. Long before these autumn attempts to
attach him to the closet, George III had been urging Lord North
to cultivate the man on his own behalf, repeatedly reminding
him that "little attentions often doe good." "I have on many Occasion seen Lord North rather jealous of him," he had written
in May.

Perhaps Lord North's love of indecision makes him fear the
advice of one who ever wishes to see business carried on with
activity, and who finds fault with his best friends if they do not
zealously support the system in which they are embarked.[2]

The people who were seeking to save North at this moment
were aware that he was unfortunate in his handling of human
beings. The man who could be whimsically evasive in the face of
his parliamentary opponents felt too bitterly the unkindness of his
friends, and Robinson's letters show him inadequate and full of
repressions when there was question of a difficult interview with an
offended supporter. Towards the close of November North was on
unsatisfactory terms with Jenkinson; was complaining of the coldness of the King, was threatening to refuse to sit in cabinet again
with the new secretary of state, Stormont, or with the Lord
Chancellor; while Wedderburn, though he had said that he would

---

[1] *Corr. George III*, IV, 495–98; Add. Mss. 37,835, ff. 5, 44; Add. Mss. 35,516,
Aust to Hardwicke, 24 Nov. 1779; Brit. Mus. Egerton Mss. 2,232, f. 21; H.M.C.
Various Mss. VI, Knox Mss. p. 164.
[2] Add. Mss. 37,834, f. 88.

support the government, had stated that he would have no personal intercourse with its official leader. According to North, the Chancellor Thurlow was using "intimidation" to drive him out of the ministry. And of Rigby, the Paymaster of the Forces, another Bedford man, Robinson reiterated that:

his language is all intimidating, that administration can't go on, that we shall be left in a minority and then the consequences will be terrible.

While the ministry was almost paralysed by these dissensions word was coming from Dublin: "There is not a moment to be lost." And Robinson was writing: "For God's sake let something be done about [Ireland] soon or it will be lost, if French money, French Emissarys and French Supplies of Arms and Ammunition have time to get there."[1]

Towards the end of November Robinson was trying to promote more confidential relations between Lord North on the one hand, and Jenkinson, Thurlow and George III on the other. He desired to arrange meetings between these men, but he had laboured for this before and he knew too well that there were many personal factors that would hamper him in this policy. He put forward the remarkable idea of the necessity for the presence of a third party to bless these interviews which he was trying to arrange between members of the same government. He wrote to Jenkinson:

Lord North is not open candid and free in these Conversations and then the other is sulky and sullen. I wish too, my dear Sir, there is not something wanting of the like full Communication in the Closet. I have pressed this often.[2]

The stages of North's deepening depression—and the attendant creeping paralysis from which he suffered—can be shown to have had correspondence with the ascending steps of the ministerial crisis. It is fortunate that, as the violence of Thurlow brought

[1] *Corr. George III*, IV, 503; Add. Mss. 38,212, ff. 225-32.
[2] *Ibid.* J. Robinson to C. Jenkinson, "Most Private", 28 Nov. 1779. Parts of this letter are printed in my article on "Lord North and Mr. Robinson, 1779", in the *Cambridge Historical Journal*, 1937, 274-75.

matters to a climax towards the close of November, Robinson put into writing one of his communications concerning the condition in which he found his leader:

He told me . . . that he was sensible that every one was leaving him, and were plotting to desert him, and overturn the King's Government, but why would they do that, why need they do it when he said only come and take his place, he was ready to quit to any proper Administration that could be formed, but that he could not form one, as he was the Man they all run at, that he saw clearly that he should be deserted on some Question, perhaps some Collateral one to Government . . . it would endanger the King, that the dread of all this and that he should be the Cause of it distress'd him beyond Measure, that his Duty, His Honour and every Tie of Regard, required him to state this to His Majesty and that it preyed on his Mind so much as rendered him incapable of anything, he had no Decision, he could attend to no Business, that his Sufferings were only felt by himself, but most sincerely felt, indeed with the greatest Torments of Mind but were impossible to be described and he could not bear to be the cause of the destruction of His Majesty's Power and Government and perhaps the Ruin of his country—He then, my dear Sir, fell into such a Scene of Distress, I assure you as made my Heart bleed for him and drew Tears from my Eyes. I pressed him to consult his friends. He said he had no friends he could consult. All seemed to have deserted, he was pleased to add except me; I then desired him to talk in the most confidential Manner with you, who I was certain would give him your best Advice for the Support of His Majesty, His Majesty's Government and Himself; He grew calmer, said he would talk with you, that he was ready to do anything that could save the King and this Country . . . if he was but supported by others . . . only he felt himself unequal to the Lead that ought and must be taken in the present Crisis, and he felt too that His Majesty was cold to him, which he was certain he did not deserve, having undergone for His Majesty's Service Torture and Anguish of Mind for some years passed at different periods which were inexpressible. I said much to him, but I will not repeat it only in general that it tended to soothe his mind and strengthen him, He was pleased to receive it kind and affectionately. I am sure it was the honestest advice if not the best and it was to the best of my abilities and I trust it had some effect to alleviate his anguish which I assure you was great indeed. In short my dear sir some measures must be taken to comfort and support him or he will fall under the burden. . . . You will see my dear sir that I write this to you in the open confidential intercourse of my mind without a reserve. I do it as I would to a Physician from whom I expect to be relieved from disease and saved from death. I see the state very sick indeed. My sovereign and my country can only be saved by wise speedy firm and vigorous resolutions and means. I see too from what I told you on Friday night that we shall have intestine commotions to contend with as well as our foreign enemies, it is necessary therefore that the government should be made as strong as may be within to be prepared to receive the shocks. As one who from various circumstances attending my situation may sooner see these evils advancing than others and urged by the most dutiful affection to His Majesty and sincerest attachment to his government and constitutional power, I can't sit an idle spectator or a silent one to the approach of that hour when all that power His Majesty is so properly invested and entrusted with by the constitution may be seized upon and annihilated.[1]

Jenkinson sent the letter to George III, and said "I look upon all this as nothing permanent but as a Disease of the Mind."[2]

Jenkinson came to see within a few days, however, that if North were allowed to go on saying that he was being kept in office against his will every public calamity would be charged to the King in person. So North was pressed for a decision on his repeated request to be released and, though parliament had assembled on 25 November, the Lord Chancellor was authorized again on 3 December to speak particularly to "Lord Shelburne and his little party" whom it was hoped to recruit for a ministry under Lord Gower. Thurlow, however, was not permitted to reveal the extent of the changes which would be allowed, apart from the resignation of North, and when he pressed for this information, Jenkinson, who wrote, "the gaining of time is of some importance," advised the King not to give way. The negotiation was doomed to failure and Thurlow refused to go further than a private enquiry in his own name; so that the result left him more recalcitrant than ever and

[1] See n. 2 p. 134.   [2] *Corr. George III*, IV, 500.

both he and George III wrote long letters of self-justification to one another.[1] We can easily imagine the mood in which he remained from this time in the ministry.[2]

Here, then, is the first of the strands which go to the making of the problem and the predicament of 1779-80. Almost against the will of North who is supposed to lead it, almost against the will of Thurlow on the one hand and Wedderburn on the other hand who belong to it, almost against the will of Eden and Rigby, for example, who represented different parties amongst its parliamentary supporters, the ministry of North continues in existence without even believing in itself. It picks up what secretaries of state it can in order to carry on, while Sandwich and Germain, the confessed source of its original weakness, have become its sole sure collaborators. And all the time the undoubted talents of Burke and Fox, Shelburne and Richmond, Dunning and Rockingham are wasting themselves in a futile opposition.

It is a ministry so torn within itself that it would seem to possess no inner principle of cohesion save in the will and determination of the King; so confessedly weak in its executive aspects that its members despair, and, as we shall see, only the activity of subordinate agents, who are really instruments of the closet, helps to cover up some of its disgraces; so distressed that if there is any will to survive, any resolution to continue in existence, this is embodied not in the ministers themselves—and hardly even in the chief of them—but

[1] *Corr. George III*, IV, 500-37, *passim*; V, 2-5; Brit. Mus. Egerton Mss. 2,232, ff. 23-33; Add. Mss. 38,212, ff. 261, 301.

[2] On 27 Jan. 1780 Robinson broke into the following lament concerning the relations between Thurlow and North: "It is cruel, it is hard, it is too much to see the K[ing] in such a situation, with two [men] who if they cou'd be united would smooth all things bad even as they seem to be at home . . . and I told the Chancellor directly that I must venture to differ with him; for though he did, yet, if it was to be my last voice, I must say that I did not despair of the state and that I should still less fear it if he and Lord North would but act with energy together; call on us all, said I, even in the most subaltern situation to act with vigour as well as those in higher situations, and if we did not with every exertion obey them send us about our business whoever we were and get those who would serve the state. His answer was, and it struck me strongly, Damn him [Lord North] that is impossible, nothing can goad him forward, he is the very Clog that Loads everything." Add. Mss. 38,213, ff. 79-82.

in the King himself, in Robinson and Jenkinson, in the men who
work and burrow underground. The influence which George III
could exercise in parliament—combined with the votes of those
independent men who supported the King's government on the
whole because it was the King's, because they would not admit
defeat in America, or because they hated the Rockinghamites most
of all—kept the North administration in existence. It was the King's
government, and though this was proper—though it would be
anachronistic to say that George was committing a breach of the
constitution at this date—there could be no doubt that he was risk-
ing his credit and staking his prestige, by persisting in the endeavour.
It was the system of George III rather than that of North himself
that was the issue. And, so far, it had been made clear that its Rockinghamite enemies could not defeat it by their parliamentary
strength alone.

§II. "IRELAND GOES THE WAY OF AMERICA"

It might be imagined that, if the use of what was called influence
had been insufficient to give Lord North a feeling of security in
regard to his majority in the British house of commons, at least the
Lord Lieutenant in Dublin would be free from any grave anxiety,
when the body with which he had to deal was as notoriously corrupt as the parliament of Ireland at that date. We have seen, however, that even the head of Lord Buckinghamshire could not rest
easily on its pillow while agitation was growing and passions were
rising in 1779. In particular he had dreaded for months the day when
he would have to meet his parliament, and he had persuaded the
government in London that the tumult would be too dangerous if
a new session were to be called in the summer of that year. He had
further pointed out that in times of great national crisis "the occasional favour of government" would hardly induce men to resist
the force of a widespread movement or brave the indignation of an
awakened people. Succeeding events were to demonstrate in fact
that the whole vast edifice of influence or corruption—the complicated system built up by a government to ensure its survival and

ascendancy in spite of the wilfulness and caprice of particular men
—could suffer landslide and slip on a sudden from the grasp of its
controllers, through the operation of a public opinion and a social
force outside the walls of parliament.

On 16 September the Lord Lieutenant had sent to London the
heads of the speech which he was proposing to make at the opening
of the new session of the Irish parliament in the following month.
He had accompanied these with an urgent request for instructions,
and once again he had given an unmistakable warning to the
British ministers:

The business to be laid before the Parliament of this Kingdom in
this ensuing session will probably be of as great extent and importance as any which ever yet came under their deliberations.

He required "very particular instructions", he said, concerning
the attitude that he ought to adopt on the question of concessions
to Irish commerce.

That the Parliament of Ireland will address his Majesty on this
subject though no notice should be taken of it in the speech will
not admit of a doubt.

His anxiety was great and in his despatch to Weymouth he alluded
to the existence of "a crisis when the difficulties of the Irish government hourly multiply". To Lord George Germain he wrote on
30 September that to offer a direct resistance to an Address in favour
of "unlimited commerce" would be "the attempting to stop the
ocean with a hurdle".

But my best efforts shall be exerted, tho' perhaps in vain, to
reduce the terms and temperate the expectations.

In the meantime the British cabinet had discussed the matter and
on the 24th Lord Weymouth had had nothing to say, save that they
had given unanimous approval to the Lord Lieutenant's draft,
which had "treated the several points with proper caution". Buckingham made the comment: "Lord Weymouth seldom enters into

any particulars," and noted that he had received no letter from Lord North for some weeks.[1]

Beresford, writing from Dublin, seemed satisfied with the Lord Lieutenant's projected speech, especially as "The terms are general and bind down to no specific measure or mode." He seems to have thought that, in spite of opposition, the government could expect to prevail. It is clear, however, that Buckingham was more apprehensive; it had been his anxious hope to secure by his importunity the permission to promise something handsome to the Irish at the opening of parliament. At a meeting held at the Castle the day before the new session began, it was decided to make one final attempt to parry the blow which everybody was expecting. It was agreed that Foster should try to forestall any amendment to the Address by giving "notice of his intention to move for a Committee to inquire into *the distressed and impoverished state of the Nation*". The advisers of the Lord Lieutenant in Dublin seemed confident that this would enable the government to evade the importunities of the opposition.[2]

It was of no avail, for when the Address had been moved in the house of commons on the 12th Grattan proposed an amendment urging the absolute necessity of a "free export trade for Ireland." He attributed the miseries of the country "wholly to the tyranny of England", praised the armed associations, "called upon the mob to do themselves justice" and "in short said everything he could to inflame people both within and without the House". His proposal was debated for many hours and amongst the suggestions thrown out during the discussion was the idea that the Irish parliament "should depute some of their members to treat with the Parliament of Great Britain." The débâcle came when two servants of the crown, who had long ago given warning of the conduct which they would pursue and had declined to attend the preliminary meeting at the Castle the day before, supported the policy of amending the Address, though they declared themselves not quite satisfied with the formula proposed by Grattan. Burgh, the Prime

[1] S.P. 63/466, ff. 214–21; *Grattan Memoirs*, 1, 382; H.M.C. *Lothian Mss.* p. 356; ibid. *Stopford Sackville Mss.* 1, 256, 258–59.
[2] *Beresford Correspondence*, 1, 52–53; *Grattan Memoirs*, 1, 391–94.

Serjeant, demanded the opening of the ports—that is to say the liberation of the import as well as the export trade. Flood, the Vice-Treasurer, threw out the suggestion which was eventually adopted, namely that the demand should be put forward for what he called "free trade." He argued that "Ireland could not ask for less," though it would be for Great Britain to "judge how much she could grant".

Buckingham reported that "the greatest part of the country gentlemen, usually the friends of government . . . sent notice that they must support the amendment." Other servants of the crown, who had flattered themselves the day before that they could steer the government through the crisis—even those who had begun to attempt various forms of evasive action—changed their minds in the course of the debate. In any case, though they were anxious to avoid the issue, some of them refused to give a straight vote against commercial concessions if, after all, the question was to be put to them direct; and as Buckingham had pointed out a fortnight before, this was only to be expected in view of the opinions which they had produced for transmission to London in the summer. The conduct of the servants of the crown "gave resolution and strength to many of their inferiors", and other moderate men like Conolly influenced the customary supporters of the government in favour of the amendment. Ultimately the Chief Secretary found himself deserted by all save a mere handful of die-hards, and these, though willing to divide with him, thought it "hard to be dragged into a division with a contemptible minority" and even said that "it would expose the great weakness of administration". It is significant, furthermore, that even these were unwilling to lay themselves open to "the resentment of a nation" in a case where they felt that no purpose could be served by the sacrifice. Again Buckingham had foreseen the situation a fortnight before: "the few moderate men will either be aw'd by national clamour into silence or their voice will be lost amidst the general cry". The Chief Secretary, though clearly afraid to have to confront the anger of the British government, finally allowed the amendment to go through without a division, and it was carried in the following form:

That it is not by temporary Expedients but by a Free Trade alone that this Nation is now to be saved from impending Ruin.

It is difficult to imagine a case in which—under the terms upon which politics were conducted in the eighteenth century—a country could have reached a greater degree of fundamental unanimity than there existed in Ireland on this point at this particular moment.[1]

"The expectations of Parliament and the Nation are fixed upon His Majesty's answer to the addresses of both Houses," wrote Buckingham on 18 October. "It will be difficult to resist Popular motions, which I understand are already in contemplation." If no concessions were granted by England the new duties would not be carried in Dublin, and the establishment would have to be reduced —even the military department would suffer. There might be fresh non-importation resolutions, carried this time by parliament itself. There might be a proposal to lay a tax on absentees. On 24 October Buckingham complained that only from the *London Gazette* could he learn that his "alarming dispatches" had been received; "yet there prevails a degree of universal impatience for [the King's] answer." On the following day there was despatched to London a note from Pery, the Irish Speaker, showing that what the Irish really wanted was permission to export woollen goods and to conduct a direct trade with the British plantations overseas.[2]

In the meantime the King's answer to the Addresses of the Irish

[1] On this debate see Add. Mss. 38,344, ff. 1–2, Proceedings in the Irish House of Commons, 12 Oct. 1779 [in J. Robinson's hand]; S.P. 63/467, ff. 17–25; *Beresford Correspondence* I, 53–60 and 61–65; Hardy, *Charlemont* I, 391–92; Add. Mss. 37,834, f. 159; Add. Mss. 38,212, ff. 159 and 164. The news of the debate reached London late on the 17th and George III's reaction to it is given in a letter to Robinson of 20 Oct. [Add. Mss. 37,834, f. 162] after the full accounts had come into his hands [*Corr. George III*, IV, 467]: "If they [the Irish] had shown moderation it would have been difficult to have got the Trading part of the kingdom to have come into anything material.... I have been tried in the School of Adversity and will certainly meet this accumulation with firmness. I am not conscious of deserving it, therefore have no regret to take up my thoughts but will alone employ them in trying to save my country."

[2] S.P. 63/467, ff. 44–46 and 56–57; H.M.C. *Lothian Mss.* pp. 357–58; *Grattan Memoirs*, II, 395–98.

parliament had been drafted by Lord Weymouth, who had not yet resigned from the office of secretary of state. North decided to harden this initial draft; and in this he was apparently under the influence of Robinson and Jenkinson, who were afraid of giving any definite suggestion that the demands of the Irish would be complied with. Robinson no doubt had been influenced in turn by a letter from Beresford in Dublin, who, as we shall see, was criticizing the demeanour of the Lord Lieutenant, sabotaging his efforts in London, and writing: "I entreat you to be cautious in your answer to the present demand."[1] North was still refusing to give any promises and the relevant portion of the King's answer to the Address was tantalizingly non-committal. It ran as follows:

The House of Commons may be assured of His Majesty's sincere concern for the Distress of his Kingdom of Ireland, of his affectionate Attention to their Interests, and of his constant Readiness to concur in such Measures as shall, upon mature Consideration, appear most conducive to the general welfare of all his Subjects.[2]

The Irish house of commons, which had adjourned on 14 October, reassembled on 1 November and discussed the sinister proposal that "a Committee be appointed to enquire into the state and management of the revenue of this kingdom for the twenty years last past". The motion was withdrawn, however, and on the following day the house even voted its thanks to the King for his reply to the recent Address. This vote of thanks was to have contained the promise: "That his Majesty may depend his faithful Commons will grant the necessary supplies to support his Majesty's government". Yelverton protested against this, however, on the ground that no weapon was left to the Irish save the resort to the expedient of granting the supplies only for a limited period. Since it was further argued that the country was too impoverished to grant the usual supplies, the engagement in regard to this matter was

[1] Add. Mss. 38,212, ff. 182, 189–90, 191; *Beresford Correspondence*, I, 53 *et seqq.*
[2] Cf. S.P. 63/471, Weymouth to Buckingham, Private, 24 Oct. 1779: "His Majesty cannot pledge himself to grant what does not depend on him and which must be left to Parliament to determine."

only carried after being qualified by the clause: "as far as the Circumstances of the Kingdom will permit".[1]

It was immediately made apparent that, even if the Irish house of commons proved amenable, the voice of the people outside its walls would not be so easily silenced on the present occasion. It happened that on 4 November the customary celebration of King William III's birthday was due to take place in the capital. At eleven o'clock in the morning the various companies of Volunteers assembled, to the number of over a thousand apparently, and turned the anniversary into a gala day of their own. They included two hundred men of the company of "Dublin Volunteers" under the Duke of Leinster; and these wore "blue uniform lined with buff, red collars and red edgings, buff waistcoats . . . the grenadiers with feathers and the infantry with caps and plumes." Also there were the "Liberty Volunteers" under Sir Edward Newenham—a body the political complexion of which was more distinctly radical— and these wore buff waistcoats and blue uniforms edged with orange. Amongst the rest were the 170 men of the Merchants' Company, who had blue uniforms faced with red, and white waistcoats, their colours orange, "with Hibernia endeavouring to support her harp and grasping the Cap of Liberty." Later in the day the official celebration occurred, and the Lord Lieutenant, followed by the Lord Chancellor, the Speaker of the house of commons, the Lord Mayor of Dublin, the nobility, the aldermen and gentry made the usual procession around the statue of King William. They were then able to read on the pedestal of this monument—in "letters of great magnitude"—the phrases which the Volunteers had left as their mottoes: "Relief to Ireland," "Short Money Bills," "Free Trade or Else?," "The Glorious Revolution," "The Loyal Volunteers," "Quinquaginta Millia Juncti Parati pro Patria Mori." The opposition press declared: "The impartial and uninfluenced are of opinion that we can neither derive comfort nor certainty from his M—y's answer to the address of Parliament."[2]

---

[1] Account of debate in *Magee's Weekly Register*, 6 Nov. 1779.
[2] *Magee's Weekly Register*, 6 Nov. 1779; *Beresford Correspondence*, I, 73-75; S.P. 63/467, f. 95.

In fact, the proceedings in the Irish house of commons at its initial meeting on 12 October had been most remarkable by virtue of the signal which they had given to the country at large. If there had been any doubt before there could no longer be any difference of opinion on the matter: the more sinister menace was the one which was operating outside the walls of parliament. On 24 September Buckingham had written:

The arm'd societys daily increase, and the whole island will be very soon, literaly speaking, *hérissé de combatants*.[1]

The Irish parliament voted its thanks to these bodies on 13 October, the house of commons with unanimity, and the lords (on the motion of the Duke of Leinster) without a division, though the Lord Chancellor and Lord Annaly drew attention to the illegality of these armed associations. When the amended Address was carried by the members of the house of commons—the speaker at their head—to Dublin Castle, the streets were lined with the local Volunteers, under the command of Leinster, and they presented arms as the Speaker passed. They had now received formal recognition. They had been able to take their place in the picture at one of the dramatic moments in the proceedings. After the opening of the Irish parliament the whole movement received a further impetus. The old companies widened their membership. New units were being formed.

Certain doubtful tendencies, moreover, were now making their appearance in the movement, or at least were becoming more clear or more explicit. On occasion we notice symptoms of an ugly mood or we see a disposition to rattle the sword. Soon after the middle of October, Buckingham was reporting that "discreet men seem terribly alarmed and wish for their own sakes to prevent that ruin and confusion which seems to threaten this country." After the opening of parliament the Tyrone Ditches and Acton Volunteers, at a meeting where seventy people were present, talked of their willingness to stand forth "against a foreign or internal foe". It was in connection with this statement of policy that they unani-

[1] H.M.C. *Stopford Sackville Mss.* I, 256–57.

mously agreed to work for the formation of larger units—"to do all in our power to aid the forming of a battalion in the county of Armagh". There are signs that the companies in the north were coming to a higher degree of organization, widening their horizon, and at the same time being brought more closely under the leadership of Lord Charlemont.[1] On the other hand there are signs that some of these bodies were becoming recalcitrant to the leadership of the gentry if that leadership was exercised on behalf of moderation. Buckingham wrote on 24 October:

> It concerns me to hear from every quarter that more corps are forming, as whatever may be their professions and avow'd principles, they are in general so independent of their ostensible leaders, that tho[ugh] sober people reluctantly speak out, they are very uneasy respecting the line of conduct which the spirit of the moment may induce them to adopt.
>
> One very serious regulation is introducing in some of them, that of appointing their officers by rotation.[2]

There were some companies, he said, "whose principles are determinedly republican".

All this was brought to a higher power by the fact that in the same period, and particularly during the recess in the latter half of October, political leaders and Volunteer officers seized the opportunity to carry the frenzy across the length and breadth of the country. They called meetings in town and country in order to mobilize public opinion behind the parliamentary campaign. They induced the constituents in one locality and another to send letters of instruction to their members of parliament. The programme of a Short Money Bill and no new taxes (until the demand for free trade should have been met) was now to be backed by the power and the passion of a galvanized people. From the correspondence of Lord Charlemont it is apparent that this leader of the north had intimated to his *clientèle* his desire to see these musterings of local opinion.[3] To a certain degree it was a case of the exasperated local gentry

---

[1] H.M.C. *Charlemont Mss.* pp. 360, 363-64.
[2] H.M.C. *Lothian Mss.* pp. 357-58.
[3] *Ibid. Charlemont Mss.* 361 *et seqq.*; *Magee's Weekly Register*, 6 Nov. 1779.

rousing the spirit of either their tenants or the freeholders of the neighbourhood. Arthur Young was not the only person who doubted the wisdom of this:

It is always for the benefit of the landed interest TO BE QUIET, he said. Let merchants and manufacturers complain, riot, associate and do whatever they please, but never unite with them, restrain but never inflame them.

As we have seen, even at the very end of September, the efforts of John Robinson at the English Treasury had failed to secure the examination of the materials on Irish trade which had been transmitted from Dublin early in the summer. It was only at the beginning of October that a regular analysis of them was started, when the most vigorous man in the ministry, the Lord Chancellor, Thurlow, had been induced to intervene and give a decided impulse to the undertaking. It would appear that Robinson, still the guardian angel of the whole administration, had been reduced to despair and had cast about him for an influential mediator. He had had a meeting with Thurlow, who after a further consultation with North had written to him in the following terms:

It [this letter] is to persuade you not to leave town whatever may be the call until something is settled which may be sent to Ireland as the best advice or instructions which the scantiness of the time and other accidents will admit of, nor until some directions are given for preparing material to be laid before Parliament in pursuance of the addresses of both houses [i.e. of the previous May.]

The Chancellor declared that Jenkinson was the person, and the only person, who would be "able to furnish the Idea of what is necessary on both Heads". Robinson promised to see Jenkinson on the following day in order to receive his instructions. In the meantime, he wrote to him:

I set to work to prepare some materials on Irish affairs and luckily I have employed all this Day in making an Extract of all the Acts of Parliament which stand on our Statute Book restrictive of their

Trade and also the like of all the acts granting them indulgences.
These will help me in forming your abstract which I will endeavour
to do for you.[1]

Work had begun in earnest at last, but not by the responsible
ministers concerned—rather in the backstairs, and indeed by the
two men whose association formed the main factor in the "closet-
influence" at this date—John Robinson, the intimate of North, and
Charles Jenkinson, the King's Friend. In October, therefore, the
first steps were being taken towards the discovery of a policy; but
in reality, as we have seen, all this was too late to forestall the long
anticipated explosion in Ireland—too late to help the Lord Lieutenant at the meeting of the Irish parliament. Still the work proceeded,
Jenkinson directing to Robinson his demands for further information; while Robinson would transmit the requests to Dublin,
partly to Heron, the Chief Secretary, and partly to Beresford at
the Treasury there—endeavouring "to keep the inquiries as much
covered as may be, to prevent as far as may be, their penetrating
your views". Alternatively he would be inquiring into "the
Accounts which were prepared relative to the Trade of Ireland in
the two last Sessions of Parliament", or seeking out the accounts
"for the Linnen, Linnen Yarn and Woollen yarn for 25 years" or
inquiring into the records at the Customs House. Some of the results of his work are to be seen in the Liverpool Manuscripts at the
British Museum—observations on the acts of parliament which
limited Irish trade; abstracts of those acts of the British parliament
which (in however small a way) had conferred benefits on Ireland;
abstracts of those acts of the Irish parliament which confessed to a
dependence on the British crown; and the long, careful summary in
Robinson's hand of all the opinions that had been sent from Dublin

---

[1] Add. Mss. 38,212, ff. 137-38, J. Robinson to C. Jenkinson, 3 Oct. 1779. In
order to anticipate a renewal of the difficulty encountered in September,
Robinson promised "that I will not let slip from me the least Thing tending to
shew that you have been so good as to take up the Business".

The intervention of the Lord Chancellor at this moment led to the despatch of
last-minute instructions to the Lord Lieutenant from Lord North and Lord
George Germain, as well as from Heron to Robinson, on 5 and 6 Oct.; Add.
Mss. 37,834, ff. 153, 154; Beresford Correspondence, 1, 60.

in the summer as a result of the Address of the British house of lords.[1] Either Robinson or Jenkinson would keep North informed of the general state of the business, or would secure his assent to the direction of the researches on certain lines. It was necessary to fight against North's indolence and evasiveness still, and Robinson would write:

Indeed my dear Sir you can't conceive what I go through. I am sure it is scarce possible to describe it. Lord North's mind is so broke and his temper altered that he is quite peevish.[2]

North was incapacitated by illness early in November and there were other occasions in this period when, as we have seen, he would be reduced almost to paralysis by his moods of depression. We have already noted that when Gower left the ministry and, later, when Weymouth resigned the secretaryship of state, the administration fell into such a state of anarchy that only the labours of Robinson and Jenkinson seemed to be holding it together. The same two men stand now at the very centre of the transactions relating to Ireland—by the very laws that governed the mode of their operations they would be active at the point where the crisis was most anxious or the conflict most intense. Now, if ever, it was possible to charge George III with ruling by means of an interior cabinet, whose responsibility could hardly be brought home to them in the ordinary procedure of parliament.

The device of secret correspondence, the system of underhand communications, and the intervention of irresponsible advisers tended to be multiplied and transported into fresh fields, the sub-terranean animals breeding more creatures like themselves. This became clear as the crisis was developing in Dublin and it transpired that a double system of correspondence had also been set on foot between England and Ireland. The whole position of the Lord Lieutenant himself was being completely undermined by com-munications which some of his own agents had established with

---

[1] Add. Mss. 38,212, ff. 140, 151, 154 etc.; Add. Mss. 38,344, ff. 5–96; a copy of Robinson's "abstract" was sent to the King, 8 Oct.; Add. Mss. 37,834, f. 154.
[2] Add. Mss. 38,212, f. 201, to C. Jenkinson, 29 Oct.

Robinson behind his back. The correspondence with Beresford had been going on for some time, as we have seen, but on 18 October Robinson received from him an account of the situation in Dublin which he described in a letter to Jenkinson as "curious". Very quickly we find that here is a systematic intrigue that is being carried on against the Lord Lieutenant, and before the end of October the Irish Attorney General is fully engaged in the conspiracy, sending letters to Robinson which exactly support and complement the information from Beresford. Under these influences, as we have seen, Weymouth's draft of a reply to the Address of the Irish house of commons had been revised, so that the British government should not be committed even now by any promises. It gradually becomes clear that Robinson is relying chiefly on the news that comes from Beresford and the Attorney General, though later, when pressed, he is able to give little reason for this confidence. He communicates their letters to Jenkinson and to the royal closet,[1] where no doubt they were very acceptable; and later he asks permission to show them also to the Lord Chancellor. But there are always wheels within wheels in this secret system, which creates its own complications within itself, and ultimately Robinson receives a communication so serious in character that he asks whether he might dare even to withhold it from the King—he talks about "sinking" it.[2] He is ready to think of taking this risk although he knows that the King will not be unaware of the fact that letters of some kind or other have been received.

The secret system had the further disadvantage that on occasion it gave a certain leverage to minor intrigues. In the subterranean activity there was much of petty-mindedness, much of the outlook of the mere political jobber. Though Robinson was justified in his anxiety in 1779, there is something in his fretfulness and activity which must remind us at times of the maiden aunt. Above all, matters of momentous importance seem to have fallen on occasion

[1] E.g. *Corr. George III*, IV, 467; Add. Mss. 37,834, ff. 161 etc. Robinson is evidently conducting the correspondence with Beresford and Scott under the King's directions; *ibid.* f. 131, 13 Aug., f. 154, 8 Oct. On 5 Nov. he shows North one of Beresford's "confidential" letters, but does this at the King's command, Add. Mss. 37,835, f. 7.

[2] Add. Mss. 38,212, f. 256, to Jenkinson, 30 Nov. 1779.

into the hands of little men. It was always possible in the eighteenth century to view events of the kind which were taking place in Dublin merely from the standpoint of the professional political agent, the dealer in patronage. Lord North himself was not exempt from this weakness, and, writing to Robinson after he had heard the news of the opening of the Irish parliament, he seems to have sent his thoughts running down a well-worn channel; he said that those who were under obligations to the Lord Lieutenant had failed to show the government in Ireland the loyalty it had had a right to expect. Robinson was the government's chief political manager. It was natural therefore that he should state the question to himself in purely professional terms. He was only too ready to ask: What has the Lord Lieutenant done to fritter away the majority which the Government once had in the Irish Parliament?[1]

Beresford and the Attorney General, Scott, sent exactly the information which corresponded with this attitude of mind. Buckingham in previous years, they said, had instituted a change of policy—he had withdrawn his support from some of the families that had hitherto been the mainstay of British authority in Ireland. The men he had patronized and brought into office had been the very ones who would turn traitor to the cause when a genuine national crisis occurred. They were the kind who would affect to be "patriots" and would turn at the crucial moment to the side of opposition. "From a mistaken and weak policy, the strength of English Government has been totally annihilated by the Administration of His present Excellency," wrote Beresford. Buckingham had allowed himself to be persuaded "that the majority obtained by [his predecessors] Lords Townshend and Harcourt ... had cost the nation an immense sum, that it was to be governed by other and

[1] H.M.C. *Abergavenny Mss.* p. 27, No. 231, North to John Robinson, 19 Oct. Cf. Add. Mss. 30,872, f. 119, T. Wilson to J. Wilkes, 23 Oct. 1779: "What do you think of Ireland, will not a few Coronets and Places properly distributed silence them. Flood is come over for the Purpose and is to return before the first of next month", i.e., before the end of the Irish parliamentary recess. On 30 Mar. 1779 J. Robinson, writing to George III, Add. Mss. 37,834, f. 60, had predicted that "in the present and probable Situation of Ireland, the Patronage of the Crown there, to its fullest extent almost", would be necessary for maintaining government and satisfying the leading men in the Irish parliament in the near future.

cheaper means". The dramatic scenes at the opening of the Irish parliament were apparently to be explained in accordance with the mechanics of conventional eighteenth-century political management.

Further than this, Buckingham was open to the criticism that he had allowed a number of sinister movements to develop until at last they had become completely out of hand. He had deprecated governmental interference as dangerous, he had been defective and partial in his reports to London, he had sought to evade responsibility. "The weakness of the present Government [in Ireland] can never disembarrass you," wrote Beresford to Robinson. If Buckingham and his friends—particularly his unsatisfactory Chief Secretary, Heron—remained in Ireland "nothing short of commands" would be necessary to "direct them in the right way". It was Beresford's view that "When Ministers give way to the desire of the public, as it is called, every man [i.e., every member of parliament] shifts for himself"—in other words, though they may vote on the merits of particular questions, there will be no solid body whose votes will envisage the general stability of the government. Beresford and the Attorney General had set to work in October to form "a connection and clitk for English Government independent of the Lord Lieutenant".[1] Early in November Beresford even argued: "Grant us free trade or . . . recall instantly Lord Buckinghamshire or at least his Secretary. I am sure that it is the only chance of escaping a Rebellion."

By this time it was becoming clear that the crisis in Ireland had not by any means reached its climax. After the demonstrations in Dublin on 4 November Beresford had written:

All my forebodings appear now to be nearly completed; and it is probable that a very few weeks if not days will produce events which will disunite the interests of England and Ireland.[2]

All attention was now being concentrated upon the policy of the

[1] Add. Mss. 38,212, ff. 204-05.
[2] *Beresford Correspondence*, I, 73. George III wrote to Robinson, 2 Nov., Add. Mss. 37,835, f. 5: "The affairs of Ireland are certainly in a most unpleasant situation and I don't see how the vessel can be steered."

Short Money Bill—of granting supplies for six months instead of two years—and the appeal to the country at large in the latter half of October had awakened such a mood in Ireland that there seemed little hope of raising an effective resistance to the measure in the Irish house of commons. The Lord Lieutenant, who certainly had it in his power to oppose the Short Money Bill whether he could secure a majority or not, was anxious to ride at this moment with a loose rein; but he could hardly pursue a flexible policy, in a matter of such moment, on his own authority—once again he asked importunately for instructions, obviously in the hope that he would be told not to offer a futile resistance. He wrote on 8 November:

If the expectations of this kingdom are not received with lenity almost every species of disorder may be apprehended. Rational men are seriously alarmed. . . . Many of the old tryd friends of government speak doubtfully of what will be their conduct respecting the question of a short money bill, and the very few who will engage to resist deem the opposing a lost cause.[1]

It is clear, in fact, that behind everything Buckingham was blackmailing the English ministers for a promise of commercial concessions. Only these would enable him to elude his immediate problem. Only these could conjure away the unknown dangers beyond.

The men who were intimately connected with the royal closet were indignant that the Lord Lieutenant should doubt for a moment the attitude that should be taken up towards the proposed policy of a Short Money Bill. Charles Jenkinson wrote that his conduct was "intolerable"; Buckingham "wished to receive positive orders" to resist, so that in Dublin he could put the blame on the English ministry. This was the period when Lord Weymouth had decided to leave North's administration; North himself was "exceedingly ill"; and Buckingham was suffering torments from lack of support and advice. One of his correspondents wrote to

[1] S.P. 63/467, ff. 101-02; cf. Add. Mss. 38,212, ff. 213-14, H. T. Clements to C. Jenkinson, 6 Nov. "The madness of the people seems to have deffened all reason"; and H.M.C. *Stopford Sackville Mss.* 1, 260. On 16 Nov. Buckingham wrote [S.P. 63/467, f. 109] that he had had no letters from England since the 3rd.

him on 3 November: "I feel exceedingly for the disagreeable situation Your Excellency must be in not hearing from Lord North." Another wrote on the 8th, "Lord North still continues confined," so that "whatever business was in his hands" was still in a state of suspension.

It was on 14 November that North broke his long silence and wrote to the Lord Lieutenant a letter as remarkable in its character as it was extraordinary in its length. We can infer from this document that the views of Beresford, Robinson and Jenkinson had the ascendancy at this date; though the time was at hand when the better North would see the realities of the situation and would come out to meet them in the grand manner. For the moment he pretended that he had no idea of the nature of the commercial concessions which would satisfy the Irish. He ridiculed the vagueness of the term "free trade", as though he had never received any information to give it particularity. He wrote without a single reference to the statistics and opinions which had been transmitted from Dublin in the summer. In any case he could not commit the British parliament, which was to meet on 25 November, and in that parliament, he said, no business relating to the commercial restrictions could possibly be carried through before Christmas. He was satisfied to declare that "neither the Irish House of Lords or Commons thought proper to inquire into the extent or cause of the present distress," and it is strange that after the events of recent months he should have taken such a line, even though the statement itself was verbally accurate. It is not even a defence for his conduct at this moment that there was perhaps a profound truth in one of his more interesting remarks, namely:

that it is totally impossible that a free trade can save Ireland or any other country from impending ruin.

Similarly, it was vanity to allude—as he did—to the minor concessions which had been made to the trade of Ireland in recent years, as though these were remarkable examples of generosity. North, in fact, gave no promises even now concerning any change in commercial policy, and it was his view that the Irish gentry—the members of the house of commons in particular—should "dare to be a little unpopular". He declared:

> There are some persons at the bottom of these proceedings and whose designs go much further than a free trade, and who have had the address to draw in the bulk of the nation. . . . All these join in availing themselves of a moment of distress to drive the people to madness. . . . Your Excellency seems aware of the dangerous consequences of a short Money Bill. . . . You will however, I dare say, exert yourself to the utmost. If it should pass the mischief would be great to England and greater to Ireland.

Jenkinson made the comment that this letter said enough to oblige the Lord Lieutenant to resist the Short Money Bill, "though he will not have it in his power to plead any orders from hence".[1]

The very day after North had written his letter to Dublin there occurred an event in that city which doubled the intensity of the crisis. Those who had belittled the power of the Irish movement— those who had thought it easy to resist the tide if one only "dared to be unpopular" for a moment—now found that events were running far ahead of them. On the other hand, those who in Ireland were trying to subject parliament itself to external pressure were forced to bear witness to the danger of that policy. We see at this moment all the ingredients of the great upheaval which was to put London into a state of terror in the following summer; and it appears to us as a miniature foretaste, or even a dress-rehearsal, of what were to become famous as the Gordon riots. Three or four thousand men were computed to have assembled in College Green, and it was apparently claimed afterwards that they had been summoned by an inflammatory letter signed "A Member of Parliament". Some of them seem to have been under the impression that they were to be assisted by "a number of armed men from the north". They sent out detachments to various parts for the

[1] H.M.C. *Appendix to 8th Report, Pt. I,* Emly Mss. 204–05; Add. Mss. 38,307, ff. 82–83, C. Jenkinson to the Lord Chancellor, 17 Nov. The Lord Chancellor saw North's letter before it was sent; Add. Mss. 37,835, f. 24. The King considered the letter "very judicious", *ibid.* f. 26. In his view "fear alone makes advice be called for", i.e. by Buckingham, "and then it is very dubious if it will be followed"; *ibid.* f. 5.

purpose of "executing vengeance" against members of parliament whose conduct had been displeasing to the "patriots". One body broke up the sittings at the Four Courts, in their search for the Attorney General, who managed to escape. Another party attacked the man's private house, and had broken the windows before they were induced to go away. Around the house of commons itself members were besieged and were compelled to swear that they would vote "for the good of Ireland, free trade and a short Money Bill". The magistracy proved defective on this occasion (as they were to be also in London in the following June) and though the Lord Mayor of Dublin was summoned to the house of commons and a few troops were at hand, the necessary orders for the dispersal of the mob were not given. The crowd appeared on the following days, and even on the 17th the Lord Lieutenant, writing to the Attorney General, was still using the phrase: "as soon as you may think it prudent to come out as usual". On the 16th J. M. Mason, another of the members against whom the mob were particularly vindictive, did not dare to go to the house though he was due to take the Chair in the Committee of Accounts. He wrote to the Speaker:

I cannot venture to go down to the House without manifest danger of my life and cannot foresee how long this prohibition may continue, since the House has not thought it necessary to take any steps towards vindicating the freedom of its members.

Now it is possible to see what dangerous fire some of the "patriot" politicians of Ireland had begun to play with—possible to learn what the subordination of the proceedings in parliament to outside opinion might be made to signify at worst. That deeper logic which underlies so much of revolutionary history, deflecting the purposes of men through the intervention of forms of violence that had never been in the original schedule, is evident even at this early date.

Even moderate men were alarmed, and on the day after the outrage the Irish house of commons carried *nem. con.* a series of resolutions against those who might menace any of its members individually or come "in a tumultuous and disorderly Manner" to "hinder or promote the passing of any Bill or other Matter depending before the House". On the 17th the Mayor and Sheriffs of Dublin were summoned to the house and told that though their humanity had been commendable in a certain light, the excess of lenity might some day "prove fatal to the Innocent."[1]

The authority of the British parliament in Ireland was being openly questioned at this time, and the men who, like the Attorney General, wished to uphold it, were being intimidated into silence and submission. Before long, an opposition newspaper in Dublin contained the threat that Ireland, like America, might appeal to the *ultima ratio* if her demand for free trade were not satisfied. The Attorney General who had no sympathy with either the Volunteers or the general agitation—and who believed that the indulgences to Irish trade would have no economic effects for fifty years since the country was not yet in a position to take advantage of them—still declared that a refusal of such indulgences at the moment would result in an upheaval like the one which had taken place at the other side of the Atlantic. Within a day or two of the Dublin riot it was being suggested that without waiting for any commercial concessions from England, a shipment of Irish wool should defy the British navy, and challenge the validity of the law of William III's reign which prohibited the export of that commodity. In other words the idea was entertained of having an Irish version of the Boston Tea Party.

From 1775 there had been voices which prophesied that if the American colonists were defeated, the power of the British legislature over Ireland herself would be extended further than ever in the future. Some were saying that at the next stage of the story it would be the Irish who would have to submit to taxation levied by the parliament in London. A year after the war with the American colonies had broken out, a reprint had been made of the famous work published by William Molyneux in 1698, *The case of Ireland's being bound by acts of parliament in England*—a work which claimed the legislative independence of Ireland and declared her union with

[1] S.P. 63/467, ff. 106-09, 117, 133-35; Add. Mss. 37,835, ff. 28-30; *Beresford Correspondence*: I, 75-85; H.M.C. *Appendix to 8th Report, Pt. I*, Emly Mss. p. 205; *Journals of the Irish House of Commons*: 17 Nov. 1779.

England to be analogous with that between England and Scotland in the seventeenth century, namely, a union of two separate kingdoms under one head. For years, in books and pamphlets, and in opposition newspapers, the fundamental constitutional issues had been ventilated in one form or another. There existed a considerable repertoire of those radical ideas which in normal times are dropped here and there but have little effect and are often wisely ignored by governments, and left to beat vainly in the air. The exasperation of the Irish in the year 1779; the aggravated discontent which the negligence of North and his government had had the effect of producing; and finally the opening of the new session of the Irish parliament in October, were analogous to the act of putting in the clutch. The more radical constitutional ideas no longer revolved aimlessly and disconnected in an unresisting medium; for now they had found something in the country which they could grip hold of; and a great issue, though not entirely a new one, had at last been put into gear. The cry for commercial concessions had been left unanswered for too long. It was beginning to pass into the more radical protest against the subordination of the Irish to the British government.

The success of the Short Money Bill was virtually beyond question after the disturbances of 15 November; but men who are like a cat in a corner may make serious mistakes out of fear or desperation, and there are certain situations in which, unless they have exceptional ability, anything that they may do will afterwards appear to be wrong. For the final sensation in this chapter of Irish history the Lord Lieutenant and his Chief Secretary managed to draw all the blame upon themselves. The latter, Sir Richard Heron, was regarded by all parties as an unfortunate leader of the house of commons. It was Buckingham himself who, eight months later, put on to paper the best description we possess of the effects of his incompetence:

Upon every unforeseen Motion the House runs wild, those who should support follow their own caprice, the originally intended measure is modifyd away, and many who in fact intended to betray the cause assert that they could not distinguish what was realy the wish of Government. Sir Richard's abilitys are calculated for quieter times, he is a most excellent Chamber Council, but cannot plead, even in the best cause.[1]

At preliminary meetings held by the confidential servants of the crown, Heron declared that in a division upon the question of a Short Money Bill the government would be left in a minority of thirty or forty. It was apparently the general view that there was "reason to apprehend the greatest violence might be shown against the supporters of Administration". It was therefore decided that in general the government should submit to the policy of a Short Money Bill, but that the house of commons should be asked first, to make good the deficiency of the revenue up to 24 June 1780, secondly to allow the funding of the new loan, and, finally, to support the Loan Fund—"on which the credit of the nation so immediately depended"—by imposing new duties, which, as assigned for this particular purpose, would be required for the full period of two years.

In the house of commons, however, the opposition refused to agree to a compromise which, they said, "entirely defeated every purpose they proposed" in their policy of a Short Money Bill. They rejected the whole policy of new taxes, and once again a servant of the crown changed his mind in the course of the debate, though Sir Richard Heron himself did not dare to give way on so important a point. At a meeting held at the Castle on the following morning Buckingham insisted that there should be no weakening in the administration on the subject of the new taxes. At a further sitting of the house of commons it transpired that members were now less willing than ever to put themselves upon the altar for the sake of a cause upon which the servants of the crown themselves had differed the day before. Grattan carried his motion "that at this time it would be inexpedient to grant new taxes", by 170 votes to 47. On the following day, 25 November, the Committee for Supply decided by 138 votes to 100 to grant even the duties for the support of the Loan Fund only for a period of six months. The violence with which Burgh, the Prime Serjeant, supported the popular

[1] Add. Mss. 34,417, f. 95, Buckingham to W. Eden, Private, 22 July 1780.

cause; the fact that the Duke of Leinster's friends opposed the government; and the Lord Lieutenant's attachment to Foster (who had given way to the opposition) all helped to magnify the disgrace of Buckingham and Heron at this moment. Men who had previously described the success of the Short Money Bill as inevitable now ascribed the disaster to Heron's incompetence, Buckingham's weakness, and the undependability of the men connected with the Castle.[1]

Henceforward, Beresford and John Robinson were working underground to secure that all the blame should fall on the Lord Lieutenant and that he should be immediately recalled. When Lord North, fearing the effect that such a dismissal would have on Irish opinion, shrank from the measure, they used every endeavour to coax or frighten Buckingham into a voluntary resignation.[2] Their efforts were assisted by the fact that certain of the leading Irishmen—particularly servants of the crown—who had voted for "popular" measures were only too anxious to excuse themselves by saying that their conduct had been occasioned by Buckingham's weakness. On this whole issue a certain tension developed in the succeeding months between the closet-advisers, particularly Robinson, on the one hand and North on the other, when the latter declared that he did not think it in the power of any Lord Lieutenant to prevent the constitutional issue from being raised.

On 1 December the English ministry was being confronted in the house of lords with a charge that was inescapable—the charge that it had completely neglected the whole problem of Irish commerce since Lord Rockingham had raised the issue in May. Lord Hillsborough, who had just succeeded Weymouth as secretary of state, made a full-scale attempt to rebut the charge and pointed to

---

[1] *Grattan Memoirs*, II, 5–11; *Beresford Correspondence*, I, 81–84, 91–94; H.M.C., *Stopford Sackville Mss.* I, 261; Add. Mss. 38,212, f. 256, 324, etc.

[2] The King was anxious for the removal of Buckingham. On 2 Nov. he had written that "no dependence could be placed on the Castle"; on 9 Nov. he had talked of "the want of Capacity or of Fairness which either attends the Castle or at least is thought to be the case by the best friends of English Government"; on 13 Nov. he had suggested "placing a more firm man instantly at the head of affairs in Ireland"; and on 21 Nov. had suggested a reversion to the older policy of appointing Lords Deputies. Add. Mss. 37,835, ff. 5, 11, 15, 30.

the important papers on the subject of Irish trade which had been transmitted to England by the Lord Lieutenant in the summer. It was in the course of this debate that Lord Gower explained his resignation from the Presidency of the Council and attributed it to the "neglect" of which he had been the witness, especially the neglect of the Irish question. And it is curious to note that on the very same day Lord Hillsborough addressed a reproof to the Lord Lieutenant for being the cause of the very neglect whose existence he denied in parliamentary debate—he levelled his reproaches against the very man whose zeal had made it possible for the government to put up even the pretence that the matter had not been entirely ignored. Hillsborough complained that since July "all correspondence between Your Excellency and my office has subsided upon a subject so interesting to the peace and welfare of both kingdoms." Buckingham's reply was laconic:

When you have at leisure investigated the official correspondence, your candour will trace the reason of its not having been more diffuse.[1]

§III. THE PARLIAMENTARY ATTACK

From the things that have been described above it will be apparent that the ministry was encompassed by crises and terrors—hemmed in by shadows that enlarged their shape and tightened their menacing circle, leaping more close at hand, and looming more ominously, as parliament reassembled in Westminster on 25 November 1779. The very prospect of the new session had been partly responsible for bringing crises to a head and producing that clatter and tumble of crockery, that crescendo of disaster, which made the autumn so heavy with misery for North. Behind the glooms and depressions of the chief minister was always the thought that he was about to be deserted by his supporters in the house of commons.

The chaotic state of the ministry, the neglect of the problem of

[1] S.P. 63/467, ff. 145–48, 215–17 and 225–26; partly printed in *Grattan Memoirs*, II, 405–08.

Irish trade, and the inadequacy of the navy, had long provided
much material for the debating-talents of opposition speakers.
Everything that had happened since June had justified the severity
of the criticisms and the darkness of the prophecies that Rockingham and Shelburne and their followers had been making in the
earlier months of the year. The new disasters—the invasion-scare,
the undefended state of Plymouth, the threat to the West India
islands, and the sensational character of the events in Dublin, now
provided spectacular themes for the critics, confirming and even
magnifying all that the gloomiest prophets had foretold. Since the
men of the opposition in those days had much skill—and took
much trouble—in the collection of intelligence, the *Parliamentary
History* was to provide the student of this period with a vivid and
highly-coloured picture of the events that had taken place since
the prorogation in June.

Certain exceptional factors, such as would only operate against
a ministry already known to be tottering, were bound to make this
particular meeting of parliament more fateful than usual, heightening the dramatic quality of the debates themselves and increasing
the tension behind the scenes. One of these factors we have already
seen at work throughout the course of the year 1779; namely, the
tendency of certain supporters and even certain members of the
government to put a higher price on their collaboration—indeed,
to think that if there was likelihood of a collapse of the ministry it
might be well to move over in time to the winning side and help
to turn the balance. Another was the tendency of the opposition
factions to unite when the government was in danger, such a union
being difficult to bring about—and still more difficult to maintain
—in normal times, (though disturbing and embarrassing for the
government when actually achieved) but most dangerous of all
and most likely to take place when the government seemed on the
point of collapsing for quite other reasons—that is to say, when the
prize seemed near enough to make it appear that a combined opposition would have some effect. Furthermore, the opposition could
argue that since the situation of the government was so miserable
the prize would be theirs if they could only make a supreme effort
now, going a stage further than usual in their resistance, and all

joining in a violent heave to make desperation more desperate, all conspiring to carry political conflict to a higher degree of intensity. On the top of all this it was significant that the time had now arrived when men began to become conscious of the imminence of a general election. At this stage in the life of a parliament the members began to be more than usually sensitive to the opinion of their constituents.

Throughout the eighteenth century it had been true that opposition to the government of the day had involved hostility to the king himself, who was still the head of the executive, still in a genuine sense a partner with the ministry in the actual conduct of affairs. A king could hardly be indifferent to the fortunes of a political game which had the effect of forcing his hands in the choice of ministers—bringing new men into office by virtue of their parliamentary strength. On the present occasion, however, George III is implicated in a peculiar way in the political system that is being attacked. The whole battle that he is fighting is his own—his rather than the ministry's—and he will fight against Lord North to save Lord North, for the administration must be continued in existence so that George III will not have to surrender to the Rockingham whigs. North's way of disclaiming the responsibilities of the head of a government encouraged the habit of throwing back the responsibility, whether for the political system in general or for the war and its mismanagement, on to the shoulders of the King himself.

When parliament opened on 25 November, therefore, there were obvious reasons why the scale of the conflict should be enlarged and the issue magnified to transcend the ordinary issues of party politics. Now, if ever, the conflict lay between a considerable section of parliament and the king; and even in debate it became clear that George III rather than North himself was the object of the new offensive, though it was admitted that parliamentary etiquette allowed the attribution of responsibility only to his servants. At first the criticism was directed against the closet influence, and Lord Rockingham himself laid down the pattern of the opposition charges in a speech in the house of lords on 25 November. Our plight, he said:

was owing to a baleful and pernicious system; it was the natural effect of causes, not perhaps entirely removed from the public eye; but then it was an effect foreseen and predicted, which he ever had, and always would, do all in his power to defeat.

He then brought out the accusation which gives the key to his programme: "The cause originated in unconstitutional control and advice." The King, he said, must give his genuine confidence to the responsible minister; "otherwise it was delusory to expect that even new counsels or counsellors could succeed." Lord Lyttelton flayed a ministry "of the most jarring councils and the most divided opinions"—"What was their government? Who could define their system? Who would be hardy enough to say that they had a settled plan?" He declared that a crisis had been reached which

demanded fair, open and avowed council, no whispering, no whiffling, no skulking opinions, no opinions delivered in the closet and disavowed elsewhere.

Shelburne said: "Ministers were no longer responsible", while in the commons James Grenville talked of them as men "under the guidance of secret advice, and that of the most hateful and pernicious kind". Here, in the commons, T. Townshend said:

But of late years, a most dangerous doctrine had gone forth, and had been most sedulously propagated by the followers of administration, and perhaps some of its members, though neither had the confidence publicly to avow it, which directly tended to overthrow the constitution, "that the King was his own minister, his own admiral in chief, his own general, his own secretary, his own president of the council, his own financier". Thus his Majesty was made the shield behind which knavery, servility, and every species of folly, treachery and villainy might screen themselves.[1]

If, however, there was to arise the kind of conjuncture which

[1] *Parliamentary History*, xx, 1029 *et seqq*. Cf. 1120, C. J. Fox: "It was not the mere rumour of the streets that the King was his own minister ... an invisible cabinet influence"; 1248, T. Townshend, "The common topic out of that House, was the influence of the crown, and secret influence."

might be regarded as providing the whigs with one of their historic moments—if the flag were to be unfurled again the King in the way they thought had happened in the time of John or James II— Charles James Fox, enlarging the occasion by his passion, and making it more dramatic by his rhetorical outbursts—was more ready to burn his boats than anybody else, more willing to startle even his colleagues by the trenchant manner in which he stated the issue with George III.

In the autumn of the year 1779, the hopes of Fox, who was now thirty years of age, had seemed at last to be on the verge of fulfilment. When the prize is so tantalizingly near, yet so evasive still, it burns the finger-tips—rising success only producing increased exasperation. It is clear at this point of the story that, to a man of the temper of Fox, every moment's postponement was maddening. In response to the crisis he took steps which increased his stature and developed his political personality, so that by the study of this chapter of English history we can see how he came to assume his characteristic rôle. Goaded by the perversity of the conjuncture and by his passions—which were mountainous—he became the figure that we know, the Fox of the great whig legend. Certainly he was angry and at the moment his wilfulness seemed to become wilder even than it had ever been before. Certainly he was over-covetous—he fought too desperately perhaps, and was willing even to gamble too recklessly in order to bring himself and his party to power. He complained more than others in these particular years of the bitterness of exclusion from office. The world said that his desperate financial need made the acquisition of an office under government a matter of urgent necessity to him. When he himself commented on the matter he did not deny that his situation was such, though he said that he had searched his heart and believed that this was not the real motive of his conduct. The very majesty of events, in any case, sometimes seems to lift men above themselves, and carries the conflict out of the region of mere faction-fights—the greatness of the issue seems to raise the stature of those who are engaged in it, forcing the triflers to become sincere, and bringing to the cry for liberty a more authentic note than before. If at the first level of analysis we must say that it is men who make history, we are not permitted to close our eyes to the fact that history itself helps to make and mould a man—that at this moment indeed the course of events was hammering out the shape of the Fox that we know.

Those who read the dull abridgements and turgid paraphrases of Fox's speeches as they appear in the volumes of our *Parliamentary History*—so often mere skeletons or diagrams of an argument without the colour, the swiftness, the warmth and the sudden gleam—will be relieved on occasion by a passage that is strangely moving, quickened by a current of electricity; as though the reporter had realized that here, if possible, he must let no word slip away, and must transcend his ordinary competence in order not to miss the authentic note. On 25 November Fox delivered a famous speech, at the climax of which we can see how the style of the reporting changes. Shelburne confessedly followed the pattern of this speech and used similar historical analogies in a remarkable oration that he delivered in the house of lords a little later. With hardly due respect to the niceties of parliamentary custom, the campaign was directed against the King.

Though in general the evils of a reign would be attributed to the wickedness of ministers, said Fox, "yet, when those evils reached to a certain height, ministers were forgotten, and the prince alone was punished. Thus it was with the royal House of Stuart"—with Charles I and James II, who for the sins of their ministers had to "bear the whole weight of their people's indignation".

There was not, (he observed,) in the whole history of this country, a period that resembled the present, except the reign of the unfortunate Henry 6. His family, like that of his present Majesty, did not claim the crown as their hereditary right; it was by revolutions that they both obtained it. Henry was an amiable and pious prince; so was his present Majesty: Henry was the son of the most renowned monarch that had ever sat upon our throne; George was the grandson of a hero: Henry lost all his father's conquests and all his hereditary provinces in France: George had already seen the conquests of his grandfather wrested from him in the West Indies, and his hereditary provinces of America erected into an empire, that disclaimed all connection with him.

George III, he continued, "had set out in life with the brightest prospects that a young man could have wished for". But "how sadly was the scene reversed! his empire dismembered, his councils distracted, his people falling off in their fondness for his person!" The people were beginning to murmur; their patience was not unlimited; "there certainly would be insurrections."

It was not a secret to that House, that the present sovereign's claim to the throne of this country was founded upon only the delinquency of the Stuart family; a circumstance, which should never be one moment out of his Majesty's recollection. . . . If there was at this day one of that unfortunate House remaining . . . could he not say "You have banished my ancestor from the throne, and barred the sceptre from all his progeny . . . and yet the ministers of the present reign are ten times more wicked and more ignorant than those were. . . ." When a nation was reduced to such a state of wretchedness . . . the people would inevitably take up arms and the first characters in the kingdom would be seen in their ranks.[1]

The parliamentary campaign, then, was being directed in a remarkable way against the King in person; and in these days, when Robinson and Jenkinson had saved the tottering ministry, it is not surprising that one of the main themes of debate should have been the "secret influence". The fight was a vain one—it was a case of lunging at shadows. The effectiveness of the parliamentary warfare depended on the possibility of bringing home to the responsible ministers themselves those acts of misgovernment which were the subject of complaint. The survival of the ministry of North, in spite of that almost universal discontent which was being displayed in this period, made more vivid the importance of another kind of influence—the influence of the King within the house of commons itself, the power of what the enemies of George III would call corruption. A narrative which is to lead to Dunning's famous motion of 1780 must note the fresh importance which this issue acquired at the opening of this new session of parliament.

[1] *Parliamentary History:* xx, 1123–25; cf. Wraxall, *Memoirs* (1815), II, 20–21. Cf. *Morning Post*, 27 Nov. 1779. "Mr. Fox in his parliamentary invocation to rebellion seems to strive as hard for a halter as any gentleman ever did in his desperate circumstances."

The opposition parties were able to announce the achievement of an important object in the early days of December. They now joined forces—the followers of Rockingham combining with those of Shelburne—"experience of what had passed, the dread of worse that might happen, had melted them into one mass." Fox pretended to claim that there were now only two parties in the kingdom—"His Majesty's ministers, supported by the influence of the crown, against all Britain".

The first men of rank, fortune and character, in both Houses, had firmly and virtuously resolved to set their faces against this increasing, this alarming influence of the crown. . . . They had resolved to act in concert, and nothing would ever content them but reducing the influence of the crown within due and constitutional bounds. The sense of danger had brought about this coalition; they were . . . . well-wishers of his Majesty, but the avowed and determined enemies of this dangerous influence, which grew proportionately strong as the empire grew weak. . . . It was a lamentable contest in which his Majesty was engaged; . . . a contest with the whole body of his subjects.[1]

One of the great issues of the year 1780 was plainly formulated in the terms of this union between the parties of opposition. But it must be noted that the battle was one which could hardly be fought out within the walls of parliament. It was precisely the complaint that parliament itself was unduly influenced by the crown.

So we note on the one side the play of closet-advisers, while on the other side we are confronted with the operation of royal "influence" upon the house of commons itself. It would seem that the politics of the bedroom and the backstairs are in the ascendant, that underground forces and left-handed agencies turn the balance, and the King prevails because he has allies who are concealed in the shadows. The enemies of George III, however, were not without resources—not unwilling to turn from the normal game of parliamentary politics, and to look for allies in what as yet was only a sort of demi-monde. If they wished to summon unrecognized forces to

[1] *Parliamentary History:* xx, 1225.

their help, however, they did not need to search in closets and cellars, but went out into the broad daylight, for their one remaining hope lay in market-place and in countryside, in the unmeasured power of extra-parliamentary opinion. That hope had become greater now that the effectiveness of this factor had become so apparent in the affairs of Ireland.

According to some hostile judgments, the troubles in Ireland had been provoked by the signals and incitations of the Rockinghamite whigs themselves. John Robinson and his Irish correspondents were only too eager to point out the connections that existed between the patriots in Dublin and the opposition at Westminster; and they noted particularly the family connection between the Duke of Richmond and the Duke of Leinster. Apart from intermarriages and political attachments some of the opposition-leaders in England were amongst the most important of the absentee landlords; and it was true that in one manner or another some of them had political influence in certain Irish constituencies. In the papers of Charles James Fox there is a letter which announces on 3 November 1779 that Fox had been in Ireland for a period of six weeks.[1] No mention is made of any political activity there, but Fox chose a curiously significant date for his visit, and was in Ireland when the new session of parliament opened in Dublin. There are letters which bear evidence to the friendship between certain of the leaders of the opposition parties in the two countries, and show that at one time and another—if not recently—Burke and Fox, for example, had been in correspondence with more than one of the Irishmen who were influential in this period. The political connections between the two countries are always interesting in the age of the Hanoverians and deserve a more detailed examination than they have yet received.

For the parliamentary opposition at Westminster the whole course of the Irish crisis in the year 1779 was bound to provide a spectacular debating opportunity. Ministers, they said, by "their total inattention towards the affairs of Ireland" had invited a new

[1] Fox Mss. in the possession of the Master of Trinity College, Cambridge; Fitzpatrick Correspondence, W. F. Fawkener to R. Fitzpatrick, 3 Nov. 1779.

range of disasters, and had "abandoned the government of that kingdom to chance". They were able to point out that the ultimate cause of the distresses of Ireland, the profounder origin of the political crisis in Dublin, was still, once again, the "accursed American war". And though some mischief may have resulted from the imprudent conduct of the opposition leaders in England during the course of the year, they were able to reply to the charge that they had provoked the upheaval: "Were there no discontents before gentlemen on this side of the House had spoken on the subject?" They were able to point to pamphlets and newspapers which had been produced in Ireland—and capable leaders there—as a sufficient explanation of the movements that had been taking place.

At a slightly later date, Edmund Burke wrote to one of the Irish politicians that, by restricting the supplies to a period of six months, "you revived the grand use, and characteristick benefit of Parliament, which was on the point of being entirely lost amongst us".[1] But it had become clear to the members of the opposition at this period that the Irish parliament had only been driven to this display of virtue by a national uprising and a formidable array of power. Exasperated by the futility of their efforts in the house of commons, the English enemies of the government were only too ready to fix their attention on that extra-parliamentary movement which had operated with such effect even upon the high throne of corruption, the Irish lower house.

So the companies of Irish Volunteers in particular formed one of the great topics of discussion in the new session of the British parliament. Lord Lyttelton on the very opening day had stated the essential thesis: "These Irish Associations are the Whigs of Ireland." For whigs, he said, were "men who detest tyranny, and execrate despotism; men who consider passive obedience and non-resistance as the slavish doctrine enforced only by tyrants". Fox declared the same day: "the situation of affairs was so very delicate that it was not easy for members to treat the subject in a becoming manner."

[1] E. Burke, "Letter to Thomas Burgh, Esq.", 1 Jan. 1780; *Works* (1812,), IX, 248.

They were almost as effectually barred from giving a free opinion on the case, as the members of the Irish House, who had the bayonet at their breast, and were sworn by compulsion to vote as the people dictated.

Now the legality of the associations would be defended by reference to the Bill of Rights or to the events of the year 1745. Now Lord Shelburne would formulate in drastic terms the ultimate political implications of the movement:

The government [in Ireland] had been abdicated and the people resumed the powers vested in it; and in so doing were fully authorized by every principle of the constitution, and every motive of self-preservation; and whenever they should delegate this inherent power, they wisely and firmly determined to have it placed upon so large and liberal a basis, that they should not be liable to suffer under the same oppressions in time to come.

In his wilful, angry mood Fox was even prepared for a real conflict in the country, the kind of conflict that should make the hills and valleys ring; for his speech of 25 November continued:

The Irish associations had been called illegal; legal or illegal, he declared he entirely approved of them. He approved of that manly determination which, in the dernier resort, flies to arms in order to obtain deliverance. When the last particle of good faith in men is exhausted, they will seek in themselves the means of redress; they will recur to first principles, to the spirit as well as letter of the constitution; and they can never fail in such resources, though the law may literally condemn such a departure from its general and unqualified rules. . . .

God knew, that he sincerely lamented the cause which produced this sad, he could not but say, this perplexing and humiliating alternative. He most heartily regretted that any cause had been administered which seemed to justify violence and resistance; he dreaded the consequences, however justifiable in their origin, or moderately or judiciously conducted; but whatever the effects might be, he was ready to acknowledge that such a power was inherent in men; as men and citizens it was a sacred trust in their hands, as a defence against the possible or actual abuse of power, political treachery, and the arts and intrigues of government; and when all other means failed, resistance he should ever hold as perfectly justifiable.[1]

Finally Fox said that what he had predicted earlier in the course of the year had "literally come to pass"; namely, "augmented armed associations, sufficiently formidable to dictate to and direct an acquiescing British parliament".

So, in this period, the whigs who were connected with Lord Rockingham found in the Irish upheaval a doctrine that could be applied in British politics—a doctrine of what might be called near-revolution. They had been moving in this direction for some time, for they had hoped to see their own country defeated in America, and Fox had expressed his sorrow when he had heard the news of what was claimed to be a British victory. Since the time of Halifax—and even in 1688 and the years immediately after-wards—the leaders of the whigs had realized that revolution was a thing which it was good to have behind one in history but which must not be allowed to happen again. It was an excellent thing to have had revolution and then a monarchy re-founded in circum-stances that stood as a perpetual warning to kings; but politics had been refined and it is almost true to say that civilization had been advanced, because the eighteenth-century whigs had been only conservatively anti-king—too conscious of their interest in the existing order to be the apostles of more revolution still. The party of Rockingham and Burke had not merely the pleasure of know-ing that there was the seventeenth-century revolution behind them. It was their good fortune that there existed a contemporary one to support the argument—a revolution happily far away across the Atlantic. It had not been without its effect nearer home, for if it had helped to originate the crisis in Ireland it also helped to induce the ministry of North to be more careful in the face of this —helped it ultimately to grant the commercial concessions instead of attempting to resist the hurricane. In spite of all this, it was clear that the deadlock in England itself was not broken and the energies and determination of George III had still not been worn down. Even the crisis in Ireland on top of all the other disasters had not

[1] *Parliamentary History*, xx, 1226–28.

resulted in the overthrow of the ministry of North. Fox and his Rockinghamite friends were fighting a real battle against a genuine king—against power firmly entrenched—and now, more than ever, the situation had come to seem desperate. These men did not know what we know, that peace would be made in America, that the younger Pitt would be skilful and wise, and that the constitution would ultimately be saved at least from monarchical despotism. They needed further weapons. They needed a *deus ex machina*; for since the battle was genuine it could not be won by a party which merely played the parliamentary game according to the rules. Now was not the moment for that conservative type of whiggism which avows that a revolution is unthinkable.

In Ireland the *deus ex machina* had intervened, and extra-parliamentary opinion, operating through channels that were bound to be irregular, had forced the hands of a parliament in spite of the resources of corruption. In other words, it was clear that there were political forces in society itself which could be mobilized certainly in a manner not quite regular but yet without a direct appeal to arms. It was to be significant that in 1780 even the Rockinghamite whigs not only desired to see in England something of the kind that had taken place in Ireland, but were prepared to make full play with what might be called the quasi-revolutionary argument. The only thing left for them to call upon was the god from the machine. Indeed they called; but for long it seemed that (in Britain at least) the god was asleep.

Before the month of December had proceeded very far the government had improved its cause in one respect, and the opposition had curiously lost ground in a field which they had made peculiarly their own. Lord North had announced a generous programme of concessions in favour of the commerce of Ireland; and these—especially as men had ceased to expect them, and as they went further than the Irish had dared to hope—released the tension, and produced an unusual display of gratitude, so that the minister became a popular figure in Ireland for a time.

We have already seen that on 20 November John Robinson—who could still say that the work on the question of Irish commerce

was the "never failing dish" of his leisure moments—had declared
that Lord North was now anxious to see something done for the
Irish, and indeed was "in a hurry about it."[1] The news of the
offences committed by the mob against the Irish house of commons
on the 15th had undoubtedly contributed to his anxiety and had
helped to bring about his change of attitude. A paper from the
Irish Speaker appears to have assisted the attempt to hammer out a
policy, since it described the concessions which would give satisfaction in Ireland—a point concerning which the men in London
had, or affected to have, been in doubt.[2] On 26 November we
learn from Lord Beauchamp, who was working hard to secure a
settlement, that the prospects of a satisfactory arrangement were
now much more hopeful. On the 29th it seemed possible that commissioners might be sent over to Dublin to negotiate an agreement
on commercial questions. The news that the Irish money bill had
been passed for only six months was said to have been not without
its advantages for the ministers, "as the country gentlemen, whom
they were afraid would oppose [concessions for] Ireland, will now
see that the matter has become serious".[3] It was pointed out in fact
that it had not been the government itself but public opinion and
the prejudices of the house of commons which had been the ob-
struction to a more generous policy at an earlier date. Nothing less
than the events which had actually taken place in Dublin had been
necessary to wear down the prejudices of the English people and
the objections of the vested interests at home.

Lord North himself, though he still drew attention to "the many
favours which had been conferred on Ireland, since he had a seat
in his Majesty's councils", now confessed that these had proved
insufficient to remove the difficulties of that country or to remedy
its distress. On 1 December Lord Hillsborough declared in the
house of lords that "Ireland was entitled to a free trade with equal
taxes", and five days later Lord Beauchamp himself, while dis-

[1] Add. Mss. 38,212, ff. 227–32. In Add. Mss. 37,835, f. 38, John Robinson
writes to George III on 22 Nov., "Lord North [yesterday] adopted very much
the Ideas which you mentioned concerning Ireland."

[2] *Grattan Memoirs*, II, 395–96; S.P. 63/467, ff. 56–57; see also p. 142 above.
Cf. *Beresford Correspondence*: I, 98–99; and the reference in note 3 below.

[3] H.M.C. *Appendix to 8th Report, Pt. I*, Emly Mss. pp. 205–06.

claiming any knowledge of Lord North's precise intentions, gave
the impression of being assured that something like this would be
granted.[1] On 8 December a series of resolutions concerning the
trade of Ireland was laid before the cabinet, and these were transmitted to Dublin, where it was necessary to discover whether they
would give satisfaction.[2] In the subsequent week, Thomas Allan,
who assisted in the final stages of the transaction, said:

I have had a continued scene of hurry; papers upon papers
though useless to the point were ordered. . . . A dozen clerks were
employed in framing a variety of accounts which had never been
looked into.

Finally, on 13 December, Lord North presented to the house of
commons a programme of commercial concessions which was
welcomed as a surprising act of generosity by the Irish themselves.
He proposed to permit the export from Ireland of "all woollen
manufactures whatsoever, or manufactures made up, or mixed
with, wool or wool flocks". He confessed that this was due to the
Irish; for he admitted one of the charges that had been made against
England, namely, that she had broken a compact made in 1692 to
the effect that she herself should enjoy the woollen manufacture
exclusively, while they should enjoy the linen in a similar way.[3]
He proposed the repeal of those parts of an act of George II's reign
which prohibited the exportation of glass or any kind of glass-ware
from Ireland, and he even described this act as "a very extraordinary
stretch of the legislative power of Great Britain, considering the
smallness of the object". Thirdly, he proposed to allow Ireland a
free—or rather, as he called it, an "equal"—trade with the British
colonies and plantations in America and the West Indies. In other
words he was prepared to open that trade to the Irish, subject only

[1] H.M.C. *Appendix to 8th Report, Pt. I,* Emly Mss. pp. 205–06.
[2] *Corr. George III,* IV, 511–13; H.M.C. *Various Mss.* VI, Knox Mss. p. 238, refers
to resolutions on this subject "drawn up by Mr. Knox". Robinson, writing to
Jenkinson, 20 Dec., Add. Mss. 38,212, ff. 299–300, refers to them as "your
resolutions".
[3] See e.g. *The People of Ireland not a parcel of lazy incorrigible Scoundrels* (1779),
p. 33.

to the limitations and burdens which had to be borne by the merchants of Britain herself. This he rightly claimed to be a genuine and generous concession, since in those days every power considered itself as having the exclusive right to trade with its overseas dependencies; and if Ireland had been an independent state—not subject to Britain in any way at all—she would have had no claim to a share in the colonial commerce. The concessions were welcomed by the parliament at Westminster. They produced shouts of joy and gratitude in Ireland itself. Lord Lucan on 15 December left England in order to work in Dublin for the conciliation of the two countries. When the first of the bills for the relief of Ireland had been hurried through parliament the King went in person on 23 December to give the royal assent, on "an occasion of so much importance to his faithful kingdom of Ireland".[1]

Only the opposition in England seemed ungracious, as though they feared that Lord North might be too easily freed from the burden of his Irish difficulties. Always they insisted that here was no beneficent gesture, no generosity of spirit—the minister made concessions merely because he had seen the pistol at his head. The opposition were nervous concerning their relations with the "patriot" party in Ireland—they would not approve the concessions lest the Irish themselves should fail to find them sufficiently generous. The ministry must take the responsibility for its own proposals, they said, while they themselves would maintain a silence that must not be construed as approbation. By their over-anxiety and their clever tactics at this moment they produced the very result which it had been their object to avoid; for the "patriots" of Ireland wondered why Fox should be unhappy when they were pleased, why the opposition whigs in England should not be the first to rejoice when concessions were being made to the commerce of Ireland. It seemed that the whigs in England desired the Irish to be unhappy so that they should have an ally to help them in harassing Lord North. On the other hand, from the English point of view it was argued that once again the whigs in Westminster were inciting the Irish to ask for something more.

[1] *Parliamentary History*, xx, 1272–84; H.M.C. *Appendix to 8th Report, Pt. I,* Emly Mss. p. 207.

The Rockinghamite whigs were much concerned to see the harm that had been done to their relations with the "patriots" in the Irish parliament.[1] The episode reveals the importance that they attached to these relations, and shows that there had been previous communications at some time or another, though it exposes also the defects in any concert that existed between the men of the English and the Irish opposition. Burke, writing to Thomas Burgh, asked why the Irish had troubled "to mix with the panegyric on the Minister so large a portion of acrimony to the independent part of the nation." He made a lengthy explanation of the conduct of the Rockinghamites, as did Thomas Townshend, who wrote almost at the same time and with the same anxiety to Lord Charlemont. A few days later Fox wrote to the Duke of Leinster:

Were we to speak out and say that their propositions, though right so far as they went, were far from sufficient? You must consider how necessary it is for us to have the confidence of the people here, and how much that would have been shaken, if it could have been raised against us with any colour of truth, that we were teaching Ireland to be dissatisfied. . . . Under all these difficulties surely it was the safest way for us, and the best way for Ireland too, to give the ministry full careers upon the subject, reserving ourselves afterwards to assist Ireland when she might want us. . . . If, after all, we are suspected of not being friendly to Ireland, it is very hard, and upon me in particular, who certainly never missed any opportunity of declaring in public as well as in private, how much I wished you success in all the points you were likely to push.[2]

---

[1] Cf. H.M.C. *Appendix to 8th Report, Pt. I*, Emly Mss. p. 206, Lucan to Pery, 7 Dec. 1779, where it is suggested that Shelburne "is afraid that Ireland will be so satisfied that it will serve no more as a tool to overturn administration here . . . . He, therefore, endeavoured to stir up constitutional grievances."

[2] E. Burke, "Letter to Thomas Burgh, Esq.", 1 Jan. 1780, *Works* (1812), IX, 226–57; Fitzwilliam *Correspondence of Burke:* II, 313; H.M.C. *Charlemont Mss.* pp. 369–70.

Part II

THE YORKSHIRE ASSOCIATION

Chapter V

THE INTERVENTION OF THE PEOPLE

A T precisely this point in English history the country itself
rises up, as though determined not to be left out of the story
any longer. Our vision, which has hitherto been focused
on the government and parliament at Westminster, has now to be
extended, so that it can scan the length and breadth of England. The
population of England and Wales would appear to have been
somewhere in the neighbourhood of seven millions in the period
with which we are dealing. Already the country was well on the
way with an agrarian revolution and the French were eager to
learn how it could be that so bleak an island should present so
rich and smiling a countryside. Long before this time the historian
traces also the incipient stages of the industrial revolution. And
trans-oceanic trade had assumed such proportions as to give a
new revelation (even at this postponed date) of the magnitude of
the consequences produced by the maritime discoveries of the
fifteenth century.

London had continued to grow, and over the area which it now
covers there existed in the year 1779 something like a million inhabitants. The demands of its markets—which were like tentacles put
out not merely upon the home counties but even upon the northern
parts of the country, even upon the cattle in the Highlands of Scotland—had helped to unify and develop the economy of England.
For a long time the city itself, and the great population of the London area, had almost stood as a separate power in politics, a separate
estate of the realm.[1] In a different sense, and particularly clearly in
the home counties, it appeared that Middlesex was already providing the country with independent political leadership. In the
eighteenth century, almost one might say for the first time, the rest
of the country began to see the rise of towns which were really

[1] For a protest against this see *An Historical Essay, wherein the Example,
Influence and Authority of Londoners in Publick Affairs are occasionally considered and
compared* (London, 1741).

181

more than villages. At a small number of places in the provinces, there had come into existence the genuine features of what might be called urban life. Bristol had 100,000 inhabitants, Norwich over 40,000, Liverpool and Manchester about that number, Birmingham and Sheffield rather less, while Hull, Leeds and Nottingham were also of appreciable size and there was a heavily-populated region in Tyneside.

Communications had greatly improved, especially by river and canal. If this had helped to quicken the pace of economic life it had also made the unity of the country more real in other ways—it had had the effect of drawing the threads together. Many towns, such as York, Leeds, Cambridge, Salisbury, Winchester, and Norwich, had their local newspaper, though it might appear only once or twice a week. Political news travelled fairly quickly, therefore, and local complaints could be merged into national ones—there could exist a rough precursor of what we describe too trenchantly perhaps as "public opinion". The high development of political life and political interest in London, which had been significant in the 1760's, had communicated itself to the home counties with which many Londoners and many members of parliament had connections. In various provincial towns there would be local radical parties—nonconformist groups for example—and local leaders (like John Cartwright in Nottingham and the dissenting minister, Robinson, in Cambridge) had begun to stir up political controversy. In Yorkshire the West Riding was rapidly becoming the chief seat of the woollen industry, and there were towns which, as we shall see, were ripe for a political awakening. In this county also we shall watch the emergence of a number of the landed gentry who were prepared to provide an independent form of political leadership. Perhaps it is not strange that, after Middlesex (and considering the predominance which London was bound to enjoy in the region of the home counties) Yorkshire should have come forward to give the lead to the rest of the provinces at this time.

Throughout the eighteenth century, and at least as early as in the time of Defoe, there had been appearing in England a fissure which at times almost seems to amount to a cleavage between two forms of civilization. And though the fact is not inexplicable, we might say that it is one of the curiosities of history that this cleavage did not ultimately split the country from top to bottom, in the way that the contemporary *philosophe* movement split both tradition and society in France. The differences were easily recognizable in eighteenth-century England, where some of the later forms of compromise and reconciliation between them were as yet un-achieved. And those differences were social as much as intellectual, however often the two currents might intermingle or their courses become blurred.

In one sense the differences go back to a religious divergence—the Church of England and the body of the dissenters had come to represent remarkably differing types of mentality and outlook. The cleavage was widened by that educational divergence which separated schools like Eton and universities like Oxford and Cambridge from the dissenting academies. On the one hand there was the traditional emphasis upon the study of the ancient classics, while on the other hand men gloried rather in more utilitarian types of teaching, and gave more place to modern languages and the natural sciences. The men who were associated with indus-try and commerce and the rising towns disparaged the traditions of the landed aristocracy and lacked the cultivated taste, the classical prejudices, of the Augustan Age. A crop of controversialists and publicists who represented the world of the disinherited—the men who had never entered into the great tradition or possessed a share in it—formed a kind of undergrowth, an underworld, vividly alive and too often overlooked by students of the more formal literature or the more academic thought of the period. These men represented common sense and took short cuts to truth, assisted by influences that either came from the French *philosophes* or are traceable to the same origin. And the significance of the breach that they made in English thought and tradition in the eighteenth century was clearest of all when these people turned to questions of politics. They made short work of the mysteries of tradition, the subtleties of historical interpretation, the complexities and anomalies, which existed in the eighteenth-century scheme of things and which were so dis-tressing to the man of "common sense". The Yorkshire movement, which we are about to examine, provided for their political thought and their historical interpretations a remarkable leverage.

Finally, from the correspondence in the newspapers and the remarks that constantly appear in private letters—from the diatribes put out by the enemies of the government, but also from the very apologies which were made in reply by its friends—we must judge that the war with the American colonies and the Bourbon powers, the increase of taxes and the disruption of trade, had begun to have an effect on the merchant and the manufacturer, the landlord and the farmer. Without over-stressing the degree of their suffering, we must note, that, on the merest hint that it was in their power to remedy matters by a protest, they were ready to rush to meetings, or bombard the newspapers with their complaints.

§I. THE MIDDLESEX MOVEMENT

Of three great political crises which threatened the system of George III, the first in 1769-70 arose out of the Middlesex election case, and the attempt to generalize the grievance of a single county by carrying the issue to all bodies of freeholders throughout the land. The second, in 1779-80, begins with an attempt—one in which Wilkes himself again plays a leading part—to fabricate a second Middlesex election controversy and to carry it across the length and breadth of the country; though on this occasion the movement led to a *cul de sac* and was quickly diverted into an entirely different channel, as we shall see. The third, in 1792, provides us with the same initial pattern, for it begins with an attempt to create a Westminster election grievance, somewhat on the lines of the earlier Middlesex cases.

This recurrent pattern illustrates not only the importance but the leadership of London in the political developments that were taking place. It shows a certain paucity of invention on the side of the enemies of the government, and enhances the importance of the ingenuity of Wilkes in the creation of opposition technique. Also it demonstrates the degree to which the opponents of George III were compelled to resort to the organization of extra-parliamentary opinion in their attempts to overthrow his system. In the two latter cases the crisis led to the establishment of what was called the Association, perhaps the most curious device in extra-parliamentary organization that our history has ever known. It is important to any one who wishes to study how the machinery of modern party came to develop. It is still more interesting, perhaps, when examined for its own sake, as involving almost the plan of an alternative system of government.

In the latter part of September 1779 John Robinson was busy trying to find a suitable candidate to stand for the government in a Middlesex by-election, necessitated by the death of John Glynn, who had been a follower of Wilkes and had shared with him the task of representing the county in the house of commons. The constituency was regarded as important by the government, and the matter gave a great deal of trouble to the Secretary of the Treasury; but by 27 September nobody had been induced to contest the seat, and when a meeting was held in the Tower Hamlets for the purpose of nominating a candidate the friends of government had to use "a little management" in order to secure a postponement. George III wrote on that day:

It is vexatious to see how little attachment men of worth seem to have for that county; if some one is not soon decided upon, I fear the populace will bring forth some not to the Credit of the County.

On 3 October Robinson had to report that he was

extremely sorry to say that no proper candidate for the County of Middlesex has been yet found, almost every Gentleman of any considerable property in the County suitable for such Station has been tried, either by the Duke of Northumberland or Mr Robinson. By a letter from the Duke of Northumberland your Majesty will see that the matter rests with Colonel Tuffnell.

By this time the government must have felt the case to be desperate, as the adjourned meeting for the purpose of nomination was to take place on the following day. Robinson reported that "although this meeting is only a partial one for the Tower Hamlets, yet if a nomination should take place there of a person not to be supported by Government it will entangle and create confusion". In order to thwart the Wilkites George III therefore gave his approval to the nomination of Colonel Tuffnell, "as the Duke of Northumberland answers for his intention to keep the County quiet, though I suppose his Vote in Parliament will generally be adverse". Tuffnell, who was already in the house of commons as the member for Beverley, had "in general hitherto gone against Administration". Anything, however, would be better than a Wilkite radical.[1]

By the perversity of fate it was the nomination of Tuffnell, so avowedly made for the purpose of keeping the county quiet, which touched the spring and released the storm in Middlesex. At the adjourned meeting in the Tower Hamlets on 4 October the popular party wished to nominate George Byng, but "questions arose whether Mr Byng or Mr Tuffnell could offer themselves, being already in Parliament." It appeared that the government had not allowed the grass to grow under their feet, for Tuffnell was able to announce that he for his own part had already applied to Lord North for the Chiltern Hundreds. George Byng, hearing this, became "very angry" and declared:

that although he had a very great regard for Colonel Tuffnell, he must now consider him as a ministerial candidate and would oppose him and apply also to Lord North to vacate his seat.[2]

[1] Add. Mss. 37,834, ff. 143-52, Correspondence between J. Robinson and George III; Add. Mss. 38,212, ff. 115-17, Correspondence between J. Robinson and C. Jenkinson; *Corr. George III*, iv, 451-52. The King wrote to Robinson on 5 Oct., [H.M.C. *Abergavenny Mss.* p. 26, No. 226] "I hope no pains will be spared to secure the election"; and to North on 16 Oct. [*Corr. George III*, iv, 459] "If the D. of Northumberland requires some gold pills for the Election it would be wrong not to give him some assistance."

[2] Add. Mss. 37,834, f. 152; printed in *Corr. George III*, iv, 451-52.
According to the *Cambridge Chronicle*, 23 Oct. 1779, Tuffnell was asked at a later meeting whether he would join his interest with that of Byng and his friends to solicit a lucrative office for Byng in order that he might vacate his seat. Tuffnell was evasive but a great majority supported a resolution to that effect. A letter from Lord North, read at the same meeting, stated that so long as Tuffnell "persists in his cause I do not think it would be right for me" to accede to Byng's demand.

This he did, but Lord North met him with a refusal—he had already promised the Chiltern Hundreds to Tuffnell, he said. There is evidence that North expected trouble over this matter in advance, and for this reason he decided that the grant to this latter should be signed by the King himself instead of issuing directly from the Treasury.[1] It is curious to note that less than four months before he had been "handsomely roasted" for "giving the Chiltern Hundreds to Lord Hyde that he might stand for Cambridge"—a thing which on some previous occasion he had apparently "promised that he would never do".[2]

The popular party—as though they had not the rest of the country to choose from—accused the government of an attempt once again to foist its own candidate upon the county of Middlesex. Some of them were even in favour of electing Byng in spite of his disqualification. It is clear that they were straining for another conflict with the government—a repetition of the movement of 1769; though this time they could only complain that a member of parliament had not been allowed to resign. Tuffnell, in fact, decided later to withdraw from the contest, alleging that he had been threatened with mob-violence.[3] The popular party, however, had been forced to choose another candidate, Thomas Wood; and he was now returned unopposed. But though they claimed this as a great victory for liberty and independence, they decided to generalize their grievance, after the manner of 1769, and to "go to the country", so to speak—to alarm freeholders everywhere—on the issue of the freedom of elections. At the same time Wilkes returned to the fray, and, as Horace Walpole remarked, was beginning to make a noise again. At this very moment he was also making a final successful bid for election to the lucrative office of chamberlain of the city of London.

[1] *Corr. George III*, IV, 459.

[2] Jesse, *George Selwyn and his Contemporaries*, IV, 196–97, Rev. Dr Warner to G. Selwyn, 14 June [1779.]

[3] Add. Mss. 37,834, f. 168. North declared later in the house of commons that he promised Byng the Chiltern Hundreds if Tuffnell withdrew. Tuffnell said that he could have carried the election but feared riots. *Cambridge Chronicle*, 18 Dec. 1779 [not in *Parliamentary History*]. A letter of 22 Nov. in the *Letters of the first Earl of Malmesbury*, I, 442–44, predicts something curiously like the Gordon riots as a possible result of this Middlesex controversy.

The recognized mode of procedure when such a protest had to be made was by the presentation of petitions to the king or to parliament; and in 1769 many of these, all to the same effect, had been sent up from borough and county meetings, so that synchronized action had produced the effect of something like a general movement. The enemies of the government, however, were greatly exercised at that period by the ineffectiveness of petitions, and after the failure of the effort in 1769 some regions had gone one step further, sending up this time not prayers but "remonstrances". Now, ten years later, many were determined not to be satisfied with an *ad hoc* meeting of freeholders, a futile petition, and then a complete dispersal. At a county meeting on 13 November 1779, on the subject of the new election grievance, there are signs not merely of discontent but also of exasperation; and many people regarded the policy of petitioning the house of commons as "too temperate" a measure, stressing its perpetual futility.[1] It was afterwards claimed that only the efforts of the more moderate party secured the acceptance of the idea of a petition. A document was produced, however, and it stated that "we have been deprived of the exercise of a most valuable franchise", while demanding "that some permanent law may be provided for the effectual security of those rights". At the same time it was decided to invite other counties to combine with that of Middlesex in the new campaign on behalf of the rights of freeholders. Also it was resolved at a meeting on 22 November that "for the purpose of preserving the independence of this county a general meeting of the freeholders be held monthly during the sitting of Parliament". When the petition was actually presented to the house of commons there was talk of the "freeholders coming to the house with other instruments than parchment".[2]

In fact this pretended electoral grievance was merely an ostensible issue and it covered what was clearly a much deeper and wider exasperation. In fact, as we shall see, men were interested not

[1] *Norwich Mercury*, 20 Nov. 1779. One objector "said we had an accursed House of Commons. Shall we ask of those whose authority we cannot acknowledge? He wished an appeal to the country at large."

[2] Accounts of meetings in e.g. *Norwich Mercury*, 20 Nov. 1779; *London Courant*, 4 Dec. 1779; *Parliamentary History*, xx, 1267-70.

so much in the avowed object of the petition, as in the possibilities of ulterior action—it was necessary for them only that the petition they delivered to the house should be rejected at the instance of the ministry. Within a short time it was being suggested that the freeholders might have found a better cause to carry to the country than this doubtful election issue; and the petition itself opened the way to a further and broader discussion; for appended to it was the demand that there be held an "immediate and thorough enquiry . . . into the true cause of those misfortunes which have reduced this once powerful and flourishing empire to a state which words cannot describe". In conformity with this demand, John Wilkes declared his intention of moving for such an inquiry in the house of commons on 3 February 1780. In other words, there was to be a great agitation in the country and a complementary campaign in parliament. As we shall see later, however, the leadership in both cases was to be stolen from Wilkes very soon.[1]

While the underlying purpose of this Middlesex movement was certainly retained, a change of plan in one respect soon became advisable, if not actually essential, however; and one of the reasons began to be clear on 10 December, when the petition was presented to the house of commons. It transpired that the subject of the petition, the topic that was to provide the ostensible issue, the question of an electoral grievance, had been badly chosen after all. It soon became apparent that in any case North was an abler parliamentary tactician than Grafton had been in a similar situation in 1769-70; indeed he showed a surprising readiness to give satisfaction at this moment to the complaining electors of Middlesex. It was North's unusual skill on such occasions as this, and particularly a whimsically disarming manner, which made him so effective in the house, so necessary to George III, in spite of his other faults, and so much more charming to his whig enemies who only saw him in debate than to his own colleagues who had to deal with him in the conduct of business. On the present occasion North explained that the right

---

[1] "Several members" in the house of commons debate on the petition said that it "was *immediately* to be followed up on the enlarged ground of the deplorable state of the nation by the city of London and the counties of Hertford, Surrey and Hampshire." *London Courant*, 11 Dec. 1779.

of granting the Chiltern Hundreds had always been an embarrassment to him as chancellor of the exchequer. He had promised the Chiltern Hundreds to Tuffnell because this man had been the first to make the application. For the rest he would be glad if parliament only would provide some fair expedient and free him from this disagreeable prerogative. When the new member for Middlesex proposed that leave be given to bring in a bill "to enable members of the House of Commons to be eligible to serve in Parliament for any other county, city, borough, town or place", the motion was passed unanimously.[1]

To support the whole programme of electoral grievance, Wilkes on the very same day, 10 December, produced a second example of abuse, on this occasion from Hampshire. He hoped to use a complaint in another county to assist his policy of extending the issue, and carrying the discontent beyond the borders of Middlesex itself. He placed before the house of commons a letter, written by the Lord Lieutenant of Hampshire, which was to serve as further proof of the interference of government in elections.[2] Even here, however, Wilkes was peculiarly unfortunate, for the Lord Lieutenant in question, though later found guilty of a formal breach of privilege, was somewhat excused by the house, on the ground that custom had long since been allowed to sanction certain irregularities in this field. And a curious difficulty arose, which made the whole episode peculiarly embarrassing to the opposition; for the very resolution of the house of commons which had been in question

---

[1] On the debate see *Parliamentary History*, xx, 1267–70; *London Courant*, 11 Dec. 1779; *Cambridge Chronicle*, 18 Dec. 1779. On the proposed legislation see also *Leeds Mercury*, 8 Feb. 1780; *Corr. George III*, v, 23; Add. Mss. 38,593, ff. 28–9, Proceedings of the Westminster Committee, 12 April 1780; *Parliamentary History*, xxi, 626.

[2] Add. Mss. 38,212, ff. 279–80, J. Robinson to C. Jenkinson, 10 Dec. 1779. "So ready an Acquiescence" by North in the debate on the Middlesex affair "made our friends burst out of the House like a Torrent." Opposition then forced on the Hampshire issue, and though Robinson "circulated double notes and strong ones" to recall supporters, the Treasury Bench had in the meantime given way once more, so that members "will not obey our call again and say that we don't know our own minds." George III's comments are in Add. Mss. 37,835, f. 71. Cf. Add. Mss. 30,872, f. 145; H.M.C. *Abergavenny Mss.* p. 27, No. 235.

in this case forbade a peer of parliament (as well as the Lord Lieuten-ant of a county) to interfere in parliamentary elections. It was possible to show that the opposition peers had contravened it very recently. In any case, though for a time some of the newspapers had been able to announce that other counties were preparing to follow the example of Middlesex, the projected revival of the electoral issue of 1769 came to nothing in fact. The main lines of the original design were indeed maintained, but the ostensible issue, the subject-matter of the petition, had led to a *cul de sac* and therefore had to be changed. The subject matter itself, as we have seen, was of little moment to some people, however, provided it were of such a character that the petition were sure to be rejected by the govern-ment.

A further meeting of the freeholders of Middlesex was due to be held a month after the previous one, that is to say, on 20 December. Its object had been formulated, and, according to the advertisement it was summoned "for the purpose of establishing meetings to maintain and support the freedom of elections". When the free-holders assembled, they did not concern themselves with the free-dom of elections any more, for a better issue had arisen to provide the pretext for "establishing meetings", in other words for devel-oping their machinery of ulterior action. It happened, however, that before the gathering took place on the 20th another important step had been taken—a disquisition had been prepared in writing and had been handed to the chairman for presentation to the assembled freeholders. We must take note of it because it contains the extreme statement—indeed we might say the most comprehen-sive statement that was made at this time—of the doctrine and pro-gramme of the Association, as the radical leaders understood it. The author claimed to be the initiator of the design and said that he had put it in writing to Sir George Savile in 1776. Possibly he desired to anticipate any pretensions to originality on the part of the York-shiremen, with whom Savile himself—as we shall see—was colla-borating so closely in this period. The speech was immediately pub-lished and ran through a number of editions, appearing later under the name of its author, John Jebb, who was to play an important part in the whole movement which we are studying.

According to Jebb, the electors of Middlesex were defective in the machinery by means of which they were even now proposing to take action. Petitions not merely from single counties but even from groups of counties were bound to be useless; for parliamentary representatives could not be controlled by the issuing of instructions, and the house of commons would refuse to submit to dictation from particular constituencies. The author proposed, therefore, a still further development in the machinery of county meetings, producing a doctrine and a scheme which in a more or less modified form gained wide currency in the country in the ensuing months. Both the doctrine and the scheme—as one of the enemies of the proposal was at pains to point out—contained the potentialities of an alternative system of government,[1] and represented the farthest point to which "republicanism", as it was then called, could very well have been driven at this date.

According to the scheme now proposed, the counties of England were to act upon a uniform plan and were to establish a system of standing committees. These committees were to send deputies to a central representative body "provided it should ever be thought requisite for them to confer upon a common cause". An estimate was to be formed of the land and commercial property in each of the areas of the country, so that the number of deputies could be properly assessed and the perfect representative system achieved. Then, once it became clear through this machinery that "a majority of the landed and commercial interest of the Kingdom had agreed upon a certain matter", the new institution could claim the supremacy—the house of commons itself, as a purely derivative body, would be superseded by a higher organ.

Jebb argued that when the new representative body had been created the house of commons must submit; "the command would proceed from the principal to the delegate," for members of parliament were mere "proxies" and their voice "must be regarded as annihilated when the voice of the Principal shall be thus distinctly heard". It would even "be constitutional to declare the House of Commons dissolved", and the act of the organized counties, once

---

[1] Add. Mss. 34,417, ff. 36–7, Adam Ferguson to William Eden, 17 Feb. 1780; "a new species of government forming in some of the countys of England".

it had the concurrence of the lords and the assent of the king, would in fact be a law of the land. "No unconstitutional coercion would be exerted against the remaining branches of the Legislature," once the corrupt house of commons had been disposed of, says our author. But he argues that even these "would perhaps perceive it to be prudent to comply with the temperate claims and wishes of the commons". He talks of the "right of the people to new-model the constitution". He suggests that the decisions of the new representative body might be "properly authenticated as the public Act of the Combined Counties". He even thinks that the people, acting directly through their own institutions in this way, might achieve a Federal Union with the American colonies.[1]

It would appear that at the time of writing Jebb was unaware of the important developments that were about to take place. He still envisaged a combination of counties on the original Middlesex issue; he still had in mind the question of a movement on behalf of the "freedom of elections". When the meeting of the Middlesex freeholders was held on 20 December, however, the original ostensible issue was abandoned, as we have seen, and it is remarkable to what a degree public attention had turned by this time to a totally different range of abuses. If the first experiment of the Wilkites had been an artificial attempt to resurrect the controversies of a previous decade, the new policy had a sounder basis—it answered a demand which seems genuinely to have arisen amongst the freeholders of England themselves.

As early as 2 November a correspondent in the *Public Advertiser* had demanded that county meetings should be summoned to protest against the waste of public money. Towards the close of November, at a time when, if Burke had thought of his scheme of "economical reform", he had not mentioned it to anybody, a number of Yorkshire freeholders decided to take action on the question of public expenditure, and summoned a meeting of the gentry of

[1] *An Address to the Freeholders of Middlesex*, 20 Dec. 1779. An advertisement, dated 30 Dec. 1779, says that this does not materially differ from the original paper read in the presence of the assembled freeholders. Cf. *Observations on an Address to the Freeholders of Middlesex*, 20 Dec. 1779, *with a clear exposition of the design therein proposed of a republican congress for new modelling the constitution.*

the county for 30 December. They advertised the purpose of the meeting as being an urgent one and made a special plea for a full attendance. The object was the presentation of a petition to parliament against the scandalous waste of public money.

On 13 December a correspondent, writing to the *London Courant*, made the complaint that attention was not sufficiently drawn to the question of the application of the public revenue. He bewailed the fact that so little reference was made to this important matter in the political discussions of the day. "Economy seems to be wholly disregarded," he said. A correspondent in another paper on the following day urged the freeholders of Middlesex to abandon their "trivial" election controversy and direct their attention to the more serious problem of the waste of "the people's money".[1] On 7 December and 15 December resolutions on this topic were proposed in the house of lords; and, though they were rejected, the decision was made that the house should inquire into public expenditure on 8 February 1780. Immediately after the second of these debates—on 16 December—the common council of the city of London identified itself with the action of the minority in the house of lords, and sent a letter of thanks to each of its members who had supported the cause of public economy. The news of what was happening in Yorkshire did not become known in London till almost the middle of the month, but by the time of the Middlesex meeting on the 20th, the waves of this agitation were rising and gathering power.

So on 20 December the Middlesex freeholders decided to change the label without changing the essential movement—they decided to support the Yorkshire freeholders, the common council of the city of London, and the minority in the house of lords on this new issue—the question of the waste of public money. Abandoning the lead they agreed to meet again on 7 January for the purpose of adopting a petition similar to the one which the Yorkshire freeholders were expected to have produced before that date.[2] They stooped to conquer, and they gained a great step towards one of

---

[1] "An Independent Freeholder", addressing George Byng in the *London Evening Post*, 11–14 Dec. 1779.

[2] *London Courant*, 28 Dec. 1779.

their essential points—for by their own example they were helping to secure the concerted action of the counties in a petitioning movement on one subject or another. Opposition newspapers, which had been advertising the readiness of other counties to follow the example of Middlesex in the electoral controversy, changed their language from this time, and spoke of Yorkshire as the leader, telling others henceforward to follow her.

In these events, moreover, we see the genesis of the remarkable programme of the parliamentary opposition in the early months of 1780. Two incidents proclaim the fact that the example given by Yorkshire had given the cue to the parliamentary leaders themselves by 15 December 1779. On this date Burke announced in the house of commons his intention of producing a plan of economical reform.[1] On the same day Shelburne, the leader of a separate faction in the opposition, raised the same issue—the question of public expenditure—in the house of lords. Shelburne took this opportunity to make for his own part a formal statement which declared that the opposition parties had now joined forces against the government. Newspapers from this moment repeat the glad tidings —nothing now divides the followers of Shelburne from those of Rockingham. Like the Middlesex Election case of 1769 the question of public expenditure provides an issue on which opposition can base their union during the coming year.[2]

The spokesmen of the opposition were anxious to make it clear to the world that the movement of the Yorkshire freeholders had not been inspired by any of the parliamentary leaders. Lord John Cavendish, for example, claimed that he knew of the Yorkshire movement before anybody had heard a whisper of Burke's scheme of economical reform. It was even claimed that some of the leaders in that movement had been enemies of Lord Rockingham's influence in Yorkshire; and it seems that some of them in fact were men who up to this time had actually been supporters of the government. The decision to make economical reform the great debating-

[1] On hearing of the plan the King wrote to Robinson [Add. Mss. 37,835, f. 77, 15 Dec. 1779] that it was "rather strange", for "certainly the times are not so virtuous that persons will labour for the Public without reward."

[2] *London Courant*, 15 and 16 Dec.; *London Evening Post*, 14–16 Dec. 1779.

issue in parliament seems to have been adopted in a hurry in the middle of December. When Burke announced it on 15th, he explained that he had not yet had time to think out his scheme or to draw it up in its main lines. Fox certainly knew little about it at that date, and Barré had to speak with reserve as he confessed that he did not know what the plan was to imply. Lord John Cavendish declared at the same time that he had only heard of the proposal very recently. It would seem, therefore, that the parliamentary leaders had decided to take advantage of a movement which had originated spontaneously in the world outside.[1] We may note that a plan of economical reform had been put forward eighteen months before by Thomas Gilbert. One writer now complained that Burke was stealing the credit which belonged to this man, Gilbert, as the real initiator of the design. Gilbert himself declared that he had been proposing to present his plan to the house of commons again at this period, if Burke had not stepped in and anticipated his intention.[2]

We have seen in a previous chapter that at the beginning of December, Fox announced the union of the opposition parties in parliament, a union which was to be directed against the influence of the crown. By the middle of December there had been added to the programme the protest against the waste of public money. It will remain for us to see how these two elements of opposition policy reinforced one another and were brought into a synthesis.

§II. THE YORKSHIRE MEETING, 30 DECEMBER 1779

On 23 November 1779, the Reverend Christopher Wyvill, a considerable landowner in Yorkshire, was staying at the house of his friend, General Cary, at Leven Grove. It was decided to propose the calling of a county meeting, but to keep the plan an absolute

[1] *Parliamentary History*, xx, 1293-1305.
[2] Letter from "A Member of Parliament" to the *Public Advertiser*, 22 Dec. 1779; *Parliamentary History*, xx, 1304; cf. *ibid.* xix, 803, 873.

secret "till it can be known whether a proper number of Gentlemen will appear in support of this measure". Alternative forms of advertisement were drawn up, but friends who supported the proposal—William Chaloner and Lieut. General Hale—sent word from Guisborough that they would only put their signature to the invitation provided a number of other men would do the same. Wyvill therefore returned home to Burton Hall on the 25th and approached certain neighbours who encouraged him in the design. On the following day he wrote to a few other people, including the Rev. William Mason, the friend of Thomas Gray and Horace Walpole; and Mason was almost the first amongst these to declare his support of the movement, replying apparently on the 27th. Hitherto he had been a stranger to Wyvill, but now he became one of the most enthusiastic of his collaborators in the agitation that was being opened. Wyvill said later that:

the idea of calling a Meeting of the County of York, had originated, not, as the enemies of the measure had asserted, with Lord Rockingham; nor yet with any other member of either of the two Houses of Parliament, but with a few private gentlemen of the North-Riding, who were totally free from all party influence, and equally unconnected with the leaders of Administration, and their opponents.

On 29 November the issue was canvassed on a much wider scale. A circular letter was sent to many Yorkshire gentlemen, suggesting the adoption of a petition against the scandalous waste of public money. This letter contained vague allusions to the possibility of combined action by several of the counties, referred to the establishment of an Association and hinted at further measures that might be adopted for restoring the freedom of parliament. On the same date a number of members of the house of commons who were connected with Yorkshire were also informed of the course of action that was being contemplated. The replies from the gentry revealed a considerable degree of discontent with the extravagance of the government, but a curious diffidence sometimes, and what a hostile witness might call a lack of spirit. One man said: "a thin Meeting at York will be a matter of triumph . . . to the cause of our

Adversaries" ; another said: "I sat too many years in Parliament not to be convinced it can be productive of no Public advantage"; a third wrote: "I have in the course of my life attended many County Meetings, none of which (one excepted) produced any-thing but disappointment"; Thomas Wilson of Leeds wrote: "People here are afraid of being left in the lurch"; and one man refused, partly because he "never attended your Meetings", though he hoped that others in his district had been approached "on behalf of so worthy a cause". By 5 December it appeared that the attempt might have to be abandoned, and one man advised the withdrawal of the proposal.[1] Wyvill persisted, however, and on 8 December Pemberton Milnes of Wakefield—the head of the dissenting inter-est in the county, a stout partisan of Lord Rockingham, and "the biggest drinker of port in Yorkshire"—sent messages of great encouragement together with a small collection of signatures. The notice of the meeting finally appeared and it was signed by men who were claimed to possess landed property to the value of £150,000 a year.[2] It was noted at the same time that nearly a third of the signatories were clergymen.[3]

In the months which immediately preceded the opening of Wyvill's campaign, the papers in York had had nothing to say about the hardships of the country in general, or even about dis-content in this particular part of it. On the very eve of that cam-paign they still contained the advertisement calling in the subscrip-tions that the men of the North Riding at a meeting in July had

[1] Cf. Add. Mss. 30,872, f. 180, Thomas Mullett to J. Wilkes, 5 Feb. 1780, for an account of the initial "want of spirit" in Bristol. Speaking of the riots in Lancashire in the autumn of 1779, Rockingham, [H.M.C. *Foljambe Mss.* pp. 152–53] declared on 8 Nov.: "I see by the newspapers that the Alarum Bell is set a ringing in Lancashire. As yet I don't hear that our manufacturing parts [i.e. in Yorkshire] have stirred at all." Mason, writing to Horace Walpole on 7 Dec. 1779, [J. Mitford, *Correspondence of H. Walpole and Rev. J. Mason* (1851) II, 53–6,] was not sure that the Yorkshire meeting would prove to be practicable. On the "coolness of Bristol," see also Fitzwilliam, *Correspondence of Burke*, II, 317.

[2] See e.g. *London Courant*, 20 Dec. 1779.

[3] The above account is based primarily on the *Political Papers of C. Wyvill*, III, 107–49, 15 Feb. 1780, and the contemporary Yorkshire newspapers. See, for further references, my article on "The Yorkshire Association and the Crisis of 1779–80", *Transactions of the Royal Historical Society*, 1947, pp. 69–91.

agreed by a great majority to provide for the maintenance of "a regiment to serve during the war". Wyvill's circular of 29 November contained a reference to a possible increase in the land-tax and on the following day the *York Courant* announced that a plan was being prepared for the more equal distribution of the burden of this tax. It was the policy of the Yorkshire leaders to enlarge upon this possibility—one which, they argued, would be disastrous for the north of England, where, in fact, the charge still virtually stood at one shilling in the pound, in sharp contrast to the four shillings which was the nominal rate and which was being imposed in many other parts of the country. From the beginning of December the local newspapers provided sundry paragraphs which illustrated the extravagance of the government, and called particular attention to this aspect of public affairs. The leaders of the Yorkshire movement sent anonymous letters on occasion to the local press for the purpose of awakening interest in their cause. On 17 December it was further reported that:

Petitions are preparing in Norfolk, Suffolk, Essex and Sussex to be signed by the freeholders, praying the attention of Parliament to the alarming situation of the whole landed interest, from the ruin of an amazing number of farmers owing to the prices of the earth's products being lower than they have been for thirty years.

A week before this, there had been an announcement in the local paper of the intention of Yorkshiremen to petition the house of commons to grant no new taxes until certain "economical" reforms had been obtained.

Great labour and much tactical skill were expended on the task of preparing the ground for this movement.[1] Before the meeting took place there was a reference in the papers to "the Committee who meet at York-Tavern" which apparently was recognized as having the management of the whole affair. Wyvill attached great importance to the advice of Sir George Savile, who represented the

[1] See e.g. *York Courant*, 14 Dec. 1779: "Many Hundreds of Circular Letters have been sent off from the Committee who meet at the York Tavern to the Gentlemen of Property."

county in the house of commons, and whose opinions he now began to consult on various quasi-technical points. He himself prepared a form of petition and some of his friends, such as Cary, Chaloner and Hale who have already been mentioned, as well as a neighbour and early adherent of the movement, J. S. Morritt of Rokeby, declared their approval of it. It was read to many "gentlemen at a previous meeting held in the York Tavern on the afternoon of 29 December"; and these preferred it to an alternative proposal understood to have been submitted by John Lee, who (whether speaking for himself or acting for his party, the Rockinghamite faction) apparently suggested a different course of action altogether. Lee wanted:

A declaration or Representation, written in a strain of dignified expostulation on the distressful State of the Country, but pointing at no specific measure of Reformation, and submitting no prayer to the wisdom of Parliament.

Wyvill's petition was referred to a committee of seven, including Wyvill himself, Rev. William Mason and General Hale, who made only one alteration—a significant one—at the suggestion of Thomas Hill of Leeds. In reference to waste of public money they added the words which were to enlarge the whole issue and were to give the song of the Yorkshiremen a new refrain:

Whence the Crown has acquired a great and unconstitutional influence, which, if not checked, may soon prove fatal to the Liberties of this Country.

From the first, as we have already seen, Wyvill had been anxious that secrets should not be disclosed too soon. He was a shrewd tactician, and since it is known that the whole of his scheme had been settled in his mind beforehand, it is curious to observe how gradually he allowed his intentions to filter down to a wider world as he saw the tactical opportunity. When the adjourned "previous meeting" was held on the evening of the 29th, a gathering which was now more hearty in its applause of the petition was thrown into "convulsions of laughter" by Sir Thomas Frankland's account of the fate such a document was likely to meet at Westminster. Wyvill replied that he was prepared for the failure of the petition and that he had a remedy—"not in measures of violence as some persons might conceive he meant, but in an Association consistent with Law and the principles of the Constitution". His Plan of Association had already been put into writing, and at one of the preliminary meetings on this 29 December it was discussed, but the decision was made not to bring it forward at the general meeting.[1] It contained more of those surprises which it might be wise to hold in reserve till the time was ripe, and the condition of the patient called for stronger medicine.

On the following day, the 30th, the great meeting took place in the York Assembly-Rooms, and it was evidently more imposing than anything of the kind that had been known before. Savile declared later to the house of commons that over 600 gentlemen were present, and that "in the hall where this petition was conceived, there was more property than within the walls of this house." Rockingham said in the lords that a total income of £800,000 a year was represented at the meeting. The supporters of the government in Yorkshire had already informed John Robinson that it would bê useless for them to attempt a counter-movement. One such man, who was present on the occasion and wrote an account of the proceedings to William Eden, said:

It must be owned that the meeting was numerous and that there was a great number of persons of property amongst those who espoused the measure. I wish those noblemen and gentlemen who disliked it would have attended that there might have been a chance of its being rejected.[2]

In view of the unanimity which was claimed for the resolutions of the meeting it is surprising to note how many of the speeches were against the petition; and it seems to have been the case that, as the proceedings lasted for a number of hours, the composition of the meeting did not remain quite constant—men were moving in

[1] *The Yorkshire Freeholder*, No. IV, 10 Feb. 1780, pp. 20–21.
[2] Add. Mss. 34,417, ff. 1–2. P. Johnson to W. Eden, 1 Jan. 1780.

and out. Wyvill opened the discussion, enlarging on "the calamit-
ous state of the nation, the immense extent of the present complicated war, the increase of the national debt, the stagnation of trade
and manufactures, the decline of public credit, and the general fall
of the land rents of the kingdom". He presented the petition and
then Mr Cholmley declared "that he had sat too long in the house,
to think that a petition would be productive of any good effect".
In any case parliament would expect some proof of the "misapplication of public money. . . . For his part, he had it only from common report". Mr Drummond said that the expenditure of public
money was a matter for parliament itself to control; "striking off
pensions, etc., is plausible in theory, but difficult in practise." He
wished to give the government a further trial, to see whether
Britain would not revive again within another year, for she was
still the terror of her enemies. "The motion," says an eye-witness,
"was then supported by a young Irishman who lately married a
widow with moderate estates in this county. He . . . recommended
the imitation of *his countrymen* with the utmost effrontery." He
seems to be the Mr Pritchard whom Wyvill quotes as saying at this
point:

> Was it love for Ireland that made Lord North so anxious to hurry
> the Irish bills through Parliament? No—it was 64,000 bayonets
> pointed at his heart.

The sensation of the day, however, was provided by Mr Smelt,
who had been sub-governor of the Prince of Wales, and who was
regarded as enjoying even now an undue degree of intimacy with
the circle around the King. It is not clear that he did not appear in
response to a royal request, for George III, writing to Robinson a
week before, had signified his wish for something of the kind—
namely, a protest which, even if unsupported, should carry some
weight as coming from a man of exemplary private character.[1]
Smelt was afterwards accused of having presented the whole
case for George III—all the appropriate doctrines—in the form in
which the system had been instilled into him during his visits to the

[1] Add. Mss. 37,835, f. 81, to J. Robinson, 23 Dec. 1779.

court.[1] He summarized indeed the whole philosophy of the Patriot King as this had been reproduced in the pamphlet literature at the opening of the reign. It is remarkable that so long a speech was able to be completed at such a meeting, especially as Smelt himself admitted at a later time that before he began to talk the day was "already far advanced". He also introduced his remarks with the confession that he had "never before the present occasion spoken in public". Even those who attacked his assertions later in the meeting confessed either warmth of affection for Smelt or admiration for his private character.

He declared himself "mortified to find that, instead of contributing to the support of Government, the avowed end of the present meeting was to divide its strength". He gave a brief account of his career and then announced that he would resign the pension that he had been receiving from the King's privy purse—"Now, Sir, I am an INDEPENDENT MAN," he said. Then, without adding anything that would make his views more palatable to the meeting —without looking for a bridge or transposing and accommodating his expressions in order that he might meet his audience half-way— he put out his doctrines in the most unmitigated terms. "It was the body of the people that was corrupt and the King was the ONLY patriot in the country"; "the influence of the Crown was not by any means exorbitant; on the contrary it required to be increased"; before the crown there was a veil, "that sacred veil behind which the vulgar eye should never be permitted to penetrate"; "the King is not the servant of the people; he is their soul; he is the soul of the constitution." A violent hissing was heard throughout the room when he said it was a misfortune that England had no minister "sufficiently firm to keep up the taxes in time of peace", and so prevent the military establishment from being allowed to fall into decay.

After the meeting Wyvill and his friends carefully collated their notes on this oration, anxious that this alone—of all the speeches

[1] See e.g. *The Yorkshire Question, or Petition and Address,* 1780, p. 4. "There is not a man in the country who enjoys so much of the *apparent* confidence of the King at this day and certainly there is not a man . . . who was ever honoured with so much of the private society and familiar intercourse with His Majesty as Mr Smelt."

delivered on that occasion—should be printed *in extenso* and widely circulated in the country. The reports of what was said by the men who favoured the petition were abridged almost out of existence and it is clear that the things that were violent and incendiary were purged away by the editor. The best propaganda that the leaders of the Yorkshire movement could find at hand was in the utterances of this man, Smelt, who was regarded as "letting the cat out of the bag", and who proved to be the worst possible advertisement for the royal cause. He himself printed a different account of his speech, and beyond doubt this version gives more adequate expression to what at least he had meant to say, and what he wished men to regard as his confession of faith.[1] It is possible that Wyvill's report did less than justice to the attack that he made on the Rockingham whigs, especially in a passage in which he brought out the anomaly of an aristocracy that was pretending to support the idea of the natural equality of men. Smelt indeed reminded his listeners of the corruption that had existed during the period of whig predominance before 1760, when "the power of the King was . . . contracted within as narrow a compass as the most zealous advocate of the present petition could desire to contract it now." These remarks drew from a member of parliament, Charles Turner, the admission that "a Whig in power was very often like a Tory."

We learn, however, that "the great tribune of the people was Councillor [William] Hill of Tadcaster, who roared out sedition to the great delight of the common freeholders for one and a half hours." Wyvill in his report gives little of what was said by this man and communicates nothing of the character and colour of his remarks. There were more speeches, and Wyvill evidently replied more than once to various objections that had been made; until "the common people in the room grew riotous and roared for the question." It is curious that, after this series of addresses, the resolution of the meeting in favour of the petition was carried "with only one dissenting voice".[2]

[1] *An Account of some particulars relating to the Meeting held at York on Thurs.,* 30 *Dec.* 1779, by Leonard Smelt [1780].

[2] For an account of this meeting see, apart from the reports mentioned above, *Wyvill Papers,* I, v–vIII and 9–40; and J. Mitford, *The Correspondence of Horace Walpole and Rev. William Mason,* II, 60–1.

That document described the condition of the country and enlarged upon the waste of public money. It demanded that no new burdens should be laid upon the tax-payer until the grievances of the people had been redressed. The demand brings to our mind the recent policy of the Irish, who had voted supplies for a period of six months only, thereby putting a pistol at the head of the English ministry. On the subject of the redress of grievances the petition specifically asked that

effectual measures may be taken by [the] House [of Commons] to inquire into and correct the gross abuses in the expenditure of public money; to reduce all exorbitant emoluments; to rescind and abolish all sinecure places and unmerited pensions; and to appropriate the produce to the necessities of the state, in such manner as to the wisdom of Parliament shall seem meet.

The adoption of the petition did not end the proceedings of the Yorkshire meeting. A second resolution was brought forward, and it was of particular significance, for it related to what we have called "ulterior action". For the Yorkshiremen, as well as for the men of Middlesex, this was more important than the petition itself, and we must regard it as the *arrière-pensée* of the whole petitioning movement. Since the second resolution was the crucial one and since it was in regard to this particular point that most of the controversy was to take place in the ensuing months, we must note the fact that the proposal was adopted very hurriedly and received little, if any, discussion. The resolution declared that a Committee should be appointed "to carry on the necessary correspondence for effectually promoting the object of the petition and to support that laudable reform, and such other measure as may conduce to restore the Freedom of Parliament". The hostile witness who sent a report of the proceedings to Eden gives the following account of the affair:

But then the Chairman read the second resolution which you see in the newspapers, and which had been *studiously* kept back till then. The consequence was that some gentlemen being gone to dinner and others overborne by noise little was said to this smuggled resolution and the few dissenting views being lost in the clamour of ayes the patrons of the measure pretended that both the resolutions were carried unanimously, though it was notorious that many gentlemen had very explicitly declared their disapprobation of the whole measure and many more had signified it by letters.[1]

Henry Goodricke, though he sat in the house of commons for a ministerial borough, was a less hostile witness, for "he went to that Meeting with the determined and avowed Purpose (as several of his friends can testify) of giving his hearty support to the great Patriotic objects of the Petition." Both at the meeting and afterwards he declared that "there is no country on earth in which so much money is diverted from public purposes into the pockets of individuals." He declared later, however, that the second resolution had taken him by surprise, even though he had attended the "previous meeting" on the day before the full assembly. He wondered whether it was "any Necessary Custom or Accident which could not allow the important Matters intended for public deliberation and resolve to be submitted beforehand to private consideration". There was no debate on this issue, he said; and in the earlier discussion on the petition itself no hint had been given that a matter "of so extraordinary, so unusual and so consequential a nature" was to be brought forward. He, for his part, had not given his assent to it.[2] And he did not stand alone in his doubts; for it soon transpired that once the resolution had been carried there were many misgivings. Wyvill was informed on 2 January 1780 that "many persons, of no mean distinction", were perturbed by the "threat" which the measure seemed to imply, and were in need of some specific form of reassurance.[3]

The Committee appointed by the general meeting numbered 61, and there can be no doubt that, if the second resolution itself was carried in a hurry at the close of the proceedings, the list of names had been prepared beforehand and was adopted in a fairly

[1] Add. Mss. 34,417, ff. 1–2, P. Johnson to W. Eden, 1 Jan. 1780.
[2] *York Chronicle*, 28 Jan. 1780. See *ibid.* 7, 21, 28 Jan.; 4, 25 Feb.; 31 March; 28 April 1780; and *York Courant*, 11, 18 Jan., for the Goodricke controversy in general.
[3] *Wyvill Papers*, III, 173–74.

summary manner. None of those who were initially invited declined to serve and the quorum was fixed at 21. It was difficult, however, especially "at this inclement season", for members from different parts of the county to make up the required attendances; on 14 January only 16 were present.[1] On 21 January, therefore, the Committee deputed such of its number as resided in or near York to act as a sub-committee for purposes of routine correspondence and for the promotion of the petition itself. Copies of this document were sent to the various parts of the county for signature, with the instruction that to every name should be appended the location of the freehold that gave the title to sign. From Halifax it was reported that leaving the petition at a public-house would not have the required effect. In Beverley the petition was not put into proper hands and it was soon discovered that it remained unsigned. The man who was to have looked after the matter in the Scarborough district "left the country", so that in this region also the matter was left stranded for a time. In Leeds a club was formed for the promotion of the petition and the furtherance of the reform programme. It was evident that the movement was one which even now had to be carefully nursed by local partisans.[2] Sir George Savile was consulted on the question of the length of time which ought to be allowed for the collection of signatures.[3] It seems that the number

[1] *Wyvill Papers*, I, 54, 61–62; cf. *The Yorkshire Freeholder*, No. IV, 10 Feb. 1780, p. 20. This paper was established to stand as the recognized mouthpiece of the movement.

[2] *Wyvill Papers*, I, 52–53, 71; III, 203. Cf. Add. Mss. 38,213, ff. 39–40, Thomas Ramsden to C. Jenkinson, 8 Jan. 1780: "The Belman here went about to say that the petition was lying at an inn here [Pontefract] to be signed by any freeholder. I dare say very few of this place will trust their hands; perhaps an incendiary attorney, the presbyterian parson and 2 or 3 republicans may."

[3] *Wyvill Papers*, III, 200–05. In the York City Library are the copies of the signatures to this petition, made at the time. The list is of 8,407 signatures, of which 652 were from the region circulated by Wyvill, 341 on the copy at the York Tavern, 437 in Bradford, and over 300 in Leeds. Lord Mulgrave stated in the house of commons [*Parliamentary History*, XXI, 80] that "he understood the county contained very near 30,000 freeholders." He also said that "not 1,500 names appeared to the petition", perhaps alluding to the fact that a single man might sign for freeholds in various localities. According to the *York Chronicle* of 3 March 1780, North said in the house of commons on 23 Feb. that there were 27,000 freeholders in Yorkshire, but Savile said that "he had exceeded the truth by much more than one half."

of signatures in a given locality depended somewhat on the energy and enthusiasm of the man who had charge of the matter there.

§III. THE SPREAD OF THE PETITIONING MOVEMENT

In the meantime the London newspapers had been preparing the ground for an upheaval which should be something more than a spasmodic outbreak of local disturbances and regional protests. By sundry news-items and anonymous letters to the press, by articles, hints and exhortations, the world was being taught to accustom itself to the idea of a great intervention of the people. Three weeks before Wyvill had begun to prepare his Yorkshire meeting, the following passage had appeared in one of the newspapers.

Let us in our Turn, unite in some Manner as the Irish have done, something, however, short of their Rebellion; let us constitutionally commune together. The Constitution allows the Correspondence of one County with another. . . . *Join as the Irish do, to prohibit your Members to grant the Supplies' till the Pilferers of the Empire are brought to Account.*[1]

Even in November 1779 it was being said:

The people of original right, as a free people, will vindicate the country, correct their parliament, and reform their throne. . . . *In England every man is a politician.*[2]

It should be noted that though some of the writers were men who had been concerned in the recent Middlesex movement, this paper campaign was not always the result of concerted action. In other words, there existed a vague idea that the time had come for an intervention of "the people", though the character of this was not clearly envisaged and the suggestions which were put forward were not of a uniform pattern. Towards the end of November the *London Evening Post* was making the conjecture that "the public danger, distress and resentment" would bring to the front a Minister of the

[1] *Public Advertiser*, 2 Nov. 1779.
[2] *London Courant*, 27 Nov. 1779; Letter from "The Whig".

People as in the days of Chatham; and it is evident that the Duke of Richmond was the man expected to emerge as the popular leader in question.[1] Repeatedly from this time we meet a suggestion which, as we shall see, by no means answered to the purposes of the Rev. Christopher Wyvill—namely, that members of the parliamentary opposition should secede from the house of commons and become the leaders of a popular movement in the country at large.

It is not by speaking or voting in the House of Commons, Sir, that this country is to be saved. Within these walls the majority are callous. . . . We have many great, many good, many respectable Lords and Commoners, zealous friends of England. . . . If they mean to do us any service—let them retire to their counties, mix among the yeomanry, explain to them their danger, put them in the CONSTITUTIONAL path to obtain a change of men and system.[2]

By December it was being said that "Associations are forming in the principal counties in England to give instructions to their Members on subjects of the utmost importance." It was being announced that if opposition did not soon prevail in both houses of parliament "they intend to appeal to the people." On 4 January "Junius Brutus", writing to the London Courant, demanded the establishment of "a Grand National Association to act by the Deputies of the respective Counties and Towns". Amid all this there is the repeated suggestion that the country ought to follow the example of the American colonists or the Irish Volunteers.

The Associations in America . . . have set an example before Free-men how to act when oppressed. This Example has been followed by Ireland. . . . When James II was driven into Exile it was by a National Association . . . Association becomes the duty of all.[3]

---

[1] London Evening Post, 27–30 Nov. 1779, Letter from "A Consistent Whig"; Cf. "Tria Juncta in Uno", ibid. 2–4 Dec. Cf. also, Fitzmaurice, Shelburne, II, 46, Duke of Richmond to Shelburne, 7 Dec. 1779: "From what I see a general spirit is rising." At the beginning of Dec., T. Wilson told Wilkes that in order to "rouse the People of England effectually" the minority ought to form an Association and "call upon the people at large". [Add. Mss. 30,872, f. 154.]

[2] Letter from "Aratus" in London Evening Post, 9–11 Dec. 1779.

[3] Public Advertiser, 4 Dec. 1779.

It can hardly be doubted that at this point of the story there existed in various parts of England a considerable degree of distress and a general feeling of dissatisfaction. In many people this would issue in a petulance, a recalcitrant mood, an unformulated type of discontent; and in such a state of mind men will clutch at anything which comes to hand in order to find reasons for their clamour or direction for their criticism. There can exist an unspecified form of general dissatisfaction which only clarifies itself after it has moved into whatever channel may be provided for it by skilful leadership. The organizers of the Yorkshire movement had chosen the issue well; for the question of extravagance in the use of public money touched the place where the shoe pinched, touched the harassed trader, the suffering farmer, the anxious property-owner, and indeed every tax-payer in the land. It could rouse members of all parties and could stir into recalcitrancy for the moment even those who were the habitual supporters of the government. It was a topic ideally suited to serve as the ostensible programme of a movement which sought in the first place to collect into itself as many as possible of the freeholders and electors of the country; and then to draw these—if not blindfold, at least only half-conscious of what was happening—along a path of which the end was not the apparent one, as was to be revealed only in due time.

So, from the very beginning of January 1780, the Yorkshire movement spread; and an observer who in London collected the news and watched the signs in the sky saw what appeared to be a mighty upheaval, an awakening of the people, which shook the solid earth and traversed the length and breadth of the country. The agitation which had been opened earlier by the men of Middlesex—the campaign on behalf of the freedom of elections—had already been directed into the new course. Wilkes and his friends moved into line with the Yorkshire movement, ready in advance to assist the swelling of the stream. Hampshire, which had been drawn into the wake of the Middlesex movement, even moved to the front for a moment, and adopted Wyvill's petition as early as 3 January. A meeting had previously been summoned to celebrate the victory achieved at the expense of the government in a recent by-election; and it proved to be "the most respectable and numerous known in that county for many years". It does not appear that a Committee of Correspondence was appointed and it is possible that the intentions of Wyvill had not been properly understood in Winchester at this early date. "Not a syllable" was uttered against the petition itself, however; and this was "unanimously agreed to". The day was celebrated with illuminations.

Then at 10 a.m. on 7 January, the electors of Middlesex assembled at the Mermaid Tavern in Hackney for the adjourned meeting which had been decided upon a fortnight previously. Though some of the great lords were present—the Duke of Portland for example —the familiar leaders of the radical party took charge of the proceedings, George Byng declaiming against the unfairness with which "the county of Middlesex in particular was oppressed by the house-tax," and stating that "all taxes considered, they paid fifteen shillings in the pound." Two points are worthy of note in connection with the Middlesex meeting. Firstly, when it was proposed that there should be inserted in the petition the charge that the government had driven the American colonists to make league with the Bourbon enemy, the suggestion, though a popular one, was dropped, lest it should alienate some who had supported the American conflict in the past but were now prepared to sign the petition. In any case it was thought desirable to set the example of unanimity by adhering faithfully to the model that had been provided by the meeting in York. Secondly, the men of Middlesex were either determined to develop one of Wyvill's ideas or anxious to make it more explicit, for they did not confine themselves to the policy of a local committee. They specifically mentioned the idea of forming a "National Association." They openly avowed the intention of organizing the country as a whole.[1]

The ball had now been set rolling and the corporation of York together with the common council of the city of London set the example for towns and cities which might be disposed to range themselves at the side of the counties in the petitioning movement. In the case of York, Charles Turner, one of the parliamentary representatives, claimed that 990 burgesses, "almost the whole of his constituents", had signed the petition, though only 940 had voted

[1] *Wyvill Papers,* I, 58–60; *Leeds Mercury,* 11 Jan. 1780.

at the last election. The county meetings varied in character. In some places—some of the counties near London, for example—the proceedings were not dissimilar to those in Yorkshire and Middlesex. They would be addressed by Middlesex radicals like George Byng or by property-owners of advanced views like Thomas Day, while a local member of parliament or a representative of the nobility might receive scant attention when he tried to say a few words in favour of the government. In Cheshire the grounds of complaint were enlarged and the petition was directed not merely against public extravagance but also against place-men in parliament and against the interference of the government in elections. According to Horace Walpole, who received his information from Lord Cholmondeley—one of those present at the meeting— "William Talmache made such a violent speech that it had near lost the petition," and "not one of the Whig gentlemen would sign."[1]

Already on 8 January a writer from Norwich had described the economic distress due to "the loss of the American and Spanish orders", and had said: "Nothing is more generally talked of here at present than an association of this city and county similar to that of the county of York." People's minds were "so much inflamed by distress against the ministry that legal and constitutional associations are universally desired", this writer said.[2] The county petition was carried at a meeting in this city on 29 January, but it is interesting to note from the following account of the proceedings how serious was the lack of that preparation and management to which Wyvill had devoted weeks of his time before the assembly of the Yorkshire freeholders.

I got to Norwich a few minutes before the gentlemen met at the shire-house. I found the business had been ill-managed, not sufficient notice had been given; some men piqued that they had not been consulted. In short no plan settled; no arrangement taken; nobody willing to take the chair. I was applied to several times but declined it. At last when the letter to the sheriff was read, requesting a meeting, and my name as one of the persons who signed it I thought

[1] Horace Walpole, Letters, (ed. Toynbee) XI, 121; Last Journals, Jan. 1780; H.M.C. Various Mss. VI, 165; Leeds Mercury, 25 Jan. For Talmache see Index.
[2] Leeds Mercury, 18 Jan.

any longer declining would appear unmanly and look as if I was ashamed of my principles.

This particular writer provides us with a further picture which helps us to realize the complicated character of the Yorkshire movement. His own political position was not an uncommon one: for he disliked the Rockinghamites and regarded them as having incited the American colonists to resistance; but at the same time he blamed the administration for providing the occasion for these troubles and misfortunes; he was hostile to the King's Friends; and he resented "the profusion of the public treasury". He desired at least an inquiry into the question of public economy, if only in order to quieten the misgivings of the people. He supported the petitioning movement, therefore; but only a fortnight after the Norwich meeting he put on to paper the following troubled after-thoughts on the subject of the "ulterior action", the Committee of Correspondence:

I for some time declined being named as one of the Committee of Correspondence, but was overpersuaded to let my name appear, though I declared my intention of not attending. The Committee of Correspondence I did not approve of and the more I think on't, the more I dislike it. It will, if anything will, prevent the design of the Petition, and can answer no end but that of faction and party. I am certain that many persons who assented to that resolution did no more than myself consider the foolish tendency of it. However, I have the pleasure to believe that if the committee confine their business to the subject of the petition their object will soon expire, and if they extend it to other matters foreign to the subject of the meeting that many gentlemen, of whom I shall be one, will go to Norwich and publicly disapprove of it and withdraw our names.[1]

The type of meeting which we have so far been considering, however, is illustrative only of one aspect of the petitioning movement of 1780. Earlier in the century No. 53 of *The Craftsman* had made an examination of petitions and addresses, and had shown how such things, emanating from corporations and bodies of

---

[1] Add. Mss. 38,213, ff. 137–40; cf. *Cambridge Chronicle*, 5 Feb. See also Add. Mss. 38,307, ff. 133–34, C. Jenkinson to Dr Lloyd, referring to "the alterations made in the petition of your county after it was signed by some of the petitioners."

free-holders, might be spontaneous in appearance and yet might be nothing more than an obedient response to a summons that came from above. John Wesley once described how "a Lord or Squire (sometimes two or more) goes and sends his steward round the town where his seat is, with a paper." He adds:

And who has the hardiness to gainsay; especially if my Lord keeps open house?[1]

In the eighteenth century, people not uncommonly talked of a local petition as though it were the property of the magnate who had sponsored it and supported it with his influence. Ten years before the Yorkshire movement took place a speaker in the house of commons had drawn a satirical picture of the local "great man", who would put out the hint that the people of the neighbourhood should approach him; who, in reply to an invitation which in reality had been "drawn up by himself", would "graciously vouchsafe to attend" the meeting which he had himself demanded; who by "preconcerted" action would then be invited to take the chair; and who would finally put to the meeting a petition, which he would afterwards flaunt in the face of the ministers, as though it had represented "the sense of the people". In the case of the Yorkshire movement the Duke of Richmond avowed in the house of lords his part in provoking a popular petition in the county of Sussex, while if Earl Temple almost apologized for leaving the county of Buckingham to its own devices it transpired that his shyness had the effect of delaying any action on the part of that county.[2] The young Lord Mahon proved to be one of the most fervent of the supporters of the movement, not only in his county of Kent, but also in Buckinghamshire, where his family had a little property; though he met with considerable resistance in both areas.[3]

[1] Cf. York Chronicle, 4 Feb., where "Veritas" writes from Doncaster, 24 Jan. "A gentleman of property in this neighbourhood who has appeared forward to join in the measures adopted by the later County Meeting, has given an order to all his tenants (who may possibly in some corner or other be possessed of the requisite 40/- per annum) to sign the petition left in this town."

[2] Richmond's letter of 8 Jan. to the Freeholders of Sussex [York Chronicle, 21 Jan.] hints at constitutional as well as economical reform.

[3] See Appendix A, "Lord Mahon and the Yorkshire Movement".

It was in Huntingdonshire, however, that the conflict between local spheres of interest was to have its most remarkable effect in the movement of 1780. There is a letter written later in the year in which Lord Sandwich describes the extreme character of the cleavage which existed in this county, where he was confronted with the influence of the Earl of Manchester.[1] The county meeting in Huntingdon on 20 January 1780 was reduced to disorder by a duel between the two factions, and the proceedings resolved themselves, we are told, into a "debate between the Principals". Lord Ludlow stated at a later time in the house of commons that when he arrived at the meeting there were so many people present from the navy hospitals—so many dependants of Sandwich—that he imagined himself in Greenwich Hospital. On the other hand Sandwich's son, Lord Hinchinbrooke, declared that the Duke of Manchester "carried down with him all his clerks from the Custom-House".[2] In the disorder that supervened it seems to have been difficult to discover which of the two parties had the majority of the meeting in its favour. The *Norwich Mercury* reports that the sheriff adjudged the majority to be against the petition. At the same time the *London Courant*, which supported the Yorkshire movement, protested against what was alleged to be a trick on the part of the sheriff. In the house of commons at a later date, Lord George Cavendish said that he "was confident that the show of hands had been greatly in favour of the Petition", but he confessed that he was "a little nearsighted". Sir George Wombwell contradicted his view and insisted that at least two-thirds of the meeting were opposed to the idea of petitioning. One report says that when a division was called for "nothing but confusion was heard."[3] The upshot of it all was that those who wanted the petition began to sign it there and

[1] H.M.C. *Dartmouth Mss.* III, 253; "There is no place in England where the parties are more at variance than in Huntingdonshire; we could not dine together on the election day, and the two members could not agree to give a joint ball to the ladies."

[2] *Cambridge Chronicle*, 11 March.

[3] *Cambridge Chronicle*, 22 Jan. This report says that "on holding up of hands the majority were in favour," but "on a separation there appeared a majority against" the petition; cf., however, *London Courant* 24 Jan., *York Chronicle*, 28 Jan.

then, and put it into circulation in the county. Those who disapproved put their signatures to a protest.[1] In spite of the local influence of the Earl of Sandwich, Huntingdonshire was able to range itself in the ranks of the petitioning counties, therefore, and formed a Committee of Correspondence.

In the whole nature of a petitioning movement in the eighteenth century there was material to provide the impartial observer with doubts and a political enemy with a wealth of debating-points; for if at first sight the picture that is presented to us appears to be one of prayer or protest that rises spontaneously from one locality or another—public opinion streaming up like a vapour from a hundred sources in town and country—there is an under-side to the theme, and here the impression is more rough and untidy, with a hint of things not only ragged but ragamuffin, not only coarse but even roguish and disreputable at times. We must forget the England which by numberless miracles of transportation and by press, post and telegraph is today so closely bound together—all things interacting and interpenetrating—that an incident in the capital city instantly beats a pulse in the stillness of a fenland village or the remoteness of a Pennine farm. We must keep in mind, even as we look at the eighteenth century itself, not the mannered and artificial world of the periwigs, not the stilted urbanities and over-polished epigrams of the Augustans, but all that arrière-world of shopkeepers, mechanics, and petty freeholders which was more coarse and rough, at once less critical and less pretentious, than its equivalent to-day. In 1770 Rigby was not indulging in merely libellous irrelevancy when he asked, "How is it possible that the farmers and weavers in Yorkshire and Cumberland should know, or take an interest in the Middlesex election?" And if at that date it was possible to raise the objection that some men became petitioners and "patriots" upon a notion that "if the minister was pulled down, there would be neither tythe, turnpike or taxes," this is not much different from the case of the poor duped workers of the borough of Horsham who in 1832 were heard rejoicing over the passage of the Great Reform Bill and shouting, "Now we are all Kings and will pay no more rent." It is not much different from the case of those

[1] *Gentleman's Magazine*, Jan. 1780, p. 46.

men in Venice, who, when Ruskin tried to discover the seat of their grievances in the nineteenth century, were only aware that they had to pay more than they liked for a pint of beer, and had been taught to blame the tyranny of the Austrian government.

We have already seen a reference to the "common people" at the Yorkshire meeting, and on other occasions—as in the case of Cambridge at a later date—an assembly not without respectable and imposing elements might possess a ragged fringe. Many different grades of social life were included in the gatherings of nobility, gentry, clergymen, freeholders, and electors; and turbulent elements would hiss in anger or stamp in impatience, so that the gentry might find it necessary on occasion to apologize to a political enemy who had been treated with discourtesy. During the discussions concerning the petitioning movement of 1769–70 Rigby declared:

But supposing that a majority of freeholders had signed these petitions, without influence and solicitation, the majority, even of this class, is no better than an ignorant multitude.[1]

We need not be too severe in our judgment of Rigby, for Sir George Savile, while fervently supporting the Yorkshire movement of ten years later, more than once cautioned Wyvill against indiscriminate signature-hunting—against any reliance upon the mere multitude of names. It would provoke the charge that the petition had merely been hawked round the ale-houses, he said:

You would be tauntingly asked, *how John and Thomas came to know of these abuses?*[2]

Gamaliel Lloyd writing to Savile on behalf of a number of gentlemen in Leeds declared in the middle of 1780:

[1] *Parliamentary History*, XVI, 698. The radical writer Robert Robinson, in his "Political Catechism" of 1784 [*Works*, II, 301–02], gives a humorous description of the inferior type of freeholder.

[2] *Wyvill Papers*, III, 200–05. The *London Courant* of 8 March quotes Thurlow as saying that the petitions were "hawked about from ale-house to ale-house". According to the *York Chronicle* of 17 March, [cf. *Parliamentary History*, XXI, 188–89] Rigby stated in the house of commons on 8 March that in his county of Essex the title of the petition had to be changed from that of "freeholders" to that of "all persons paying taxes," since so few of the freeholders signed.

And what recommends the Association the more, is, that it has been promoted by so many Gentlemen of large independent fortunes, who from education and other circumstances, have had much better opportunity of being rightly informed in politics than ourselves.[1]

At the Nottinghamshire meeting it is curious to see the Rev. George Walker talking down to the crowd and explaining why they had been summoned by their betters to confer on matters so high as those of politics.[2]

John Wesley in 1771 told of a petition in a town in Kent. "None to whom he spoke had read it or heard it read," he asserted; this had not prevented them from signing it, however. In 1780 Mr Burrell in the house of commons described how in Kent the ignorant had been told that if they accepted the resolution in favour of the Committee of Correspondence their taxes would be abolished in a fortnight; but if they did nothing more than send up a petition praying for public economy, "they would not have a bed to lie on in a month." Henry Shifner at a meeting in Hereford on 11 March 1780 asserted:

I have seen many instances of it, where two-thirds of the subscribers have, some by importunity, some for company sake, some by threats, put their hands to Petitions of which they hardly knew the contents, much less could see into the views of the Patrons of such Petitions.[3]

One further feature of the petitioning movement of 1780 is so significant that we must regard it as essential to the understanding of the structure of the whole; and it is interesting to note from a parliamentary debate on this subject ten years before[4] that it had already been a characteristic of the parallel movement of 1769. Rigby declared on that occasion that "a few factious and discontented people . . . go round the country," secure meetings and communicate discontent.

[1] *Wyvill Papers*, III, 259–63.
[2] *Substance of the Speech of Rev. Mr Walker at . . . Mansfield, 28 Feb. 1780.*
[3] *London Chronicle*, 6–9 May.
[4] *Parliamentary History*, XVI, 668–727.

If it were not for the petition-hunters, who travel from North to South, and from East and West, who tell them there are grievances which they do not feel and apprehensions which they do not conceive, I am sure the name of a petition could never have been heard in more than three counties throughout the kingdom.

Lord Clare related the case of a travelling petition-hunter, who recounted the crimes of the government before a rustic audience, when "not one of the neighbouring gentlemen were present." Clare described how "the countrymen, thinking there could be no harm in taking a chance at least for putting an end to these practices, if such there were, signed the paper and went home to their families." Lord North pointed out how men who had freeholds in many counties, went from place to place inducing the inhabitants "to set their hands to petitions which they have never read, and give countenance to complaints which they never heard".[1] In 1780 we frequently see how the same man will be leader and organizer, speaker and member of the Committee, in one locality after another. It was amongst the enthusiasts who travelled from place to place that there was to emerge later the group that acquired a kind of directorate over the whole movement.

In spite of what we might call the anomalous texture of an eighteenth-century petitioning movement, it is impossible to deny the imposing character of the upheaval which was taking place in England in January 1780. It was ragged and untidy in several respects, and on occasion it was disreputable from some points of view, as many momentous things are at the very beginning, when new forces are being released and these are not yet disciplined, or adjusted to their constitutional function, or conducted into regular channels. The Yorkshire movement, however, still forms an important chapter in the political education of the British people. And the men who had challenged the very integrity of the petitioning cause in 1769 did not dispute the reality of the complaints or the genuineness of the protests of 1780. The hardships of farmers and landlords, the distresses of cloth-workers in Leeds[2] and Norwich,

[1] Cf. Sandwich in the house of lords, 8 Feb. 1780, *Morning Chronicle*, 12 Feb.
[2] *Cambridge Chronicle*, 5 Feb.

were themselves not denied, though the spokesmen of the government might claim that they were a natural incident of so great, so desperate a war. One writer attributed the sufferings of the farmers to the whig aristocrats—the landlords who at a moment of artificial prosperity had fixed the rents unduly high. It is clear at the same time that Wyvill and his friends made great use of the argument that worse hardships were to come—that Yorkshire was likely to lose the special advantages it had enjoyed in regard to the land-tax, for example. And throughout the correspondence of Savile with Wyvill in 1780-81 there is a curious strain of pessimism which seems to contradict the public utterances of Savile himself on the state of public opinion in the country—seems to contradict the view that the distresses of the people had become intolerable. At bottom he is convinced that it will not be possible to arouse the country and maintain popular fervour—it will even be necessary to wait until the situation becomes worse. There is a lack of political sense and of foresight in the people whom Wyvill and the other leaders of the movement are seeking to rally behind them. They will not be stirred by any calculation of future dangers or anticipated ills—indeed they will not move until they actually feel the pinch. Savile certainly seems clear that, as yet, the people have not sufficiently felt the pinch.

§I.V. FOX BECOMES "THE MAN OF THE PEOPLE"

Before the Yorkshire movement had been formally inaugurated, Wyvill found himself embarrassed by the evident intention of the Rockingham whigs to take the enterprise under their wing. Besides Lord John Cavendish, Sir George Savile and other members of the house of commons, a handful of peers attended the Yorkshire meeting on 30 December—Lord Rockingham, the Duke of Devonshire, the Duke of Rutland, the Earl of Scarborough, the Earl of Effingham, Earl Fitzwilliam, and the Earl of Egremont. "The Great Barons pour in upon us," wrote William Mason two days before the meeting; "and yet all we could do was done to prevent it."[1] During the proceedings at York, however, the magnates of the whig party were kept in the background, apparently as a matter of policy, and the members of parliament in general were almost regarded as an alien group—not part and parcel of the assembly as a whole. By a special resolution they were thanked for their presence and support, but Horace Walpole wrote to Mason:

> I like your committee's thanking the Barons for their appearance, which was a very civil way of marking the impertinence of their intrusion.[2]

Replying to the letter of thanks, Rockingham and the other lords expressed their "entire and hearty approbation of the principles which prevailed at the meeting at York". They added: "the interposition of the body of the people of property in this country in their affairs is naturally rare; no art of designing men for their own private purposes can produce it". Members of both houses of parliament, "instead of being constrained or superseded in their parliamentary capacity", would be assisted by such an intervention, provided they were intent upon their public duty.[3]

It would seem that at this stage of the proceedings the Rockinghamites had hardly the shadow of a misgiving—hardly the ghost of a fear that Wyvill might have any intention of superseding them "in their parliamentary capacities." They failed to discern the possible implications and the ulterior purposes of the agitation. Alternatively we may say that they were under an illusion concerning their ability to bring it under their control. Christopher Wyvill foresaw the difficulty from the first; and to a certain degree he was conscious of an aspect in the Yorkshire movement that was "anti-parliament". At any rate there was a certain streak in his thinking which amounted to a distrust of parliament-men. The failure of the Rockinghamites to bring the Yorkshire meeting under control and to harness the movement to their party-purposes in the month of January soon led the magnates to more sober second-thoughts.

---

[1] J. Mitford, *Correspondence of Horace Walpole and Rev. W. Mason*, II, 59.
[2] *Ibid.* 62.
[3] *Wyvill Papers*, I, 44–46.

They welcomed the movement as a support to their own party-cause and as a fulfilment of their prophecies. They took care, however, not to surrender to Wyvill and his friends.

Two men marched ahead of the rest of the Rockinghamites, however, and were caught more completely—affected more profoundly—by the sweep of the current. Charles James Fox and his uncle, the Duke of Richmond, had had their minds prepared in advance, and all their expectations were awake—they had been playing with radical ideas, dreaming of a great movement on the Irish model, and threatening something like a popular upheaval that would complete the discomfiture of George III. Even before the close of 1779 Fox's opponents were affecting to regard him as a revolutionary and his extravagant language had made him notorious. One paper supplied the story that a minister had gained a footing in an opposition house by paying court to the cook, and had overheard Fox explaining "a new plan for exciting an insurrection to reform the constitution".[1]

The Fox *coterie* threw themselves into the new adventure, behaving still as a flying squad or a free company, able to pierce far ahead or to conduct guerilla warfare on its own account, and only loosely attached to the Rockingham connection. To both Fox and Richmond the ostensible programme of the Yorkshire movement was the point that mattered least; what they loved in it were precisely the ulterior implications, the oblique suggestions of menace; and the subject of public economy was not the one upon which they could feel most happy or could meet their enemies without embarrassment. Both indeed were particularly vulnerable when the world began to cry out against the waste of the people's money. Fox, apart from holding a sinecure which he had mortgaged, was the son of the famous "defaulter of unaccounted millions", the Lord Holland who had aroused an unusual degree of resentment by the way he had enriched himself as Paymaster-General. The

---

[1] *Public Advertiser*, 22 Dec. 1779. For the increase in the "popularity" of Fox, as a result of a recent duel arising out of a parliamentary debate, see H. Walpole, *Last Journals*, where we are told that his health was toasted at a meeting to celebrate Wilkes's election as Chamberlain, and the *London Courant* of 6 Dec. where there is a report that he was being considered for the freedom of the city.

father's accounts were not yet closed and the public had never forgotten the matter, while Fox himself would show an unusual sensitiveness and a certain feeling of alarm whenever any reference was made to that question. His own recklessness and extravagance were notorious and in the debate on the Budget early in March Lord George Gordon made fun of "his great and superior knowledge in the business of making loans"—"the honorable orator", he said, "knew how to borrow money on better terms than the noble lord [North] in the blue ribbon."[1] For years the Duke of Richmond had been subject to reproach because, as the descendent of one of Charles II's illegitimate sons, he had inherited the profits of a penny a "chaldron" on coals coming to London, and these were supposed to supply him with an income of no less than £16,000 a year. It was argued by some that what at its very inception had been a gross plundering of the poor had not become anything else by prescriptive right—had not been turned into righteousness by the mere passage of time. At an early stage in the history of the Yorkshire movement it was suggested to the ministry that the demand for economy might well be directed against the profits of paymasters and the vested interests of those who were descended from the illegitimate children of Charles II. The supporters of the government did not miss the opportunity. The Duke of Grafton, another descendant of Charles II, had to apologize for his heritage in the house of lords.[2]

Fox himself soon found that he was open to another attack; for the wheel had made its full cycle and he who ten years before had been so prominent amongst the supporters of North and the opponents of Wilkes might well be asked to explain why now he should go so far beyond even other enemies of George III in identifying himself with something more Wilkite still, and in asserting the supremacy of that "voice of the people" which was to be heard outside the walls of parliament. In the course of the famous Middlesex election controversy he had claimed that the voice of the people was only to be found in the house of commons. His enemies

[1] *Parliamentary History*, XXI, 162; cf. Letter II from "An Old Freeholder" in *London Chronicle*, 25–28 March.
[2] *Parliamentary History*, XX, 1338; *Gazetteer*, 11 Feb.

in the early months of 1780 were quick to remind him of the escapades of his youth.

Yet it was through the Yorkshire movement that Fox came into the limelight as never before, and in the course of it he emerged—if only for a moment—as "the man of the people". He was more deeply affected by it than any other person in the aristocratic political world of the time; and it was the most important political movement which went to the shaping of his mind; apart from his friendship with Edmund Burke, it was perhaps the most enriching political experience that he ever had. Precisely because he was a parliament-man, and one who was in connection with the Rockinghamites, any success that he gained would be a challenge to Wyvill and to the original conception of the Yorkshire movement. His sensational success at the Westminster meeting on 2 February, after Wyvill had edged out the great barons so skilfully in York, was bound to give a different complexion to the agitation as a whole.

His first contact with the movement had taken place a few days before, on 27 January, when the Wiltshire meeting—a gathering of about 150 people—was held in Devizes, and he made his first speech outside the walls of parliament, declaring that he had never before "spoken to an uncorrupt assembly". He came forward, "though not a Freeholder himself, yet as nearly connected with a great property under his care", and he addressed himself—as we might expect—not to economical reform as such but to the question of a great movement of popular protest that should alter the existing political balance in the country. He repeatedly stressed "the great advantage which the people might gain by insisting firmly on their rights". He urged them to "consider their own weight and consequence in the state", and to "depend chiefly on themselves for a redress of grievances"—not to "sit still in expectation of it from any statesman". It was his argument that the spirit of the American colonists ought to make itself felt in Britain, and that nothing had been done for Ireland until the Irish had learned to look after their interests themselves. If he mentioned the question of public expenditure, it was only to insult the King and say that since princes were so fond of war they should share its inconveni-

ences at a time when their subjects were "obliged to deny themselves . . . even the decent conveniences of life".

In God's name was the King to be the only person who was to
feel nothing from the distresses of his Kingdom?[1]

Fox was made a member of the Wiltshire Committee of Correspondence; and a few days later a much more imposing meeting in
Westminster Hall—a meeting which supporters represented as
having been three or four thousand strong and very "respectable"
—gave him a moment of triumph such as was rare in his life. The
news that he and his friends were connecting themselves with the
movement must have spread abroad already, for before the meeting the court party sought to discredit the Duke of Richmond and
dispersed handbills calling attention to the dearness of coals. And
once the proceedings had been opened Fox, "by the unanimous
voice of the Assembly", was asked to occupy the chair.

It is curious to note that here, as so often elsewhere, the Middlesex radicals were evidently intending to take charge of the proceedings from the very start. Sawbridge made the original proposal
that a petition like the one from the county of York should be
addressed to the house of commons. Wilkes then seconded the
motion in what seems to have been regarded as one of his ablest
speeches. He expressed the happiness he felt at "that spirit of Association which at this period pervades the Kingdom". Yet, as Middlesex had been superseded in the first place by Yorkshire, and
Wilkes by Wyvill, so now and henceforward the city of Westminster had the front place on the stage, and Charles James Fox
managed at this moment to run away with most of the glory.
Having been "unanimously" called upon to deliver the petition
of Westminster to the house of commons, he took the opportunity
to make a long and "remarkably brilliant" speech, in which incidentally he mentions that Wilkes was sitting at his right hand. On
this occasion he committed himself to the fundamental principle of

---

[1] *Copies of the Proceedings of the General Meetings of the County of Wiltshire*,
published by order of the Committee (1780), pp. 4–10. See also *Wyvill Papers*,
I, 108 *et seqq.* and *Gazetteer*, 1 Feb. 1780.

the Yorkshire movement. If that purely delegated body, the house of commons, failed in the execution of its trust—in particular if they refused to grant the purpose of the present petition—"from that moment they passed the line—from that moment they ceased to be representatives of the people; and it was legal, constitutional and necessary for the people to assume that trust which their delegates had thrown off."

What would that people suffer in the annals of time who permitted themselves to be enslaved in a reign not immortalised by enterprise and glory. . . . The people must be the ministers of their own deliverance and the road to it was open. They had seen the effect of manly resolution. Their brethren in America and their brethren in Ireland had taught them how to act when bad men forced them to feel. Are we not born from the same original? . . . Shall the heart of the empire be tame and lifeless while the limbs are in activity and motion?

Sitting at the side of Fox at this moment was not only John Wilkes but John Jebb, the gentlest of the agitators and one of the most attractive of the radical influences into the orbit of which Fox had moved. We have already met him in connection with a paper which he addressed to the Middlesex freeholders in December and which presented in an extreme form the doctrine of the Association. Jebb, in what he describes as his first attempt to speak before a political audience of this kind, now proposed that Fox should be adopted as the future parliamentary candidate for the constituency. So was inaugurated Fox's political connection with the city of Westminster.[1]

A Committee of Correspondence was appointed and Fox's chairmanship of this Committee at its weekly meetings was to be one of the chief aspects of his political activity in the months which followed. The importance of the whole episode was heightened by the fact that from this moment the Committee of Westminster became the most famous of all the committees that had been established in connection with the petitioning movement. Already the

---

[1] St. James's Chronicle: 1-3 Feb. 1780; The Speech of the Hon. C. J. Fox delivered at Westminster on Feb. 2, 1780.

leadership, which had passed from Middlesex to Yorkshire in December 1779, as we have seen, had returned to Middlesex in the following January, when many of the leaders, including Christopher Wyvill himself, had gone to London, making the capital the centre of their operations. Amongst the various Committees in the metropolis from the beginning of February, however, it was the one in Westminster which was to maintain its own identity and hold the centre of the stage. Partly because of the spectacular character of the original meeting of electors, and partly because Fox as chairman was so picturesque a figure-head, the proceedings of this body came into the lime-light from the start. The Westminster Committee held the attention of the press; in more ways than one it took a significant line of its own; and soon it was to become the seat of the most remarkable new developments, so that it came to acquire a special position of leadership. In any case Fox stood out as the principal man in parliament who in any thorough manner had thrown himself into this new enterprise—had walked out of the governing classes, so to speak, not merely to bless and patronize it, but to become a part of it himself. Both he personally, and the Westminster Committee in general, formed the chief liaison between the movement in the country and the men who belonged to the parliamentary world. Finally, Wyvill contrived to leave the Rockinghamites on the shelf at the Yorkshire meeting. But at Westminster, as we have seen, it was rather the radicals who were put in the shade—the day was a triumph for Fox and the parliament-men.

"It was curious," says Horace Walpole, "to see Charles Fox, lately so unpopular a character, become the idol of the people." Fox had accepted the Yorkshire movement blithely, but henceforward all was not to be clear sailing by any means. He had found a boat, but he was not the master of the direction it would follow, and from the moment that it took to the water it carried him into new pressure-regions, and exposed him to wind and weather. We know that he tried to tack, but we also know that he was carried away a little—carried away almost in spite of himself. There were guiding hands behind the movement—influences at work underneath the apparent freedom of the public meetings—and they were not the hands or the influence of Fox; rather it was the case that he was now uncovered, he had made himself more amenable to the pulls and pressures. In the days of Burke and of aristocratic leadership he more than anybody else is responsible for the fact that a party calling itself whig did not in the spirit of a blind oligarchy oppose the rising political consciousness of county and town, but made a bridge for the future, and enabled a political transition to take place without cataclysm. And in his very violence he more than anybody else helped to bring eighteenth-century whiggism into touch with the more drastic seventeenth-century doctrine— with the view that in the last resort the enemies of entrenched power must be prepared even for revolutionary action. He was not a radical, concerned to remodel society and government in a permanent manner. He was a whig who judged that the crisis of English liberty, the quasi-revolutionary moment, was at hand. In his mind the aims of the American colonists, the Irish Volunteers, and the Yorkshire movement had been synthesised into one grand whig cause—a mighty upheaval against a King whom otherwise it seemed impossible to dislodge from a power apparently beyond constitutional control.

Chapter VI

THE CHARACTER OF
THE YORKSHIRE MOVEMENT

§1. ECONOMICAL REFORM

IF we were to ask: What was the actual point at which the Rockinghamite party in parliament found that the shoe pinched at
this time? the answer would be clear—it was their view that
the margin of difference was made in the house of commons by
what they described as "royal influence". If, on the other hand, we
were to ask where the mass of the petitioners in the country felt the
pinch, they would be ready with their answer, and would say, in
their rents and farms, their shops and factories and warehouses; but
the marginal pressure which they resented came from the taxes,
it is clear, and they diagnosed the evil as the "waste of public
money." By the parliamentary followers of Rockingham and
Shelburne on the one hand, and by the leaders of the Yorkshire
movement on the other, these two grievances had been dove-tailed
into one another, or brought together in a single synthesis. Edmund
Burke's plan of economical reform catches both birds in the same
net. Its checks upon public extravagance are *ipso facto* a reduction
of the resources that the King can use for the purpose of influencing
parliament.

The impression of wastefulness was widespread, and we to-day
can hardly withhold our surprise when we see the multiplicity of
useless or redundant offices which were tolerated in an age when the
operations of government were comparatively few and simple.
While things run smoothly—while the engine can take the burden
comfortably, even as it works at low pressure—the world is content to go on carrying the extra passengers, so that custom is
allowed its due career. But such survivals and redundancies are
liable to be questioned when the machinery is strained so that a
great many people have begun to cry out that they are feeling the
pinch. At this point in the argument there can be no doubt that the

war made the difference in 1779–80, especially as it was now proving so intense and was lasting so long that the nation could not easily take it in its stride. No doubt there was much truth in the assertions of government spokesmen who argued that the hardships of which men were complaining were in reality the results of the war. Of the Yorkshire movement—as well as the Irish one—it could be said that the heat and the pressure had risen earlier than would otherwise have been the case, because of the strain which the conflict with the American colonies had placed upon the whole system.

The effect of war upon the development of a country's economy and upon the structure of the state itself is one of the topics which must constantly engage the student of modern European history. The use of mercenary armies affects the relations between kings and capitalists, and is already helping to change the character of the body politic in various regions, in the fifteenth century. The development of national standing armies intensifies the character of seventeenth-century states, and the increase in the magnitude of military operations is connected with the development of mass-production and the rise in the scale of government contracts. The wars between Charles V and Francis I of France, or between Louis XIV and William III of England, seem sometimes to turn into conflicts between vast financial systems. And in modern times neither England nor France nor Spain could meet the demands of a time of war by the traditional methods of government—indeed, even where bankruptcy and revolution were avoided, it appears that governmental finance was only rectified by methods which involved a change in the character of the state itself. The reason of men has imagined that it was directing the destiny of the world and the progress of the nation-state in one direction; but the needs of the state in time of war have been pulling the universe all the time along a very different course. In the nineteenth century the two movements seemed to be reconciled, and the liberals who clamoured for a more general education and a wider franchise seemed to be in line with all those military developments since the outbreak of the French Revolution, which required more and more the intelligent and conscious co-operation of men of all classes in the work of the state—required an extension of the franchise and of education if only in order to strengthen the hands of government. Only now, after two large twentieth-century wars, do we see that even in the days of our grandfathers it was the liberals who were deceiving themselves with the illusion that they were victorious in the concealed tug-of-war that was taking place. Only now do we realize to what an extent, even in the nineteenth century, a profounder movement was taking the world (as the Jacobins, under the pressures generated by war, took the French Revolution itself) away from the paradise of the individualist, and in the direction of the insatiable, inexorable, high-powered state.

The strain which the American war had put upon the country and the stimulus which it gave to public opinion were to lead in Burke's plan of economical reform to a process of rationalization in government, which implied a change in the character of the state itself. The men who thought that they were only clamouring against wild prodigality here and there were in reality asking for a transformation in the very pattern of the body politic. The case is illustrated at the opening of Burke's account of his proposals, in his speech on economical reform.

I must observe, Sir, that whoever takes a view of this kingdom in a cursory manner, will imagine, that he beholds a solid, compacted, uniform system of monarchy; in which all inferiour jurisdiction are but as rays diverging from one centre. But on examining it more nearly, you find much eccentricity and confusion. It is not a monarchy in strictness. But, as in the Saxon times this country was an heptarchy, it is now a strange sort of *pentarchy*. It is divided into five several distinct principalities, besides the supreme. ... Cross a brook, and you lose the King of England; but you have some comfort in coming again under his majesty, though "shorn of his beams," and no more than prince of Wales. Go to the north, and you find him dwindled to a duke of Lancaster; turn to the west of that north, and he pops upon you in the humble character of the earl of Chester. Travel a few miles on, the earl of Chester disappears; and the king surprises you again as count palatine of Lancaster. If you travel beyond Mount Edgecombe, you find him once more in his incognito, and he is duke of Cornwall. ... Every one of those principalities has the apparatus of a kingdom.

Burke mentions how, recently, "that pert, factious fellow, the duke of Lancaster" had presumed to go to law with King George III—that is to say with himself—at a cost to the country of fifteen thousand pounds. He attacks on similar lines the forest rights of the crown, and in particular that "useless piece of antiquity" which made the Speaker of the house of commons one of the chief justices in eyre for the forests, though his dignity put him "too high for jurisdiction over wild beasts", and by his learning he was "too valuable to be wasted as chief justice of a desert." Burke described the royal household as "formed upon manners and customs that have long since expired"—formed indeed, "in many respects, upon *feudal principles*"—and at the same time "upon the principles of a *body corporate*; it has its own magistrates, courts and by-laws." He proceeded against things like "*the great wardrobe* (which has the care of the king's furniture)" the *jewel office*, which existed "for the sole purpose of taxing the King's gifts of plate"; and he pointed out that for the payment of such useless establishments "there are no less than *three useless* treasurers."

Burke proposed to unite the separate principalities more closely to the crown, suppressing the various useless offices attached to them, selling the forests, and disposing of the crown-lands in a similar way. He intended to regulate the King's civil establishments, to limit the pensions, and to abolish altogether the useless, expensive, and inconvenient offices in court and state. The board of works, which concealed its good works so that they were "perfectly invisible", and which had its own treasury and paymaster, was to be destroyed and its functions put "into the hands of a real builder, who shall not be a member of parliament". The mint should be turned into a factory (which was what it really was) and not be allowed to continue as a corporate body, like the Bank of England, when it had long ago ceased to act as a bank. Such offices as that of the paymaster of the land forces should be treated, he said, as "no longer *banks* or *treasuries*, but mere *offices of administration*".

Burke not only attacked these and many similar things, which represented the fossilizations of an older state of society—great slabs of antiquity still embedded in our system of government—but he thundered against their modern parallels, against the creation of a third secretary of state when for almost a year one of the normal secretaryships could be left vacant, as had recently been the case. He declaimed against a Board of Trade which had not come into operation even to take over our commercial controversies with the American colonies in the last decade; or to examine our difficulties with Ireland in the last twelve months. "The perpetual virtual adjournment, and the unbroken sitting vacation of that board was no more disturbed by the Irish than by the plantation commerce or any other commerce." He shocked the prejudices of the time by proposing that the Lord Steward should maintain the tables in the King's household by contracts which should initially be examined and approved at the Board of Treasury, and discharged at the exchequer. This was the process of rationalization which he envisaged in response to the cry of the petitioning movement, the cry of the men who declared that now, at least, the country could not afford the luxury. It was by other men than Burke at this time that the representative system itself was being re-examined and exposed on similar lines; for that, also, was open to the criticism that it contained too many of the fossilizations of the distant past. The whole character of the English body politic was, therefore, the question at issue at this date.

Once the issue had been raised, it transpired that Burke and his friends were not alone in the view that the government of England was clogged and encumbered by these specimens of archaic survival. North himself said, for example:

It was very certain that the present course of the Exchequer was inimical to a speedy and effectual controul. The system was unequal to the extent of the business; and it created delays and inconveniences exceedingly disagreeable, and which tended to obstruct, instead of expediting the national service.[1]

It was Burke's claim, however, that no mere love of archaism, no mere fanatical devotion to tradition, kept so much of the ancient system still embedded in the structure of the body politic. "For the purposes of influence, and for those purposes only, are retained half

[1] *Parliamentary History*, XXI, 76; cf. *ibid.* 97, 179–80, 278.

at least of the household establishments." At the same time it was no mere love of rationalization, no deficiency in any historical sense, we can be sure, which provided the impulse to Burke's remarkable crusade. For him and for his political friends, as we have seen, the campaign was directed in reality against royal influence. Not only ancient survivals of the kind that we have just observed, but also novel developments in society had worked for the increase in the sources of that influence. Not only the fossilized remnants of a feudal age, but the multiplication of customs-officers, exchequer officials, and colonial services in the new commercial and imperial age, had helped to add to the resources at the disposal of the King. "The increase, too, that had been made in the military establishment, in the raising of new corps, and the appointment of officers to them had . . . augmented the sources of corruption." The country at large, in the protests that were being made at this period, was no doubt seeking primarily a relief from financial burdens in difficult times. It was still true, however, that, in the speeches, the pamphlets, and the petitions themselves, the complaints were made more pointed by the prevailing assumption that too much of the money was being lavished in the cause of what they regarded as "corruption".

Patronage was the system of the eighteenth century and without it the aristocratic cliques and connections would hardly have held together, the magnates would have lost much of their own local influence. Burke seemed to suggests in his *Thoughts on the Cause of the Present Discontents* that such patronage was "natural" when the nobility used it, but became illegitimate and turned into "corruption" when it was employed by the King. In spite of this no one could deny in those days—any more than in these—that when governments have offices to distribute it is not unnatural for them to favour those who support them, rather than the men in opposition. And in those days—as in these—it was not unnatural that any party, whether in office or out of office, should seek a certain degree of party-discipline, and employ very definite "sanctions", very concrete forms of persuasion, in order to induce it. It was not unreasonable to argue that for ordinary purposes, and for the routine of daily life, a working majority was necessary for any ministry that existed in the eighteenth century. Neither then nor now would it be feasible to leave every single issue to the caprice of a house of commons that behaved every day as a free and open public meeting. This argument was all the more cogent in the eighteenth century when for so long no great political issue divided the parliamentary world, and opposition to the government was so often a mere bid for spoils and offices. In general it was not unnatural that there should be some bias in the system of things— some understanding as to the place from which favours were to be expected—which told in favour of stability and the King's government.

Patronage was not merely consonant with the social structure of eighteenth century England; it was essential to it; indeed it was almost the cement which held it together. There was a legitimate influence attached to aristocratic position, and there was a legitimate influence—one which might even operate in the house of commons —which was attached to the crown itself. The two were not unconnected; a man might use his interest to support the government —in local elections for example—and expect the government to give him some of its patronage in return. A faction-leader could always say to the head of the government: If you do not put my nominee in as harbour-master here, or as excise-officer there, I shall lose my local influence and will be unable to give you the support I have hitherto given. When a man belonged to the governing classes his interests in his own locality dovetailed into a national organization of interests, in this and other ways.

Under such a system it was always possible for any man who was displeased, and any party which was in opposition, to allege that the government was guilty of corruption. The whole system had the serious disadvantage that it was open to corruption, liable to become a great abuse if the competition either for votes or for favour became too intense, or if, as a sanction for party-discipline, it operated too directly and too often. A man might have given Sir Robert Walpole his independent support in parliament for ten years or more, and might then feel that he was being "neglected" if he was passed over when favours were being distributed. Here the services had been rendered long before any reward for them was in question; and the reward might be particularly appropriate if the man had long been at considerable expense in the local elections which he had conducted in support of the government. Amongst those, however, who in the eighteenth century quite accepted the system of patronage, there were some who valued their honour and independence, and on occasion they made it clear that they resented many of the developments that were taking place.

It was considered unfair, even by people who were whigs and regular supporters of the government, when Walpole withdrew his favour from men who had been faithful to him for years, but who voted against him on a single issue—the Excise Bill in 1733, for example—an issue in which they considered that their principles were involved. It was considered particularly unfair, in that many of these were not in any sense to be construed as registering any lack of confidence in Walpole's general system of government. It was often considered unfair by the same people when the punitive measures of the government in the time of Walpole operated so directly and extended so far as to result in the dismissal of army officers. Both Walpole and George III were attacked by the governing classes for promoting men without property, men who had no independent standing, so that they were bound to be more servile supporters of government, less ready to risk their careers, when a loss of place was bound to mean ruin for them.

In the period of the Yorkshire movement there are a number of tangible reasons for saying that the system of patronage had led to the prevalence of a certain degree of "corruption". George III once wrote to North that he had thought that at least a Headmaster of Eton might have been appointed on other than political considerations.[1] It was too clear that the members for Cornish boroughs did not show the independence that was the well-known feature of much of the county-representation. Abrupt changes of party—or covert menaces in house of commons speeches—were too directly connected with the distribution of favours and offices. In conversation and in letters, political comment was too often transposed into terms of jobbery, and the result was a current cynicism. Amongst the troubles and vicissitudes of North, as we have seen,

[1] *Corr. George III*, v, 307–08, Dec. 1781.

there was too great a preoccupation—too perpetual an anxiety—concerning the question of promises and rewards. In any case North, himself, as we have already noticed, would too often try to foreclose a political dispute by asking a man what he wanted for himself; and it is clear that the whole system tended, along these lines, to produce a decline of a healthy public spirit. The Rockinghamites claimed that the sources of influence at the disposal of the King tipped the balance in the house of commons—to them, therefore, it presented the critical issue. And we might say that if, apart from producing a working majority for government in normal times, it turned the scale when a great national question was at issue—if it decided the result even against the voice of the nation outside parliament—then this royal influence was indeed the menace that it was alleged to be. As we have seen, however, corruption lost some of its power over men at the critical moment in Dublin. We shall find later that the emergence of the Yorkshire Association was to put the matter to the test in the British parliament.

Even Burke, who was more cautious than some of the Rockinghamites, had welcomed not only the petitioning movement but the formation of Committees, the project of some species of ulterior action. Indeed, he had urged his constituents in Bristol not to waste their energies on a petition if they did not "in some way or other resolve to correspond with other places which have a common object in view, for the support and pursuit of it through more sessions than one". As he paraphrased it in the house of commons, he said to them:

You know the common fate of petitions; if you do mean to present a petition, do not let it be forsaken, like an ostrich's egg, to be fostered by the accidental rays of the sun in barren sands; but follow it up at least with as great care as you would show about an inclosure or a road bill.[1]

For Burke, however, it was essentially a petition against corruption, a petition on behalf of economy. His party for the most part

[1] Fitzwilliam, *Correspondence of Burke*, II, 316–18; *Parliamentary History*, XX, 1383.

followed him in this, secure in the thought that, if they could trim and pare the royal influence by their "economical" proposals, they would then have a stronger footing in the house of commons for further projects of reformation. Fox set the issue clearly in the house of commons on 8 February when he produced a famous argument from the judgment of Solomon, an argument which became a favourite weapon of the Rockinghamites in the subsequent period. It was easy for the supporters of the government to say that the whigs attacked corruption merely because they were out of office, and that in reality they were fighting only for a change of ministry, scrambling for places and profits themselves. Very well, argued Fox:

We say to the ministry, You misapply the public money; nay, you do worse, you apply it to bad purposes: ministry say to us, You want our places; and thus the charge of corruption is given and retorted. Come now, let us see whose child corruption is; opposition are willing, are desirous, that it should be sacrificed; ministry have often made similar professions; the time is come to prove the sincerity of both; see who will now acknowledge; see who will father this dear but denied child, corruption![1]

If Burke were to attack the problem of royal influence by the series of bills comprised in his Plan of Economical Reform, that is to say, by an attempt to uproot historic institutions—to tear out of the fabric of the state those fossils which were so deeply embedded in the structure—he was bound to meet with great difficulties in the eighteenth century, which, precisely because it was lacking in historical-mindedness, was liable to be superstitious on the occasions when it did cling to the past. The men of that time hesitated to pull out even the weeds, fearing that too drastic a policy of reform would bring up also the roots of society. In particular, it was difficult to carry out such a programme as that of Burke without touching the question of the rights of property; and the strength of those rights is illustrated by the fact that even the advocates of parliamentary reform often shrank from any attack on rotten boroughs. The crucial issue was raised in respect of those parts of the

[1] *Parliamentary History*, xx, 1380.

new proposals which affected the King's control of his civil list. It was pointed out that Burke had been tender to the sinecures of his fellow-whigs (where he had been prepared to continue them for the lives of existing holders) but had been less considerate for the King, whose civil list represented his private property, and stood in place of ancient forms of income which he had allowed to be commuted. Since the salaries of ministers, judges, and ambassadors were then paid from the civil list, we can see again, even in this aspect of the question, how the deposits of history still encumbered the present time. Now, as in ancient days, there was confusion and overlapping between the king in his private capacity and the public functions and ministrations of the crown.

Burke made his great speech on the economical reform on 11 February, when, though he impressed his hearers, he did not capture them with his oratory in the way that he captured his readers by the version that appeared in print.[1] Not until 23 February did he present the most important of the bills that were comprised in his far-reaching project: namely, the "Bill for the better Regulation of his Majesty's Civil Establishments, for the Limitation of Pensions, and the Suppression of sundry useless, expensive and inconvenient Places". When on 8 March the house of commons began to go into committee on the separate clauses of the bill, it was Rigby who rashly hurled an explosive into the proceedings, asserting that parliament had no right to control the expenditure of the King's civil list, "which was an interest no power on earth could deprive him of without manifest injustice".[2] Burke asserted that such a doctrine "went equally to the defeating every part of the Bill"; and North, whose tactical sense often saved him from serious errors on such an occasion, refused to challenge the issue by a direct motion— he knew that if he was victorious in the division his very success

[1] On the whole occasion see H.M.C. *Appendix to 6th Report*, Sir R. Graham's Mss. 341–42. "The tumult was great; the swords of the Deputy Serjeant at Arms and the Speaker's train bearer were broken in an instant ... The Rev'd Orator Wyvill and three or four hundred gentlemen could not gain admittance; more than six hundred persons were present when prayers were read. Mr Burke was very ingenious and temperate. Many believe it was a plan concerted between Lord North and him."

[2] *Parliamentary History*, XXI, 180–81.

would have an alarming effect on the country outside. In any case it was North's policy not to defeat the purposes of Burke's bill at the start by a vote on general principles, but to begin with fair words and then to carry on a kind of rearguard action over the particular clauses as they came up one by one.

Nothing could have dismayed the opposition parties more than the emergence of this technical issue. Nothing could equal the exasperation which they showed when they saw themselves endangered by what seemed a standing threat, but at the same time a menace that could not be located and fastened down. For their purposes it would have been infinitely better if this question of the civil list had been brought down to earth, down from the region of cloud and fog—better if they could only have goaded North (as they tried to do) into putting the matter to the vote—so that at least they might have made capital in the country from their very defeat. If the heart of the whole matter, so far as they were concerned, was the question of "royal influence", the heart of the heart, or the cream of the cream, was this question of the right of parliament to control the civil list. Now, more than ever before, they seemed to see the shadow of a coming defeat, and read the signs of future discomfiture and thwarting. At this point their parliamentary speeches reached the maximum of violence and exasperation.

Fox challenged the house to come to a resolution if it regarded the civil list as beyond its jurisdiction:

If such a vote should be agreed to by a majority of that House, he should look upon his toils and labours to be at an end; and the people would have recourse to other means of redress, when parliament had precluded all possible expectations through the ordinary methods prescribed by the constitution; they would have recourse to other arguments, than what might be urged in the course of debates in that House, in order to rescue themselves and their posterity from the chains which were forging for them. He would not presume to point out the means the people in this last extremity would resort to; he was persuaded they would be wise, salutary, and adequate to the object proposed to be attained. Should such be the necessity, he never would again enter that House; his presence there would be of very little consequence. He would unite himself with those out of that House, whose sentiments corresponded with his own. He hoped he should acquit himself like a man; and he knew of nothing in his own disposition, which would prevent him from bearing him out with firmness and perseverance in the struggle. He was persuaded the measures adopted by the people would be peaceable; but at the same time suited to the exigencies of the occasion; in such measures he was prepared to co-operate; and he did not doubt but the friends of legal liberty and the constitution would prevail in the contest.

It is worthy of note, that at a later point in this debate even Burke himself spoke to much the same effect, declaring that the principle put forward by Rigby implied the annihilation of the constitution. The acceptance of this view by the house of commons, however:

would not, though it might be intended to effect it, destroy the liberties of Britain. Debate, it is true, would be at an end, because it could answer no useful purpose. The duties of those, who had struggled for a long series of years against every disadvantage, that it was possible to conceive against large majorities, public obloquy, repeated defeat, and daily mortifications, would cease; their un-availing opposition would be terminated. The people must do what parliament had refused, or rather what they were resolved not to do, or had declared themselves incompetent to effect; but he trusted, that health would follow. A fever purged off and puri-fied the blood, gave it a more happy circulation, and renovated or corrected a weak or disordered constitution. . . . Every right his Majesty enjoyed, as sovereign, was a delegated right, and conse-quently subject to examination, correction, and controul.[1]

All these things which were being thrown out even by a Burke inside the walls of parliament had a definite relationship with the events that were taking place outside, and had their counterpart in the utterances of the leaders of the Yorkshire movement. In a fur-ther debate in committee, on the same 8 March, on one of the clauses of Burke's Establishment Bill, Fox returned to the theme and made his meaning even more clear than earlier in the day:

[1] *Parliamentary History*, XXI, 184–85, 190–91.

If the maxim, that the House really had no power over the civil list, should be established, a rebellion, and nothing but a rebellion, could possibly save the constitution, and restore it to that state, from which the establishment of so vile a doctrine would inevitably reduce it. But why would not ministry stand forth, and fairly try the question?[1]

A few days later, Rigby modified his original assertion. According to his revised statement he had never meant to suggest that parliament had no over-ruling power in regard to any possible case which touched the expenditure of the civil list. Fox still maintained his point, however, and said that "he would not retract from the declaration he had made on a former day." Concerning the view that the expenditure of the King's civil list could not be controlled by parliament, he asserted, that "if such a doctrine was established, they must go to another place and rescue themselves from slavery by other arguments than words."[2]

§II. OPPOSITION TACTICS AND COUNTER-MOVEMENT

A few days before Christmas 1779, George III was urging that the friends of the ministry should not allow Wyvill and the opposition leaders to have everything their own way at the forthcoming meeting in York. He wrote to Lord North:

I cannot conclude without strongly pressing that every measure may be taken to get the friends of Government in Yorkshire to attend the Meeting on the 30th at York not that I suppose they will be able to stop the violence of the Meeting, but it will show that the County is not Unanimous in this business, and it may decide whether any contrary Resolutions should be taken.[3]

[1] *Parliamentary History*, XXI, 216.
[2] *Ibid.* 258.
[3] *Corr. George III*, IV, 526; cf. Add. Mss. 37,835, f. 81, George III to Robinson, 23 Dec. 1779: "I trust Mr Robinson is leaving no stone unturned to get friends of the Constitution to attend." Robinson, replying 24 Dec., *ibid.* ff. 85-8, said he had spent "the greatest part of the day" on this business.

Later, when he had heard the result of the meeting in York he declared that it would be wise to exercise much care in the appointment of sheriffs in 1780 "and to be as much as possible acquainted with their political sentiments, that meetings may as much as possible be discouraged".[1]

On 23 December a group of lords and gentlemen from Yorkshire were collected at 10 Downing Street by Robinson, but their discussion "ended in an unanimous Opinion that they had better not attend" the Yorkshire meeting, "nor collect numbers to attend to oppose the Measures there, but privately to discourage and if proper and necessary to protest". Robinson commented:

Thus the field is left fair for our Antagonists and my labours hitherto fruitless, and now, on this, at an end.[2]

Lord Carmarthen, who appeared before the close of this consultation, refused to join the rest in "preventing our friends from attending" the Yorkshire meeting. "If they were apprehensive of any improper or dangerous proposals being made at the meeting," he said, he "rather should think it a reason for encouraging our friends to attend in order to oppose such proposals."[3] Lord Carmarthen was soon to make it clear that he had a certain sympathy with at least the ostensible objects of the meeting.

We have seen also, however, that the Earl of Sandwich was not content to leave the enemy unchallenged in the way that had been allowed to happen in Yorkshire. As early as the morning of 10 January he was discussing with William Eden the form of resistance which might be offered to the petitioning movement at the Huntingdon meeting which was due to be held on the 20th. Eden was prepared to draw up a draft of suggested counter-resolutions; but, being unable to meet Sandwich again at a whist-party as had been arranged, he sent them by letter, saying, "I entreat Your Lordship not to shew anything in my hand-writing on this subject." The gist of the proposed resolutions was: "that no regular

[1] H.M.C. *Bathurst Mss.*, p. 18.
[2] Add. Mss. 38,212, f. 316; Add. Mss. 34,416, f. 489.
[3] *Political Memoranda of the Fifth Duke of Leeds*, pp. 171-9.

charges or proofs of the misapplication of the public money have been exhibited to satisfy this meeting"; "that it is not the sense of this meeting upon loose and unsatisfying surmises to impede the deliberations of parliament . . . more especially at a moment when this Kingdom is engaged in a necessary war against the united strength of the perfidious House of Bourbon"; and "that this meeting does not see any present reason to withdraw their confidence from their representatives in Parliament . . . upon the mere suggestion of circumstances which are the natural and perhaps inevitable consequences of an extensive war".[1] Sandwich copied the resolutions and returned the manuscript to Eden; but, as we have already seen, had no chance to present his proposals in proper form to the Huntingdon county meeting, which broke into confusion after the question of the petition had been put to the vote. Something similar to these, however, was to appear when in Huntingdonshire and other counties the dissidents drew up their formal Protests against the movement that was taking place.

Somewhere in the back-stage, amongst the minor agents of both government and opposition parties, there were men who carried on a kind of guerilla warfare, discrediting "personalities", exposing vested interests, disseminating scandal, and generally playing a game of catch-as-catch-can. Before the Westminster meeting, as we have seen, they circulated hand-bills calling attention to the dearness of coals—a thrust at the Duke of Richmond. On the morning of the Cambridge meeting of 25 March some members of the University circulated a printed extract from a sermon delivered in 1769 by Dr. Watson, the Regius Professor of Divinity—a sermon "which absolutely contradicted the radical sentiments which he was to utter at the meeting". A curious figure in this political demi-monde was Thomas Ramsden of Pontefract, a correspondent of Charles Jenkinson, who was not content to leave the field to Christopher Wyvill and his friends, but attempted to conduct a Yorkshire campaign of his own. Before the general meeting in York he had sent a paper to the York Courant, and had tried to have it printed as a handbill, but was compelled to report:

[1] Add Mss. 34,417, ff. 13-14; ibid. f. 289 [enclosed in f. 13].

that no printer there would venture to print it unless some gentleman's name was attached to it. They are said to be intimidated; but
whom they fear is not said though one may easily guess that it is
the powerful patriotic power [i.e., the Rockingham interest in
Yorkshire.]

A few days later he wrote:

I am very clearly of opinion that something should be done by
administration not only to inform the ignorant but to prevent the
mischiefs intended by disappointed faction, from sacrificing everything to their ambition. If anything is thought proper to be printed
on a separate sheet and in the newspapers it may very properly (as
heretofore) be sent by the several postmasters to distribute in their
neighbourhood and particularly in the market towns; some also to
the Mayors of Boroughs and Corporations, only in such counties
however as are threatened with their meetings.

Ramsden even had a plan to suggest; and his secret diplomacies,
his conspiratorial tactics, were not unlike those of Wyvill himself,
and some of the men who assisted him. "Unless it is possible and
proper to avoid doing anything in consequence of the petition intended to be presented", he said, the government might

move immediately on the meeting of the House of Commons and
before the first petition is presented, for a Commission to be chosen
by ballot consisting of 21 members who shall enquire into the
salarys and profits arising to the auditors of the Exchequer, the
Tellers of the Exchequer; the Paymaster-General of the Forces; and
Treasurer of the Navy ... Also the grants of King Charles II to his
Bastards and their successors and particularly the duty on coals
imported into London which is so heavy a tax and load on the
inhabitants and manufacturers there.

This is to be kept an entire secret till the day before the meeting
when lists of the 21 are to be delivered to all friends.[1]

In these minor engagements—and in this kind of trick-warfare—
the Rockingham connection as a whole was vulnerable at the
moment, as we have already seen. When the aristocratic party

[1] Add. Mss. 38,212, ff. 318, 328, 330, 332; Add. Mss. 38,213, ff.39-14.

tried to join hands with a movement that had democratic leanings there was an anomaly to be exploited. When the word went round that the farmers were in distress, men could argue that not the King but the mighty landlords were to blame.[1] When there was a movement to purge the electoral system of its evils and abuses, it was possible to draw attention to the effect of wealth and influence in the aristocracy. The *York Courant* for 1 February 1780 contains the following satirical conjecture:

1st. That the pernicious custom at City Elections of distributing half a Guinea to each voter, and that more expensive one of Balls and Treats, after the important Business of the Day is finished, shall be discountenanced by them and if possible for ever abolished.

2. That not one of the Minority Lords will endeavour to support a future Election with Their baleful Influence, not even should a Brother or any of their numerous Relations stand for candidates.

At the general meetings it would often happen that some supporter of the government would enlarge on the same type of argument, though his words might be lost in the hubbub or summarily brushed aside. At Chelmsford Herbert Croft referred to the corruption of the whigs at an earlier period, and the great fortune acquired by Sir Robert Walpole, "who had built a fine seat, enriched his family, and collected at immense expense a fine collection of pictures which had recently been sold to Russia", He then reminded the audience of Lord Holland:

Happy Lord Holland to leave behind him at the same time the rarest example of eloquence [Fox], and its fittest subject [i.e. his own corruption].

Why did the petition not become more specific and "point out particular grievances", such as Mr Townshend's Tellership of the Exchequer, and Lord Camden's reversion, Croft went on to ask. Then as a shrewd thrust against the Yorkshiremen, who dreaded

[1] See e.g. H.M.C., *Rutland Mss.* III, 22-23, The Duke to the Duchess of Rutland, 8 Dec. 1779: "Almost an universal bankruptcy among the tenants if rents are not lowered is constantly expected." Cf. *Gentleman's Magazine*, Feb. 1780, pp. 120-21, and April 1780, p. 187.

the proposal, he suggested that the burden in the country would be more fairly distributed if the petition could secure an equalization of the land-tax, which bore heavily on Essex.[1] It is to the credit of Horace Walpole, that he recognized and faced one of the prime anomalies, and, when invited to sign the petition of Westminster, recalled that he possessed nothing in the world save sinecures and pensions that he owed to his father.[2] He was a friend of Rev. William Mason; he sympathized with the Yorkshire movement; and he said that he would even submit his fate to the popular decision. He would not affect to sign a petition, however, when he was one of the abuses that were being petitioned against.

Those who were opposed to the petitioning movement, however, soon found themselves confronted by a curious difficulty. It was obvious that they could not adopt a direct counter-petition and send to the house of commons a document that deprecated economy in public expenditure. And when they resolved to issue protests—manifestoes that had no actual prayer to put forward—it was not technically possible for the house to accept these, or to bring them under formal consideration. In so far as they attacked the men who had petitioned, Fox could declare that the protests themselves were libellous and were controverting the ancient right of Englishmen—the right to petition king or parliament. Protests were drawn up and signed, however, where, as in Hertfordshire, Huntingdonshire, Norfolk, Sussex, and Surrey, a section of the country objected to the course that the critics of the government had chosen to follow. And these protests tended to adhere to a certain pattern, the basic formulas having already been put into circulation by the supporters of the ministry. The impulse behind them came at least in part from government influence in one locality and another.

In these counter-manifestoes it would be urged sometimes that the meeting of the freeholders had been called at too short notice, or that in some manner the business had been carried through without an opportunity for due consideration. Generally it would be asserted that no proof had been given of the grievances in question; allegations and insinuations had been inserted in the address to the

[1] *Norwich Mercury*, 29 Jan., *York Courant*, 1 Feb.
[2] *Letters of Horace Walpole* (ed. Toynbee), XI, 236–39.

house of commons, but there was no evidence in support of these. The demand that there should be a certain withholding of supplies until specified reforms had been undertaken was an attack on the freedom of the legislative body, an encroachment on the house of commons in a sphere peculiarly its own, and a form of blackmail directed against the government. It represented a policy fraught with danger when the country stood desperate in the midst of a war, not only against the American colonies, but also against the combined Bourbon powers. The distress in the country was the natural accompaniment of such a war. In any case the petitions, the committees, the underlying tendencies of the whole movement, were of no assistance to the nation—they operated to divide the country. The result could only be dissidence and mutual suspicion; this, at a moment when the crisis called so loudly for unanimity.

Finally there was a resolution of protest which in varying forms of words was almost universally adopted by the critics of the movement. It referred to the creation of Committees of Correspondence, and the talk of the possible establishment of an "Association". Even amongst the petitioners as we have seen—even amongst Yorkshire supporters of the movement at the beginning of January—these measures of "ulterior action" had already produced a certain doubt and misgiving. Even amongst those who had voted in their favour or had agreed to become members of the Committee, there were regrets, there was sometimes an inclination to believe that one had been carried further than one had meant to go. "The measure of forming committees and entering into associations was a great stumbling-block in some of the counties," says the *Annual Register*. "Associations and committees had produced such recent effects in America, and even in Ireland, that the very terms were suspicious." Suffolk, Derbyshire, Hereford and Northumberland adopted the petition but declined to form committees. In Kent we shall see petitions produced by two different parties at the general meeting; and while the one party wished only to appeal for an economical reform, the other would have nothing less than the Committee of Correspondence too, with the object of arriving later also at a Plan of Association. The Lord Lieutenant and gentry who met for purposes of protest in Surrey declared their intention of refraining from any attack on the petition itself—they would confine their objections, they said, to the Committee and the intention of associating. In Sussex the protesting parties declared that "public œconomy is undoubtedly necessary," but rejected "the declared purpose of forming General Associations apparently tending to overrule the Legislature". At Northampton the original general meeting was persuaded to drop the plan of producing a petition at all. This county was anxious, indeed, to see public economy, but decided merely to instruct its parliamentary representatives to work at Westminster on behalf of the good cause.[1]

The formulation which was given to the protest against this aspect of the movement is illustrated in one of the resolutions put forward by those who had disagreed with the course of the proceedings at the Hertfordshire meeting. Here the minority had vainly attempted at the "previous" meeting to separate the petition from the rest of the programme—to confine the object to a prayer for public economy—if only for the sake of procuring unanimity. The Hertfordshire Protest runs:

> We do most particularly protest against the Resolution for appointing a Committee of Correspondence, apparently tending to over-awe the Legislature, by collecting and combining the factious Discontents of the several parts of the Kingdom into one System upon which to found Powers, and introduce Measures, inconsistent with and subversive of our present happy Constitution and to establish a Plan which appears to us to lead to the greatest Calamities which can befall our Country: namely, *Insurrection! Confusion!* and *Anarchy!*[2]

The corresponding Nottingham Protest ran:

> We conceive that combinations and associations, such as now are attempting to be established in this country, have a manifest

[1] *York Courant*, 8 Feb. According to the *London Courant* of 13 March, Mr. Trevelyan at the Northumberland meeting of 8 March supported the petition "only on condition there were no committees or associations".

[2] *York Courant*, 8 Feb. There is a reply to this Protest in *The Yorkshire Freeholder*, No. V, 17 Feb. 1780. Cf. *ibid.* No. VI, 24 Feb. 1780, p. 34.

tendency ... to [render] Parliament the mere register of the edicts of the Committee and [to transfer] the sovereignty from the senate to private cabals and self-created assemblies.[1]

Here, then, the issue was drawn, and it was precisely to this point that the parliamentary enemies of the Yorkshire movement chose in turn to direct their attacks. In the house of commons there was no large-scale attempt, of the kind that there had been in January 1770, to discredit the petitions in themselves and to analyse away the virtue of the petitioning movement altogether. North was amiable and tactful in response to the bombardment that he received, when on one occasion after another he was told that "the people" had made known their demands, the counties had spoken, the freeholders of England had issued their fiat. It was he who remained sober and quietly reasonable while the frantic members of the opposition stormed. And he did not join the disreputables in the arguments *ad hominem,* the taunts about Lord Holland, the outcry against the Duke of Richmond. He said that he would not identify himself with an attack on property—even on the sinecures of his aristocratic whig enemies. North, in fact, conceded the right of petition with both hands. He conceded more than he was asked to give, more than it was convenient for his enemies to have granted to them—he said that a petition, even if it came from three people only, had a claim on the attention of the house of commons.[2] His tactics were shrewd, for in the very act of showing generosity, he undermined the opposition more completely—he emphasized the fact that the petitions in any case only came from individuals. He drew a clear line, and pointed out that the petitions adopted in York and elsewhere comprised the prayers of only those people who had signed them—not the demands of "Yorkshire", or the desires of "the freeholders of England" or the instructions of the

---

[1] *Morning Chronicle,* 9 Feb. 1780. On the Nottingham Corporation 18 of the members forming a body that renewed itself by co-optation, carried the petition. The six "junior counsel" who were elected by the burgesses protested. For the Surrey Protest see *York Courant,* 15 Feb.; for the Norfolk Protest, *Morning Chronicle,* 24 March.

[2] *Morning Chronicle,* 11 Feb. 1780; *Gazetteer,* 12 Feb. 1780. *Parliamentary History,* XX, 1388. Cf. *The Yorkshire Freeholder,* No. VI, 24 Feb. 1780, pp. 34–5.

nation; not necessarily even the wishes of the majority of the free-holders in whatever locality might be concerned. Neither would he consent at a later stage in the proceedings to recognize the petition of a quasi-political organ, a delegated body, a self-styled "representative group", whether it claimed to stand for a county or for the country as a whole, whether it was a local Committee or an Assembly of Deputies.[1] Still he would hold to his argument that a petition carried no more than its own weight, and amounted to no more than an expression of the desires of those men who had appended their signatures. By this method he challenged the Yorkshire movement at its most sensitive point, and denied to the local Committees that representative character which was essential to their argument. There were men very ready to point out that the signatures to the petitions, numerous though they were, did not comprise the majority of the freeholders of the various localities. Within the ranks of the radicals themselves there was liable to arise a discordant note: Why the majority of freeholders only? Why should they have the weight, while all the rest of the people were allowed to count as nothing?[2] Savile, therefore, was wise, when, on presenting the Yorkshire petition to the house of commons on 8 February, he stressed not so much the number of the petitioners but their imposing character—the weight of property which they could claim to have behind them.

Furthermore, though North had been so willing to grant that even the petition of only three freeholders had a claim on the attention of the house, he drew a further distinction: he would not admit that the petition of 3 or 3,000 or 30,000 could claim to have a thing conceded merely because it was asked for. He repudiated the suggestion that now the house, without inquiry into the matter, without reflection upon its own responsibilities, should instantly grant what the petitions were alleged to demand.

It happened that Savile, when he presented the Yorkshire petition to the house on 8 February, overplayed his argument and showed his hand too completely, evidently becoming indiscreet in his threats and insinuations. "I make no threats," he said at one

[1] E.g. North's remarks of 11 Feb. 1780, York Courant, 22 Feb.
[2] See pp. 297, 342 below. Cf. William Hussey in Parliamentary History, xxi, 177.

moment; "this petition is not presented by men with swords and muskets." But then he went on to declare: "But if it should be refused—here I leave a blank, that blank let the consciences, let the feelings, let the reason of ministers supply." North, never the man to miss such a debating-opportunity, met the menaces with that tranquillity which was calculated by contrast to make them appear the more disreputable. "He had been threatened with unknown but severe consequences," he said, "if he should so much as delay granting the requested redress until an enquiry should be made into the existence, nature and extent of the alledged grievances." Fox replied that Lord North had not been so slow and cautious when it had been the case of an Irish petition, backed by sanctions and charged with menace. Obviously he wished to teach the English not to expect redress unless their prayers were similarly supported. Obviously he wished it to be known that he would only give way to that kind of pressure which had coercive effect. Fox repeated the thesis:

The people are not in arms, they do not menace civil war. They have in their power, legal, constitutional means of enforcing their petition.

He then reduced the menaces to the mere suggestion that, if their petitions were ignored, the people "would lose all confidence in their representatives, all reverence for Parliament". Even here he added a sting, however, for in tones of menace, he threw out the comment: "The consequences of such a situation I need not point out."

North had other arguments against the petitioners on occasion. These latter were ill-informed, for example, and "the true state of pensions was but very imperfectly known," so that complaints were sometimes built on misunderstandings. But with North, as with the supporters of government in general, one final distinction was all-important. Men had a right to petition, it was true, but "Associations at present he held to be highly dangerous." There was a tendency to confuse the existing Committees with the Association, though this latter was still strictly speaking only a plan for the future as yet. Lord Mulgrave declared that "the associations had

as much as declared, that if parliament did not grant the prayer of
the petitions other means would be taken than those the petitioners
had used." Wedderburn stated one point with accuracy, as we
shall see:

> He believed the motives of far the greatest part of the petitioners
> were perfectly pure, but . . . there were persons who signed the
> petitions, who, if he should gravely state to them, that he believed
> they entered implicitly from conviction into the measure, would
> laugh at his folly. . . . That class of petitioners were incited by
> motives of a higher cast, and of a more extensive nature.[1]

William Adam declared that he did not fear the present associations (that is to say the Committees) "because he trusted to the
moderation of the gentlemen engaged in them". In themselves
they were of dangerous tendency, however, and

> if they should become general they might at last degenerate into
> meetings absolutely dictatorial, and which, in the end would
> render parliament a mere court of record to register their arbitrary
> edicts.

The burden is always the same. William Burrell on 8 March said
in the house of commons:

> He for one approved of petitions; he was himself a petitioner, but
> he totally disapproved of committees and associations. . . . He
> knew of no way to collect the voice of the majority of the people,
> but by the majority of the freeholders; and . . . not above an eighth
> of that description had signed the petitions. . . .
> They [the petitioners] plainly aimed at the destruction of the
> independency of parliament, by tying down the members to
> certain measures.

Earliest of all, on 8 February the Earl of Hillsborough had stated
this side of the argument in the house of lords. "They [the Com-
mittees]" he said, "were set up as another estate unknown to the

---

[1] *Parliamentary History*, XXI, 96; cf. *ibid.* 107, where he quotes a judgment that
associations, "though for legal purposes, were in themselves illegal".

constitution. They would, if not timely suppressed, lead to anarchy and public confusion."[1]

Here, then, were all the materials for a counter-movement, and in the course of February it was no longer so plausible to claim that the nation rose as one, surging up in a single resistance-movement that was all the more imposing because it seemed to be above politics and party. No longer did the cry for public economy produce the unity that transcended faction, the unity that could be said to over-ride the divisions of classes. The leaders had to be careful. Always they reiterated the words "legal and constitutional" when they spoke of the Association, declaring rightly that they were meditating no appeal to force. But by their very insistence they reveal perhaps a doubt; or they seemed to assume that the prefix "legal and constitutional" would suffice to put things right; or—on occasion one may feel—they even protest too much. Wyvill had set to work to reassure the Yorkshiremen in the middle of January and had disclosed to the public what we might call the minimum definition of his intentions in regard to the Association. Later it became a custom for the Committees to prefix a set of resolutions (or preface their Plan of Association) with a formula which put on record their satisfaction with the form of government by king, lords and commons, already established. At a comparatively early date the Committees set out to publish reassurances, as in the case of the Essex County Committee which made the following announcement on 5 February:

To obviate misapprehension . . . the Committee . . . declare that they do not now nor ever did mean to promote the reform aimed at by any other mode than that of a peaceable demeanour, steady loyalty and respectful application to the legislature.[2]

---

[1] *Parliamentary History*, XXI, 1352. Cf. *Political Memoranda of the Fifth Duke of Leeds*, 18n: "No one could know to what dangerous lengths such institutions might proceed, tho[ugh] perhaps originating from the best and most constitutional principles." See also Letter IV by "An Old Freeholder" in *London Chronicle*, 15-18 April, drawing analogies between the Yorkshire Association and the League in sixteenth-century France; and the remarks of the Bishop of Peterborough, p. 374 below.

[2] *Cambridge Chronicle*, 12 Feb. 1780.

The Committee of Flintshire published a more remarkable disclaimer which ran as follows:

> The Committee of the County of Flintshire take leave to inform the public, whose opinions they respect, that they have no factious or seditious objects in view; that they wish only to co-operate with those national endeavours that are now become general to recommend that economy and good management to the Legislature which our public and private wants have rendered so necessary. We wish not to weaken the powers of government. . . . It is the farthest from our intention to influence Parliament by other means than respectful Petitions, reason and good sense, for we wish always to see our representatives equally free from fear as from corruption. . . . Should we fail in our endeavours, this good at least will result from the design itself, that we shall hereby furnish the people at the approaching elections with an unerring rule to distinguish the true friends of their country.[1]

§III. THE ASSOCIATION

In the process by which we come to apprehend our history more profoundly and to rectify anachronistic crudities or faults in interpretation, it often happens that much importance will attach to the meaning of a term, and especially to those insinuations and implications, those flavours and nuances, which carry us beyond mere dictionary definitions, and at a particular period of time endow an apparently plain and simple word with a peculiar stimulus and a fringe of super-added suggestiveness. Something of this is clearly the case with the word Association at the point we have now reached in English history; and we must not imagine that we are merely concerned with a society for the propagation of a doctrine or with an institution that seeks to bring into fraternal contact with one another a number of like-minded men. Even in Johnson's *Dictionary* some critics were ready to pounce on the sinister connotations of the synonym "confederacy", and the defenders of the Yorkshire Association can be seen deprecating this resort to a

[1] *London Courant*, 9 March.

dictionary definition. Wyvill himself said that he wished he could drop the word Association if the word itself was the stumbling-block.[1]

In 1780 we shall find this particular word reaching the peak of its notoriety, as more than one movement which helps to load it with significance now comes to its culmination. To understand what happened we must try to contemplate the crisis with which we are dealing, not as it appears to us to-day (when we can see how, in fact, all the weapons of the opposition were to misfire) but rather as it impinged on the consciousness of contemporaries, whether they were the friends or the enemies of Lord North. That Wedder-burn was right in saying that this was more than an ordinary peti-tioning movement, and that some of its partisans would laugh at the naivety of those who imagined them to be merely anxious to remedy the waste of public money, is clear in a hundred ways. The point becomes explicit in the speech of Thomas Day to the free-holders of Essex on 25 April 1780:

The ostensible object of your meeting was a petition for a re-form in the public expenditure. . . . But however necessary might be the measure, I must here publicly confess, that had I bounded my hopes with the mere objects of the first petition, I should no more have interested myself in its fate, than in a project for a turnpike-road, or a navigable canal.[2]

In the middle of December a London paper made the announce-ment of the forthcoming Yorkshire meeting and declared that it was going to be "a second Runnymeade".[3] Sir George Savile, a comparatively moderate supporter of the Yorkshire design, used the word National Assembly when he spoke of the projected organization, and admitted that the nickname of "anti-parliament" would be justified. Over and over again the supporters of the

[1] *The Yorkshire Freeholder*, No. 1, 20 Jan. 1780, pp. 2 and 5; *York Chronicle*, 28 Jan., p. 4, col. 1–2; *Wyvill Papers*, III, 175.
[2] *Speech of Thomas Day at the General Meeting of the Counties of Cambridge and Essex* (1780), p. 11.
[3] *London Evening Post*, 14–16 Dec. 1779.

movement refer to two imposing historical precedents: they say
that the body which forced Magna Carta on the King was an Association, and so was that "Convention Parliament" which placed
William and Mary on the throne at a time when a legitimate parliament could not be brought into existence. Throughout the literature of the movement there runs the idea that now the quasi-
revolutionary moment, the crisis of English liberty, has arrived.
Thomas Day, in his above-mentioned speech at the Essex meeting,
said that "forms and ceremonies must yield to the extremity of
your danger." "It was now as expedient for the people at large to
interfere", said N. Calvert at the Hertfordshire meeting, "as at the
time when Magna Charta and the Bill of Rights were granted."[1]
Even the Rockinghamite peers in those early days when they supported all that had been set on foot at the meeting of the Yorkshire freeholders, took the line that here was one of those rare
occasions when the direct interposition of the people over-rides the
normal operations of government.

If in the eighteenth century the term whig so often implied the
man who meant to conserve the results of the Glorious Revolution
and the Hanoverian Succession, it now seemed to be used on
occasion in an older, larger and more striking sense. There was a
tendency to argue that the Yorkshire Association was a whig
movement; for, to be a whig, was it not to be essentially and cosmic-
ally anti-King—to be willing to summon the people at the critical
moment to a campaign which was directed against nothing less
than the throne itself? "Assemble the Freeholders," said a letter
in the *London Courant* of 23 December 1779; then came the remark
which reveals so much, even in what it thinks to concede: "They
are not however called upon as their ancestors have often been to
take up arms in defence of their rights."

Once again had come what to the whigs was their historic
moment—the day when gloves were taken off and the issue was
finally drawn between monarchy and "the people". It was an interim version of the day of judgment, and in his address to the

---

[1] *York Chronicle*, 21 Jan. 1780. Cf. note 1 p. 193 above: "a republican congress for new modelling the constitution.".

electors of Middlesex in December 1779, Jebb spoke of

that solemn hour, when the delegates of a state chosen according to forms, which not law and custom, but necessity or expenditure shall prescribe, and assembling for the purpose of inquiring into the abuse of power shall sit in awful judgment upon the traiterous invaders of their rights.[1]

To such delegates, to such an assembly alone, he continued, "the tremendous name of majesty may, with propriety, be attributed." Not only did the movement invoke the more drastic doctrines to which the whigs had resorted only at moments of extreme urgency —at the final settling of accounts so to speak—but in a large and at the same time definite sense it took from the ancient whigs its object and purpose—the restoration of the constitution to its original principles.[2] Lord Carysfort, writing to the Huntingdonshire meeting, gives an example of the way in which the teaching of Locke was used to support the argument:

Mr Locke is of opinion that "there remains inherent in the people a power to remove or alter the legislative, when they find the legislative act contrary to the trust reposed in them" . . . W en the Constitution has been corrupted . . . it has been usual to have recourse not to the ordinary forms of Parliament, but to an extraordinary delegation from the people, chosen for the express purpose of enquiring and ascertaining the laws and liberties of the kingdom.

He refers to the delegations of twelve members sent from each of the counties in the time of William the Conqueror, which "according to Sir Matthew Hale . . . appears to have been as sufficient and effectual a Parliament, as ever was held in England". He

[1] *Works*, II, 469. Cf. "I.A." writing in the *Public Advertiser*, 31 Dec. 1779: "This Meeting at York it is hoped will not be considered as a County Meeting only, but be resorted to as a national Consult on public calamity." Robert Robinson in a sermon of 30 Jan. 1780 [*Works*, III, 301,] says "judging [government] belongs in ordinary cases to the delegates and in extraordinary cases it reverts to the people."

[2] *Constitutionalists' Letters to the Electors and People of England preparatory to the approaching General Election* (1780), p. 4.

quotes a further case in 1223, during the reign of Henry III; this, he says, led to Magna Carta.[1]

The *Leeds Mercury* for 25 January announces:

The intention of assembling the independent gentlemen of the different counties at this alarming juncture, is to elect Committees to whom the power of the people is to be delegated, and which Committees, or a delegation from them, is to form a convention, to consult and agree on the most effectual and constitutional measures to stop the progress of corruption.

It is curious to note that one political writer of the previous decade had set out to show that the historic moment, the quasi-revolutionary crisis was approaching; and this was in the work which laid out the programme of what we might call the Association *par excellence*. The work is one which was quoted on a number of occasions by Jebb in our period, and was referred to by Wilkes when he brought forward his motion for parliamentary reform in 1776. It became the subject of a curious remark by Dr. Parr, who, when asked if he had read it, answered: "Have I not read my bible, sir?" The author in question was James Burgh, who had produced in 1754 a book entitled *The Dignity of Human Nature*, dedicated to the Dowager-Princess of Wales; had meditated the writing of a political treatise for the education of the Prince of Wales; and in 1766 had published *Crito*, dedicated in advance "to the good people of Britain of the twentieth century". He was evidently a fanatic on the subject of associations, for in *Crito* he tells how he had hoped to found a Grand National Association for the production of more virtuous periodical literature that would seek to counteract the influence of the philosophy of Bolingbroke.[2] Two years before that

---

[1] *A letter from the Rt. Hon. Lord Carysfort to the Huntingdonshire Committee* (dated from Dublin, 27 Feb. 1780), pp. 7 and 15; cf. Jebb, *Works*, II, 471–72 n. Cf. *The Yorkshire Freeholder*, No. XII, 6 April 1780. Also *The Association vindicated*, (1780), p. 11, which adds: "The people must necessarily judge for themselves when . . . to put in force this dormant principle," the mode of action varying "from the humble Petition . . . to the last solemn and awful appeal to Heaven."

[2] *Crito*, II, 207 *et seqq.* Cf. the Dedication, p. 18: "We read newspapers. We dispute in coffee-houses and taverns. We drink party-toasts. But we have not yet come to a resolution for associating, petitioning, or instructing."

—in 1764—he had proposed an association "against the iniquitous Practices of Engrossers, Forestallers, Jobbers, etc., and for reducing the Price of Provisions, especially Butchers' meat". He suggests elsewhere an association for the support of public credit which was "to prevent the diminution of the Stocks". He also makes reference to an association of people who would engage to give domestic servants their true character in testimonials.[1]

It was in 1774-75, however, that he published his three volumes of *Political Disquisitions,* a curious compilation, packed with long extracts from ancient writers, modern historians, political philosophers, publicists like Davenant and Bolingbroke, and speeches, chiefly of members of the opposition in the time of the first two Georges—the whole directed to the study of the evils of corruption, of placemen, of an inadequate representative system, etc., on the theory that the entire body politic was becoming corrupt. Practically two hundred pages—which amounted almost to a half —of the third volume are devoted to an imposing Conclusion "addressed to the independent Part of the People of Great Britain, Ireland and the Colonies". This section codifies Burgh's teaching on the decline of liberty in a state—much of it in the manner of Bolingbroke and with references to some of Machiavelli's theses on this subject—and it predicts that the final crisis is near. Indeed, while referring to the dangers of insurrection and the possible emergence of tyrants like Cromwell, it attacks as the ultimate evil the inertia of the people and even says that "desperate diseases require desperate remedies." But, says Burgh:

All sound patriots will avoid rousing the people, if redress can be any other way obtained. Therefore I do not propose having recourse to force. What I propose is, to apply the power of the people, guided, limited, and directed by men of property, who are interested in the security of their country, and have no income, by place or pension, to indemnify them for bringing slavery and ruin upon their country. . . .

Before all other things, there must be established a GRAND NATIONAL ASSOCIATION FOR RESTORING THE CONSTITUTION. Into this must be invited all men of property,

[1] *Crito,* II, 87.

all friends to liberty, all able commanders, etc. There must be a copy of the ASSOCIATION for every parish, and a parochial committee to procure subscriptions from all persons whose names are in any tax-book, and who are willing to join the Association. And there must be a grand committee for every county in the three kingdoms, and in the colonies of *America*. . . .

By the readiness of people to enter into the associations, it may be effectually determined, whether the majority are desirous of the proposed reformations. This, as has been observed before, is a matter of supreme consequence, for resistance to government, unless it be by a clear majority of the people, is rebellion.

When he asks who should be the head of the Association, he suggests first of all the king; and, picking up one of the themes of the earlier "Patriot" literature he says: "Would to God, the Father of his people would lay hold of such an opportunity of declaring himself a friend to independent parliaments." Alternatively he thinks of the "independent nobility", by which he means roughly speaking the Rockinghamites. But if these should fail, he declaims: "let the great, the rich, the independent city of London take the lead." Very soon in fact he is calling it the *London* Association.

The objects of such a general association as I propose are 1. The securing of public credit. 2. Obtaining the undoubted sense of the people, on the state of public affairs. 3. Presenting petitions, signed by a clear majority of the people of property, for the necessary acts of parliament. 4. To raise, and have in readiness, the strength of the nation, in order to influence government and prevent mischief.

The initial example of the London petition was to be followed by "all the great cities, towns, counties, corporate bodies and faculties". The acts of parliament required would be ones "for restoring annual parliaments, for making representation adequate, for exclusion by rotation, and for limiting the number of placemen and pensioners sitting in the house". What is interesting is the bold suggestion that there should be some form of action to render the petitioning effectual, "to raise the strength of the nation against the government". For Burgh, though he talks of peaceful methods,

gives now a series of examples to show how governments and parliaments have been coerced and overborne by the direct action of
the people in the past. He says:

Members of parliament would hardly dare to reject the proposed
reformation-bill, as knowing themselves not to be invulnerable,
and remembering that they could not command a guard of 500
soldiers each at their country houses at all times.

He uses the language of desperation at this point:

Ten millions of people are not to sit still and see a villainous junto
overthrow their liberties. Formalities are then at an end. The
question, in a season of such extremity, is not, who has a *right* to do
this or that? Any man has a right to save his country.

He betrays the quasi-revolutionary implications of his plan when
he writes:

If the contest is between a designing minister, a mercenary army,
and a corrupt parliament on the one hand, and on the other, the
body of the independent people, the decision may prove difficult
but is most likely to be in favour of liberty, if the people can only
unite, and act in concert. For if the cause be unquestionably good,
the people will soon have purse, and army, and every thing else
in their hands.

Finally he says: "I know nothing of war, and therefore can propose
nothing concerning the conduct of it; but to wish that it may be
avoided if possible." He refuses to go into further details lest he
should "alarm the more timorous part of readers, and render them
less inclined to join the grand national association".

Cartwright at the end of his famous booklet, *Take Your Choice,*
1776—so long reputed the pioneer work in the movements of this
period—makes great use of Burgh and reproduces at considerable
length his plan of an Association. He deprecates, however, the suggestion of violence and the hint of a *coup de main,* and he sees a way
out of the difficulty—recommends an alternative method that will
overcome the inertia or the resistance of parliament. He points

out that if the membership of the new organization is widened in order to include all Englishmen (not merely property-holders) the proposed system of delegation will be too imposing for anybody to resist—by its own weight it will carry everything before it. It is interesting to note that Cartwright in 1776 says that he has reason for believing in the early emergence of such a movement—the necessary leadership is going to appear in the near future. Jebb, whose recommendations to the county of Middlesex were founded on Burgh—and who often quotes this writer—speaks of having talked of the plan to Sir George Savile in the same year. The indications would suggest, therefore, that 1776 is a significant date. It was at this very time that Wilkes alluded to the authority of Burgh, when speaking on behalf of parliamentary reform in the house of commons.

The movement of 1780 is permeated with these ideas and packed with the identical insinuations. The quasi-revolutionary character of the scheme is demonstrated when we examine the attitude it adopted in regard to the question of "sanctions", the question of the actual pressure to be applied in order to achieve the desired end. Those who feared the unpredictable things that might issue from such a movement would not be reassured to see how imprecise were the prevailing ideas in regard to this matter, how much the leaders relied on a vague feeling that possessed them—an assurance that here they had discovered a form of power. The government and the parliament were repeatedly informed that the people had their own means of redress if their petitions were not granted. Lurking somewhere in speeches and pamphlets there always seemed to be a more or less unspecified threat.[1] In any case there is constant reference to the Associations in America and Ireland, where the people had learned that if they desired redress they must gird their loins and secure the reformation for themselves. With the Volunteer Associations in Ireland the English counterpart was to conduct a correspondence, and the two movements were regarded as one. "Take the Irish receipt in order to turn members of parliament into

---

[1] See e.g. *Rockingham Memoirs*, II, 393–95, where William Cowper writes, 13 Feb.: "They tell the Government that the spirit of resistance is gone forth . . . and bid them slight the York petition at their peril."

honest men," said one writer. On 5 January 1780 we read in the *London Courant*:

The House of Commons of Ireland were never remarkable for patriotism or independence until their constituents obliged them to [be so].

In England in 1780 various devices were being considered and discussed. The demand that no new taxes should be granted until some measure had been adopted to remedy public extravagance was itself an ineffectual attempt to impose a "sanction". Again it was urged in England that if the petitions were rejected the minority in both houses should secede from parliament, put themselves at the head of the Association and then confront what would be merely the rump of the corrupt legislature. Fox and Richmond, who went further than the rest of the Rockinghamites in support of the movement, were threatening this policy in parliament in March, May and June 1780, and Jebb wrote in its favour to the Huntingdonshire Committee.[1]

The Rev. William Mason in a letter to Horace Walpole gave his approbation to the idea of a refusal by the people to pay taxes.[2] Burgh had suggested the policy of electing members of parliament for one year only and then refusing obedience—refusing to pay the taxes, for example—if the house of commons pretended to sit after the expiry of the period of their delegation.[3] A correspondent who signed himself "Alfred", and who may have been Jebb, wrote to the *London Courant* on 30 March 1780, declaring that the extension of annual parliaments to the septennial period had been *ultra vires*, and that there should be an Association of men refusing to pay taxes levied by a parliament that had outlived its proper period. Horace Walpole, when he was hearing the Yorkshire news direct from William Mason, told how one of the leaders of the move-

[1] Cf. *Public Advertiser*, 21 Dec. 1779; *London Evening Post*, 14–16 Dec. 1779; *Leeds Mercury*, 1 Feb. 1780; and *Gazetteer*, 15 May, 1780.

[2] Mitford, *Correspondence of H. Walpole and Rev. W. Mason*, II. 90.

[3] See e.g. a letter signed "Buckingham" in the *London Chronicle*, 5 March 1780; "Anglo-Saxon": *The Duty of a Freeman, addressed to the Electors of Great Britain*, 4 Sept. 1780, p. 9; and letters from "Alfred" in *Cambridge Chronicle*, 15 April.

ment in that county had advised the preparation of arms, though his proposal had been suppressed. In any case the question would be raised at times: The Irish have arms; why not also the English? And particularly after the Gordon riots we hear much about the right of freemen to carry arms in the defence of their property and liberty. Burgh had made side-glances at direct mob-action—had recalled how the Irish had formed an Association, and the populace had exerted pressure in Dublin, to secure the act of 1768 which reduced the duration of the Irish parliament to eight years. One writer acknowledged that the proposed new organ, like the house of commons itself, might be subject to imperfections as a representative institution; even he, however, claimed that its decisions were beyond question once they had been reported back to the county meetings and ratified by the direct action of the people. And when it was urged against the Association of 1780 that such a body was bound to be dangerous if the house of commons failed to satisfy its demands, the very men who bitterly resented the imputation provided further reinforcement for it; they argued that the case could not arise—that the house of commons would never dare to contravene the wishes of the people so unmistakably expressed. Even men so moderate as Lord Rockingham and his friends, in a Protest of the minority in the house of lords on 8 February—actually in the very act of defending the constitutional character of the Yorkshire movement—could say that, if people were apprehensive concerning what might happen in the event of the petitions being rejected, such a dangerous contingency was not at all likely to occur. The house of commons certainly had the power "to vote as they think fit",

but it is not possible to conceive that so wise an assembly will ever be rash enough to reject such petitions and by that means cause the dangerous question to be broached and agitated, *Whether they have not broke their Trust*.[1]

There was one "sanction", however, concerning which a wider measure of agreement could be obtained. It represented Wyvill's

[1] *Parliamentary History*, XX, 1369–70.

minimum definition of his plan, a definition which concealed some of his intentions, but reassured the timid. The Association was to combine in one body those freeholders and other electors who would engage to vote for no parliamentary candidate save such as would commit themselves to supporting its objects, by either becoming members of it or issuing an explicit statement. The Society of the Supporters of the Bill of Rights had been moving towards this, and the scheme was a development of the principles adopted by Wilkes and his faction in the general election of 1774.[1] There can be no doubt that Wyvill, in promoting the Yorkshire movement, had in mind—apart from more radical projects involving what Savile called the "anti-parliament"—the idea of influencing the next general election which was to take place fairly soon. In the course of the movement the whole policy of issuing "tests" to candidates for parliament and transmitting instructions from constituencies to their members became alive again, as we shall see. Burgh on one occasion had noted that the eve of a general election was an excellent time to chose for the formation of the Association.[2]

This whole scheme envisages the Association as something like a modern political party, where electors and elected are pledged to a general programme or system of policy; and it calls to mind an advertisement which appeared in the papers in 1774, inviting all who wished for the overthrow of the existing ministry to join in an Association for that specific purpose.[3] We are at a stage in the evolution of the modern kind of political party based on an agreement concerning specific ideas or cooperation in regard to certain issues; and it is difficult to imagine any other way in which something of this kind could have inserted itself into the eighteenth-century system, where political groups were based so largely on family connections, personal attachments, and private influence. This whole aspect of the Association—which had in view a body of people merely pledged to an electoral programme—had its

[1] Add. Mss. 30,895, f. 51. Engagement taken by Wilkes and Glynn, 26 Sept. 1774.

[2] In the closing weeks of 1779, attention was being called to the possibility of an early dissolution of Parliament; e.g. London Courant, 6 Dec. 1779; Jebb, Works, II, 459n.

[3] London Evening Post, 5-7 July 1774.

classic statement in an anonymous *Historical Essay on the English Constitution*, published in 1771. It is interesting to note that this work was used by Burgh and provided some of the constituents of his theory.[1]

All this represents the crown and culmination in the development of the idea of the Association which had had an increasing importance in the preceding period and marked the growth in independence and consciousness—the impulse to self-help—in an advancing society. The scheme envisaged by the Yorkshire leaders put an arch over all the others. It was to be a combination of all the men of property in the kingdom—these acting in their capacity as ultimate holders of sovereignty. Henry Neville had written in *Plato Redivivus* in 1681 that the wide distribution of property had "made the country scarce governable by Monarchy". In the reign of William III a pamphleteer could argue that if the king bought up all the freehold land of the country he could elect himself knight of every shire "and so become absolute monarch". Though a statute passed by king, lords, and commons had a sovereign validity in the eighteenth century, there was an internal check upon the legislature —a kind of inhibition; for both logically and chronologically property was anterior to the house of commons. It would not have been thought proper for parliament to change the place of the house of lords in the constitution. How much less proper it would be for either the lords or the commons to prescribe the revision of the representative system itself! Just as it could be argued that an association of fund-holders was the proper body to deal with the problem of the national debt—since, so to speak, they were the property-owners concerned—so it was claimed by Granville Sharp in 1777 and by the radicals in the Yorkshire movement that the king must consult the constituencies directly if he thought of moving towards

---

[1] See e.g. p. 62. "The barons . . . immediately entered into an association . . . to obtain the re-establishment . . . particularly [of] the elective power of the people. This was the first association that was ever made in England. . . ." p. 161. "The only effectual remedy . . . is to enter into legal associations. . . . The head of these associations should be in London. And the friends to the constitution, in every market-town in England, should establish the like there, and mutually correspond with each other. I could even wish to see a constitutional club established in every parish."

parliamentary reform. The writer of the *Occasional Letters upon Taxation* in 1780 agreed with Jebb in suggesting that the county committees might bring about a Federal Union with the American colonies.

Finally, the leaders of the Yorkshire movement were "cataclysmic" in the idea that they had of the process of things in time, and held a conception of "decadence" which was already in some respects out of harmony with the age. They saw the necessity for an immediate success, for if there was the least delay it would be too late to attempt anything; there was a point where corruption became complete—the hated system of George III, clamped down, and with everything interlocked, would have established a permanent despotism. "One more Septennial Parliament", wrote "Alfred" (probably Jebb) in the *Cambridge Chronicle* for 15 April 1780, "will inevitably prove the ruin of old England." And it meant misery and failure to them when occasionally they thought of themselves in the way we now think of them—namely, as serving for nothing but to educate the people and to be an example for future times.

Chapter VII

THE DECISIVE CONFLICTS

§1. FOX *versus* WYVILL

THE Westminster Committee—like the others that had been formed in town and country—was constituted in a manner ideally calculated to permit its domination by a handful of men. The quorum was fixed at seven and it appears that, out of over ninety members, just over twenty were present at the first three meetings, and approximately thirty-six on the three following occasions. Of the whole body only a few were virtually continuous in their attendance in the early period of the movement— indeed, apart from the case of a dozen men or so attendance was casual, and many people would turn up perhaps for only a single meeting. Of the twenty-two who were at the opening meeting some seven do not reappear for a considerable time. It was a body in which a group of men who attended regularly and knew what they wanted had the opportunity to gain an extraordinary predominance. It was the ideal example of the kind of committee in which those who disagree with the proceedings—especially those whose dissent proceeds from their love of moderation—can achieve very little by their presence and in any case almost inevitably cease to attend. And amongst the persistent absentees were often distinguished peers and politicians whose names on the list of membership had merely helped to give the Committee an enhanced prestige. The effect of all this was increased by the fact that the Committee—or at least that part of it which was earnest and attended the meetings—could enlarge its own numbers by co-optation. After the first week the Westminster Committee added twenty-four new names to its list of members, and the process was repeated at succeeding meetings. On 15 March, when the original list of over 90 had swollen to something in the neighbourhood of one hundred and fifty, it was decided that in future more care should be taken in this process of self-recruitment:

Resolved: that in future every person proposed as a Member of this Committee be elected by ballot and that two Black Balls appearing against such Election shall exclude such person from being a Member of this Committee.

The stricter balloting rule at this stage would not necessarily diminish the power of a determined inner group.[1]

If the Westminster Committee had consisted entirely of blind followers of Fox, or had been packed with Rockinghamite whigs, it would still have found itself (as we shall see) a single unit, a single cell, in a general organization curiously compact and firm. The truth was, however, that in Westminster itself two separate groups held the strategic position and divided the leadership—on the one hand the circle of Fox's intimate friends and on the other a handful of Middlesex radicals who tended to go a great deal of the way with Jebb. A double play of forces came into operation—firstly a tension within the Committee itself and secondly a tendency to friction between the Westminster unit and the organization as a whole. At the first stage of the story the presence of Fox and his friends on the Committee, the weight they possessed in it, and the active part they played, were the primary reasons for the controversies that took place.

The controversies were brought to a point—brought to a nicer issue—precisely because the structure of the movement as a whole, as well as of each separate Committee, was such as to give a particular leverage to the efforts and influence of a handful of individuals. In one locality after another the general meeting had accepted, with little variation, the same set of "stock" resolutions.[2] As a contemporary critic said, a few active men drew up a list of committee-nominations (occasionally a list of sixty or ninety), and these would be adopted by acclamation—in reality "this Provincial Congress is chosen by itself."[3] Some of the leaders of the movement, holding

[1] Add. Mss. 38,593, Proceedings of the Westminster Committee.
[2] A hostile witness of the Exeter meeting describes the "clapping of Hands, thumping of Tables, kicking the Floor … and a String of Resolutions entered on the Minutes without the ordinary sanction of a previous Motion". *St James's Chronicle*, 3–6 April 1780.
[3] Letter from "An Old Freeholder" in *London Chronicle*, 23–25 March 1780.

land in various counties, passed from one local meeting to another, and were appointed to a whole series of local Committees. Though in fact it was the leadership which counted for so much, these Committees now arrogated to themselves what they had previously claimed for the full county meeting—the direct body of property-holders—namely, the power to speak as the authentic voice of the people of England, and the right to correct the wickedness of a corrupt house of commons. They spoke as though public opinion was behind them, streaming up, so to speak, from a hundred sources in town and country. In reality they had secured a remarkable position from which to lead public opinion or manufacture it—to guide the political education of a wider class.

If Fox and the Westminster Committee came into friction with the general movement, they were at issue then with an easily recognizable group of people who claimed to be its spokesmen, and the issue itself was one relating to the kind of leadership that should be given to the organization. Once again that issue was sharpened—it was made more definite, and was given a more precise location—by the fact that with remarkable speed the headquarters of the whole movement had been transferred to the capital. Indeed, once the original general meeting had taken place, it was not the events or proceedings in county or town that mattered, it was not even the men of Yorkshire or the decisions taken in York that provided the leadership. Now, more than before, the various local Committees surprise us by their uniformity, the subservience of their procedure and activities to a given pattern, and their willingness to accept an extraordinarily rapid process of centralization. Since a number of men belonged to more than one local Committee, and many of these were the leaders—were also people who would foregather in London in any case—a small circle acquired a kind of directorate of the whole movement, and conducted their operations from the capital. Many of the chairmen of the various county Committees were members of the Westminster Committee or would be elected to honorary membership. Soon we see delegations from the London, Westminster, and Middlesex Committees coming together and at an early date it was proposed that all the members of the various Committees who happened to be in London should regularly confer with one another. By a number of different processes the centre of gravity of the whole movement was shifted to London; as when the first meeting of the Wiltshire Committee—one which Fox attended—decided that those of its members who belonged to either house of parliament and who were in London should be instructed to form themselves into a committee there. Wyvill himself had moved from Yorkshire to London in January, as we have seen, and his Committee, when questions were submitted to them by those who desired to follow their lead, replied that they preferred matters to be addressed directly to him in London, especially as there were grounds for believing that the post office was interfering with correspondence.[1] The Kent and Buckinghamshire Committees found it useful to meet in London, and in the latter case Shelburne once protested on the ground that the "country members" would find it so difficult to attend. The total result of all these tendencies was greatly to lessen the influence of the ordinary Committee men, whom Shelburne called "the country members". The thing which we describe as "the Yorkshire movement" had in fact come to mean a small body of men who were working together in a fairly regular manner in London.[2]

Now the one local Committee which did not seem to lose its importance and its identity in this way was the Westminster Committee under the active and zealous chairmanship of Fox. It maintained its autonomy, marching ultimately into what in some respects was a form of leadership, because Fox and some of his intimate friends stood out against Wyvill and his allies amongst the radicals—stood out primarily in their capacity as parliament-men, drawn into an anti-parliament organization not originally quite intended for them. It must be remembered, however, that from

[1] *Wyvil Papers*, I, 80-81; cf. Add. Mss. 38,593, f. 5. See also the resolutions of the Common Council of the City of London, 10 Feb., in favour of meetings between members of Committees who happened to be in London, in *Gazetteer*, 15 Feb.

[2] So early as 10 Feb. *The Yorkshire Freeholder*, No. IV, found it necessary to deal with "certain Suspicions, which some of the best Friends to [the] Petition have entertained concerning the Conduct of the general Committee". The author writes of "a Letter which I received lately from a Gentleman, who tells me that some Persons believe Measures of the utmost Consequence are decided upon by a *Junto* and only brought into the Committee for their Confirmation".

January it was not any of the elected Committees—not even West-minster—which controlled the course of events and directed the movement. The primacy really belonged to the informal gather-ings of the leaders in London, gatherings in which Wyvill had a remarkable influence. Wyvill refused to become a member of the Westminster Committee when invited. He maintained the inde-pendence of his position and on occasion firmly refused to be drawn into a circle where he might be seduced. He had the prestige of the Yorkshire Committee behind him. He possessed a well-pre-pared plan. And he was gifted in the arts of management. The stage was therefore set for tension and conflict between Wyvill, the leader in the informal conferences, and the Committee of West-minster under Fox.

The conflict occurred precisely at the point where we might have expected it to arise—on the question of the relations of the whole movement to parliament, and the function in it of those men who were members of parliament. Within ten days of the West-minster meeting the promised opposition campaign had been launched in both houses, and Shelburne said "the temper of the nation was such, as not to bear to be much longer amused", while Rockingham threatened "horrid scenes" and "civil confusion" if the demands of the petitioners were not satisfied. The Committee of Westminster kept watch on the debates and votes in the house of commons as plans of public economy were being discussed; and announced their thanks or denunciations, or circulated their in-junctions, as though they were the sovereign people, conveying their wishes to members of parliament who were mere delegates. Wyvill's plans went further than this, however, and though in January, when he had been asked to reassure doubters, the public statement which he was induced to make only made reference to the economical reform, he had already made it clear in private that his authentic purpose was a change in the representative system it-self.[1]

---

[1] *Wyvill Papers*, I, 54, III, 174-78. Letter from "A Freeholder of Yorkshire", (Wyvill) in *York Courant* and *Leeds Mercury*, 18 Jan. 1780 (with association re-stricted to public economy.) Cf. Letter from "A Yorkshire Freeholder", *York Courant*, 25 Jan. 1780, evidently intended to reassure the timid, and *The Yorkshire Freeholder*, No. IV, 10 Feb. 1780, pp. 20-21.

In the last week of February the matter came to a climax, for it happened that on the 21st, or just before, Wyvill discovered that his Plan of Association had fallen into the hands of his enemies. "The Ministry have got possession of the paper by some means or other," he wrote; and he advised the Yorkshire Committee to publish it immediately, securing at the same time that copies of it should be transmitted to Fox and the other chairmen of Committees.[1] It would seem that a decision was taken to hasten the progress of the movement at this time, for it happened that on this same 21 February Lord North secured the amendment of a motion by Savile for a list of pensions that were being granted by the crown; and as he had gained his end only by two votes Fox wrote in high glee to the Yorkshire Committee: "If such are the effects of your exertions, even in the first instance, I need not say how sure you are of success, if you persevere."[2] Yet by the very day after Fox had written this letter, a different word of command evidently went out, for a number of Committees in the neighbourhood of London, including Westminster itself, began to sing a different tune. They decided that the victory of North in the debate of 21 February "amounts to a direct refusal of one of the great objects of the petitions".[3] Zero-hour had come. The "anti-parliament" was to be called to life.

At this point we can clearly recognize the importance of those informal conferences in London which were stealing the leadership of the movement from the Yorkshiremen, and indeed had superseded the local Committees in general. On 24 February such an informal conference—without consulting the local Committees in the first place, as Fox and others expected—drew up a circular inviting each Committee to send three Deputies to a General Assembly of Deputies which was to be held in London on 7 March "to consider of a Plan of Association". It led to a serious crisis with the Westminster Committee, because, at the insistence of Wyvill, it was stipulated that the appointed Deputies should not be members of

[1] *Wyvill Papers*, I, 98–99.
[2] *Ibid.* I, 100–01.
[3] Add. Mss. 38,593, ff. 6–8, (Westminster); *Morning Chronicle*, 29 Feb. (Sussex); *Gazetteer*, 1 March, (Middlesex). Cf. *Morning Chronicle*, 24 Feb. (Essex, 22 Feb.).

parliament. For Wyvill regarded the movement as being directed not only against the King and the government but in the last resort against the existing form of the house of commons itself. He was not only unwilling to see it tainted with "an air of party", but felt it incongruous if leading members of either house were to gain an ascendancy in the movement or were allowed to have a place on the general staff. "My objection is not personally to Mr. Fox," he wrote, "but . . . to all great Partizans and Parliamentary Leaders of either House." This determined leader, who had done so much to manufacture his own public opinion behind him, could now make his own call upon it and bring it forward almost as a trump card. He declared that "from his knowledge of the sentiments of the Independent Gentlemen of Yorkshire, he conceives it proper and advisable for him to take this line; he ever conceives himself pledged to do it."

For four days he refused to give way, until—as we learn from his papers—"the Parliamentary Leaders . . . desisted from their design to sit in the First Meeting of Deputies." He finally consented to a withdrawal of the original circular provided the members of parliament whom he had in mind would promise not to serve even if they were elected by a local Committee. The General Meeting was postponed until 11 March, and instead of being summoned to prepare a Plan of Association it was to be empowered under the revised scheme "to form . . . plans of public and constitutional reform". Wyvill and his two Yorkshire colleagues still appended a note to the circular, to the effect that in their opinion the appointment of members of parliament was undesirable.[1] By this time we learn from a letter of Lord Rockingham that great agitation and controversy had arisen in the informal conferences on the subject of rotten boroughs, the duration of parliament, the varied possible alterations in the representative system, the question of compensation to dispossessed proprietors, the problem of the enfranchisement of industrial and trading towns, and even the project of universal manhood suffrage.[2] It is clear that in the closing days of

[1] *Wyvill Papers*, I, 111–12; III, 179–81.
[2] *Rockingham Memoirs*, II, 395–400, Rockingham to Pemberton Milnes, 28 Feb. 1780.

February the Yorkshire movement was being carried through clashes and crises to a further stage of its development.

What Wyvill hoped to secure from the general meeting in London is illustrated by the covering letter which he inserted— along with a copy of his own Plan of Association—in the invitation which was sent out to the local Committees.

And each county, city, and town, having first associated separately and apart, on grounds which have received the general approbation, the whole body of the petitioners, in due time, may be collected and firmly consolidated in one great National Association.

The consequences of this, he argued, "must be certain and compleat success to the constitutional reform proposed by the people."[1]

The short interval between the despatch of the invitation on 29 February and the arrival of the Deputies in London on 11 March left little time for discussion, and no time for a reference of the matter to the full meetings of gentry and freeholders. The response to the appeal must have been disappointing to the leaders, for the result was only a broken fragment of the magnificent edifice that had been initially designed. Twelve counties and four cities or towns sent Deputies; and, in addition, a representative from Cheshire attended a single meeting, though it was afterwards said that he had presented himself without authorization.[2] The list was again augmented when, at the last meeting of all, Dr Barrow, one of the representatives for Gloucestershire, entered his name also as the Deputy for Gloucester City. The whole body came far short of that vast counter-system of representation, that imposing "anti-parliament", which some of the leaders had hoped for, and some of the doctrine of the movement presumed. Members of parliament were admitted, and the Westminster Committee took excellent advantage of the fact. It seems to have been the great parliamentary leaders to whom Wyvill took exception, and he still declared that he would refuse to attend if any of these should make their appearance even in the event of their being appointed. Colonel Fitzpatrick,

[1] *Wyvill Papers*, I, 113-15.
[2] *Letters of H. Walpole* (ed. Toynbee), XI, 165.

Thomas Grenville, and T. Brand-Hollis represented Westminster—a predominantly Foxite group, who supported Fox's more conservative policy at this time. Other members of the Westminster Committee attended the meetings as representatives of other regions—Jebb, for example, on behalf of Huntingdonshire, where he possessed a little property, Sir Francis Vincent on behalf of the county of Surrey. Wyvill, Jebb, Major Cartwright, Lord Mahon, J. Townsend, Trecothick, Frankland, and Brass Crosby were amongst the more prominent of the delegates. The radicals held the field.

At the first meeting, held on 11 March, Wyvill was appointed chairman, and it was agreed that the voting should be by deputations. It was also resolved that no Deputy should be admitted "until he shall have produced such proof of his appointment as shall be satisfactory to this meeting". Though whispers from various sides make it clear that storm and controversy were raging—if not in the formal sessions themselves, at any rate in the wings, and in various quarters in London—little of the actual proceedings seems to have leaked out. The formation of a General Association was resolved upon, and if a committee consisting of Wyvill, Mahon, Baker, Bromley, and Fitzpatrick failed to produce a plan, Wyvill was left with a clearer opportunity of leadership, since he could provide in Yorkshire a model for the other regions. It was resolved that the objects of the Association should be three: the securing of a diligent examination of the receipt and expenditure of public money; the addition of at least one hundred county members to the house of commons; and the establishment of annual parliaments. It was agreed that at the next election voters should be urged not to give their support to candidates who declined to commit themselves to the promotion of this programme. A later resolution declared the necessity of a law to prevent "both expense in elections and the operation of undue influence therein".[1]

The movement was marching ahead, therefore, with great rapidity; and some who had been patrons or benevolent spectators—like Horace Walpole—were coming to be in a frenzied state of mind.

---

[1] On the resolutions of the Deputies, together with a Memorial written by Bromley on their behalf, see *Wyvill Papers*, I, 116 *et seqq* and 426 *et seqq*.

Nothing could exceed the dismay of the Rockinghamites as they saw the directorate of the Yorkshire Association moving away from economical reform at the very moment when that issue was reaching its highest degree of intensity in debates in the house of commons. Already, on 28 February, Lord Rockingham had sent out a cry of alarm, as, writing to a member of the Yorkshire Committee, he complained of the whole idea of imposing "tests" on candidates in parliamentary elections, especially as there was such difference of opinion, even amongst reformers themselves, on the programme to be promoted, and on the very question of annual or triennial parliaments. The real grievances "arise from the *corruption of men when chosen into Parliament*", he said:

There are so many visionary schemes and expedients *by way of reforms on float,* that a *general* confusion and disagreement will ensue.

Some at least of the Rockinghamites were prepared to see the localities consulted on the question of parliamentary reform. Even Burke was prepared to admit that, supposing the great majority of the people were united in such a desire, misguided though it might be, it would be sinister and scandalous if there existed in the country a force that should be capable of resisting the demand. It was a different matter, however, if a General Meeting of Deputies gave the lead, decided the issue before the localities had been consulted, and presented the counties with a project which they were merely asked to ratify or reject. It would be a different matter, too, if the machinery of the Yorkshire movement were used to stampede the country into a decision or to produce a so-called mandate from the people, when the genuine voice of the nation had not been heard. The Rockinghamites put their finger at this early date upon what has been one of the unfortunate excesses of many pseudo-representative bodies.

Most curious of all, however, were the repercussions of this controversy on the development of the Westminster Committee. While the General Meeting of Deputies was still in session, that Committee received an interim report from its own delegation; and the evidence seems to show that it was unprepared for the pace

with which things were moving. Stimulated by clash and controversy, the more radical party issued the declaration that even the
ostensible objects of the Yorkshire meeting of 30 December could
never be achieved by any measure short of parliamentary reform.
Indeed they moved

That a more equal representation of the people and annual parliaments are the constitutional and the most effective methods of
reforming the present abuses in government and of preventing
them in future.

No decision was reached. The consideration of the motion was
adjourned to a special meeting of the Westminster Committee to
be held on the following Monday, 20 March. It was no doubt as a
result of the growing tension that this meeting decreed the abandonment of the system of wholesale co-optation, and agreed that
two blackballs should serve to exclude in future. It is probable that
Horace Walpole was correct in his view that Fox used his influence
on the more conservative side in the important debates of this day.

Another motion which was put to the Westminster Committee
on 15 March was to prove significant, and it did not admit of the
use of the same argument for delay or fuller attendance or previous
notification. The Rockinghamites had been prepared to agree that
it might be proper to learn the views of the local Committees on
the question of parliamentary reform, and a proposal that a sub-
committee should be appointed in Westminster to inquire into the
matter was clearly more difficult to resist. It was adopted, but the
members elected were no longer a Foxite group, for apart from
the chairman Sheridan—who was becoming closely associated
with Fox—they comprised Vardy, Vincent, Jebb, Hollis, Cromp-
ton, and Hartley, so that there was little to act as a brake upon the
radical theorists.[1] With remarkable rapidity they produced an important series of decisions at their first meeting on 17 March.

The Yorkshire movement had brought vividly before the public
much of the early literature of parliamentary reform, some of
which was reprinted, some paraphrased in open letters to the papers,
some further reproduced in the resolutions or manifestoes of Com-

[1] Add. Mss. 38,593, ff. 12–15.

mittees or sub-committees in one locality or another. The report of 17 March codified the teaching of Granville Sharp and John Cartwright, behind which, as we have seen, lie the *Political Disquisitions* of James Burgh. All these appear to have been curiously influenced by Malachy Postlethwayt, whose *Universal Dictionary of Trade and Commerce* reached its fourth edition in 1774 and contained important articles on "Parliament" and the "Land Tax". Postlethwayt had used the statistical methods which were to become so familiar, in order to expose the anomalies of the existing state of the representation. He was the third writer mentioned—along with Burgh and Sharp—in Wilkes's speech on parliamentary reform in 1776.

The Westminster sub-committee declared that "*new Parliaments to be holden once in every year were the antient usage*" and are "the hereditary and indefeasible right of the People of England". Their report attacked the Septennial Act as "a direct infringement on the Constitution", since it was made "without communication with the constituent Body of the People". It announced that "by stat. 8 Hen. VI., the Parliament, then elected by the commonalty at large", disfranchised the greater part of their constituents. And, after testing the statistical anomalies in the existing representative system, it declared that

a number scarcely above six thousand, being a majority of the voters of a hundred and twenty-nine of the boroughs, return two hundred and fifty-seven representatives, which is a majority of the whole English House of Commons . . . many of these boroughs are immediately under the influence of the Crown.[1]

The effect of the sub-committee's report at the special session of the full Committee of 20 March would seem to have been remarkable; and by the 25th a specific adhesion had been given by the Committee as a whole to the reform proposals of the General Assembly of Deputies.[2] By 21 March Horace Walpole could report that Fox himself was "pushing them impetuously"; and if he was wrong in diagnosing this change he was not many days ahead of the truth. To complete the paradox, on 20 March the General

[1] Add. Mss. 38,593, ff. 16-19; printed in *Wyvill Papers*, 1,212-17.
[2] *Ibid.* ff. 15-23.

Assembly of Deputies itself met for the last time; and the Foxite delegation from Westminster were still trying to apply the brake—leading Devonshire, Sussex, Gloucestershire, and Buckinghamshire (with Hertfordshire also on one of the issues) in an attempt to secure that annual parliaments and the additional knights of the shire should at least not be made articles of association, or treated as a *sine qua non*, or turned into a fundamental purpose of the movement. On this issue the deputies for London and Middlesex voted against the Westminster delegation. In fact the supporters of the more moderate programme were out-numbered by two to one.

Almost immediately afterwards, it was Wyvill who retreated: Fox moved over to the idea of annual parliaments, while he himself withdrew in favour of the triennial principle.

Nothing is more essential to the wise conduct of public and private affairs than the power to distinguish between those matters which are to be treated with diplomacy and those to which one must hold fast with the fervour of men who are confessing the faith. Those who are concerned with the latter must be prepared to be defeated in their short-term objects; and Wyvill very soon learned that if he wished to achieve results in a reasonable period of time, he must use diplomacy and secure the alliance of "the nobility". It is arguable that, jostling as they were in a rough and tricky world, the leaders of the Yorkshire movement might well have followed the advice of the Rockinghamites in March 1780—guarded the unanimity of the movement, pared down the effects of corruption in the house of commons, and then, with a more favourable balance of forces, considered the next step in reform. For the time, as we shall see, by attempting too much they perhaps lost all; for not even the minimum programme, not even economical reform, was achieved; and as the turmoil threw much of the nation back to the side of the government, the administration of North was able to survive for two more years.[1]

Since Wyvill was fighting for parliamentary reform in itself,

[1] *Political Memoranda of the Fifth Duke of Leeds*, p. 28, They have "let go the substance through eagerness to grasp the shadow." Cf. *Rockingham Memoirs*, II, 408–09; letter from C. Turner, dated 10 April, in *York Courant*, 9 May; and *A Speech on the Nomination of Candidates to represent Middlesex*, 7 Sept. 1780, p. 11.

however, it is not to the point to say that he ought to have changed his object; though he was bound to learn sooner or later that he was working for a distant end in spite of himself. He and his collaborators launched upon the country, and set fairly and squarely on its course, the most important of the movements that have made the modern world.[1] The Yorkshire Association bridges the gulf between Middlesex radicalism—Wilkite, undiscriminating, and half-disreputable—and the national movement of parliamentary reform. It assists the transition from eighteenth-century parties based on "connection" to the modern kind of party which is a matter of issues and principles. It contributes to the political education of Englishmen, and indeed of the Rockinghamites themselves, helping ultimately to produce the transformed party of Fox and Grey, the development from the Old Whigs to the New. The year 1780 sees both Fox and the younger Pitt—who was elected to Mahon's Kent Committee—caught into the Association and committed to parliamentary reform.

There is little that cannot be traced back to the seventeenth century when the overthrow of the very bases of government and the exhilaration in men's minds threw up even Bellairs, to whom Robert Owen declared his indebtedness, and brought out ideas that have never since been seriously taken up—like that idea of "exclusion by rotation" (intended to stop the development of the professional parliament-man) which Burgh vainly tried to revive, which Jebb once or twice mentions, and which Cartwright did not quite approve of, in the 1770's. In the early half of the eighteenth century those who opposed the ministry of the day, easily criticized the parliament which supported the government, and naturally complained that it failed to represent the constituencies. Hatred of corruption, placemen, rotten boroughs; demands for "tests" and "instructions"; and prejudices in favour of independent county members—all these were old—and the speeches and literature of an earlier generation had provided an admirable quarry for Burgh, the

---

[1] *Political Memoranda of the Fifth Duke of Leeds*, p. 28 [April 1780.] "The shortening the duration of Parliaments, a new mode of election [etc.] . . . seem'd to meet with more advocates (both as to respect and numbers) than would have been, I think, imagined."

prophet of the Association. The quarrel with the American colonies and the cry "No taxation without representation" had provoked perhaps a more authentic inquiry into the idea of parliamentary government. It was the Middlesex election controversy of 1769–70, however, which first raised in a vivid manner for Englishmen in general, the question of the relations between the house of commons and the constituencies. The development in the 1770's— when Alderman Sawbridge, for example, annually moved for shorter parliaments—comes with increasing weight until Wyvill sees his opportunity.

It should be noted, however, that it is the freeholders who are being summoned to a higher form of political consciousness, by the efforts of Wyvill; and they are people who are assumed to possess a vote. This is no rebellion of the "have-nots" against the "haves"—it is grounded in the rights of property; and the addition of knights of the shire is meant to increase the power of those who already possess a degree of power. They are to have added weight in the constitution, according to the Yorkshire plan, in order to "balance" the increased power of the crown. The report of the Westminster sub-committee of 15 March, however, points to objects that lie beyond any scheme that Wyvill has in mind. Rôles in fact are to be reversed in the near future. There are men on the Westminster Committee who will not consent to be held back by Wyvill now.

§II. THE OPPOSITION BEGINS TO DISINTEGRATE

As March drew to its close the scene shifted away from the capital and the story was enacted on a stage that was nothing less than the broad expanse of England. The ring-leaders in London had done their work; the General Meeting of Deputies was over; and it remained to be seen what the local Committees would have to say about the decision which had been made. Yet when it had been decided on 24 February to summon the General Meeting in London, it was still the case that many regions had not yet held their original assemblies of freeholders—had not even presented the petition for public economy. Sixteen counties had followed the example of Yorkshire before the end of January, but during almost the whole of February it had been the cities and boroughs which had been enrolling themselves in the Yorkshire movement. Only from the time when the events in London had begun to be exhilarating did the remaining counties give signs of commotion, as though the movement had got its second wind. On 26 February Buckinghamshire joined the petitioners, while in March there were half-a-dozen county meetings, beginning with that in Kent on the 4th which is discussed below in an appendix. A remarkable one took place in Cambridge on the 25th of the month.

The meeting—like one which had been held in Nottingham—illustrates the importance of the connection between nonconformity and the more radical political tendencies existing at this time. The Yorkshire movement, in the early stages of which, as we have already seen, a remarkable part was played by clergymen, provided an opportunity for these more radical tendencies, and even at the very first we saw how the nonconformist, Pemberton Milnes of Wakefield, intervened to save the situation. In Cambridge the nonconformists were the centre of opposition to the existing municipal régime and the government influence in the locality. The growth of the spirit of party in this region had shown itself in a contested parliamentary election in the borough in 1774—the first for nearly forty years. The refractory party were assisted by landowners like the Presbyterian Alderman Purchas, and by John Mortlock, who had married into a well-to-do dissenting family. In Chesterton lived one of their more violent and doctrinaire spokesmen, the dissenting minister Robert Robinson, whose *Political Catechism* illustrates the radicalism of this period.

One of the members for the county, Sir John Hynde Cotton, complained in the house of commons at a later date, that the Cambridgeshire meeting had been held on a market day:

that he did not see one face in 20 that he had ever seen before, though no member was better acquainted with his constituents; that the country folk, *tag, rag* and *bobtail*, attended and converted the meeting into a downright mob.

The meeting was not summoned by the sheriff, but as a result of the efforts of the nonconformist opposition. It was known in advance that it was to have the support of Dr. Watson, who was Regius Professor of Divinity, so, during the morning of the stipulated day his opponents distributed circulars among the crowd, including an extract (printed in London, for the Cambridge printer was a patriot) from a sermon preached by Dr. Watson at the Assizes in Cambridge in 1769, at the time of the previous Wilkite disturbances. Watson had described then how "the licentious spirit of faction hath been let loose, and groundless suspicions, jealousies, distrusts and discontents infused into the bulk of the people." He had complained of an age in which "every citizen affects the authority of a senator, every mechanic becomes a new modeller of our constitution." He had shown how "a riotous contempt for decency, order, and all kinds of subordination, have been studiously excited", ... Finally, he had set out to scourge "the dissolute luxuriancy of an overgrown metropolis".[1] His own previous opinions could now be offered to the public as the best antidote to any influence which he might have in this new form of Wilkite upheaval which was taking place.

According to William Cole:

The Duke of Manchester, Wilkes, Mr [Crisp] Molineux & a Mr. [Thomas] Daye, a man of some Property, lately acquired, near about Ongar in Essex, where he had distinguished himself as a busy & noisy Patriot, being a ready Speaker, who was inticed down to this Hot-Bed of Faction, the dissenting Interest in & about Cambridge, with Dr. Watson, Regius Professor of Divinity, Archdeacon of Ely, Rector of Somersham, at their Head, assembled about 11 o'clock in one of the Courts of the Town Hall, where they waited a long time for the Duke of Rutland & his Company.

It was found necessary to move away from the court in the Guildhall when the meeting had begun to assemble. A friendly witness tells us that this was because the place was not large enough

[1] *London Chronicle*, 13–15 April 1780. See also Watson's letter in support of the Huntingdonshire meeting, *Cambridge Chronicle*, 29 Jan. 1780, and his attack on the influence of the crown on p. 11–12 of his University Sermon of 4 Feb. 1780. William Cole, in a letter to H. Walpole, (see note 1 p. 288), says that Watson did not speak at this meeting but prompted the other speakers.

to contain the crowd, and there appears to be no reason for thinking that this account of the situation was untrue. There seems to have been another motive for the transference which took place, however; for Cole tells us that the Duke of Rutland, who had much local influence, had assembled with his company in the other court; and each of the parties insisted that the other should come to join it, so that a deadlock seemed likely to occur.

To qualify this Jarring, it was proposed by Wilkes, as no unusual measure, & which would much better answer their design to seduce the People, to adjourn to some Bowling Green, or open Space, where the greater number of people might hear their Harangues: this was agreed to & Clare Hall Peice, & Parker's Peice were named: however, the Senate House Yard, as it was Market Day, & the Market Hill full of Stalls, was pitch't upon, as having a Flight of Steps very suitable to the orators for Display of the Talents . . .

It is clear that the meeting was less "respectable" in character, and less imposing in its proceedings than that which had inaugurated the movement in York[1]; for if Hynde Cotton spoke of the "*tag, rag* and *bobtail*", there are other evidences that the assembly had at least a disorderly fringe. The temper of the whole gathering was in any case more radical than in other places, and it is curious to note that here at last was a meeting that turned out to be a triumph for Wilkes. Cole wrote in bitterness that it was

a Mob of Dissenters of all Hues, Colours & Denominations in every part of the County, called together . . . in order to draw up a Petition of Oeconomy, Alterations in the Method of Parliament, & other wild and republican Schemes, first engendred at Mr. Robinson's Conventicle, & then recommended to the notice of the Corporation by a modest Republican, if that is compatible, Alderman Burleigh.

[1] Cf. H.M.C. *Rutland Mss.*, III, 25, the Duke of Rutland to Lord Robert Manners, 10 March 1780: "You are the declared candidate . . . you have not an inch of property in that county [Cambridgeshire]—it will be indispensably necessary that you should attend and make a most violent speech." On the candidature of Manners see H.M. Cam, *Proceedings of the Cambridge Antiquarian Society*, XL, 1 et seqq.

The "Anabaptist", Purchas, opened the proceedings, and Lord Duncannon, who had been made chairman, read the petition, "but not to the Satisfaction of the Party, who had it bellowed out by Crisp Molineux". The petition was adopted and there was a proposal that the two members for the county should present it to the house of commons. The two men in question, however, were not happy, and though Cotton agreed to submit the document, the meeting itself did not seem to be happy either.

On that, Wilkes, to make himself popular, offered his Service to lay it [the Petition] before the House, recounting the Inconveniences that had occurred where members, who were not hearty in the Cause, had delivered these Petitions. This occasioned a Roar among the populace for Wilkes for Ever.

Gunning, who attended the meeting at the age of twelve, afterwards said that, so far as he could remember, nobody spoke against the petition save Sir John Hynde Cotton and Sir Sampson Gideon, the representatives of the county in parliament—"both of them remarkably bad speakers", and the former, on this occasion "extremely violent", taking "no pains to conceal his contempt of the persons assembled."[1]

Since the Cambridge meeting was held after the Meeting of Deputies in London, the ulterior projects of the movement were not unknown, and were not allowed to pass unmentioned. The Duke of Manchester seems to have been "inflammatory", making a speech which was "addressed wholly to the People, telling them that they were the sole Origin & Fountain of Laws, & that since such as He, & Parliaments were become so corrupt, it was from them alone that Protection was to be sought". Thomas Day gave a speech, to which, when he printed it later, he gave the title On the Necessity of a Reform in Parliament. He asserted that "Kings must expect allegiance no longer than they deserve it," and he talked of the plan of shorter parliaments and an improved representation. Cole tells us that a Plan of Association was actually proposed, but without success, "for there was not, to Appearance a Gentleman of the County with them." At any rate a Committee was

[1] H. Gunning, Reminiscences of . . . . Cambridge (1854) II, 330.

formed, including peers like the Dukes of Manchester and Rutland, radicals like Wilkes and Thomas Day, and local opposition leaders such as Purchas.

Finally, we are told, "the Patriots" adjourned to the Rose Tavern with their petition, "amidst the applauses of the Mobarchy."

Robinson, the Anabaptist Teacher, who lives at Chesterton, set the Bells a Ringing in that Church as soon as he got Home, & made a great Supper at night for all his Party, where strong Liquors, good Cheer, & Zeal for the Cause, so far got the better of their discretion, that many of the Ebenezers were laid flat on their Back, & had Assistance to convey them to their several Habitations.

"Sir," said Crisp Molineux, when he presented the Cambridge petition to the house of commons on 6 April, "the voice of the People under the open canopy of Heaven, called aloud for a redress of grievances".[1]

In the meantime, the programme of the Meeting of Deputies had been circulated, and was referred first to the local Committees and then to the full general meetings that had originally appointed them. In a definite manner the question of parliamentary reform—hitherto ventilated in a few pamphlets—was presented as a political issue to large sections of the public. Now that the Plan of Association was submitted to the country, there was offered to many people—under better conditions perhaps than in elections at this time—an actual exercise in self-government. For the last word lay with "the people"—whether freeholders or other electors, or even, as at Westminster, mere tax-payers—convoked in direct assembly from city and country-side.

Defeated in their objects at the Meeting of Deputies, the Rockingham whigs were determined to carry the battle to the local Committees and the resumed county meetings. No sooner had the

[1] *York Chronicle*, 28 April 1780. Molineux was seconded in the house of commons on this occasion by Wilkes. On the Cambridge meeting see G. W. Gigniliat, *The Author of Sandford and Merton* (N.Y. 1932), pp. 181 et seqq., based on the account given by Cole in Add. Mss. 5,855, ff. 140–44. *The Correspondence of Horace Walpole and Rev. Wm. Cole* (ed. by W. S. Lewis and A. D. Wallace,) II, 206–08, provides another account of this meeting by Cole. Cf. *Wyvill Papers*, I, 130–35.

delegates in London completed their conferences than this party re-directed its guns and turned them against the enemy's next position. Rockingham held that the resolution concerning annual parliaments would secure no following *"if the County of York* are not led into that decision"; and the importance of the leadership which this county was now in a position to give, as well as the influence which he and some of his friends possessed in that part of England, induced him to make a strong initial effort there. He had little time for this, since the Deputies had ended their sessions only on 20 March, while the general meeting of the county was due to take place on the 28th.

Repeated attempts were made by Lord Rockingham and his friends to induce members of the Yorkshire Committee to resist the novel proposals that had been introduced into the movement by the zeal of their own leader, Wyvill. In one of his letters Rockingham even went out of his way to defend rotten boroughs, arguing that Yorkshire was *"low rated to the Land Tax"* because it sent thirty-two representatives to the house of commons, "sixteen of which may be deemed to come from what are called *Rotten Boroughs".*[1] Wyvill says that one of these letters promised the support of the Rockinghamites for the Plan of Association provided the policy of triennial parliaments should be substituted for the resolution in favour of annual ones. Since he claims that this letter determined the Committee's course of action it is unfortunate that he does not supply a copy of it in his *Political Papers*, for his summary of it cannot be reconciled with those letters of Rockingham which we do possess, including one written immediately after the document in question and equally intended to be communicated to members of the Committee. Wyvill conce¹˙ᵈ the point concerning triennial parliaments, and expressed himself with some bitterness afterwards because this did not secure him the support of the Rockinghamites after all. According to his account "Lord Rockingham, it was soon found had answered for more than he was able to effect, and his powerful Friends disavowed their having previously authorized such an engagement." If this were

[1] H.M.C. *Lonsdale Mss.* 136–8; cf. *Rockingham Memoirs*, II, 405; cf. also *ibid.* 395–400.

the case it is curious that in the following August Wyvill should have been hoaxed again and should have written to Lord Mahon that "Lord Rockingham is on the point of joining us." And if in March the Cavendishes—who were notoriously hostile to Wyvill's scheme—had disavowed their leader, we may be entitled to wonder why in August Wyvill could believe that they would follow him this second time—could even say that Rockingham "governed them entirely".[1]

At the full county meeting in York on 28 March even Sir George Savile, who had acted as a confidential adviser to Wyvill from the first, declared that he would not commit himself to the policy of an increase in the county representation, though he agreed that it "might be a good measure". He declined to support even triennial parliaments, and though he said he would promote this change if he could be convinced that the majority of his constituents were in favour of it, he declared that he would not be convinced merely by taking "the sense of that room"—a point which was significant, for he had not previously paid attention to such a distinction.[2] He, like Lord John Cavendish, declared his preference for an Association on the issue of public economy; while the latter put forward the view that more frequent general elections would only be likely to do more harm than good. All this failed to secure any further concession to the Rockinghamites however; and it is with some surprise that we learn from the official minutes that the Plan of Association was adopted "unanimously".[3]

It sometimes happened that the course of discussion in a given locality would fasten upon a particular aspect of the problem of association, as the one in York had centred upon the question of triennial parliaments. And if we have already noted that the Rockinghamites objected to "tests" and to the extended programme of the movement, we may observe how a further line of protest was

---

[1] *Wyvill Papers*, I, Preface XIV–XIX; Mss. of Earl Stanhope at Chevening, B, [i.e. in the correspondence with Shelburne because it had been forwarded to Shelburne.] Wyvill to Mahon, 28 Aug. 1780.

[2] For Savile's views see also *Wyvill Papers*, III, 205–08, 254–59.

[3] *Wyvill Papers*, I, 148–50; (cf. however, Wyvill's reports, *ibid.* Preface XVI and 164); Add. Mss. 34,417, f. 43, P. Johnson to W. Eden, 30 March; *Morning Chronicle* and *York Courier*, 4 April.

developed in Wiltshire, where attention became concentrated to an increasing degree upon the question of the competence of the local Committees. The mandate which had been given in the first place to these Committees of Correspondence is marked by those prudences and suppressions which betray the tactical skill of Wyvill. It authorized these bodies not only to further the cause of the petition itself but to "prepare a Plan of an Association . . . to support that laudable reform, and such other measures as may conduce to restore the Freedom of Parliament". It can hardly have been without forethought and calculation that a formula was produced so capable of infinite extension in the hands of men who were ready to exploit the technicalities. When we consider the hurried manner in which the original county assemblies carried out this part of their proceedings, we can appreciate the fact that a great number of those who had signed the petitions regarded the Committees only as the means by which greater effect could be given to the demand for economical reform. On this assumption even Burke, as we have seen, had supported the establishment of Committees and had declared that without them a petition would be sheer futility. On the same assumption some men had protested against those suspicious critics of the movement who had accused the Committees of aiming at wider purposes. Those who, as we have seen, had been confused in their original acceptance of the idea of a Committee of any kind, would hardly be prepared for those technical distinctions which purported to cover the extraordinary enlargement of the functions of these bodies.

One county—that of Wiltshire—pressed this argument to the utmost, with the result that it behaved in a more cautious and conservative manner than even Lord Rockingham desired, displeasing him as much in this direction as the Yorkshiremen were doing at the opposite side of the compass.[1] The suspicions of the Wiltshire Committee were awakened early, for when at the end of February they were invited to send a delegation to the Meeting of Deputies in London, they determined to fight shy of this development and instructed their chairman to reply that they would refer the matter to "a more mature and ample Discussion in a Meeting of the County

[1] Fitzmaurice, *Shelburne*, II, 50–51.

at large"—a procedure which, they said, "the Importance of the Measure absolutely requires." Since they declined to act with that haste which the plans of Wyvill demanded they were unrepresented at the Meeting of Deputies. They were confirmed in their policy by a long letter dated 18 March from one of their influential members, the Earl of Radnor, who at the same time drew attention to a further constitutional issue which had evidently emerged:

> To confer upon the Deputies (which some Persons have supposed) a Representative Power obligatory upon the Committees, is as contrary to the Design of the Invitation, as it is inconsistent with every Principle of Prudence and Propriety, and beyond the Powers of the Committees to confer.
> I understand the Line taken by this [Wiltshire] Committee . . . was, that their Appointment extended only to promoting the Objects of the Petition. It certainly only did so . . .

On 27 March the same Committee was called upon to consider the Plan of Association which had been communicated to them by the General Meeting of Deputies. Two of their important members, Charles James Fox and the Earl of Shelburne, who were unable to attend, sent written statements of their views and attempted to persuade the county to play its part in the general movement. Their letters differed very greatly and showed how far the party of Lord Shelburne was coming to diverge from even the extremist wing of the Rockinghamites on the question of the Yorkshire movement. For, while Fox emphasized the considerable effect which the popular awakening had had on the proceedings of parliament, and urged the possibility that a moderate form of Association would make the success complete, Shelburne for his part enumerated all the disappointments that had been suffered—he was concerned to whip up exasperation against both the ministry and the parliament. He drew attention also to the recent increase in the salt-tax and the levy against private breweries, "bearing very hard upon our County in particular". Whereas Fox made no mention of annual parliaments or a strengthening of the county representation, Shelburne proclaimed that the rights of Englishmen were stronger than acts of parliament and that the voice of the county meetings was superior to "the present defective Representation" which in any case was "the mere child of Accident or Intrigue". To him triennial parliaments and a moderate increase in the number of county members would be a prudent compromise—wiser perhaps than "pushing the Right of the People to its utmost extent".

Refusing to be moved by the encouraging words of Fox, or quickened by the goadings and incitements of Shelburne, the Wiltshire Committee doubled the degree of its cautiousness and armed itself afresh against all those drifts and tendencies which during February and March had been carrying the Yorkshire movement into radical courses. It resolved unanimously:

That it is the Opinion of this Committee, that towards forming a Plan of an Association according to the original Appointment of this Committee, the County be moved to-morrow—
That if this Committee shall hereafter think it adviseable to send any of their Members to meet Gentlemen sent from other Counties, that the Persons so sent be restrained to promoting the Prayer of the Petition—Public Œconomy.
That the Chairman do . . . acquaint the County Meeting, that many Subjects materially connected with the Prayer of the Petition are now depending in the House of Commons.

On the following day, 28 March, the general meeting of the county broke up without establishing an association even for limited purposes of public economy. It went further than the Committee had done, and succeeded in putting its finger upon another of those technical features of the movement which in recent weeks had so often enabled the extremists to secure the upper hand. In order to forestall more effectively any *coup de main* on the part of a radical minority, it resolved unanimously:

that if the Committee shall hereafter think it adviseable to send any of their Members to meet Gentlemen sent from other Counties, that the Persons so sent be restrained to promoting the Prayer of the Petition,—Public Œconomy. And that no Members of the Committee be so appointed, but at a Meeting to be holden for the special Purpose of such Appointment, on the Notice by circular

Letter of ten Days at the least; and unless such Appointment be made with the Consent of the Majority of Twenty-one at least assembled at the said Committee.[1]

Intense controversy was produced in various other counties when the Plan of Association was discussed—controversy between radicals and Rockinghamites even at the resumed general meeting in Huntingdon for example. It was perhaps in Buckinghamshire, however, that the longest and severest conflict took place and the resistance of the Rockinghamites was to prove most remarkable and persevering, the activities of Lord Mahon, supported by Shelburne, finding themselves here in opposition to the local influence of Earl Temple.[2] In the closing days of March even the parliamentary opposition parties were losing the appearance of unanimity, and were beginning to dissipate their ammunition in skirmishes against one another.[3] The followers of Rockingham were moving away once again from the party of Shelburne, for this latter party lacked that weight of vested interests which tended to keep the former in a conservative frame of mind. By traditions that extended back to the days when the elder Pitt was young, the Shelburne faction tended to look to the people, while its weakness in the face of the Rockinghamites put it under the necessity of drawing on the power which would come from popular favour, unless by a stroke of good fortune it could reinforce itself on occasion by an alliance with the closet. In any case it had always been less attached than the main body of the whigs to the traditions of patronage and the cur-

[1] For the events in Wiltshire, and the correspondence associated with its Committee, see *Copies of the Proceedings of the General Meetings of the County of Wilts.*, pp. 35-62, *passim*. Cf. note 1, p. 272 above.

[2] See Appendix A, "Lord Mahon and the Yorkshire Movement."

[3] Add. Mss. 37,835, f. 108, J. Robinson to George III, 31 March 1780: "The difference of Sentiment which so evidently appears among the Heads of Opposition may possibly create such a Schism among them as may enable government to render abortive all their designs." Cf. *Political Memoranda of the Fifth Duke of Leeds*: pp. 29-30, (c. April 1780), where Shelburne, complaining of the "material difference of opinion among the Principal leaders of Opposition", says: "But what can we do? Nothing upon earth, there is no dealing with Mr. Burke . . . no arguing with him . . . and [he] has got so much ascendency over Lord Rockingham."

rent conceptions of party—less inclined to base its views and build its prejudices upon a faith in the eighteenth century structure of society and government. Shelburne himself, moreover, affected to be free from superstition, and made himself the patron of some of the most progressive minds of the time.

From the moment when they had refused their support at the Yorkshire meeting of 28 March—from the moment when they declined to be won over by Wyvill's concession in regard to triennial parliaments—the Rockinghamites, on the other hand, found themselves the object of the hostility of the radicals, who showed the resentment of disappointed and disillusioned men. The resentment was greater in that the weaknesses of the Yorkshire movement—the faults in its nature, as it had been originally conceived—were becoming apparent, and even Wyvill had come to the view that he would be able to do nothing without the aid of "the nobility". Thomas Day, who was to become memorable as the author of *Sandford and Merton*, brought out the full force of this ill-feeling in a speech which he made at the Essex meeting at Chelmsford on 25 April:

> I derive the worst omens for the public cause from the unwillingness [of the Rockingham Whigs] to satisfy the public apprehensions [i.e. by accepting tests and engagements when standing for Parliament].—Does it then become a set of men, who have been reviling the established Government for years, under the plausible pretext of zeal for the rights and liberties of the people, to refuse that very people the just and trivial satisfaction they demand?—Are heaven, and earth, and hell, to be moved ... not that the great causes of all our miseries may be removed ... but that one garrison may evacuate the place, and another march in; while we, like the wretched inhabitants of contested territory, gain nothing by battles, sieges, and defeats, but a change of masters?
> ... I have never yet heard of an aristocracy, from ancient Rome to modern Venice, that was not the universal tyrant and inquisitor of the species.[1]

[1] *Speech of Thomas Day to the Freeholders of Essex*, 25 April 1780; see also G. W. Gignilliat, *op. cit.*, pp. 188–89. On the quarrel with the Rockinghamites, see also Appendix B, "Horace Walpole and the Yorkshire Movement."

To crown the misfortunes, the emergence of the more speculative issues, and in particular the quarrel with the Rockinghamites, had the effect of producing dissensions within the ranks of the movement itself. The very attempt which had been made in York to placate the opposition nobility by revising the original plan of annual parliaments only served to provoke new trouble on what we might call the left wing of the movement, without removing any of the difficulties that had existed on the right. Wyvill was open to the reproach that he had been the first to break the unanimity—the first to forsake the programme which he himself had induced the General Meeting of Deputies to adopt.

Granville Sharp himself plunged into the heart of this new controversy and set out to show that Wyvill had affronted the fundamental idea which underlay the agitation on behalf of annual parliaments. Some of his previous writings had already been re-printed[1] but in the new conjuncture he issued frenzied protests against the compromises of Wyvill, printing now a letter to "a Member of the Surry Committee", now a letter for Hertford, now *A Circular Letter to the several Petitioning Counties*. To Sharp—and indeed to many of the spokesmen of the new movement, including Bromley, who had drawn up a manifesto on behalf of the General Meeting of Deputies—the matter at issue was neither a disputable reform, nor a speculative proposition nor even in any sense an innovation.

We are far from desiring that "*the constitution may be new-modelled;*" we only pray, that the unjust *usurpations,* (made without the consent of the people,) the *corruptions, and other such abuses,* may be taken away and reformed: and then the ancient constitution of *annual* elections, and "*more often if need be,*" will recover its full vigour without any other alteration.

Sharp declared that "All . . . Statutes against Fundamental Rights are null and void by their own intrinsic iniquity." The Septennial

---

[1] Cf. Add. Mss. 30,872, f. 168, Granville Sharp to Wilkes, 12 Jan. 1780, enclosing copies of his *Legal Means of Political Reformation* for use in connection with the county meetings.

Act was *ultra vires*, and no legislation could have validity which affected the duration of the mandate given to elected members of the house of commons, unless the assent of the constituencies had been secured. Now was not the moment for the constituencies to recognize the usurpations never before admitted by them, or to give the stamp of their authority even to triennial parliaments.

The *concession* [i.e. surrender] of a popular right, made by the people themselves in their collective capacity, at their several county-meetings, is infinitely more binding upon them (to exclude any future claim to this ceded right) than the same *concession* would be, if made merely by their *representatives* in parliament, without the instruction or concurrence of the people.

Wyvill, by his compromise, had struck a wedge into the whole ideology of his radical friends, the whole theory of fundamental rights, and the whole interpretation of English history upon which the claims of the Yorkshire movement had been based. He had even infringed the constitutional theory of the Association itself, for if compliances had been necessary *"for the sake of unanimity"* these ought to have been made to the "unanimously agreed" decisions of the men who had been *"deputed to a national conference* by freely-elected committees from a very considerable proportion of the counties and most populous cities and towns in England".

The striking similarity also of *this deputation*, in many respects, to an ancient example of a *national deputation* from all the counties, cited, on this occasion, by Lord Carysfort, from Hoveden, adds great weight to the resolutions in question.[1]

Apart from this particular difficulty, there were men who were running far ahead of the Association in their zeal against rotten boroughs or their desire for universal manhood suffrage. The ideas thrown out by Wyvill and his friends had dropped into a living world and had taken on a life of their own, refusing to dance just to Wyvill's tune or to stop just where he told them to stop. The

[1] *The Legal Means of Political Reformation*, pp. 76, 91–92, 85–86.

"speculative issues" had been raised and were producing new controversies and tensions at the heart of the movement itself.[1]

§III. THE DEFEAT OF THE ECONOMICAL REFORM

By this time the parliamentary conflict on the subject of economical reform had virtually been decided; the crucial debates having taken place just before and after the middle of March, in the days when the General Meeting of Deputies was being held in London. The story had had its picturesque moments; on the 8th, for example, when the house was about to go into committee on Burke's Establishment Bill, Lord George Gordon had been in one of his obstreperous moods, arguing that Burke had "evidently taken care of his friends" by allowing their sinecures to continue in existence for the life of the present holders. In the case of a reform "which directed its attention to the King's very bedchamber" and which "was to prevent him from eating, unless the very bread and meat he eat should be served by contract", it was at least the duty of the proposers of the scheme—he argued—"to clear themselves of all grounds of suspicion". He was told that he would be able to propose an amendment when the relevant clause came up for discussion, but he replied that this point would never be reached— "it was so far off, being in the 16th page." He demanded an immediate decision which should serve as an instruction to the committee; and continued his obstructive tactics for some time.

Then, from nine o'clock in the evening till 2.45 in the morning, the committee discussed the first clause of the Establishment Bill—the one which abolished the third secretary of state, otherwise known as the Secretary of State for the Colonies or the American Secretary. George III expected to see the government beaten on this issue, in view of "the disinclination that has in general existed

---

[1] See e.g. Add. Mss. 34,417, ff. 41–42, North to W. Eden [? 24 March 1780]: "I do not wonder that the Committees have overleaped all bounds. If they had kept within the limits their leaders prescribed . . . they would have been more orderly and governable than any such popular meetings have ever been from he first origins of faction to this day."

against that Arrangement, and no small prejudice against the present Possessor" of the office, Lord George Germain. Horace Walpole noted that the ministry were pessimistic and gave as a reason "the evident inutility of a Secretary for America when it [that continent] was lost." Now, as in the great speech in which he had introduced his economical reform, Burke made capital out of the fact that during most of the year 1779—during the illness of Suffolk and then for months after his death—the ministry had been able to carry on without the services of one of the secretaries of state. When it was argued that there had been a third secretary in the reign of Edward VI, as also for a number of years in the time of George II, the opposition replied that "the office was discontinued, because it was discovered to be useless." In any case, the country had "raised itself to the utmost pitch of national glory" when it has possessed only the customary two secretaries of state. "A third was however appointed, and from that instant the picture was completely reversed in all its features." During the course of the debate the Lord Advocate, Dundas, asked "why, if the influence of the crown was so excessive, the minister carried his questions by so small majorities?" Almost as if in order to add to the cogency of this remark the ministry saved the third secretary of state only by 208 votes to 201.[1]

A few days later, on 13 March, there occurred one of the most colourful of the house of commons debates in this period, when the committee considered a further clause of the Establishment Bill, namely the one which decreed the abolition of the Board of Trade. Gibbon, a member of that Board, has described "the delight" with which Burke was listened to on this occasion "even by those whose existence he proscribed". If he considered it "as an academy of Belles Lettres" Burke had every admiration for this Board of Trade, in which "every department of literature, the solid and the entertaining, the instructive and the amusing, had its separate professor." He had flowers to offer to the historical researches of Gibbon, to the letters published by Eden, and to the poetical accomplishments of Lord Carlisle, who in an age of poetry would have ranked amongst "the best of our minor poets," and in the

[1] *Parliamentary History*, XXI, 193–217; cf. *York Chronicle*, 17 March.

eighteenth century, "which was of a more serious form", was "deservedly regarded as a great poet". He wished to rescue these "professors", he said; for the Board of Trade was "a crow's nest, in which nightingales were kept prisoners". Their incomes were too great for their good. Like the authors endowed by Francis I they had been too well provided for. They had become "too rich to write".

Against this glut of imagery, this almost baroque *extravaganza* and the riotous cascade of hyperbole and fancy, William Eden, ponderous and humourless, conducted an unequal campaign. He traced the history of councils of commerce back to 1636 and said of the Board of Trade that

it owed its birth to William 3, it was nursed and educated by the great lord Somers; its farther progress in life was in the society of Mr. Locke, Mr. Addison, and all the first men in point of abilities within the kingdom.

He referred to 2,300 volumes in folio which demonstrated the activity and industry of the Board during the period of its existence. Burke refused to be nonplussed.

He thanked the hon. gentleman for his historical account of the origin and utility of the Board of Trade; he was ready to accept that, but not his 2,300 volumes, which he begged to be excused from taking; he would not look into one of them. They would serve, however, as a monument, under which both he and his clause might be buried, and form a funeral pile for them as large as one of the pyramids of Egypt. Alas, poor clause! (exclaimed he) if it be thy fate to be put to death, thou shalt be gloriously entombed.

Repeatedly Burke went back to the theme and rang the changes on it, ridiculing "the dull, senseless, sluggish contents of 2,300 volumes in folio". Much as he admired Locke, Addison and Prior, "he could not undertake to study the 2,300 volumes, nor consider them as any part of the productions of the great authors alluded to. He revered literature, but he did not wish to be overwhelmed with it."

Throughout the dispute with America "not so much as a single scrap of paper had been laid by that board before parliament respecting the state, condition or temper of the colonies." The only pretence it had made to any interest in British commerce had been the production of a report on the African trade a few years before —a document extraordinary in its display of "gross ignorance and partiality". William Eden had produced no evidence on the other side. He had merely pointed vaguely to the 2,300 volumes in folio—"sources of information . . . by which they could only profit in the other world". The whole system of our trade laws, the establishment of our colony governments, the granting of charters etc., had been effected by other bodies altogether—alternative institutions which the supporters of the ministry now affected to disparage.

The Lords of Trade themselves—including Gibbon, who was "brought down in a fit of gout" and was severely attacked by Fox —were induced to vote in their own cause on this occasion, though they had been asked to abstain at a time when the divisions were so close that they "might have it in their power to turn the scales in their own favour." Only Soame Jenyns declined to vote; but the Board of Trade was unpopular, Burke had shown himself a master of the field covered by the debate, and the recent revival of the office of President of the Board for the benefit of Lord Carlisle had been an acknowledged job, so that the motion for abolition was carried by 207 votes to 199. Horace Walpole seemed to think that the fate of the ministry was virtually decided by this division. He wrote on the following day, the 14th:

The court still holds out; but there is no recovering the ground that is lost. An opposition so successful will not loiter at Capua. . . . A speedy change is the best event that can happen.

The parliamentary struggle was now reaching a climax. The battles were more intense in that the divisions were so close and the opposition had had a taste of victory. Also, the most critical of all the struggles that were due to take place over the Establishment Bill—the conflict over the question of the household—was now at hand. The King wrote to Lord North on 16 March:

No one can feel more sincerely than I do for the immense fatigue he [Lord North] has at this busy moment, and hopes that He is not worse for the late days he has had this Week.

On the 20th the *Morning Chronicle* announced:

The sole cause of this paper's having been published very late several mornings last week, was the late hour at which the House of Commons rose.

Two days later, the same paper reported that Fox, Burke and Barré

were yesterday so hoarse and so ill, in consequence of their hard parliamentary duty for these ten days past that they could scarcely make themselves heard, and severally complained of the great pain in which they spoke.

When on the 24th the Easter recess occurred and Burke was able to go to Beaconsfield, he reported:

When I came hither I was so wasted by fatigue and want of sleep, which with me is always attendant on heavy labour, that it was thought advisable that I should not concern myself about any affair whatsoever for several days.

According to his own account it was not until 4 April that Burke returned to business or even took up a pen again.[1] At times it became clear that the stress of parliamentary business wore down the health of Lord North, and it was later recognized that it had helped to aggravate the illness of the Speaker.[2]

It was on 20 March that the discussion of Burke's economical reform reached what we must regard as its most critical stage. On this occasion the question concerned the regulation of the king's

---

[1] Fitzwilliam, *Correspondence of Burke*, II, 335 et seqq.

[2] In the *York Chronicle* for 19 May it is reported that the gallery of the house of commons was closed on 12 May, and that the reason was said to be that four members of parliament were "now lying dangerously ill in consequence of the great heat occasioned in the House of Commons by the concourse of people who crowded to hear the debates".

household—the abolition of the treasurer of the chamber, the treasurer of the household, the cofferer and the like. Burke, though he claimed that it meant the sacrifice of "about £12,000 out of his projected savings", had consented to withdraw the clause which stipulated that the king's household should be served by contract. Concerning the office of the treasurer of the chamber, however, he was adamant. He resolutely and consistently maintained that if the clause was defeated "his Bill was gone."

In the treasurer of the chamber consisted the very pith and marrow of his plan. . . . The treasury of the chamber was the very first office of the household that he had laid his fingers on; it therefore led the way, and involved all the rest.

One great end of his Bill was "the rendering it almost impossible in future for the King to run in debt", and to come to the house of commons for retrospective grants to cover an expenditure that had been beyond parliamentary control. For this purpose it was necessary "that the first lord of the Treasury should be answerable", should be responsible for the operation of the rule "that the expences of the civil establishment should not exceed the money allowed for that purpose by parliament". But

How could it be expected that the first lord of the Treasury should be responsible, if a variety of lesser treasuries were to exist, each of which would govern the branch of the public expenditure under its direction, just as it thought proper?

It was inevitable that as the committee of the whole house were dealing with the successive clauses of the Establishment Bill the discussion of each particular office in turn should be thrown back against a set of fundamental principles which served as a continual basis of reference. And perpetually it proved to be the same two issues that recurred, so that these were examined now from one side now from another, the successive debates almost coming to present the continuity of a developing theme. These two constitutional issues dominated the whole chain of debates at the committee stage of the Establishment Bill, and we are already familiar with them for they were the ones relating to the increasing influence of the crown and the right to control the expenditure of the civil list. It has already been mentioned that at the very beginning of these proceedings, on 8 March, Rigby had raised the latter of these two points, while Burke and his friends had not failed instantly to realize the momentousness of the issue. Burke claimed that "the King was only a trustee for the public. Property and subjects existed before kings were elected." The supporters of the ministry argued that the civil list was the king's private property; that William III had found his situation intolerable—had even threatened abdication— until he had been granted the civil list for life. It was maintained that owing to the decrease in the value of money, the £700,000 granted to William went further as a "means of influence" than the £900,000 which George III had been receiving since 1777.

It is often assumed that Burke's Establishment Bill was defeated by sheer corruption, and it can hardly be denied that some who voted with the ministry were under an obligation to it; since in those days, as at all times, a governmental majority was cemented by forms of vested interest. The narrow escape of the third secretary of state and the marginal defeat of the Board of Trade, however, show that at a moment of intensity an independent body of voters—who must normally have supported the government— were in a position to hold the balance. In the light of these two divisions we shall find that the critical clause in the Establishment Bill was to be defeated by what we must regard as a very considerable majority. That the issue was decided by independent voting, and upon a point of principle which at that date and in that particular context was understandable, is a judgment which can hardly be questioned in view of the development of the controversy concerning the right to interfere with the civil list. Those who may imagine that the objects of Burke and Fox in this period were self-evidently right, and were defeated only by corruption must answer the argument that two of the most important strategic interventions against the principle which they regarded as crucial, were made by friends of the petitioning movement, supporters of the Establishment Bill, and enemies of the influence of the crown.

In the middle of the debate of 13 March on the Board of Trade, Fox called upon the Speaker, Sir Fletcher Norton, "as the highest legal authority in the kingdom", to give the committee his ruling on the disputed question, namely the control of the civil list. He would hardly have called for such a statement if he had not been aware that Norton had come into a bitter feud with North; and the whole debate took a sensationally ugly turn when the Speaker accused the minister of using bribery in a negotiation to induce the Chief Justice of the Common Pleas to retire in favour of Wedderburn; while it transpired that he himself had only accepted the Speakership on the condition that it should be accompanied by the gift of a sinecure and the promise that it should not interfere with his promotion to one of the principal judicial posts. Not only did Norton make a bitter attack on Lord North in the course of his speech, but he declaimed against "the influence of the crown", which he said was "palpable and notorious".

It was impossible for any person, who sat so many years in that House as he had done, not to perceive both its actual existence, and apparent increase; consequently, it was the duty of every member in that House, who was himself a stranger to its effects, to do all in his power to reduce it, within such proper limits, as the constitution had marked out. . . .

Norton, however, was curiously judicial and discriminating as he discoursed in committee on the whole range of issues which the Yorkshire movement had provoked; and even if we say that he was meanly calculating—determined at this moment to show that it was in his power to sell himself to either of the contending parties —still this only had the effect of putting him in a position in which he could afford to be impartial and to distinguish all the more nearly the rights and wrongs of both sides. He announced his private opinion that the civil list itself was unnecessarily high, but he would not admit that it would be proper to reduce it now. In 1777 the house itself had declared £800,000 insufficient, and had agreed to increase the amount by £100,000. If the sum was so great as to involve a gross constitutional abuse, the house ought to have taken a different stand altogether when this question of an increase had been raised three years before.

Some time ago, he went on, he had thought it necessary to distinguish

between that part of the civil list appropriated to the special purposes of government, and that other part applicable to the expences or maintenance of the King's household. The former he thought directly and immediately within the controul of parliament, or indeed rather resulting from the nature of a public trust. The latter he thought stood upon a very different ground, and bore as near a relation as possible in its nature to private property.

Norton did not deny that there might be occasions when parliament might interfere even with this latter part of the civil list, even with the more private side of the King's expenditure. But, far from thinking that such interference could take place as an ordinary thing, he declared that even in regard to the other part, the more public side of the King's expenditure, parliament ought to be austere, not making any intervention save on serious grounds. Even in regard to "the salaries of judges, ambassadors, etc.", it was necessary to withhold any action except for cogent reasons. Norton wished success to Burke's Establishment Bill, but he disagreed with the critical part of it "which proposed the abolition of the several royal domestic establishments". This was precisely the issue on which Fox had obviously been counting on his support.

Indeed, when on 20 March this section of the bill came before the committee it became clear that, however mixed might be the views of members of the house of commons concerning the right of parliament to interfere with the civil list in general, there existed a strong repugnance to any legislative interference in its more private sections, and particularly with the management of the royal household. On this occasion another friend of the petitioning movement, another enemy of royal influence, Governor Pownall, made the strategic intervention, and it is interesting to note that he had spoken to the same effect, even before the Speaker had delivered his opinion, in the debate on the Board of Trade a week before.[1] He had attacked the Board of Trade and had approved of the interference of the house of commons in this matter, particularly as the Board "originated in parliament, was a parliamentary arrangement, began as an experiment and had at different times taken different shapes". But he had declared himself convinced "of the impropriety both in point of policy as well as justice" of interfering in anything that concerned "his Majesty's personal dignity or the support of the royal family or his household".

On 20 March Pownall's further statement on this subject was more effective since it was accompanied by a frank confession that he agreed with Burke in the object he had in view—he regarded the reform of the king's household as a necessity. He declared his conviction that parliament "had never meddled or interfered in the King's household, except in times from which he was unwilling to take his precedents".

He said, that in the 5th. Edw. 2, a commission, in consequence of proceedings in parliament, was issued, for enquiring into and reforming and new modelling the king's household. That a commission of the like sort, in consequence of like proceedings in parliament, was issued in 10th. Rich. 2; but when he looked to the consequences to which those measures lead, he should not take them as his precedent. The first ended in deposing Edward, and the second in dethroning Richard. There was a wiser and a more temperate measure taken in a period between these two—in the 50th Edw. 3—and that was, an address of parliament to the king; praying him to institute an enquiry into the state of his household, and pointing out to him the abuses which they apprehended reigned there.

Pownall did not see the necessity of even going so far as this. If the King should learn from his ministers that "though the clauses were rejected, the idea of the necessity of the reform was universally received and established . . . on all sides of the House," he

---

[1] Cf. *Parliamentary History*, XXI, 302, where Pownall claimed that "he was the first who had made the distinction between that part of the civil list, which went to the offices of the state, and that part which went to the King's household".

would not hesitate to carry out the desires of his people. Pownall "was sure, therefore, that the matter (i.e. the reform) must and would originate with his Majesty". If the ministers failed to inform or advise the King in the way that was expected, Pownall himself would take the lead in promoting an address in accordance with the precedent he had quoted. Pownall, indeed, left no doubt of the strength of his conviction that "such reform ought to be, and must be made."

If even the sympathetic were capable of such misgivings, Burke could expect little assistance at this point from those independent people who were customary supporters of the government. He still insisted that "if the present question was carried against him, he should consider his Bill as gone." He would not

> put his weak and disordered frame and constitution to the torture, in order to fight his Bill through the House inch by inch, clause by clause, and line by line . . . but would leave it to the people to go on with it, and let them judge by the issue how far their petitions were able to procure the redress of grievances they complained of.

When the division went against him by 211 votes to 158 he "declared his indifference to what became of the rest of the Bill". Fox attempted to rouse him, and convinced him that "even . . . if they could not obtain more than the abolition of the seven lords of trade" they "would have seven of the enemy less to fight against".[1] On various parallel motions relating to the royal household, however, the opposition were unsuccessful during the remaining part

---

[1] *Ibid.* XXI, 303–07. In the debate of 28 April on the clause for abolishing the Great Wardrobe etc., it was agreed "both by members and strangers" that Burke was a more "agreeable" figure than he had been for many years. "He evidently came down with his mind made up to the fate of the remaining clauses . . . and therefore treated them with all that ready wit, pleasantry, and good humour, which are the real features of his character." *Ibid.* 551–2 n. On 18 May a ludicrous situation arose, for while Burke wished to "get rid of his Bill, that it should be neither an eyesore to his adversaries, nor call for the tiresome and useless attendance of his friends", North declared his attachment to the idea of one of the clauses, so that Burke was put in the position of having to say that "his patience and spirits were both exhausted" and to beg Lord North "to be so kind and merciful, as to put an end to his sufferings". For the moment, however, he was defeated even on this issue.

of the day. Writing to one of his Bristol constituents, Burke declared on 4 April: "I must fairly own that I feel myself totally defeated. . . . By refusing to destroy the subordinate treasuries, or to enter into the household, the House has, in my opinion, rejected the whole plan." He glanced obliquely once again at the petitioning movement, and said in conclusion, concerning the whole scheme: "It now lies with the nation at large, whether it is to be received again."[1]

§IV. 6 APRIL 1780

By the beginning of the Easter recess—by 24 March—it had become clear that, in its more considerable aspects, the project of the economical reform was doomed. The whole campaign had been grounded upon a strategic mistake—a serious miscalculation concerning the state of even what might be called independent opinion. On 13 March, the Speaker of the house of commons had almost said as much, after Fox had called for a statement from him. And he had pointed to what he thought a better way of doing justice to the demands of the petitioning movement.

He had to lament, that [Burke's Establishment] Bill had engrossed so much of the time of the House. The time was wasted, and so far as the subject matter of the petitions was concerned, he did not think that their [i.e. the committee's] proceedings wore the appearance of doing business. The petitions should not have been permitted to lie upon the table so long without notice. Certain days, in each week, ought to have been allotted for taking them into consideration. The session was already far advanced; . . . The House should proceed to consider them with all imaginable dispatch and alacrity, to avoid every thing which might give a reason to doubt their sincerity; for it was scarcely possible that the petitions could be disappointed, if the prevalent language of that House, for some days past, might be safely trusted. . . .[2]

At the next stage of the story this procedure was actually fol-

[1] Fitzwilliam, *Correspondence of Burke*, II, 339.
[2] *Parliamentary History*, XXI, 265–66.

lowed and it was decided that on 6 April all the petitions which had been submitted should be referred to a committee of the whole house. Fox moved a call of the house on that day, "when he hoped he should see as full a House as ever had been known, and the People of England would then know who did their Duty, by attending to their Petitions, and how they voted".

The time was well chosen; for at their original meeting on 2 February the electors of Westminster had decided that on the very morning of 6 April they would hold their second assembly; so that the most spectacular of the resumed general meetings in connection with the Yorkshire movement in this period exactly preceded the parliamentary debate which was to be the crowning moment of the story. A correspondent, writing to the *Morning Chronicle* of 5 April, was indignant that Fox should have summoned the West-minister meeting for the 6th, "the very day that the House of Commons have set apart for the purpose of taking the Petitions . . . into consideration"; but he was inverting the chronological order of the decisions. There was reason for misgiving; for according to Horace Walpole "the court . . . expected that Fox would be attended to the house by a great mob." The analogy with the situation that pro-duced the Gordon riots is very remarkable; and the fact that on this occasion the government took precautions which afterwards gave the appearance of having been unnecessary, may help to explain their unpreparedness in the face of the Protestant Association two months later. On 6 April, however, the 3rd regiment of the Guards "were under arms till late at night; each man was provided with ten rounds of ball, and the horse had the same".[1] It was the regiment which had drawn upon itself the hostility of the popular party because of its conduct in the so-called "massacre" of St. George's Fields during the Wilkite troubles of a dozen years before. On 8 May the government was called to account for this measure in the house of commons, and when it was declared that the troops had been ordered out on an ordinary requisition from the civil

---

[1] *London Courant*, 11 April. According to the *York Chronicle* of 14 April the Guards were to wait "not only while the Westminster Association was holding in the Hall but also till the House of Commons should rise after the grand debate"

magistrates, Burke and his friends scourged the Middlesex justices as mere "carpenters, brick-makers and shoe-makers" and "generally the scum of the earth".[1]

On 6 April, says the *Morning Chronicle*, Fox, Byng, Sawbridge, Cartwright, Jebb, Turner and others of the Westminster Committee

met at the King's Arms, Palace Yard, and about one o'clock went in procession from the same place, preceded by a number of inhabitants of Westminster, and a person bearing a blue flag, with the following words in large white letters: "*Annual Parliaments and equal Representation*". In this manner they entered the Hall, and ascended a large platform, built for the occasion, over the steps of the Court of Common Pleas. Upwards of three thousand people ... received the Committee with three cheers.

Some of the newspapers claimed that the crowd numbered 6,000, but an account of the meeting which was sent to George III estimated that about 2,000 people were present, the great part "Spectators from curiosity". Fox and his friends Fitzpatrick and Sheridan had acted as a sub-committee and had drawn up a Plan of Association, which included "shorter parliaments" and the addition of a hundred county members, though it evaded the actual imposition of a "test". It contained a pledge not to vote for any parliamentary candidate "from whose known integrity and attachment to the constitution, we shall not have good reason to expect that he will give his utmost support in Parliament to the above propositions".[2]

Fox spoke for three-quarters of an hour, and, in a manner curiously similar to that of Dunning in the house of commons later in the day, enumerated the occasions on which the ministry of North had thwarted the desires of the petitioning movement. Declaring that George III's maxim of government was *Divide et impera*, he made a great call for unanimity. He then set out for his own part to make the best of both the worlds between which he was trying to

[1] *Parliamentary History*, xxi, 591–94; *London Chronicle*, 6–9 May. Similar attacks were made on these justices during the Gordon riots.

[2] Add. Mss. 38,593, ff. 23–4 [3 April]; ff. 25–7 [5 April.]

act as a bridge. He managed to give all possible assurances to the reforming party, while carefully avoiding the peculiar technical implications of an actual "test".

I was called upon (he said) by your voluntary Voice to offer myself next Election, a Candidate for the City of *Westminster*. Your Offer being made without any Solicitation on my Part, but originating in your own free Choice, it cannot be deemed necessary that I should mention any Part of my parliamentary or political History, as a required Test and Criterion by which you are to judge of me. I shall not say one Word therefore as a Test; but this much I cannot but say with the same unextorted Freedom that distinguished you in your Nomination, that I will ever . . . [do] my utmost to introduce œconomy into the Management of public Affairs . . . [promote] an Equal Representation by adding One Hundred Members to the existing Number, and [attempt] to shorten the Duration . . . of Parliaments to . . . one Year only.[1]

The radical leaders pressed the extremist arguments in favour of annual parliaments. Charles Turner gave a speech which "was, perhaps, the most extraordinary ever delivered within the walls of Westminster-hall, since the days of Oliver Cromwell". He told the people that they might alter government in any way they pleased and had the right to change to a republic, "and, in fact, that they were the Lords of the creation."[2] It does not appear that the meeting was unanimous on all points, for there were signs of dissension and, if not disorder, at least impatience. A Plan of Association, largely on the Yorkshire model, was adopted, however, and was presented for signature.[3]

The house of commons—which had met, for the first time after the recess, on the preceding day—presented an imposing appearance when the members had assembled on the 6th. It was "one of the fullest Houses that we have ever known", wrote Fox afterwards. The newspapers spoke to the same effect: "There was the

[1] *London Chronicle,* 6-8 April.

[2] *Ibid.* 8-11 April; cf. *ibid.* 13-15 April, and *Parliamentary History,* xxi, 409, where Turner gave certain explanations of this speech.

[3] *London Courant, Gazetteer* and *Morning Chronicle,* 7 April 1780; cf. *Corr. George III,* v, 175, Minutes of Meeting at Westminster Hall.

fullest House of Commons which has been known for many years."
One member declared:

> The number actually in the division in the House were 445
> [which is probably a misprint for 448] beside the tellers and those
> who paired off. This will [show] how anxious each party was to
> have the attendance of their friends. Every creature was forced
> down that could be carried into the House. . . .[1]

All the world realized that this was to be a great parliamentary
occasion—that the issue between the government and the Yorkshire movement was now to be finally drawn. Even certain members of the house of commons who held official posts in Ireland had
been summoned across to England to give their support to the
ministry.

The last few petitions—the ones from Denbighshire, Cumberland, Buckinghamshire, Nottinghamshire, Kent and Cambridgeshire etc.—had been presented on the previous day, or were submitted to the house at the opening of proceedings on the 6th.[2] The
speakers who introduced them would enlarge on the number of
the signatures that were attached to them, or the "respectability" of
the petitioners, or the voluntary character of the support which the
movement had received in the locality concerned. A critic might
then arise and object to the disorderly nature of the meeting in
Cambridge, or the indiscriminate way in which signatures had
been gathered in Retford, or the small proportion of genuine freeholders amongst the subscribers to the Nottinghamshire petition.
Nothing could disguise the fact that the government was faced
with a protest from the country at large—a protest very imposing
in its character. At the same time, it could hardly be denied that this
popular movement also had its seamy under-side, its ragged fringe.

In the committee of the whole house on the 6th it was Dunning's
duty to open the discussion upon the whole collection of petitions
—forty or so—that had been presented to the house of commons
during the previous months. Like Fox at the Westminster meeting

[1] H.M.C. *Rutland Mss.* III, 26–28.
[2] *London Chronicle*, 4–6 April; *Cambridge Chronicle*, 8 and 15 April; *York Chronicle*, 28 April.

earlier in the day, he began by recapitulating the course of events in parliament since the beginning of the year, in order to show that "no redress could be, or was meant to be given to the petitioners, by the modes already tried."

The whole of what has been done in consequence of that pile of parchment now on your table, containing the sentiments, the prayers, and petitions of above 100,000 electors, amounts, in the whole, to a single clause in my hon. friend's Bill [the clause relating to the abolition of the Board of Trade], which standing naked, as it does, is of little or no importance; the proposition [of a Commission of Accounts] snatched out of my other hon. friend's hands, [Barré's] by the noble lord [North], and only snatched to insult you in this House, and mock your constituents out of it, and the Contractors' Bill, which ministers, or at least their friends and confidents, pretend to predict, will miscarry in another place [i.e. in the house of lords.]

Dunning made it clear that he was determined to bring the whole issue to a head in a manner that would permit of no further evasion. He said he would challenge the committee with two resolutions which would settle the matter unmistakeably in one way or another:

If the committee should agree with me in the resolutions, I mean to follow them up with real, substantive, practicable measures; but should they disagree or dissent, or endeavour to evade or procrastinate, there will be at once an end of the petitions, and a full answer to the petitioners.

In the course of the debate the supporters of the ministry objected to this mode of procedure, this way of codifying the demands of the petitioners and offering so to speak the cream of all the prayers of the various localities in two comprehensive resolutions. Governor Pownall contrived to add to the magnitude of the whole occasion as he replied to this criticism, for he drew attention to a precedent which had the effect of measuring the present crisis against one that was curiously analogous in the reign of Charles I.

There never was, he said, but one period when there were so

many petitions of this sort preferred to the House as at present; that was now just 140 years ago. In 1640, there were petitions of this kind preferred in this manner to the House.[1]

He reminded his hearers that on 10 November 1640 the house had appointed a committee "to draw out of the petitions presented to the House, some such declaration as may be a fair representation of the sense of the petitioners". Dunning, in his resolutions, claimed to be summarizing the whole purport of the petitioning movement exactly in this way, discovering what was universal and what was fundamental in the prayers that one locality and another had presented to the house of commons.

Even so, the supporters of the administration were undoubtedly taken by surprise. Dunning had not disclosed his intentions and the ministry had not known what to expect from a discussion of the combined petitions. The ostensible subject-matter of these had been economical reform—a topic they had thoroughly traversed, and one in connection with which they had generally had successful divisions. If they expected anything further on the lines which had been laid out by Burke, however, Dunning from the very start set the direction firmly at right-angles to all their anticipations.

His first resolution declared:

That it is the opinion of this committee that the influence of the crown has increased, is increasing, and ought to be diminished.

We have seen that this point had been embedded in the logic of Burke's economical reform; but it was certainly by an afterthought and almost by an accident that it had been explicitly formulated in the petitions themselves. The one part of the original Yorkshire petition which is known not to have come from the pen of Wyvill is the phrase which, after a reference to the waste of public money, states:

Whence the Crown has acquired a great and unconstitutional

---

[1] References to the analogy with 1640 were common; e.g. Lord Verney in presenting the Buckinghamshire petition on 5 April, *London Chronicle*, 4–6 April.

Influence, which, if not checked, may soon prove fatal to the Liberties of this Country.

It was argued during the course of the debate on 6 April that the question of the influence of the crown was an extraneous one—an issue that had not been really part of the subject-matter of the petitions. Dunning was ready with his answer: "Nine out of ten of the petitions on the table contained this general proposition," he said; and probably even he had no idea by what a narrow margin it had come to be there. On the other hand, even the opposite complaint was brought forward, namely, that Dunning, on his own terms, ought to have gone further still and more faithfully repeated the words of the petitions. His enemies would have had an easier game if he had been more explicit in his description of George III as one whose influence "may soon prove fatal to the Liberties of this Country". The truth was that, in the course of the Yorkshire movement and the parliamentary debates connected with it, something like the formula employed by Dunning had gradually been hammered out in the early months of 1780.

Dunning quoted Hume to show that the increasing influence of the crown had been foreseen so early as the year 1742, and he mentioned Blackstone as an authority for its existence. "He cited a passage from Hume's Essays, to show that that able writer had prophesied, that arbitrary monarchy would one day or other be the euthanasia of the British constitution." He made it clear that in the reproach that he had to make against the crown he did not have in mind "that Influence which arose from its Virtues, or the just Exercise of its Prerogative, but that which arose from Corruption and other undue Practices". He showed how that influence had grown "with the increase of taxes, with the increase of commerce"; he mentioned the partiality in the distribution of military promotion, lottery tickets and subscriptions to the loan—"no less than a million of this Year's Loan had been distributed to members of parliament." Amongst other things he read from the Parliamentary Register a list of newly-raised offices and increased salaries. "He found another great source of influence in the patronage of the East-India Company. Directors were made contractors, and contractors directors, to serve the purposes of ministers." In India the ministers had also "acquired the appointment of the Supreme Council, the judges and almost every important officer".

Many men in that House could point to their next neighbour, and say he was corrupted, and was actually to be paid in hard, sordid, dirty guineas. . . .

He pledged his honour that he personally knew "upwards of fifty members in that House"—and would name them "if the House desired it and if the issue of the debate were to depend upon it"—who always voted with the government, yet confessed outside the house that the influence of the crown had dangerously increased.[1]

Dunning announced that he would later move a second resolution which would run as follows:

That it is competent to this House, to examine into, and to correct, abuses in the expenditure of the civil list revenues, as well as in every other branch of the public revenue, whenever it shall appear expedient to the wisdom of this House so to do.

North had sought to avoid a motion which should treat this matter as a question of principle; but the opposition had now decided that they would not allow him to evade the issue in this way. Dunning had his own tricks of evasion, however, and had framed a motion which the Speaker himself might have supported, and which could be carried by a house which disapproved of any interference in that portion of the civil list expenditure which concerned the royal household. Rigby, who had been an extremist in this matter on the government side, claimed that he had intended to propose: "That it was unjust in parliament to diminish the civil list revenue, without proof of some abuse of it". This, too, was not without its ambiguities, and conformed equally well to the views which had been put forward by the Speaker in a previous debate.

[1] *Parliamentary History*, XXI, 340–49; cf. *York Courant*, 11 April; *York Chronicle*, 14 April.

Rigby himself added that Dunning's second resolution was "not inconsistent with the one he had intended to propose".

After Dunning's magnificent opening one might have expected a great oratorical display. In the subsequent events of this 6 April, however, the surprises are great and the paradoxes abound. And, though the popular cause prevailed in a signal manner, the success had an element of the ludicrous, and the glory was streaked with irony. The inadequacy of corruption could hardly have been more clearly demonstrated than in the carrying of the very resolution that deplored its power. Under a king to whom the commons had shown such fidelity—not to speak of subservience—how could it happen that the loyalty should have found its breaking-point on a motion which more than all others struck at the monarchical element in the constitution? And if the King possessed this dangerous influence, why did it fail to operate on the issue that was crucial, that is to say at the moment when its own basis was precisely the subject of attack? Even if too many members of the house of commons were "under influence"—for this was admittedly the point in question—why should they confess it now, when it had been hinted that this would be an admission of the corrupt nature of all the votes they had previously given? Finally, why was it so much Dunning's debate—why from Fox, Burke, Savile, Barré and Lord John Cavendish was there no great speech—nothing to mark the fact that the petitioning movement had come to its crowning demonstration and its critical test? Why was there on the part of these men no pretence at more than a few tactical interpolations that have come down to us in unimpressive and inadequate reports?

The supporters of the government from the first showed an unskilfulness for which it would be difficult to find a parallel. Their speeches and arguments were unconvincing, their leaders made repeated mistakes in tactics, and this is one of the very rare occasions on which North himself not only lost his temper but came near to disgracing his cause. It is difficult to understand, furthermore, why a man so clever as Dundas, the Lord Advocate, should have blundered so seriously as we shall find him doing in this debate. Barré, who like Dunning was a follower of Lord Shelburne, explained in a letter to his leader how at an early stage in the proceedings "the disorder in the Ministry was so great" that the opposition leaders determined to have a division as quickly as possible. It soon became clear that the best tactics for them would be to sacrifice any desire to distinguish themselves by great orations, and to leave their enemies no opportunity to recover, no chance to remove the bad impression that had been created.[1]

As we have seen, the supporters of the ministry had been taken by surprise, and they vainly attempted to show that Dunning, by his whole mode of procedure, had given an improper turn to the controversy. They tried, further, to convince the committee that Dunning's resolution was inadmissible because it was merely the statement of an abstract proposition. In any case the thesis was a mere assertion on the part of its author; and they could argue that it was unsupported by any information which could be regarded by the house as "evidence". One man fell to niggling and said that those who believed that the power of the crown had increased might not be the people who regarded it as still increasing, while all might in any case differ on the question whether it ought to be diminished. In general the supporters of government were harassed furthermore by a bad conscience, and by the thought that virtually nothing at all had as yet been done to satisfy the demands of the petitioners. And North himself must have sounded unconvincing when he pointed out that a number of measures were still pending—still not yet defeated by the votes of government supporters—which were relevant to the petitioners' demands. Even leading government speakers seemed to have a bad conscience—they slipped into damaging admissions concerning the influence of the crown. Certainly they failed to face the issue—failed to state all that might have been said in favour of the King's constitutional influence; though Nugent added the point that the existence of a state of war "had thrown a sudden weight into the hands of the crown", and that this might be expected to continue only for a limited period.

North did not intervene until attention had been called to the silence of the ministers and he had been goaded to fury and exasperation by a direct personal attack. With regard to the policies re- .

[1] H.M.C. *Rutland Mss.*, III, 26-28.

lating to America, he said, "they were not his measures as a minister, they were all grounded on the acts of the legislature."

In proposing and consenting to those Bills, he had acted as a member of parliament, and as such only was responsible.

To the argument that his continuance in power, while opposition to him was mounting, was itself a proof of the excessive influence of the crown, he made the reply that his position was indeed reinforced by the fact that his enemies were threatening the constitution. He was called to order. He lost his temper. "Am I to hear myself charged as the author of our present misfortunes?" he said. The cries came across the house, "You are, you are." The opposition maintained that they had the right to arraign his conduct "as a minister". He, however, was not within his rights at this moment, for he was arraigning their conduct "as men". Other interpolations occurred. "Considerable confusion ensued."[1]

Dundas, who, by moving "that the chairman do leave the chair", found himself open to the retort that the prayers of the petitioners could not be dismissed in so summary a fashion, changed his tactics and suggested that Dunning's motion should be preceded by the words: "It is necessary to declare." A few days later he said that he had made his proposal "in the hope that it would more forcibly impress the minds of the committee with the propriety of negativing" the whole proposition. Fox hastened to accept the proposal, and the opposition afterwards claimed that Dundas had served their purposes by improving on the form they had devised.[2] But in assenting to the amendment Fox is reported to have said:

that if ever he should set Foot in that House again, (which was a Matter of Doubt with him) he would always oppose the second Sitting of that Committee, because the Samples already given sufficiently satisfied him that it would be no more than a Mockery.[3]

[1] The fuller account in the York Chronicle, 14 April, makes more clear the reason for the upheaval described in Parliamentary History, xxi, 363.

[2] Four days later Dundas admitted that he had unintentionally strengthened Dunning's motion: Parliamentary History, xxi, 380.

[3] York Courant, 11 April.

This first resolution was then carried by 233 votes to 215. Dunning then proposed the second, concerning the control of the civil list. North "expressed his wishes very strongly, that the Committee would not proceed", but the motion, as we have seen, was not without its ambiguities, and it was agreed to without a division. Thomas Pitt moved "that it is the duty of this House to provide, as far as may be, an immediate and effectual redress of the abuses complained of in the petitions", and though North again implored the committee not to proceed, the motion passed unanimously. Fox, now moved that the resolutions "be immediately reported to the House". This was agreed to, and the report was made, though North had attacked the procedure as "violent, arbitrary, and unusual." Once they had realized that fortune was with them, the opposition were determined to take every advantage. They carried one place after another by storm.

Dundas, when replying to another speech by Dunning a few days later, complained of the way in which the house was being hustled and surprised, as had been the case, he said, in the debate of the 6th.

Gentlemen were called on instantly to decide upon an extensive and important proposition, popped out of a member's pocket and wholly new to those whom it most immediately concerned . . . the learned gentleman [Dunning] who made it, should he carry it, would not be content with that, but contrary to all parliamentary rule, would proceed a step further, and report it instantly . . . not giving gentlemen time to sleep upon their opinions, not affording them an opportunity to recall a rash vote . . .[1]

If we argue that the members of the house of commons on 6 April were merely awed by the proximity of a general election, we possibly do them less than justice. Such a mode of reasoning assumes that they were corrupt in their general conduct, and only now—in view of the approaching contest —took heed of the wishes of the people. And it assumes that save on this particular occasion the people as a whole were accustomed to feeling themselves betrayed, accustomed to having their wishes flouted. All this, however,

[1] *Parliamentary History*, XXI, 383.

would not explain why afterwards—still nearer the general election —the same men returned to their customary support of government, and why the majority of the house of commons at a later date did more to offend the petitioners than at this moment they were doing to please them. It would not explain the fact which both parties (and outsiders like Horace Walpole) were prepared to recognize, namely, that the balance had been turned by the independent country members who were regarded as the salt of the constitution. We must not forget that though corruption might be strong enough to contribute some degree of stability to a government—might bring the additional weight that would provide a "working majority" for ordinary purposes in normal times— though the royal influence might even be excessive, so that it permitted the North administration to endure too long—it did not entirely enslave the house of commons, or decide the result when a great issue confronted the nation. North, as we have seen, was constantly in fear for his majority, and the votes of the country gentlemen were always a special anxiety to him. Under these conditions the things which were said in debate were not an idle entertainment; and the parliamentary skill of North, if it was a reason why the King desired, also explained why the house of commons so long permitted, his continuance in the leadership.

In any case it would not be impossible for men at the present day to deplore the increase in the power of government departments without either wishing to overthrow the ministers who happen to be in office, or accepting any particular remedies which might be suggested at a given moment. In 1780 men could privately complain of the weaknesses of North without wishing it to be understood that they advocated a surrender to the Rockinghamites. They could privately regret the increasing influence of the crown without agreeing that the constitution should be changed or George III be deprived of anything that was essential to his dignity. They could vote for Dunning's motion (though it jeopardized the position of Lord North himself), and yet be sure that they never intended the King to come into the power of the opposition whigs. No matter what interpretation we may adopt, however, it is difficult to see how Dunning's motion could have been carried if many honest supporters of George III had not had genuine misgivings concerning his increasing influence. And the Speaker was not peculiar when he shrank from any interference with the royal household and yet, almost in the same breath, cried out against corruption and the excessive influence of the crown.

For Lord North it was as though the end had come. He wrote to the King at 2 a.m.

If I had not for four years past apprized your Majesty that this event would happen & if I had not made it my constant prayer that I might be allow'd to quit your Majesty's Service, I should feel very unhappy now at what has happen'd & may further be expected. I humbly submit once more to your Majesty that it is absolutely necessary that I should be permitted to retire at the end of the Session. . . .

George III replied that the resolutions could by no means be looked upon as personal to North. "I wish I did not feel at whom they are *personally levelled*."[1]

Even Horace Walpole found his cheerfulness restored at this moment, and regarded Dunning's success as a proof of the fact that the radical programme of the Yorkshire movement was an unnecessary extravagance. He wrote to Mason:

The 6th of April ought for ever to be a red-lettered day, and at least as solemn a festival as the 29th of May, for the question carried was, that the influence of the crown has increased, is increasing, and *ought to be diminished*. I adopt the whole sentence into my revolution-creed. . . .

Six days later Walpole returned to the matter in a letter to Mason, which on second thoughts he decided not to send:

When in less than five months the spirit of *part* of the people can force, or intimidate the most corrupt and most Tory Parliament that ever was, to add a codicil to Magna Charta, the House of Commons does not want an hundred members more. Few Houses of Commons ever did so much for liberty. . . .[2]

[1] *Corr. George III*, v, 39–40.
[2] *Letter of H. Walpole* (ed. Toynbee), xi, 149; 155.

It was the victory—but at the same time it was the dismay of the Yorkshire leaders; and a number of places found it the reason or the pretext for regarding Wyvill's Plan of Association as unnecessary for the time being. Their faith in the existing house of commons had been restored, and they were prepared to put their hopes in the immediate future on the body that had shown such a change of heart.

In one sense, however, the events of 6 April provided an argument not only for the enemies of corruption in general, and not only for the Rockinghamites who had looked for just this kind of result from the Yorkshire movement, but also for the more radical party that was dissatisfied with the representative system. The number of the county members supporting Dunning's resolution, compared with the borough and Scottish members on the other side, gave striking confirmation to the view that the former were the virtuous element in the constitution.

§V. THE DEFEAT OF DUNNING

"The blow seems to me decisive," wrote Horace Walpole to Sir Horace Mann, two days after the victory of Dunning's motion. Then, with a zeal unusual in him, he risked a prophecy—possibly the worst of the predictions which he attempted to make in the whole of this period:

> This committee is to continue sitting on the petitions, will exclude any other business, will extract from the petitions whatever propositions it pleases ... and will carry along all those who have already voted on that foundation; so that, if the ministers attempt to make a farther stand, nothing seems so probable as their being personally accused. To combat on the same field of battle after being vanquished, will, in my opinion, be frenzy.

It is not clear that Dunning had quite expected the success which was achieved by his resolutions on 6 April. It is not clear that he knew what was the next move to make, though he had promised to follow up his resolutions "with real, substantive, practicable measures". The house of commons went into committee on the petitions again on 10 April, and he declared that since the complaints of the petitioners had been admitted to be well-founded, remedies must be discovered—"it was incumbent on the Committee to go from generals to particulars." He moved first of all, therefore, the further resolution: that "for preserving the independence of parliament, and obviating any suspicion of its purity" the house should receive at the beginning of every session an account of any sum paid "out of the produce of the civil list, or any other branch of the public revenue" to any member of either house of parliament. Dunning made it clear that when this and other resolutions had been carried "he certainly did not mean to leave them as mere resolutions of the House, but should . . . bring in one or more Bills." North was not prepared to resist this new resolution which "he thought every way fair and reasonable"; and it was carried without a division.

Then, since Burke had been unable to abolish the subordinate treasurers, the cofferer, comptroller and master of the household or their clerks, Dunning sought to gain the principal object of the proposal by a declaration that it was "incompatible with the independence of parliament" that such officers should hold seats in the house of commons, assuming that "such places shall be permitted to exist." The motion was carried by 215 to 213 votes; for five supporters of the government failed to arrive in time and the fact that they were locked out was sufficient to turn the scale. Three days later, on 13 April, there took place the second reading of Crewe's bill for disabling revenue officers from voting in parliamentery elections. Here it was not a mere resolution that was in question; and the sentimental heart of the English country gentleman would appear to have been strangely touched when confronted with the thought that he might be voting for "a total disfranchisement of a large body of the electors of Great Britain". It was pointed out that "in truth, the revenue officers had no franchise,"since "it was absolutely impossible for them to give their votes freely." The bill was defeated, however, by 224 votes to 195.

It would almost seem to be the case that the opposition whigs had come to the end of their resources; for, though the parliamentary conflict was to continue for some weeks longer, they were baffled and exasperated; and it appeared that they had nothing really new to suggest. Indeed there was little that the opposition could do now if they wished to capture the votes of the independent gentlemen. There was little scope for them, even if they allowed plans of actual reform to fall into abeyance—even if ambition were bounded by the idea of merely devising motions of any sort which would enable them to collect majorities against the government, and go on collecting them until Lord North had to bow to the repetition and the accumulated force of these. Burke's programme had failed; Dunning's policy seemed to be advancing into the wilderness; even the glorious 6th of April was coming to appear as almost a barren victory. Three significant events occurred on 14 April which, though not decisive yet, left the impression that the enemies of the government were in disarray.

Firstly, in the house of commons on this day, Dunning was "about to propose a matter of the first consequence", but asked first of all whether the Speaker would be able to bear the strain. Since Norton gave a pathetic account of his state of health, Lord John Cavendish proposed a recess; and it was Lord North who, owing to the pressure of business, discouraged the idea, favoured a shorter period of recess if there had to be one at all, and deprecated the waste of time that would be suffered if Norton found that he would have to resign the speakership at the end of the recess in any case. In the closet it was held that the Speaker was still waiting to see what each of the parties would be willing to offer him. It was known that the race-meeting was due to take place in Newmarket in the following week, and the reckless blades, the irrepressible bloods of the Rockinghamite faction, would never stay in London —they were too wild to be held on the lead. George III wrote: "I have not the Smallest doubt that the Speaker has pleaded illness to enable the Opposition to pursue the amusement at Newmarket the next Week." The Speaker was genuinely ill; but the opposition were short-sighted if they expected that a recess would operate to their benefit, save perhaps by covering their shame during Newmarket week. The ministry disliked the suspension of business, but were in a better position than the whig magnates to make use of the interval for the purpose of consolidating their faction.

Secondly, on 14 April, the ministry took the offensive by mobilizing their forces against the Contractors' Bill in the house of lords. The house of commons recess (which lasted until the 24th) gave time for passion on this subject to grow weary, and indignation to wear itself out. The ministerial success on this issue was not without reason, for the opposition peers could be wildly wilful and almost childishly unconvincing on an occasion like this. When they argued that the bill represented the "unanimous" desire of the house of commons, it was easy to show that this was not at all the case, even though the resistance in that house had not been carried to a division. When they urged that the rejection of the bill "might, in fact, create a quarrel" or "lay the foundation of perhaps a fatal misunderstanding, and create an incurable difference" between the two houses, the insincerity of this was only too patent. When they pointed out that the house of commons could claim a special compliance in this matter, since it had the right to decide the qualifications of its own members, the Lord Chancellor Thurlow had no difficulty in exposing the fallacies in this argument. This was a bill; it was not even a bill to define the qualifications of members; it involved the question of contracting in war-time; it was a matter of national concern, "a clear measure of state". Finally, when the opposition peers said that the lords were bound to give their assent to it, because "it was not only the unanimous wish of the House of Commons; it was the wish of the people of England," they were answered by a clear and not unimpressive piece of reasoning. Lord Hillsborough gave a discourse on the function of the house of lords, saying:

that the time was now come, when the consequence of the House of Lords would be fully apparent—its use, and its necessary influence in the constitution. It was their duty, when the prerogative of the crown was extended to improper bounds, to connect themselves with the people; and again, when the people were warmed either by enthusiasm or error into madness, when they were mad from virtue, and were bent on reforming and amending the constitution on erroneous principles, which he conceived now to be the case, it was their duty to check and resist that delirium of virtue, that rage and tempest of liberty, and bring them back to coolness and sobriety.

The Duke of Grafton might retort: "It was impossible to say to what lengths the resentments of the people might not proceed." The Earl of Shelburne might describe "without doors, the people clamorous for redress of grievances, ripe for any violence, and easy to be led to such measures as would shake the kingdom to its centre". The government merely made more capital out of these unfortunate indiscretions. It was not plausible to argue that the right of free deliberation had been taken away—or ought to be abdicated—in the case of a house of parliament. Apart from all this the bill itself was shown to be open to objections and even the Duke of Richmond declared that he did not quite agree with "the mode of disqualification proposed". The supporters of the bill were even unfairly handicapped; for if they alleged the existence of corrupt practices, they were asked to give "Westminster-hall proof", and yet if this could be provided they were open to the retort that the legal system already provided the remedy. Above all, how could that house of commons be called corrupt which had carried Dunning's motions on 6 April and had sent the Contractors' Bill itself up to the house of lords?

The third of the events which distinguished 14 April was the revelation which the King and the closet-advisers received that day, of an interview between Fox and North, and the existence of a disposition to negotiate. Jenkinson, who was watching every move of North with the greatest suspicion, was satisfied that the initiative had not come from his side; and he knew not only the story which North had told the King, but also the account which had leaked out through the indiscretions of Sheridan. This latter had negotiated the affair with North's secretary, Brummell, and Fox had extracted a promise that no mention of it should be made to anybody save the King. Jenkinson wrote: "I think it clear from all this, that Opposition want to treat & for some reason or other are afraid to go on." He advised George III "to be very carefull of the Conversations You have" with Lord North and "to hold such sort of general Language as You used to hold before Christmas".[1]

The decisive moment at last arrived and the house of commons reassembled on 24 April. The Speaker said that he would continue in his function in spite of his doctor's instructions, and the day was to provide an unusual ordeal for the holder of that office. The assembly was larger even than that of the famous 6 April, and those who took part in the division were slightly greater in number. Once again Dunning himself was to open the proceedings, and he was the first to note the advantage which the ministry had taken of the recent recess.

Observing that the House was more than commonly full, he said he was glad to address an assembly so crowded, and though he applauded the industry of those who had even fetched patriots from the other side of St. George's Channel, where they were engaged in discussing measures for the preservation of Ireland and brought officers of the navy and army from their professional duties to their duty within those walls, he hoped the new comers would shew their zeal for their country ... by voting for the motion, and that the 233 of the 6th of April would cut a still more respectable figure by the addition of twenty or thirty. . .

Dunning did not stand before the house, however, with a new remedy for abuses, and perhaps it was his weakness at this moment that he pursued tactics for the sake of tactics and, instead of bread, offered the people a stone. He built his argument first on the rejection by that house of the bill for the disfranchisement of revenue-officers, and secondly on the defeat of the Contractors' Bill in the house of lords. These things, he said, showed that the ministry were determined to thwart the objects of the petitioning movement, and that if they failed in the case of one branch of the legislature they would not hesitate to use their power in the other. In order to deal with this position of stalemate he made a proposal not merely unusual but admittedly unprecedented in character. He would confront one deadlock with another deadlock, and secure that, till the

[1] *Corr. George III*, v, 42–47; H.M.C. *Dartmouth Mss.*, I, 441.

grievances were redressed, the existing parliament should neither be prorogued nor dissolved. He moved:

That an humble Address be presented to his Majesty, praying, that he will be graciously pleased not to dissolve the parliament, or prorogue the present session, until proper measures have been taken to diminish the influence, and correct the other abuses, complained of by the petitions of the people.

The motion was opposed by Lord Nugent who, though he had become an enemy of the war with the American colonies, refused to admit that the influence of the crown prevailed "to a degree which should alarm the people". Dunning's proposal, he said,

smelt too strongly of the year 1641, and called to his mind the violent measures which marked our history soon after that period, staining the pages of the historian with blood, producing the violent death of the prince, and the destruction of regal government, and which was followed by a republican system of the grossest tyranny that ever a people groaned under.

On this occasion, however, it was William Adam who, speaking for the ministry, expanded the scope of the whole argument and projected the issue against a wider background. He pointed out that when a bill had been rejected by one House, "it is impossible, according to the law of parliament, to bring that Bill back again during the same session." In any case "it is probable that the same parliament that rejects the Bill this session, will reject the same Bill next session." Dunning's new motion, therefore, would not, in fact, assist the reforming party out of the deadlock which they had reached. It was an unprecedented motion, he saw, for, though an analogy from the year 1641 had been mentioned, it had then been a bill, not an address from a single house, that had been in question. The rejection of the present proposal would not in any case imply that parliament was to be immediately dissolved.

Then Adam widened the whole range of the argument and denied that the demands of petitioners could be regarded as binding upon the legislature. "The petition prayed for three things—an abolition of unmerited pensions, of useless sinecures, and of the exorbitant emoluments of necessary offices." By a construction which was being placed upon these demands, it was now claimed that the petitioners were seeking something else, namely, the establishment of a free parliament. By a further extension of the terms it had come to be asserted that nothing less than annual parliaments and an increase in the representation were the objects in view. All this only served to illustrate "the strides that reformation had taken from the first York meeting to the last meeting in Westminster-hall".

The history of all ages evinces, that reformers have always exceeded their original designs. . . . The madness of popular reformation had never failed to deprive those of power who wish to check it, and to place it in the hands of those, whose desperate situation makes them rejoice in changes.

Though it had been necessary to resist the tyranny of Charles I, Adams declared, even "the virtues, the abilities, of those times were not able to stop the wild spirit of reformation when it had once got loose."

Dunning's resolution must be regarded as an unfortunate one, and seems to confirm the view that the opposition were at the end of their resources. Fox might declare that it depended on the fate of this question "whether Englishmen were again to fight for their liberties, were again to take the field in opposition to arbitrary power". He might claim that if Charles I had only given way to "the just grievances of the people", all the dreadful horrors of civil war would have been avoided. The government carried the day by 254 votes to 203, however; and the occasion was an important one; for both sides had realized its significance as a trial of strength.

Amid scenes of confusion which taxed the powers of the Speaker, Fox claimed a further hearing and staged a remarkable demonstration at this point. He declared "that he, for one, was determined, so far as related to himself, to adjourn over the business of the present session, and never more enter that House, so long as the majority entertained similar sentiments to those they apparently embraced by the vote they had given that night". He would attend on Monday next, since Dunning had moved the adjournment of the committee on the petitions to that day.

He would make one trial, one effort more, in expectation that those who had deserted their principles would endeavour to retrieve their public character. If that last effort should miscarry, he should then know what to do. . . . He would quit that House, and leave ministers responsible for the consequences. . . . the people had resources still left; they were furnished by the constitution.

Fox could not contain his bitterness against the men who had betrayed the promises of 6 April and had given that "scandalous, treacherous, and disgraceful vote". He despised "those who were at the devotion of the minister" but they at least had the virtue of "fidelity, gratitude, and consistency". Those who had voted with Dunning on 6 April, however, and had deserted the cause now— he was "at a loss for words", he said, with which to describe them. "It was shameful, it was base, it was unmanly, it was treacherous."

The defection which he had alluded to originated chiefly among the county members, many of them of great weight and respect; but however high they might stand in the estimation of their friends in their counties, or in that House, he should ever judge of men by their conduct, and not by their professions. . . . The last vote, most probably, was agreeable to their real sentiments; the vote of the 6th of April was to answer ends merely personal. We were on the eve of a general election; the gentlemen alluded to would soon go down to their constituents: the first and most natural question would be, "What have you done in consequence of our petitions? . . . Has a more œconomical expenditure of the public money been determined upon and adopted?" . . . "No: but look at the resolutions of the 6th of April: you will there find that I and my colleague have voted [for these]."

So, Fox attacked those very county members which the Yorkshire movement had so far prized that it had determined to add another hundred of them at least to the house of commons. It was North who broke out into reproaches when he heard such a diatribe "against a set of men as respectable as any in that House".

Fox seemed to make it a complaint against them that they had voted in his favour and put him in a majority on 6 April. Yet North, as he pointed out, had been "left on that night in a very considerable minority"—deserted by men who had so often voted for him—and he had not risen, "in the anguish of defeat and disappointment", to charge them with baseness and treachery. He adjured Fox "not to despair, but rather hope, that upon some future day he might again vote in a majority". For the rest, neither the session nor the parliament was to be concluded yet; for the government still had "a great deal of business" to put before the house. Neither was it proper to behave as though the vote of this evening had denied everything to the petitioners. "No one measure whatever had been either negatived, or by inference disposed of, by the vote of that night."

The tide had turned. The issue was virtually decided. Members of the opposition attributed their subsequent defeats to the period of the recess which had recently ended. Later, on 18 May, Sawbridge declared that since 6 April "the influence of the crown had been in a progressive state of increase." He attributed it to the "tampering" with members of the house of commons, which he said he could prove had taken place at the time of the Speaker's illness and during the recess.

Part III

CONCLUSION

Chapter VIII

THE FRUITS OF
EXTRA-PARLIAMENTARY ACTIVITY

§I. THE EDUCATIVE RÔLE AND HISTORICAL IDEAS OF
THE YORKSHIRE MOVEMENT

IN the meantime the very success of Dunning's motions of 6
April had proved to be if anything a misfortune for the Yorkshire movement. The Committee of Correspondence which
had been established in Cambridge carried the county meeting
with them on 10 April, when they referred to that victory and declared that

> desirous of shewing a proper respect to the deliberations, and of
> placing a due reliance &c., on the discretion and integrity of the
> representatives of the people, [they] had ... declined for the present
> proposing any plan of association, sincerely trusting the House of
> Commons ... [1]

In Gloucestershire, Bedfordshire, Buckinghamshire and Sussex[2]
—three of them counties that had taken part in the Meeting of
Deputies—there was a similar unwillingness to commit oneself
immediately to Wyvill's plan. At the Cheshire meeting in North-

---

[1] Concerning what is presumably this second General Meeting in Cambridge,
see Mss. of Earl Stanhope at Chevening, *A*, the Duke of Rutland to Mahon, 26
March 1781, where he says that though it "had been long advertised, not above
thirty freeholders attended, so that we were compelled abruptly to adjourn".
Rutland says that "the most zealous Whigs", when he asked them to summon
the Committee again, declared at this time that "the Party" was "not yet strong
enough to act effectively". Cf. on this meeting, H.M.C. *Rutland Mss.*, III,
28; *Cambridge Chronicle*, 29 April, and Parliamentary History XXI, 499–500.

[2] Concerning the Sussex meeting, see *London Chronicle*, 18–20 April: "It
turned out long and tedious, owing to the opposition most of the motions
met." The Duke of Richmond evidently soon lost some of his ardour, for on 12
March 1781 we find him writing to Lord Mahon [Mss. of Earl Stanhope at
Chevening, *A*] "I have not attempted to assemble the County again because I
have not had any application ... no good can arise from any such steps while
men's minds are so divided upon what is proper to be recommended."

wich on 11 April, after an able speech by Sir Thomas Broughton, it
was resolved:

that on the fullest consideration it is the opinion of this Meeting
that the Committee of Correspondence appointed at the original
meeting at Northwich is not necessary, and that the same be and
is hereby dissolved, and that this Meeting be adjourned *sine die*.[1]

In Wiltshire the efforts of Fox and Shelburne had failed to overcome the suspicions of both the local Committee and the county
meeting. In Huntingdonshire the adjourned assembly had resulted
in a bitter conflict between the radical leaders and the Rockinghamites.[2] One important county—that of Lancashire—had all the time
refrained from joining the movement and even from sending up a
petition for economical reform. An open letter addressed to the
gentlemen, clergy and freeholders of this county on 29 March
ascribed this misfortune to a defect in the aristocratic leadership,
showing incidentally that little hope could be placed even on the
town of Manchester.[3]

Due time had now been given, however, for the adjourned
county meetings; and it remained to be seen what would be
Wyvill's next step—what course the new Association would take.
If Dunning's success of 6 April had led only to fiasco, even his
subsequent failure did not rally public opinion to the movement,
and came too late to affect the decision of those regions which had
preferred to give the house of commons a further trial. Sir Robert
Smyth, the chairman of the Essex Committee, became perturbed;
and on 4 May we find him writing in some anxiety to Wyvill.
"We lament very sensibly the secession of some Counties and
suspect that the Rockingham Party have thrown this damp upon

---

[1] *London Chronicle*, 18–20 April; *Parliamentary History*, XXI, 477.

[2] *Corr. George III*, v, 47–8; Mss. of the Marquis of Abergavenny, No. 254,
[not printed in H.M.C. *Abergavenny Mss.*, p. 29].

[3] *Morning Chronicle*: 29 March. Yet the *Leeds Mercury* of 4 Jan., after reporting
the original Yorkshire Meeting, made the announcement: "A Meeting for Lancashire, on a plan like the above, is soon expected to be called at Lancaster." In
the *London Courant* for 8 Jan. there is an open letter to the Earl of Derby asking
why Lancashire is not taking part. Cf. note 1 p. 198 above.

the ardor of the People."[1] He was very eager to be sure that, the Association now being established, Wyvill still meant to go forward—meant not to be deterred from summoning a further session of the General Meeting of Deputies. "If we should stop here," he wrote, "we shall have made but a ridiculous figure."[2]

Wyvill had been learning something from experience, however; and it would appear that the recent disappointments had completed the change which had been taking place in his general attitude. He replied that there would be no immediate Assembly of Deputies in London.

The present Session draws near a conclusion, and as several Petitioning Bodies have deferred entering into an Association till that event had ascertained how far this Parliament would redress the grievances complained of, it seems advisable not to meet in deputation again till our numbers are complete.

In fact, no such assembly was summoned until the general election had been held; and the next meeting occurred only in February 1781, almost a year after the first. The high politics of the Association were to suffer a long suspension, and in the mind of its leader the Yorkshire movement was already beginning to change its character. It was shedding some of its quasi-revolutionary features, giving up any hope of taking parliament immediately by storm, and losing all except the most remote and theoretical connection with that national upheaval which had taken place in January and February. The original petitioning movement had been left far behind, and what remained was the skeleton of an organization which survived to pursue a somewhat different purpose, settling down into the ordinary modern kind of agitation for more or less long-term objects. Instead of a grand, sudden *tour de force*, there was to be a persistent plodding labour in the cause of parliamentary reform.

Parallel with this change—and in some respects no doubt a

---

[1] Cf. Rev. Thos. Northcote, *Observations on the Natural and Civil Rights of Mankind* (1781): "The county associations, committees and delegations have evidently to deal with a rival treachery from the party contending for power."

[2] *Wyvill Papers:* III, 193.

symptom of it—was the curious reply which Wyvill made in the same letter to Smyth's suggestion that the Rockinghamites had "thrown this damp upon the ardor of the People". Smyth had been severe on this party and had said, "we are resolved if one set of men will not assist us to relinquish them totally, and adhere to those who will." It was Wyvill's turn to throw a damp upon the zeal of his followers, and—forgetting the transcendental faith which he had communicated to others—haul the question back into the normal realm of eighteenth century power-politics. He answered:

If the People divide among themselves, they will lose their weight and importance and then it will be unreasonable to expect the great body of Nobility will declare in their favour, without whose concurrence it is plain enough the whole popular Party never can prevail against the over-ruling power of the Crown. . . . [We must cautiously avoid] whatever may disgust and alienate that respectable body which holds the balance between the Crown and the People. For reasons which it is unnecessary to enumerate, it is surely not surprising that the Nobility pause and hesitate to adopt the popular Plan; but there are among them many men of Virtue and of just Political Principles, who are alarmed for the safety of the Constitution, who dread the increasing power of the Crown, and who may be expected to take a decisive part in support of that Plan which the People propose for its reduction, if their hesitation is treated with that candour and patient good nature, to which the doubts and difficulties of real Friends are always intitled.[1]

The walls of Jericho were not to collapse at the mere sound of the trumpet, after all.Wyvill was discarding what had been over-pre-sumptuous and quasi-messianic in his original scheme. Even now he could hardly have conceived that he was only at the beginning of a task which it was to take more than his life-time to complete.

In the new situation of things the Westminster Committee, holding its regular weekly meetings under the chairmanship of Fox until well into the month of May, began to assume additional importance. Now it issued an angry declaration against Lord North who had said "That the people of England *collectively* could only

[1] *Wyvill Papers*, III, 194-96, 14 May 1780.

be heard by [through] their representatives in Parliament". Now it gave instructions to those of its number who were members of the house of commons—requested Fox, for example, to bring forward a bill to allow members of parliament to resign without having to ask for the Chiltern Hundreds. Now it would declare that any minister who advised the King to prorogue or dissolve parliament until the petition had been answered would be "considered as an enemy to the liberties of his country". By a curious paradox, moreover, this Committee, which in the earlier stages of the movement had tended to be somewhat conservative—had sought to apply the brake—seemed to catch the revolutionary ardour just as Wyvill was losing it, so that the original relationship was reversed. It became associated with more radical programmes, raised new constitutional issues, and went a stage further in its promotion of parliamentary reform. It was no mere cell in Wyvill's Yorkshire movement, even now, but had become a virtually autonomous body—an institution in itself.

Like the Yorkshire Committee itself, the Westminster body created a sub-committee to devise a plan for preventing bribery and undue influence in the general election that could not now be far distant. This sub-committee (determined apparently not to be fobbed off with a minor or incidental rôle) secured the authority to widen its terms of reference and report on all relevant matters "relative to the election of members of Parliament". Taking into its survey the whole story of the previous five months, it came to the very judgment which the freeholders of Middlesex had started from in the previous autumn—and which they had reached by reflection upon the events in their own county ten years before—namely, that it must be useless to petition a house of commons already acknowledged to be corrupt; that it showed a total ignorance of the operation of human motive to expect any result from a petition to the King himself; and that, by "the natural effect of disappointment upon the human mind" the whole policy of petitioning would "probably impair the vigour of every future exertion".

To what earthly tribunal, therefore, shall an injured people have resort? . . . One hope still remains in the native energy of the great collective body of the people . . .

Concerning the particular evils upon which they had originally been constituted to report, they declared:

No effectual reformation of the abuses in question can take place, unless the people exercise their . . . undoubted right of reviewing the whole plan of delegation, and by recurring to the first principles of our constitution, again establish it upon its ancient foundations of equity and right reason.

Their report was dated 27 May—that is to say, after the parliamentary defeat of Burke on the one hand and Dunning on the other had become total. It traversed the whole question of parliamentary reform in a more comprehensive manner than any previous document connected with the Yorkshire Association had pretended to do. And it travelled much further than Wyvill, for, while admitting that there was some justification for a doctrine that connected parliamentary representation with the payment of taxes, it claimed that previous discussions in this field had been vitiated by too great a regard for the rights of property. "A portion of the soil, a portion of its produce, may be wanting to many; but every man has an interest in his life, his liberty, his kindred, and his country." In any case practically all the male inhabitants of the country were subject to the obligations of the militia. Therefore, besides annual parliaments and an equal representation, the sub-committee regarded universal manhood suffrage as a "transcendent" right, and went so far as to insist that nothing short of this would cure the ills of the time. "The exercise of the poor man's elective right is . . . essential to his freedom."

No consideration would have a stronger tendency to generate proper sentiments of affection to the community, and more effectually recall the minds of the rising generation from a course of dissipation and attachment to unworthy gratification, than the perception of that share of political consequence, which the restitution of the universal right of suffrage would afford.

And "altho' . . . in ordinary cases [a man] may sometimes dispose of his suffrage without a proper regard to its importance", he will be instructed by common sense when public calamity has brought the seriousness of the matter home to him. Now, at last, those who talked of "the People" made it clear that they meant *all* men. The standard was raised against the worship of "property, the grand enchantress of the world".

The sub-committee in fact had a plan of total reform; and they insisted that the whole interlocking system should be put into operation at a single stroke.

The circumstances of the times, and the peculiar nature of the means, which must be employed for effecting our deliverance, require, that the proposed plan be exhibited complete in all its essential forms; and that its various parts, being combined in strict and necessary union with each other, be established at one and the same moment of time.

They were not egalitarian, and they thought that "the alarm of the nobility for the very existence of their present splendid distinctions" would bring the Rockinghamites into alliance with the people for the establishment of the new scheme. Under this scheme the counties were to be divided into equal electoral districts, and the basis of assessment was to be the number of males who were competent to vote. The elections would be held annually on the first Tuesday in July, and the poll would be taken "by ballot, under the conduct of the churchwardens of the parish". All members of parliament would receive "reasonable wages" but would be required to swear that they held no office or emolument "at the will of the Crown, or its servants, or any Lord of Parliament". Disputed elections should be decided by jury before the judges of assize. Every qualified elector should be capable of election to parliament. And the sessions would normally run from November to April.[1]

The Yorkshire movement, as we have seen, had had conservative roots. The whole logic of the affair had rested from the very first on the idea of the supremacy of property over parliament. It

[1] Add. Mss. 38,593 ff. 38–44; printed in *Wyvill Papers*, III, 228 *et seqq*.

could not move even from county to town, however, without
changing something of its character. And it could hardly avoid
giving a further impulse to Wilkite radicalism, which represented
not the landed interest as such but the ferment in the capital city.
In the work of the sub-committee at Westminster the movement
broke through the limits of its original design and came out with a
programme more extreme, a challenge more bold, than anything
Wyvill had intended. If only through the tumult of controversy,
when men were exhilarated by contact with ideas which they had
never seriously confronted before—if only through the fact that
fundamental issues had been agitated—the events of 1780 brought
into the open the whole problem of the nature of representation
itself. The question of universal manhood suffrage came out of
dark corners, out of its hiding-place in the writings of cranks,
philosophers and pamphleteers. And those who had so often talked
of the People, hardly realizing that what they had in mind were in
reality "the rights of property", were called upon to be as good as
their word and to answer the challenge of "the rights of men".

Since so radical a programme had been devised, it is curious to
note with what fervour and fanaticism its authors attached themselves to history. And now that they had decided to regard people
rather than property as the subject of rights—now that a political
mentality was taking its shape from an assumption so significant—
it is interesting to see how they were unable to avoid carrying this
outlook back into the remotest centuries of the past, construing
antiquity itself in terms of it. Like men in all ages they did not
realize that what they took out of the past was the very thing they
had first put into it. By a piece of sleight-of-hand which would
have defeated a Scotland Yard detective at the time—obvious
though it comes to appear to a later generation—they pulled out of
early history the shapes they had manufactured in their wishful
thinking, and furnished their generation with just the type of
anachronism that it required.

Towards the end of the sixteenth and in the early part of the
seventeenth century there emerged in England a set of ideas which
long formed the structural basis of what we call the "whig interpretation of history" and which underlay the resistance to Charles I—

underlay, for example, the whole historical debate that issued in the Petition of Rights.[1] The Yorkshire movement of 1780, which made great play with the appeal to history and maintained the traditional claim that it sought only to restore the constitution to its original principles, owes much of its teaching to the historiography of the seventeenth century, and sometimes ignored the revisions that had occurred in one writer and another since 1660, so that even now we find Magna Carta ascribed to the reign of Henry III on occasion.[2] Many of the propagandists of the movement, furthermore, sketched the history or dipped into the record of Associations, tracing the precedents for the policy of 1780 back to the time of the Anglo-Saxon kings. It was as though they had determined that if their project had no roots in history they would create roots and connections, and tie the present to the past if only by pursuing all possible analogies.

Concerning the instruction of members of parliament by constituents, men still followed Sir Edward Coke, who had used a mediaeval precedent to support the thesis that representatives, when confronted by a new proposal, should go back to consult the opinion of their counties. An extended construction was given to the principle; for since constituents were particularly interested in the question of the duration of the mandate which they had given to their delegates in the house of commons, the makers of the Septennial Act were particularly culpable in lengthening the period of delegation without reference to the electors themselves. From Prynne, primarily, the writers associated with the Yorkshire movement drew evidence for the view that in the earlier history of this country it had been the custom to hold elections "once a year and more often if need be". Sometimes we meet with the further opinion which had been common in the seventeenth century: that

[1] This point is discussed in my book on *The Englishman and his History.*

[2] *Bibliotheca Politica,* (1694), 373–614, gives a detailed survey of the state of the question of the antiquity of the house of commons, as exhibited in the literature available at that time. Much of the more scientific side of this work makes little show even in the larger writings of the eighteenth-century historians. The historical assumptions of the Yorkshire movement seem for the most part to represent a throw-back to the ideas and prejudices of a period earlier still.

the first invasion of English liberties had occurred in the reign of Henry VI; or that the right of representation in parliament had been curtailed perhaps, but by no means originated or enlarged, in the reign of Henry III. Those who desired an increase in the number of county members in the house of commons could point to days when the counties had been more generously treated, and could show how the rights of boroughs had been enlarged to serve the purpose of kings, "till at length the Representation of the landed interest had become totally inadequate to the mercantile".[1] So, against the Rockinghamite criticisms of the movement, one of the advocates of parliamentary reform could state what was the current view amongst the more radical thinkers of this period:

This is no "new Speculation", for the first Parliaments we have a record of had many more Knights of Shires, than we have now; and they were at first annual, that is for one Session only; for we have more than one example of two Parliaments being called in a year.

These historical views are to be found in the *Political Disquisitions* of James Burgh, and, behind him, in the *Historical Essay on the English Constitution*, which had been published in 1771. They were proclaimed in the house of commons by Alderman Sawbridge when, on 8 May 1780, he brought forward his annual motion for shortening the duration of parliaments. They occur either explicitly or by implication throughout the propaganda of the Yorkshire movement—in the *Letter of Lord Carysfort to the Huntingdonshire Committee,* for example, and in the avowed organ of the movement, *The Yorkshire Freeholder,* of which No. XIII, 13 April 1780, was devoted to the historical ideas behind the agitation. Above all, they formed the staple argument of Granville Sharp, and they acquired greater force through the increase of his influence in this period. One of his tracts is entitled "Equitable Representation necessary to the Establishment of Law, Peace and good Government; shewn in some Extracts from Mr Prynne's *Brevia Parliamentarii Rediviva. . . .*" In *The Legal Means of Political Reformation,*

[1] See e.g. the long letter from "Aratus" in the *London Chronicle,* 18–20 April.

which in 1780 assembled a number of his treatises in one collection, he uses Lambarde's *Archaionomia* to prove that in ancient Saxon times provincial parliaments were held twice a year; the speech of Sir George Crooke at the ship-money trial to support the view that parliaments were held twice a year in King Alfred's time; and Brady's *Treatise of Cities and Boroughs* to show that both knights and burgesses were elected in county courts before the twenty-third year of Henry VI's reign. He declares that "in ancient times [and up to 8 Henry VI cap. vii] ALL MEN in each county, that were free, however poor, enjoyed a share in the legislature."[1]

In all this we can see some of the dangers of self-taught history, and some of the traps into which men fall when they satisfy themselves with the first appearance of things, or when they merely pick out from the past certain items which serve their purposes. These men were not historians or careful students of the past; and if they had looked about them they might have found in the historiography that was already available to them a certain corrective to some of their hasty conclusions. A political enemy could laugh at them for going back to days when the house of commons had merely been the tool of faction. Earl Nugent could declare in the House:

What! was it meant that parliament should be degraded to that state in which it was, when the service was so disagreeable that men were obliged to be paid for sitting and doing the public business? When that business was so unwelcome, that there were frequent instances of persons begging to be disfranchised, in order to prevent their being sent up to parliament?[2]

Above all, these men had not learned what Brady in the latter half of the seventeenth century had tried so hard to point out—namely

[1] See *Legal Means*, 29, 73n. Sharp also refers to *The Mirror of Justices*, Browne Willis's *Notitia Parliamentaria*, and De Lolme's *Constitution of England*. See *ibid.* 40–1, 46, for his attack on Blackstone who had argued that the historical cases under discussion (36 Ed. III, cap. 10 and 4 Edward III, cap. 14) only referred to parliament *sitting* every year "if need be".

[2] *Parliamentary History*, XXI, 595. Cf. *York Courant*, 16 May, where Nugent is further reported as asking in the same debate what period Sawbridge had had in mind in his historical disquisition. "Was it to those Ages when the Commons were Slaves to the King, to the Barons, or both? Was it to those Ages when the House of Commons was a very insignificant Part of the Constitution?"

that things are only understood when seen in their proper context. In particular, the technical terms in ancient documents must not be construed after the meaning which the words may possess in popular speech at the present day.

At the outer edge of error, however, beyond the bounds of the other anachronistic fallacies, there was a view that democracy must have existed in Anglo-Saxon times—however slight the surviving evidence—because these were virgin days and the constitution must have begun by being pure.[1] Natural rights here became almost merged into historical ones; and the eighteenth century *philosophe* wears the costume of the seventeenth century student of antiquity. The Westminster sub-committee's programme of 27 May is projected against that whole interpretation of English history which has been described, and it may not be irrelevant to note that if Granville Sharp had influenced the earlier sub-committee of 17 March, he may have particularly affected this later body, which had been formed to suggest precautions against bribery at the forthcoming election; for this body was authorized so drastically to enlarge its scope just after he had sent a letter to the Committee along with fifty copies of his latest circular—his latest attempt to check the kind of retreat which was being conducted by Wyvill in this period.

In any event, the Westminster sub-committee afforded an extreme example of the unconscious discrepancy between the idealized history, which looked to primitive Teutonic freedom, and the actual history which is always so sordid in comparison. It declared:

An equal representation of the people in the great council of the nation, annual elections, and the universal right of suffrage, appear

[1] Cf., however, Robert Robinson, "*Political Catechism*" 1784, in *Works*, II, 289: "Have you not also heard people talk at large about framing our excellent constitution, as if all our ancestors met in one large plain at one time. . . . Others again talk as if our immunities proceeded from the condescension and benevolence of our princes. Both sorts discover gross ignorance. Our constitution, like our language, is a fineness produced by the friction of contending interests, and we ought to ascribe the delicacy and elegance of it to providence working by time, and the course of events." Robinson still gives it to be understood, p. 285, that the declaration of rights and the British constitution go back to the time of Alfred.

so reasonable to the natural feelings of mankind, that no sophistry can elude the force of the arguments which are urged in their favour; and they are rights of so transcendent a nature, that, in opposition to the claim of the people to their enjoyment, the longest period of prescription is pleaded in vain. They were substantially enjoyed in the times of the immortal Alfred; they were cherished by the wisest Princes of the Norman line; they form the grand palladium of our nation . . . they are the birthright of Englishmen. . . .

Yet against this they have to state:

Your Sub-Committee . . . have examined the voluminous system of laws relating to the subject of Parliamentary elections, and find themselves under a necessity of pronouncing the far greater part of them to be founded upon partial conceptions, unjust restrictions, and false measures of expediency, which will not stand the test, when contrasted by the acknowledged principles of the Constitution of this country.

The ideal history of England was contrasted with the actual; the dream of the remoter period with the reality of the more recent ones—the ones that could be seen with the naked eye. What the sub-committee called "the first principles of our constitution" or "its antient foundations of equity and right reason", were a sublimated form of history—a doctrine of the rights of man transposed into one's picture of the past.

The extreme example of the operation of this whole method of interpretation, however, is to be found in a work that has already been mentioned—a work used by James Burgh—and very important amongst the antecedents of the Yorkshire movement—namely, the *Historical Essay on the English Constitution* of 1771.[1] The Society for Constitutional Information reprinted a significant passage from this book, in an Address which they issued to the public in April

[1] The National Library of Scotland ascribes this work to Allan Ramsay, Jr., the painter, and the *Dictionary of National Biography* appears to do the same. It is difficult to reconcile this radical reforming treatise with other writings attributed to Ramsay, e.g. condemning the radical movement of 1771, and, unless some precise evidence exists, I am unable to regard the matter as settled.

1780, in order to explain how our Saxon forefathers had enjoyed democratic liberty, though the records of this were so defective:

Our Saxon forefathers established their government in Britain, before the transactions of mankind were recorded in writing, at least among the northern nations: they, therefore, handed down to posterity the principles of their government, BY THE ACTUAL EXERCISE OF THEIR RIGHTS; which became the ancient usage and custom of the people, and the law of the land. And hence it came to pass, that when this antient custom and usage *ceased* to act, the *remembrance* of the custom ceased with it. We may add to this, that since the Conquest, our arbitrary kings, and men of arbitrary principles, have endeavoured to destroy the few remaining records and historical facts, that might keep in remembrance a form of government so kind, friendly, and hospitable to the human species.[1]

Nothing could better serve to illustrate the stage which the whole movement had now reached and the educational rôle to which its leaders had had to resign themselves—as well as the function which historical study itself had to perform in its teaching and its propaganda—than the establishment in this period of the Society of Constitutional Information, and the fact that it took upon itself the most curious of all imaginable historical rôles, namely, the office of "supplying, as far as may be, the want of those destroyed records". In this way, as it explained in its original Address, it proposed to revive, in "THE COMMONALTY AT LARGE, a knowledge of their lost Rights". That society was created at an initial meeting which was held in London in April, and which was attended by fourteen men, including Cartwright, Jebb, Day, Brand-Hollis, Bromley, Capell Lofft, R. B. Sheridan, Trecothick and Vardy, whose names have figured in the story of the Yorkshire movement. At the beginning of May it commenced its task of preparing those addresses and reprints which appeared, now in their hundreds and now in their thousands, and which early in June it was arranged to

---

[1] Printed in *York Chronicle*, 2 June 1780. The Address also quoted De Lolme's *Constitution of England*: "When a PEOPLE have lost the power of legally asserting their Rights, they are exposed to that which is THE HIGHEST DEGREE OF POLITICAL RUIN, the loss of even *the remembrance* of them."

distribute more methodically—always gratis—through suitable agents in towns and cities. The subscription might run from one to five guineas—fifty guineas for perpetual membership[1]—and meetings were held twice a week at first, but only every Friday after 16 June. Cartwright was the founder of the society, but of the half-dozen people who generally attended the meetings in this period, Jebb and Capell Lofft were perhaps the most assiduous. On 12 May it was resolved:

That it be requested of Mr. Lofft to compile a Tract or Tracts, consisting of Extracts from the Mirrour of Justices, Fleta, Bracton, Fortescue, Selden, Bacon, Sir Thomas Smith, Coke, Sidney, Milton, Harrington, Nevile, Molesworth, Bolingbroke, Price, Priestley, Blackstone, Somers, Davenant, the Essay on the English Constitution, and other Authors, as may clearly define, or describe in a few words, the English Constitution; and particularly what relates to the Rights of the Commons to an equal and complete Representation in Parliament; to their Independency as the Third Estate of the Realm; to the Powers delegated to their Representatives, and the Limitations of the same; and to the Abuses of those Powers.

A week later it was resolved:

That it be requested of Dr. Jebb to select the best-written Letters and Essays, in Favour of Annual Parliaments and an equal Representation, which have appeared in the Public Prints since Christmas last, to be printed hereafter.

Later in the year there was a project of publishing a monthly paper under the title: *The Historical and Constitutional Magazine.* Amongst their early reprints were speeches and letters connected with the development of the Yorkshire movement, such as the ones by Day which have been noted on various occasions above, and one by Rev. George Walker of Nottingham, who joined the society almost immediately after its formation. When they printed Lord Carysfort's *Letter*, however, which contained some interesting historical exposition, the original publisher, Almon, demanded

[1] Manuscript Resolutions, Public Record Office, T. S. 11/1133 and printed notice Brit. Mus. 8133 i 14(9). Cf. however, later, Brit. Mus. E2101 (12); "thirty pounds".

an indemnity; for, by the effect of their bounty, he was left with his own copies on his hands.

When they held their first audit dinner, in the following December, their long list of toasts, which included "Annual Parliaments", "America in our Arms", and the "Irish Volunteers", contained the item, "Universal Philanthropy". This last, however, was so near the end that, along with some others, it is deleted in pencil, presumably because the time ran out before the programme had been completed.[1]

§II. THE QUESTION OF IRISH LEGISLATIVE INDEPENDENCE

The period after the carrying of Dunning's famous resolutions of 6 April saw a significant development of the situation in Ireland—one which throws light on the importance of extra-parliamentary movements at this time. It is necessary, therefore, to pick up the threads of this story again and to see how the significant transition took place.

In proposing his remarkable commercial concessions in December, 1779, Lord North had hoped to swallow up all the resentments of Ireland in a blaze of unexpected generosity. He took particular care to inquire in advance whether his propositions would meet the needs of that country and put an end to the long period of friction and controversy. As early as 13 December we find him writing to Pery, the Speaker of the Irish house of commons:

Should they fail of giving satisfaction, I am afraid that it will be worse with us both than if they had never been made.[2]

There were many reasons which made it unlikely that England and Ireland had come to the end of their controversies in December

[1] The Resolutions and Orders of the Society for Constitutional Information (to 7 March 1783) came into the hands of the Government during the French Revolution. They were removed from the Treasury in 1847 and were for a time classed for some reason with the Records of the African Company, but are now amongst the papers of the Treasury Solicitor, T.S. 11/1133.

[2] H.M.C. *Appendix to 8th Report, Pt. I*, Emly Mss., p. 207.

1779. Already in November Thomas Waite had written from Dublin that the action of government in acceding to a six months money bill "is a record that will hang about our necks as a millstone". On hearing of the commercial concessions he wrote to a similar effect: "We shall have the same disagreeable road to travel every Parliament winter, for we shall always have something to wish and to raise mobs for." It had been stated by Lord North in the middle of November, as we have seen, that the grant of "free trade" would never be sufficient in itself to save a country from "impending ruin". Sir Lucius O'Brien had pointed out in the previous summer that commercial concessions would not bring prosperity as an automatic consequence; and early in 1780 the Irish were reminded that they must not permit themselves to be dazzled with visions of sudden affluence. When, on 12 December, the Lord Lieutenant announced the concessions to a meeting of those "usually called upon to hear the speech read at the opening of the Session", together with members of the privy council, there were three important leaders, Pery, Flood and the Provost of Trinity College, who maintained a certain reserve, principally because there was an act still restraining the importation of hops into Ireland, and they held that its retention might provoke a dispute concerning the legislative authority of Great Britain in that country.[1] In any case, since the Irish parliament in the early months of 1780 would have to establish new regulations and duties, there was an obligation to put the country on an equal footing with Great Britain, the whole question of Irish trade would come under discussion, and every vested interest would have its case to make, while it was hardly to be expected that the business should be carried through without providing occasion for further jealousy against the British. Some men even declared that the parliament at Westminster, having granted the commercial privileges, would always be in a position to take them away. Lord North was quoted as having comforted the British merchants with the assurance that the concessions were "a boon resumable at pleasure". The con-

[1] S.P. 63/467, ff. 247–49. Buckingham to Hillsborough, 14 Dec. 1779, with a list of the people invited and the people present; cf. *Beresford Correspondence*, I, 112–18, and H.M.C. *Stopford Sackville Mss.*, I, 264.

cessions themselves had been so long delayed in any case that opinion had been moving forward to more momentous constitutional issues already, as we have seen. Even on 17 December the Irish Speaker wrote to Lord North:

> It is unfortunate that the extent of the sovereignty of Britain has ever been defined. It should have remained a mystery, and never called forth but upon the utmost necessity to save the empire. . . . My fears of some disaster upon that head are still very strong.[1]

In spite of this it seemed for a time that all might go well; for there was great rejoicing in Dublin when the news of Lord North's commercial concessions was announced. As Yelverton said later, "When we first received it an intemperate burst of applause broke forth, like the extravagance of lunacy or the giddy joy of a child." Even the Provost of Trinity College, who in this period gave the ministry in London as well as the Lord Lieutenant more than one reason for complaint—and who as we have seen had expressed a misgiving in private—wrote to his constituents in Cork, "I know not what can be reasonably asked for the encouragement of the commerce and manufactures of Ireland that is not now in a course of being obtained." He added that in view of the vast expense to which Great Britain was put for the preservation of her empire and the guarding of her commercial routes, no one could doubt the good fortune which permitted Ireland "the full advantage" of these, without involving her in "any part of those great burdens". In the Irish house of commons on 20 December one speech after another sang the praises of both the British government and the Lord Lieutenant, as though there had been a general agreement to take this as an opportunity for leadership, and to guide the nation into a spirit of thankfulness. The proposals would "form the cement of an indissoluble union", said one; while another pointed out that "posterity would be surprised at the difference of England's conduct in America and Ireland." "The Lords North, Hillsborough and Buckingham would be of glorious and immortal memory in this Kingdom," said another, "and posterity, till time should be no more, would sound their praises." Burgh declared, "This coun-

[1] H.M.C. *Appendix to 8th Report, Pt I*, Emly Mss., p. 207.

try, Sir, is now in that state in which Virgil described the husband-men, happy indeed if they but know their happiness."[1] The opposition party in Great Britain, who had stood aloof, refusing to support Lord North even when he was making concessions to the Irish, were repeatedly condemned. It is clear that in Dublin a serious attempt was being made to create such a mood of rejoicing, such a disposition to gratitude, as would bring Ireland and Great Britain into friendly relations again. "Even the Patriotic News-papers," wrote Buckingham on 28 December, "have adopted a favorable cast."

In spite of these demonstrations, the Lord Lieutenant had to report that "Every effort has been exerted by the emissarys of faction, France, and America, to check this gratitude." In the course of that very debate of 20 December Grattan declared, "I am guarded, however, in the praise of ministers": C. H. Coote said, "The echoing of the praises of administration in England could produce no advantage to Ireland"; oblique references were made to constitutional grievances still outstanding; while Burgh, even in the act of depre-cating further controversy with Great Britain, offered the disquiet-ening statement: "The chimerical idea of binding us by foreign laws will drop by its own weakness." On 9 January Lord Macart-ney, who had been sent to Ireland with the secret intention of seeing if Buckingham could be induced to resign, wrote a confidential letter to John Robinson, in which he declared that the Irish were now on their good behaviour but that this was only for the time being.[2] The country was likely to be peaceful only until the trade concessions announced by Lord North had actually been placed upon the statute-book. Then, when all was safe in this field, there would be a demand for the total or partial repeal of Poyning's Law; an attempt to bring a case to vindicate the right of the Irish house of

---

[1] *Some Authentic Minutes* [of debate of] *20 Dec. 1779* (1780); S.P. 63/467, Heron to Anthony Chamier, 20 Dec. 1779; *ibid.* f. 299 Buckingham to Hillsborough, Private, 22 Dec. 1779; H.M.C. *Stopford Sackville Mss.*, I, 264–65, Buckingham to Lord G. Germain, 21 Dec. 1779. In Add. Mss. 38,212, f. 326, however, Robinson complains on 27 Dec. that Heron allowed the resolutions of the Irish house of commons to be "cut down" (in preliminary discussion) by the Speaker.

[2] Add. Mss. 38,212, ff. 299–301; H.M.C. *Abergavenny Mss.*, pp. 27–28.

lords to hear appeals; a claim that the Irish judges, like the British ones, should hold office *quamdiu se bene gesserint*; a movement to make money-bills annual, instead of biennial, so as to secure a session of the Irish parliament every year; and finally an insistence that Ireland should have her own separate Mutiny Bill. "The idea of a union [between the two countries] would be sufficient at this time to excite a rebellion," Macartney added. The Lord Lieutenant had said very much the same on this latter subject a few days before:

> Let me earnestly recommend to you not to utter the word Union in a whisper or to let it drop from your pen. The present temper will not bear it.

It is hardly possible that anyone who reads the correspondence of this period should fail to be moved by the unhappiness of the predicament in which the Lord Lieutenant now found himself. "No Crime is more Capital than the being unfortunate," he wrote to the secretary of state on 2 January. In the previous summer, he said, he had repeatedly sent warning that if nothing was done for Ireland "the Government of the Kingdom would dissolve in my hands." He knew that Robinson in London was conspiring with Beresford in Dublin to secure his recall or alternatively "to frighten me into the solliciting of it". He seems to have learned very soon that the visit of Lord Macartney early in January had been planned with the secret design of securing his resignation. In February he made a pointed allusion to "Lord North's interior cabinet" and declared that "a man of the first consequence" had described the situation as very "awkward" when, as Lord Lieutenant he "could not despatch an express without it being accompanied by another calculated to cut my throat".[1] He repeatedly complained that, through the instrumentality of Robinson, his enemies in Dublin would receive accounts of British ministerial action—including the commercial concessions themselves—a week before he himself had been notified. When he was advised to return to the policy of "attaching the friends of Lord Townshend and Lord Harcourt to his administration", he retorted that this could not be the secretary

[1] H.M.C. *Stopford Sackville Mss.*, I, 266–67.

of state's own suggestion, but must have been "insinuated" to him by Beresford and Robinson. He showed how Beresford was working to secure still greater benefits for his own faction, and how the excessive favours to this man's friends had tended to weaken the loyalty of others—the Duke of Leinster and Conolly for example.[1] Buckingham was popular in Ireland, but it did not strengthen his position in London when the commercial concessions were ascribed to his importunity rather than to the generosity of North; or when a Volunteer company which addressed its thanks to him declared: "We have armed ourselves at our own Expense in Defence of His Majesty and of our constitutional rights as Irishmen." On the 13 and 22 January the British Cabinet virtually decided to recall him, but North thwarted them by his very inactivity and said that he did not see how any Lord Lieutenant could prevent the revival of controversy with Ireland. Buckingham attached North more definitely to his cause by asking for William Eden as Chief Secretary in succession to Heron—a matter upon which North came into a state of serious tension with the closet and refused to be overborne.[2] At the end of January Buckingham pointed out to ministers that any insinuation of their disapproval of his conduct while he was still in office "may essentially prejudice the public service".

Towards the close of 1780 he confessed that "though my health is not particularly impair'd, an unremitting solicitude of a year and an half has very sensibly affected and enervated my mind."[3] He who, throughout this period, was always so much more skilful in diagnosis than firm in action, had undoubtedly reached some such condition as the one he describes, even by the opening of the year. He would be garrulous on the subject of his personal anxieties, now setting up a whine, now uttering a cry of anguish; and in the State Papers for this period his personal effusions—he was once reproved for sending private letters even on matters which had to be officially

[1] S.P. 63/467, ff. 237–44; cf. H.M.C. *Stopford Sackville Mss.*, I, 266–67. By this time Robinson was working to secure that Lord Townshend should become Lord Lieutenant, with Beresford—a connection of Townshend's—as Chief Secretary.

[2] Add. Mss. 38,213, ff. 89–112.

[3] S.P. 63/471, ff. 296–97 to Hillsborough, 22 Nov.

communicated—stand strangely juxtaposed with the stiff, laconic reproofs of the Secretary of State, whose private communications (which may have somewhat softened the effect of these) are not inserted in the correspondence.

Against the narrow views of Beresford, Robinson and the closet, Buckingham had been correct in diagnosing the troubles of 1779 not as a mere game of manoeuvre in parliamentary politics but as an imposing and dangerous movement amongst a people who were restless for greater liberty. Where his enemies insisted on a tightening of the eighteenth century forms of parliamentary discipline and party-organization, he had all the time recognized that the essential danger lay not in the house of commons itself but in the turbulence of the country at large. His very weaknesses—his habit of bowing before the wind—may have been right for this particular situation, right in the sense that it may have prevented catastrophes which could easily have been worse than those that actually occurred. At any rate his enemies are not the ones who can convince the historian that he was wrong; for it was they who by their narrow-mindedness had plunged into the American conflict without realizing that they were confronted with one of the world's great movements for liberty. Since he had convinced the Irish leaders of his goodwill, he was able, as he showed in one of his despatches,[1] to secure their sympathy and exert a moderating influence over them—able to persuade them that a breach with England would be ruinous to their country and subversive of the Protestant interest there. Pery, whose opinion was greatly respected in England, praised the accuracy of his despatches; and Lord Hillsborough told him when he left Dublin that no other Lord Lieutenant had done so much for Ireland, though we may wonder if this latter compliment was not double-edged.

We may say that in 1779 he was not unwise in making himself, so to speak, the accomplice of the imposing handful of Irish leaders —some of them servants of the crown—who were determined to secure an amelioration in the commercial status of the country. If the British ministers had felt able to respond to his importunity at an earlier date Ireland would have been pacified on this point before

[1] S.P. 63/468, ff. 205-08 Buckingham to Hillsborough, 9 Feb.

the country at large had been galvanized into an awareness of the further constitutional anomalies which the agitators were anxious to exploit. Buckingham, with all his weaknesses, was a Lord Lieutenant who had a policy, therefore, in 1779—a policy which he pressed in an importunate manner upon the British ministers until finally he secured its acceptance—and his critics were unwise when they pretended to regard him as the accomplice of wild agitators who were enemies of Britain. He made mistakes, however, and even his friend and supporter, Lord George Germain, complained in the middle of 1780 that he read his instructions and despatches "to twenty people" in Dublin—a use of official letters which, he said, "is rather new". Germain moreover was ready to believe that Buckingham would present a "formal opposition" to popular measures in Dublin "to shew he is obeying his instructions and to throw the odium upon administration here". Buckingham, exasperated by the conduct of the ministers in London, had become too eager to make it clear in Dublin that they—not he—were responsible for the resistance to the Irish demands.[1]

In 1780, indeed, when his whole predicament had become more delicate, it is arguable that the weaknesses in his personality and his situation were a misfortune; though, as Lord North confessed, it is very doubtful whether any Lord Lieutenant could have prevented trouble in Ireland in this period. The Yorkshire movement was developing in England and Buckingham could write:

Can it be conceiv'd that the embarrassments of Great Britain are not known and even exaggerated in Ireland, and that such knowledge will not [have] influence upon the temper of this kingdom.

Surveying the whole story in the following July, he wrote to William Eden:

Tho the present Government of this Country has in many instances betray'd very inconvenient weakness, it should be consider'd how very similar is now the state of every part of the British Empire, the heart not excepted. And can any Man of Reflection

[1] H.M.C. *Various Mss.*, VI, Knox Mss., p. 238.

and Candor conceive that the Idea of being able to carry unprecedented measures with impunity, from the difficultys of the Mother
Country has not been the first spring of every disagreeable innovation here. To have uniformly preserv'd the tranquillity of this
Kingdom very much contrary to the general expectation carrys
surely a degree of negative merit.[1]

It was regarded as his duty after the opening of the year 1780
to see that Ireland should become reconciled with Great Britain
and in particular that no controversy of a fundamental character
should be allowed to develop.[2] He found that he was expected to
put a check upon certain constitutional proposals (such as an
Habeas Corpus Bill for Ireland, and a bill to enable judges to hold
office *quamdiu se bene gesserint*), which had always been allowed to
go unopposed through the Irish house of commons and had hitherto been annihilated by action taken after their transmission to
England. When he expressed doubts concerning his majority in
parliament, in view of the fluidity of political conditions at that
time, he received from Lord Macartney a letter, probably calculated to provoke his resignation, and informing him that after all
they had done for Ireland, the ministers in London would be satisfied with nothing less than certainty.[3] This made him all the more
nervous and in the days just before and after 1 February he sent
long disquisitions on his political prospects to the ministers
in London, explaining that he would have a majority in ordinary
circumstances, and for the most part would be able to check any

---

[1] Add. Mss. 34,417, ff. 94–97, 22 July 1780.

[2] Buckingham's correspondence in Dec. 1779 and in the succeeding weeks
[S.P. 63/467–68] shows how he fell into further disgrace concerning large con-
signments of provisions which were being prepared in Cork for consignment to
the Dutch, who were certain to transmit them to the French. Even when he was
pressed to discover a member of parliament who would raise the issue and secure
that the embargo should come as an Irish suggestion, he replied that it was impossible—an embargo would undo all the good that might have been done by
the commercial concessions. He was taunted with the comment that, according
to his reports, government in Ireland must be regarded as having been dissolved;
but he argued that what was required was the stationing of cruisers off the coast
of France and the French islands, and he pointed out that the British government could save a lot of trouble by simply purchasing the provisions themselves.

[3] H.M.C. *Lothian Mss.*, p. 361, dated 21 Jan.

new constitutional demands if the enemies of the government were to make them, but that the real difficulty lay in the pressure of extra-parliamentary opinion at a time when "not only the Electors but even the Mob are instructed that their opinions are to determine the suffrages of Members." Under these circumstances members of the house of commons, he said, would not commit themselves in advance in the way that had been usual "when the Contest was between Factions". Even promises and the ties of connection proved weak, and "I scarcely can conceive how it will be possible to secure a decided majority by that best tie, their own emolument." He felt sure of success "barring Insurrection or something near resembling it" but he insisted that it was not possible for him to give the government in England an absolute guarantee. Against those who pretended to know about Ireland from earlier residence there, he declared that "No retrospective knowledge of Ireland can enable any Man to form a judgment of the present situation."[1]

When matters came to a test, and business was resumed in the Irish parliament on 9 February, it transpired that Buckingham had not been mistaken in either his hopes or his misgivings. Constitutional proposals were announced—Sir Richard Johnstone gave notice in the commons of an intention to move a question upon Poyning's Law, for example, while Lord Carysfort in the lords declared that he meant to bring in a motion for an Irish Mutiny Bill. Buckingham was able to report, however, that he would be in a position to defeat the proposals, provided he could meet them at an early date, though he still maintained that it would not be possible to check an attempt to secure an Habeas Corpus Bill for Ireland. The proposals in fact did not lead to anything, for those in the commons were withdrawn and the others were defeated in the house of lords.

It was at the next stage of the argument that Buckingham's hopes were to be cheated, and this in the very manner in which he had feared that it might happen. The opposition realized that it was

[1] Buckingham's official correspondence in S.P. 63/468 is occasionally accompanied in this period by his unofficial letters to Lord G. Germain in H.M.C. *Stopford Sackville Mss.*, Vol. I, and contains at ff. 210-17 his detailed estimate of the parliamentary numbers on 9 February at the end of the recess.

necessary to modify the existing state of forces in parliament and determined to postpone the great attack until they had canvassed the constitutional issue in the country at large. Grattan and his friends had a grand extra-parliamentary campaign in mind and it was not their intention to let their motions be put to the vote until the members of the house of commons had felt the pressure of public opinion in town and countryside. The assizes were shortly to take place; and they afforded an excellent opportunity for conducting an agitation and securing addresses and instructions. If the opposition were determined to consult the nation in this manner the supporters of the government could not afford to stay away; in other words there was a general recognition of the need for a parliamentary recess. Even amongst those who had supported the patriot cause in 1779, however, there were some who could not reconcile themselves to this new attempt on the part of Grattan and his friends to generate a ferment amongst the populace. Conolly said that he deprecated alterations in the constitution at this critical period, but particularly disagreed with the policy of postponing them—if they had to be raised—until "addresses and instructions had been prepared in the country by those whom too many in the House endeavoured to inflame".

The Lord Lieutenant thought to thwart Grattan by using the third and final act of parliament implementing Lord North's promise of commercial concessions—that is to say the act which opened the plantation trade to the Irish—to produce a great demonstration of gratitude in the country and a parliamentary Address which should be imposing enough to check the threatened agitation. And though the act was almost too late in coming, the Duke of Leinster, a man who in the previous autumn had done much to embarrass the government, carried in the house of lords an Address in which something like censure was passed upon the attempts of Grattan and his friends to raise "groundless jealousies in the minds of the people". Leinster declared that he had been "long enough a slave to popularity", but he had no intention of forcing constitutional issues at the point of the bayonet or seeing them agitated in the assemblies of the city. In the house of lords, however, the resistance to Leinster's motion—though small—was arresting in its character. The Address of the house of commons came far short of any similar condemnation of the policy of the agitators. The plan of presenting a firm parliamentary front against further controversy—giving a lead to the whole country in favour of peace—failed to achieve the success which Buckingham had obviously intended. Leinster himself became the object of much slander from those who had previously been only too happy to have him at their side. His attempt to rally the country behind Britain had itself precipitated a division and created a new controversy.[1]

Before the parliamentary recess had begun, the movement in the country had already started. The city of Dublin, the county of Armagh, the county of Donegal, the town of Drogheda and the city of Londonderry had held meetings and had drawn up instructions for their parliamentary representatives. "All declared that they are not satisfied with Commercial Advantages without better securing the Liberty of the Subject." The city of Dublin on 21 February instructed its members to procure a declaratory act which would guarantee Ireland "against all foreign Legislation whatsoever" and also to modify Poyning's Law by preventing the interference of the privy council of Ireland in the processes of legislation. In the ensuing weeks county meetings, corporations, grand juries and volunteer associations made similar statements concerning the legislative independence of the country. They were able to argue that since England's legislative supremacy could have had no object save the purpose of commercial tyranny, there was now no reason why she herself should wish it to continue. Further publicity was given to the agitation by the declarations exchanged when men like Walter Hussey Burgh, Henry Grattan and Denis Daly were given the freedom of certain corporations, such as the Guild of Merchants in Dublin. On the other hand, the supporters of the administration were induced to flock to the assizes in order to forestall the agitators where possible, or to secure that addresses of gratitude and loyalty should be drawn up. Some regions thanked the British government for the commercial concessions and declared their intention of promoting good relations between the two coun-

---

[1] S.P. 63/468, Buckingham to Hillsborough, 25 and 26 Feb.; *Grattan Memoirs*, II, 19–30; *Hibernian Journal*, 6–8 March.

tries, while also joining in the demand for legislative independence.[1] The Lord Lieutenant reported that most of the men of property wished "to stifle ill-humour", but declared that "the temper of the Inferior orders is certainly in an unpleasing state of fermentation."

In the meantime the Volunteer movement was perceptibly developing and was showing more definite signs of political consciousness—a further symptom of the power of the extra-parliamentary agitation in this period. Early in 1780 the organization of these bodies was proceeding to a further stage: for we find that battalions were now being combined to form regiments. On 23 February a body of Volunteers in Dublin refused to give way in the street to a detachment of regulars, and an ugly scene was avoided only because the captain of these latter ordered his men to stand aside. On 18 March the delegates of 17,000 Volunteers in the neighbourhood of Belfast invited Lord Charlemont to be their reviewing general on 12 and 13 July; and he, a little later, appointed Grattan as his aide-de-camp. In April it was agreed that various of the companies in the capital should be reviewed together once a month, the superior officer acting in rotation as the reviewing officer for the day. A little later, Napper Tandy, of the Dublin Volunteers, proposed to expel the Duke of Leinster, the commanding officer, because he and his friends were behaving in an unsatisfactory manner in parliament. Tandy himself was expelled but he was almost immediately elected to the Liberty Corps, forty or fifty representatives of which resolved at one of their meetings to withdraw from the Duke of Leinster's command.

While these developments were taking place in the country at large, the Lord Lieutenant was taking advantage of the parliamentary recess in order to make a final attempt to modify the intransigeance of the British government. He had decided—as during the critical months in the earlier half of 1779—that his Chief Secretary should make a considerable stay in London in order that the ministry should have first-hand evidence from a source that his administration could rely upon. Heron's visit to England was regarded with great jealousy by the Irish Attorney General who feared that,

---

[1] On these events, see the *Hibernian Journal* during March; *Grattan Memoirs*, II, 32 *et seqq.*; and Buckingham's official correspondence, enclosing loyal addresses.

since Eden had declined to become Chief Secretary, the Lord Lieutenant would use the opportunity in order to intrigue for the appointment of one of his collaborators, Foster. By the weakness of North and the support of Lord George Germain, however, Sir Richard Heron was in fact allowed to continue in office, and Robinson's intrigue in favour of Beresford was defeated, especially as a change in the middle of the parliamentary session would have had obvious inconveniences.[1] Buckingham furthermore induced Pery, the Irish Speaker, to go to London during the recess on the pretext of private business; but though many people—even Charles Jenkinson—declared their attachment to the man personally, George III resented his visit "for He cannot I trust persuade this Country to give up Ireland being bound to obey British Acts of Parliament, and He will not relinquish his National prejudice." And Pery, though he gives the impression that he found particular ministers not unreasonable when he talked to them individually, leaves a distinct suggestion that the compound body—the total effect of governmental action in England—was less generous; a point which is observable on other occasions during the ministry of North, and which was due no doubt to the operation of closet-influence. North communicated to Pery the decision of the cabinet that any constitutional change—even the repetition of old demands for Habeas Corpus in Ireland or for an alteration in the commissions of judges —would be regarded as inadmissible. North for his part gave the impression however that he was "not unwilling to relax on some points; yet he could not take upon himself alone to do it". In regard to a further controversy on the subject of the Irish sugar duty North "seemed to be directed . . . rather by the opinion of Mr. Robinson, who does not appear friendly, than his own". Wedderburn had an interview with the Irish Speaker and gave the same impression of a personal sympathy that was not quite in conformity with the policy of the cabinet as a whole.[2] On 28 March the issue was decided and there was despatched to Buckingham an utterly

[1] *Beresford Correspondence* I, 128–34; Mss. of the Marquis of Abergavenny, No. 247, (not printed in H.M.C. *Abergavenny Mss.*, p. 28).

[2] H.M.C. *Appendix to 14th Report, Pt. IX*, Emly Mss. pp. 156–57; Add. Mss. 38,307, f. 154; Corr. George III, v, 30.

intransigeant instruction which prescribed the terms of his commission for the ensuing period. In a formal and final manner he was now told to "oppose and resist" all constitutional attacks "in every stage of their progress, in order to prevent if possible any proposition for innovation upon, or alteration in, the Constitution, from being transmitted to this Country".

The stage was now set, and the effect of the parliamentary recess in Dublin had been to produce a hardening of opinion on both sides. The Irish house of commons resumed its session, and Grattan on 11 April gave notice that on the 19th he would move certain resolutions which would be declaratory of the rights of Ireland. When it is recalled that Dunning had carried his resolutions in the British house of commons on 6 and 10 April, it will be realised that events were moving to a climax in both countries at the same time. The discomfiture of the North ministry in England gave a further stimulus to the activity of the patriots at the other side of the Irish Sea. By this time the influence, and even the terminology, of the Yorkshire movement were beginning to have perceptible incidental effects on the Irish agitation. There had been a stir even early in January when the town of Newry, acting on an invitation from a committee in Belfast, had held a meeting to discuss the formation of Committees of Correspondence. Newry had agreed upon the necessity for such committees, but it had been possible to secure a decision that these should deal with "commercial not political" affairs. During the parliamentary recess Ireland exulted in the news that thirty counties had joined the Yorkshire petitioning movement, and that these paid over seven-eighths of the land-tax, representing ten times more property than the silent counties and a hundred times more than all the protestors in England. The freeholders of county Armagh spoke of the necessity of "the Constitution resuming its true and native vigour". A petition from Newry in April drew attention to the fact "that no motion has hitherto been made for retrenching the Expenditure of public Money." Another petition demanded the "total extinction of all superfluous Places and Pensions". When on 12 April Barry Yelverton announced his intention of raising the question of Poyning's Law, he declaimed against the influence of the crown and said that "When Great

Britain was effecting the great Business of Reformation in the Constitution, it would be wise in this kingdom to follow the Example and make the best advantage of so auspicious a moment."[1] On 17 April leave was given to bring in a bill to limit the number of placemen who should be allowed to sit in parliament.

The crisis had come, but Buckingham was not submerged by it, and in the parliamentary proceedings of April 1780 he avoided the formal defeats as well as the extremities of disgrace which had been suffered by Lord North in this period in England. On 19 April Grattan proposed his famous resolutions, the chief of which ran as follows:

> That His most excellent Majesty, by and with the consent of the Lords and Commons of Ireland, are the only power competent to enact laws to bind Ireland.

In spite of the fact that he made on this occasion one of the great speeches of his life, and in spite of his argument that Britain could not refuse to the loyal Irish the thing that they had already been prepared to concede to the rebel colonists in America, he failed to carry his motion. It was agreed that all property would be insecure if the validity of English statute-law in Ireland were called in question; but the result was not determined by any hostility to the nature of his proposal; the truth was that men who at this moment hardly dared to resist the popular cry or oppose the demand in itself could be induced to question the expediency of the motion. This was made more easy because it was discovered that under the date 26 July 1641 there was "an equivalent resolution already in the Journals of the House".

A few days later on the 26th, the motion on the subject of Poyning's Law was defeated by 130 votes to 105, partly on the view that it was inexpedient to change the constitution at the moment, partly because it proved possible to defend the intervention of the Irish privy council in the processes of legislation, and partly because it could be argued that that council under the existing Lord Lieutenant had merited better treatment than the proposers of the motion

---

[1] Report of parliamentary debate in *Hibernian Journal*, 12–14 April.

were giving it. So far as the formal issue was concerned, therefore, Buckingham had just managed to keep head above water in parliament and had checked the enemies of government on those very points which had formed the subject of agitation at the time of the recent recess. An initial attempt to secure an Irish Mutiny Bill had been thwarted for the time being. The house of commons had even decided to grant the government one of its primary objects—the supplies for the eighteen months that had been left unprovided for in the previous November—so that the enemies of the administration were deprived of one of their powerful weapons. This, wrote Buckingham, "puts an end to the attempt to repeat the expedient of short money bills or the idea of annual Parliaments". On 7 May, in fact, Lord Hillsborough congratulated Buckingham on his parliamentary success. The Irish opposition papers complained that Irish politics had run back into their old course.

Once again, however, the story had shown—and was to make still more manifest very soon—the power and importance of extraparliamentary opinion. The administration in Dublin had prevented those actual votes in parliament which would have brought constitutional issues directly to a head and might have produced a deadlock or a more catastrophic cleavage between Great Britain and Ireland; but the popular leaders had secured all the advantages of a great demonstration, and, by showing how far public opinion had moved, had contrived that it should move further still—had given it in fact an additional momentum. The essential paradox of the situation lay in the fact that men who had initially deprecated the raising of further controversies in Ireland tended to be moved by the force of the agitation that arose, the pressure of opinion about them, or the course of parliamentary debate, and would find themselves converted to the programme of the reformers. They would promise their support to the administration, but many did desert at the crucial moment, so that Buckingham would cry out: "How can the Lord Lieutenant speak with confidence upon any point at a period when no fix'd principles direct, no obligations attach, and no assurances can bind?"

Most curious of all—the government might still retain its majority and prevent a proposal from being carried; but the men who declared their regret that constitutional issues were being raised at this moment, the men who threw the proposals out on grounds of their inexpediency, often did not choose or did not dare to make a direct attack upon the principle of the measures themselves. They regretted Grattan's resolution concerning legislative independence and were willing to assist the government in its attempt to evade the whole issue; but they made it clear in the debate of the 19th that if the issue were presented directly to them after all, they would have to join Grattan in his demand for emancipation. "It is with the utmost concern," wrote Buckingham,

> that I must acquaint your Lordship that . . . the sense of the House against the obligation of any statutes of the Parliament of Great Britain within this kingdom is represented to me to have been almost unanimous.

Lord Charlemont was correct therefore when he called the 19th of April "a great day" because "though not precisely in the manner intended, we most certainly gained our point." As an index of the general state of opinion that debate was disastrous for the government, and its effects were to become clearly apparent in the more critical controversy which was to supervene.

The maximum intensity of the crisis in this period was to come once again upon a particular type of issue for which the ordinary resources of government influence and parliamentary management were inadequate. The very argument from expediency, which had helped to defeat the Declaration of Independence and the attack on Poyning's Law, now worked in reverse; for in this particular instance it pointed to a legislative innovation as a thing not merely expedient but urgently necessary. The issue in question on this occasion was the demand for an Irish Mutiny Act, a demand which —since it postulated the invalidity of the English Act in Ireland— had already been declared by Hillsborough to be "big with the greatest mischief". It happened that in this particular case extra-parliamentary opinion possessed an effective weapon and was able to secure that its wishes should make some impression upon the proceedings in Parliament; and a remarkable example was given of the way in which in the eighteenth century the operation of government depended on a form of general consent, the importance of which might only be vividly realized when on some particular occasion it was withdrawn. On 8 April the Lord Lieutenant had to report that deserters from the King's army were being discharged by justices of the peace on the ground that the British Mutiny Act was invalid in Ireland. On 18 April he announced that "some friends of Government, amongst whom was General Cuninghame" believed it necessary to take action "to prevent the danger which may arise from doubts in the army and the disinclination of magistrates to enforce the Act of Mutiny". When Grattan proposed his Declaration of Independence on 19 April "many gentlemen who were magistrates declared they would never execute for the future any part of the British Act of Mutiny." The people of Ireland were later called upon "to follow the great Example of the Members of the House of Commons" in this matter, and at a meeting of servants of the crown at Dublin Castle on 21 April "a total disbanding of the army" was feared, for "the soldiers ... will desert in great numbers," since "few magistrates . . . would enforce the Mutiny Act." It was also feared that officers might be "prosecuted for the inflicting Court-Martial sentences" and that juries would "find indictments and verdicts" against them every time.[1] On 27 April the *Freeman's Journal* contained a threat of prosecution against any magistrate or civil officer who would presume to detain a certain named deserter "on the pretended authority of an English law".

The Lord Lieutenant, who was still under orders to resist every constitutional innovation, sent repeated demands for further instructions, and became almost hysterical in his importunity, while securing—only with the greatest difficulty—that the parliamentary motion on this subject should be postponed until the instructions arrived. He showed how in 1692 England had been in favour of a separate Mutiny Act for Ireland. He reported a revised opinion of his own Lord Chancellor who, though he thought that the Mutiny Act travelled with the King's soldiers wherever they might be, now

---

[1] *Grattan Memoirs*, II, 71 *et seqq.*, and 418 *et seqq.*, which also reprints a number of Buckingham's despatches relating to the parliamentary affairs of April and May.

suggested that it would be expedient to have an enactment since it was so necessary "to quieten the question". The British cabinet decided on 6 May "that the passing a Mutiny Bill in Ireland, upon a supposition that the Mutiny Act passed in the British Parliament is not binding there" came within the class of constitutional innovations which the Lord Lieutenant had been ordered to resist. Buckingham read this decision as an order to oppose an Irish Mutiny Bill, and kept the instruction secret for a time, lest the news should hamper the passage of his money bills in Dublin. For once he had failed to read between the lines of his instructions and to find a loop-hole that existed there; and it was Lord Hillsborough himself who had to point out that he had mistaken their tenour and that he must consider the terms of them again. Henceforward Buckingham devoted his attention to securing such a draft of an Irish Mutiny Act as would not contain the implication that the English one was invalid. He was nervous even now concerning the interpretation of his instructions, for he knew that the movers of the bill were seeking in reality to undermine the validity of British legislation—he did not feel quite sure that the British ministry would approve of the way in which he was taking advantage of the loophole. Therefore with one hand he guided a band of friends who sought to secure the drafting of an Irish Mutiny Bill in terms which would be acceptable in England. With the other hand he still felt it necessary to repel the whole project of a legislative enactment in the Irish parliament. To the ministers whose anger still made him tremble he was eager to report that Sir Richard Heron had voted against the bill, though behind the scenes he had been working for it himself.[1]

Before these developments had taken place in the closing days of May and the early days of June, Buckingham had suffered a more palpable defeat in a further matter—and this time the issue was one

---

[1] At this period, i.e. towards the close of May, William Knox was sent to Ireland, presumably to make observations on the spot and to give advice. He reported that "Lord Buckinghamshire is not ignorant of anything it behoves him to know . . . and were he unconnected with the families he is related to in Ireland and had an abler Secretary, no man is fitter for Lord Lieutenant in the House of Peers, but Conolly and Heron are two millstones about his neck." H.M.C. *Stopford Sackville Mss.*, I, 270; H.M.C. *Various Mss.*, VI, Knox Mss. 167–68, 238.

which admitted of neither disguise nor evasion. A direct and un-avoidable clash of interests had occurred between Great Britain and Ireland in regard to the sugar duties which the latter country was expected to impose as a result of her admission to direct trade with the overseas colonies. On 17 May the administration in Dublin managed after great difficulty to secure that the additional duty on refined sugar imported from Britain should be 5/10¼ per cwt., as the ministry in London required, but there had been a motion that the sum should be altered to £2/1/0, and "several old Friends and old Servants of Government" had supported proposals ranging from 9/3 to 11/1, which were only defeated by a narrow margin. It is surprising that Buckingham should have secured this initial success in favour of the British figure; for a straight clash of interests had occurred and the Irish were clamouring to have the higher duty imposed.

The success did not prove to be lasting, however, for, as Sir Richard Heron reported later, "The truth is, that a real and general alarm took place." Within two days of the committee's decision the country was in an uproar, and Heron was reporting that non-importation agreements were being proposed "by many merchants who are usually very moderate". The merchants of Dublin announced their opinion that the smaller duty which England demanded was a "measure destructive of the sugar refinery of the kingdom". It would frustrate all the advantage Ireland could hope to gain from the plantation trade, since sugar was "the principal return to be obtained for any manufactures of Ireland". The British government, it was alleged, were deliberately taking away with the one hand all the benefits of the commercial concessions which they had granted with the other in the previous December.

"The Duke of Leinster and his friends, and some other gentlemen" announced on 19 May that they could not support the government in any attempt to resist the re-committal of the question of the sugar duty. When the matter was referred back to the committee, Barry Yelverton declared that "free trade" had been "the *lullaby* which hushed your necessities to rest" and proposed that it should be hurled back in the face of the British unless a duty of

16/7½ were accepted. It was felt that if the original figure—5/10¼ —were retained the Irish refineries would be ruined within the eighteen months that would probably have to elapse before the direct import from the colonies had been properly established. The committee regarded 16/7½ as "amounting to a prohibition", however, and a compromise duty of 12/- was carried by 107 votes to 71.

In regard to the Mutiny Bill and the duty on the importation of British refined sugar, Buckingham was compelled to bow to the storm and face the displeasure of the ministry in England. The peculiar force which extra-parliamentary opinion possessed in the former case, and the way in which the public protests secured the reversal of an initial decision in favour of England in the latter case, confirm the general impression that during the development of this large-scale crisis even the Irish parliament could not escape the effects of a form of pressure which was now being exercised upon it from the country at large.

§III. THE GORDON RIOTS
AND THE RECOVERY OF THE MINISTRY

The upheaval in Great Britain had begun to subside. It had been provoked by the wretchedness and inefficiency of a government which it had seemed impossible to destroy by normal parliamentary methods. Some men had begun to be weary of the tension, however; some were apprehensive when they discovered the radical nature of the constitutional changes which the Yorkshire and Middlesex leaders were in reality working to secure. The adventitious strength which the radicals had hoped to gain from the popular discontent and the widespread exasperation had proved a disappointment, and gone was the hope of a second Runnymede, an immediate effective display of the power of the awakened people. What was left was the band of convinced parliamentary reformers —these now increased in number, stimulated by contact with one another, and strengthened by that cellular organization which the Yorkshire movement had produced and which persisted in the local Committees and constitutional clubs. So there came into existence that national movement of parliamentary reform which, having failed to achieve its ends by *coup d'état*, learned that education and propaganda were its essential work for the time being.

Before the turmoil had ceased, however, there occurred at the opening of June those Gordon riots which in a different field made clear the dangers of the policy of association and the sinister consequences of the attempt to make effective the pressure of extra-parliamentary opinion upon the House of Commons. The story has often been told and lies largely outside the range of our present discussion; but we may note certain features of it which throw light on the issue presented by both the Irish and the English aspects of our narrative. When the Catholic Relief Bill was introduced into the house of lords on 25 May 1778, the Bishop of Peterborough, who declared himself a "friend to the principle of this Bill," expressed the wish that it had "been brought in sooner . . . that it might not have appeared to be hurried through both Houses". He regretted that there was no time to consider and weigh the matter and "to know the general disposition of the nation". He stated the necessity of preventing "alarms of imaginary danger"

with which ignorance and malice have heretofore, and may again kindle such a flame, as the authority of law will find it difficult to extinguish.

After the Gordon riots he stated that he would have said much more even at this early date, if he had not feared that his words would generate the very kind of commotion which he had apprehended; for he had thought that "nothing but the phrenzy of religious zeal was wanting to fill up the measure of our national calamities." His warning was impressively prophetic, and the Protestant petition that occasioned the Gordon riots specifically complained that the Relief Act "was so suddenly introduced and so hastily passed, before the sense of the nation at large could be obtained or any opposition formed to it". The very unanimity of government and opposition—of the majority of the governing class in one of their most enlightened acts of leadership—proved to be a pitfall, offending not only rational prejudice, but deep dark passions, strange as Nazi hatreds, and as baffling as anti-semitism. In June 1780 the Bishop of Peterborough underlined the moral. Attention should be paid not only to the abstract justice of a measure but to the possible effects on the prejudices and passions of a people.

When the repeal of the analogous penal laws in Scotland—which were prior to the Union—was proposed, a Protestant Association was formed and early in 1779 there occurred those riots in Edinburgh and Glasgow which led to the abandonment of the intention. This was often quoted as a demoralizing precedent for the abdication of governmental and parliamentary leadership in the face of violence, and Charles James Fox pointed out that "it became the honour and dignity of Parliament . . . not to be deterred by little insurrections in a small corner of the empire." In fact, the terrorized Roman Catholics of Scotland had themselves requested that the plans for their relief should be postponed; but the incident had its regrettable consequences, for the Protestant Association in that country, having felt its power, moved forward to an aggressive policy and demanded, for example, a more rigorous enforcement of the law in future. In February 1779, a Protestant Association was founded in London, and on 12 November Lord George Gordon, who had distinguished himself in the Scottish movement, was asked to become president of the English body, which grew with great rapidity. It was less than a fortnight later that the Bishop of Peterborough, in another of his prophetic utterances, pointed out that, "however weak and inconsiderable they may be in their beginnings", such associations could become "of the most serious importance in their consequences". It happened that on the same day Gordon was issuing the warning that the government would find 120,000 men at his back. As on other occasions in other centuries, the idol of the masses in a time of hysteria was a man psychologically unbalanced, an orator who could be quietly moving at one time, but picturesque in his very violence at another.

The Protestant Association proved to be more firm and formidable than the purely political body which Christopher Wyvill had inaugurated at York. It reached a lower social class and it was often noted that its petition contained in many cases not signatures but the marks of men who could neither read or write. Once again there was an attempt not merely to inform parliament of a grievance but to organize what we to-day so often call a pressure-group. It was afterwards said on Lord George Gordon's behalf that when the petition was to be presented to the house of commons he was persuaded to secure the attendance of petitioners in person, lest he should be charged with offering a document supported only by pretended signatures. If so, this man who had often talked bloodshed and even of the decapitation of the papistical George III made a virtue of necessity, for he announced at a final meeting in the Coachmakers' Hall on 29 May that if less than 20,000 attended him he "would not present their petition".

For his part he would run all hazards with the people, and if the people were too lukewarm to run all hazards with him they might get another President, for he would tell them candidly that he was not a lukewarm man himself, and that if they meant to spend their time in mock debate and idle opposition they might get another leader.

In this, as in the case of the Yorkshire movement—and particularly the case of the Westminster meeting of 6 April—it was the unrehearsed results of the measure that were chiefly to be apprehended. If we accept the accounts of those observers who said that it was a respectable hymn-singing throng, dressed in their Sunday suits, which assembled in St. George's Fields on 2 June, it was still true that the "weavers from Spittle Fields were mustering" and disorderly elements either joined the procession or swelled the mob in Palace Yard. The analogy with the events in Dublin on 15 November 1779 is illustrated by the fact that a section of the crowd early burst into Westminster Hall and stopped the proceedings of the Court of King's Bench, at a moment when Dunning, the seconder of the Catholic Relief Bill of 1778, happened to be speaking. It is seen again when the violence of the mob was directed against members as they approached both houses, and particularly against those who had favoured indulgence to the Roman Catholics. The proceedings of the house of lords, where the Duke of Richmond was proposing parliamentary reform and universal manhood suffrage, had to be stopped owing to the interruptions, though the peers were able to steal away by nine o'clock. The house of commons was kept imprisoned until between ten and eleven, and for a long time it was impossible to divide on the date for the consideration of the petition, since the lobby could not be cleared; while Gordon was able from time to time to resume contact with the mob, to inform them of the degree of success which attended their business, and to announce the names of those who were advocating postponement of the matter. Although the charge was denied it is not easy to resist the evidence that the later attacks on the chapels of the foreign ministers—chapels that were often attended by well-to-do Roman Catholics in London—were incited by a remark which would certainly have been typical of Gordon, to the effect that "The Scotch had no redress until they pulled down mass-houses."

All this occurred on Friday, 2 June, and on the following day there seems to have been an idea that the city was beginning to settle down after the storm. It was during the course of Sunday, 4 June, that more sinister developments occurred and we begin to realize the subtle nature of those sanctions and that self-discipline upon which the order of society and the peace of a great capital depend. The weak conduct of the city magistrates, some of whom were prominent in the "No-Popery" movement, convinced both the ministers on the one hand and the trouble-makers on the other hand, that they were in actual complicity with the rioters. There were sinister rumours on occasion to the effect that the opposite faction were about to raise a mob and that Presbyterian chapels were to be burned by the Roman Catholics in revenge. The house of Commons had postponed the consideration of the Protestant petition only until the following Tuesday, and efforts were being made to see that the mob should be reassembled for the occasion. Blue cockades became more numerous in the streets, apparently because they were a guarantee against molestation—a tendency which was calculated to develop further by its own internal logic. The whole predicament became more serious when the mob turned its attention to the rescue of the few men who had been apprehended, or to the punishment of those constables, justices and military officers who had sought to check the outrages; while it was difficult to secure evidence that the men who had been arrested had not been innocent bystanders. It had been clear on the first day that a concourse "so greatly beyond all former and common mobs" would have defeated any precautions which a ministry could have dared to take when there was great prejudice against the resort to military force; but now, when the magistrates were so often weak—as they had been in Dublin and apparently in Edinburgh—the military might have to submit to insults while unable to defend themselves, and very soon the outrages were so numerous that the government could not find the troops to dispatch to places which were known in advance to be threatened. This failure on the part of government to perform one of its primary functions led to forms of precaution or self-help which were calculated to make the situation worse. Those whose houses were endangered by neighbouring fires would request that the hoses should not be allowed to play, those who knew themselves threatened would refuse to have soldiers stationed on the spot, lest they should invite the hostility of the rioters. Some Roman Catholics would ply the mob with ale in a desperate attempt to stave off the threatening disasters. The point was to be reached at which the city authorities would actually release the prisoners in their charge, in order to save the prisons from being set on fire. The situation was rendered more difficult by the long-standing anti-government spirit in those sections of the London population that made most noise, as well as by more than a decade of incitement and agitation among them.

Between that date and the war of 1939 it is much rarer than many people realize to find a European capital which exhibits the scenes or goes through the terrors experienced by London during the Gordon riots. The memory of these days had a great part in that fear of popular demonstrations which seized upon both the ministry and the governing classes in England at the time of the French Revolution. It is not to the point if historians condemn the younger Pitt on the ground that there is no evidence of a large-scale combination for the purpose of overthrowing the existing order by violence. What men were afraid of were the unrehearsed results of various forms of association and agitation; and it was the Gordon riots that repeatedly haunted their minds. It is possible that all the extra-parliamentary agitations of the years 1779–80, and the Gordon riots themselves, were part of the growing pains of a new type of state necessitated by the increase in population, the great agglomerations in towns, and the changes in the technique of life itself. It is significant that from this time until the year 1848, comparatively small risings of the mob, processions that ran amok and almost incidental riots in the streets could overthrow a government, so inadequate for the new age was the policing of towns and cities. The evil was later remedied by the strengthening of the arm of government itself, and at the same time by the regularizing of the power of extra-parliamentary opinion, as wider classes were brought into a more genuine sense of co-operation with the ends of the state. At the same time Lord Gower, when he resigned from the ministry in October 1779, had complained that there was no "discipline" in the state. Thurlow in the following month had insisted that the strength of a government must be measured by its power to impose itself on all parts of the empire, to secure respect from the great bodies in the kingdom, and to keep its hold on the fleets and armies. During the Gordon riots it was complained that all the nerves of the state had become relaxed. The ministry of North was partly responsible for the evil, but the opposition whigs had also contributed to a loosening of the fabric of the state. And it was perhaps the fault of both that parliament and the organs of government were brought too generally into contempt.

If we consider the Irish movement, the Yorkshire Association and the Gordon riots together it is difficult to escape the issue that the years 1779–80 see an unusual stirring of the waters, as extra-parliamentary opinion not only finds a voice but discovers what as yet are irregular means of making itself effective at the very seat of government. Because recognized channels have not been found for it—normal machinery has not been produced to register its direction and to measure its power—it runs to untidiness and tends to resort to forms of menace, so that even the Yorkshire movement tries to rattle the sabre it does not possess, and seeks to dismay the enemy by unspecified threats. The unintended disorders and the unpredictable accidents that are likely to occur under these conditions were a special danger at a time when the paralysis that afflicted the arms of government, the bitterness of the conflict amongst the governing classes, the continued disparagement of the house of commons, and the special problems of the capital cities were weakening the brakes of the whole vehicle, making the traditional inhibitions less effective, and robbing authority of its former majesty. All this was happening at a time when the country was failing—and suffering—in a major war. It represented a problem which in any case could hardly be solved until the fabric of the State was renewed, the new forces regularized and the structure of government brought into line with the new conditions—in other words, until parliamentary reform was achieved. The accident that many people feared in this period— and feared again over a decade later, though many historians have pooh-poohed the fear—did actually occur when the Gordon riots reduced London to terror. This helps to explain why the country consented to endure the ministry of Lord North for nearly two years more.

The restoration of order vindicated the authority of government and raised the prestige of the King. The whole ordeal was taken into that body of experience which Englishmen thereafter had to reflect upon; and if Wilkes himself showed his zeal in the suppression of the riots, Mr. de Castro has noted that there were also some of his followers who suffered a change of heart. Volunteer defensive associations assisted in the defeat of the rioters, and this in itself might have led to danger. But when Lord Amherst issued orders directed against any persons whatsoever who were found with arms in the streets, he had to face a parliamentary storm for a contravention of the Englishman's right to carry arms in self-defence, a privilege which had been guaranteed by the Bill of Rights itself. The radicals took the opportunity to make great play with the Englishman's right to carry arms, and one discerns something of a desire that England, like Ireland, should have armed associations. The total effect of the Gordon riots, however, was to make the average Englishman a little more afraid of playing with fire.

Since we cannot rid ourselves of our knowledge of the issue of the War of American Independence it is not easy for us to realize to-day the further increase in credit which the ministry was to secure as the result of a success in the very field of its main weakness, namely, in the conduct of the colonial struggle. The importance of the news of the capitulation of Charleston, which arrived a few days after the quelling of the Gordon riots, can be measured by the anxieties expressed in correspondence and in the newspapers in the preceding weeks, when various rumours and sinister doubts were abroad. Lord George Germain repeatedly said that he nursed no vain dream of an actual conquest of the American continent by British forces, but conceived this country as rather assisting the mass of the loyal Americans to liberate themselves from the tyranny of a revolutionary Congress. The success in South Carolina was significant in the hope and the opportunity which it presented for precisely this policy. It seemed that at last the turning-point had come. Even Rigby declared that if it did not prove to be the turning-point he would consider the further prosecution of the war an act of madness.

In the middle of June arrived news from Dublin which showed that the lessons of the Gordon riots had had their part in preventing a serious disturbance. Thousands of journeymen had assembled in Phoenix Park to protest against the passage of a bill on the subject of combinations. Dublin had been "filled with consternation"; the military had been held in readiness; the Volunteers had appeared in the streets for the purpose of maintaining order. It appears to have been the intervention of Grattan himself and Sir Boyle Roche which prevented the march upon the city—a march from which the most serious consequences were apprehended. In regard to the Mutiny Bill and the sugar duty, which had given the Earl of Buckinghamshire so much anguish, and which had been transmitted to London, the British ministry showed a firmness which was rewarded by a further political victory. After ignoring the Lord Lieutenant's frantic appeals for haste, and his repeated warning that any amendment of the former measure would be disastrous in its consequences, they altered the Mutiny Bill to make it perpetual—Buckingham having failed in an unconvincing attempt to secure this amendment himself at the last moment in Dublin.

The mere rumour of this decision induced Grattan to declare that the passage of the amended bill by the Irish Parliament would be followed by a secession of the Patriots from that body and an appeal to the people. Yet on 17 August the perpetual Mutiny Act was carried by 115 votes to 63 and "the spirits of the opposition appeared to be greatly sunk." And whatever part may have been played by corruption in securing this result, it was also true that the factors previously operating against England now in a paradoxical manner worked in her favour; for the old argument from expediency—the argument that the needs of the army demanded the enactment of military legislation for Ireland—though it had favoured the passage of the original bill was equally valid in favour of the revised one. Similarly the English Privy Council reduced the duty on refined English sugar from 12/- to 9/2⅜, and this was carried in Committee in Dublin by 119 to 38 votes. The view was held that, in spite of the cries of anger, the upheaval in the country which Buckingham had apprehended was not likely in reality to take place at this time. The parliamentary session had involved the administration in heavy commitments to individuals. Buckingham was succeeded a little later by the Earl of Carlisle, who took William Eden as Chief Secretary, though this latter arrangement nearly came to shipwreck at the last moment through Eden's tenacity in regard to his personal interests as a supporter of the ministry. Wedderburn had become Chief Justice of the Common Pleas at the time of the Gordon riots.

A number of new factors, therefore, suggested the wisdom of a dissolution of parliament in the summer, and help to explain the success of the government in the general election of September 1780. But, if the immediate crisis was surmounted, it must not be imagined that either the Yorkshire Association or the Irish Volunteer movement had come to an end.

APPENDIX A

Returning from Switzerland while still almost a boy, Lord Mahon in September 1774 had stood as a Wilkite candidate for Westminster, promising to promote bills to destroy or diminish bribery and all undue influence in elections, to strive for the repeal of the Septennial Act, "thereby to strengthen and encrease the due and necessary relation between the representative and constituent bodies", and to seek the repeal of the Quebec Act and the expunging of the vote of the house of commons which had unseated Wilkes. His relationship to Lord Chatham had been one of his political assets, and certain members of the Grenville family had encouraged his attempt to gain a parliamentary seat, after his initial failure in Westminster. John Robinson mentions him as one of the people whom there was an intention of nominating as the candidate for Middlesex in the by-election of 1779.

He quickly took an interest in the Yorkshire movement and strove to promote a meeting in the county of Kent, but in a letter to Lord Shelburne on 17 January he spoke of the difficulty of getting "these slow Animals called Counties to move", and expressed the fear that the petition from Kent would not be ready for presentation to the house of commons by 8 February, when he thought that not only the Yorkshire petition but also the rest of them were due to be delivered. He met some resistance in his locality, and on 23 February we find him indignantly repudiating the suggestion of the Duke of Dorset that he was proposing to pack the proposed county meeting with the freeholders under his influence. It is clear, however, from a letter which was addressed to him at a later date, that a party of freeholders in Kent were ready to accept his candidate at a parliamentary election and looked upon him as their leader in the petitioning movement itself. Furthermore, Mahon suggested to Shelburne on 17 February, that since the county of Buckingham was proving backward, he himself was thinking of taking action there, "where," he said, "we have an estate". And later in the year it became apparent that he was ready to enter the political game in Buckinghamshire—to collect his forces for a conflict of local "influence" on behalf of the Yorkshire Association—in the familiar eighteenth century way.

In spite of his efforts in January he did not secure a meeting in Kent until 4 March, and even when this was brought about he found himself faced with serious opposition. One section of the gathering desired not merely to petition the house of commons but also to form a local Committee; and of this more radical section he was the leader. The others objected to the idea of establishing machinery for ulterior action and adopted a different petition of their own. Each party then set about collecting signatures in the county, and Mahon, who secured the formation of a Committee and was made the chairman of it, claimed to have collected 3,120 names, while, according to his report, the rival party only gained 1,830. The Committee usually met in London, and Mahon was one of its representatives at the General Meeting of Deputies.[1]

In regard to Buckinghamshire, Mahon's original complaint had not been unreasonable—here the Yorkshire movement had been slow in producing any effect. On 8 February Earl Temple, speaking somewhat by way of apology in the house of lords, explained how he had determined to leave the people "to judge for themselves"; and not until the 26th had a meeting taken place, and a Committee been formed, just in time for the appointment of representatives to the General Meeting of Deputies.[2] It was to become apparent that the attitude of Earl Temple was of major importance even in the conduct of a body so seemingly democratic as this, but it soon transpired that Lord Mahon, for his part, became the leading spirit amongst the promoters of the Association on the local Committee. It is curious to note that in regard to a motion that was extraneous to his main purpose Mahon made the confession to Shelburne:

[1] The activities of the Committee, the resolutions of the general meetings, and some of the associated correspondence are in the Chevening Mss., especially the volume entitled "Resolves of the Committee of the County of Kent".

[2] According to *The Yorkshire Freeholder*, No. x, 23 March 1780, p. 62, one hundred and ten freeholders summoned the meeting, and it was "equally attended by the Nobility and Gentlemen of the largest Property in that County, as if it had been originally called by themselves".

I should prefer *not* to be forward . . . in the Committee of a County where I am not resided and where I have not property enough to assume any kind of lead.

To this self-denying ordinance he made a specific exception, however, in respect of anything that related to the Plan of Association. He was prepared, indeed, to appeal on behalf of his plan to the general county meeting over the heads of a Committee that had decided against this policy.

His connection with Lord Chatham had brought him into association with the party that came under the leadership of Lord Shelburne, which was more congenial to his radical views than the Rockinghamite party in any case. With Lord Shelburne, as well as with some of the radical writers who were attached with him, he established therefore a confidential relationship. On 1 April he wrote to Shelburne, reporting that all was well on the Buckinghamshire Committee—Earl Temple, he said, was amenable on "all the Points" of the Yorkshire Plan of Association, though he had some reasonable objections in regard to certain words in the preamble. It was on 4 April that Mahon learned, to his great surprise, that Temple was in disagreement with him after all—unwilling to see a hundred additional knights of the shire, and unable to reconcile himself to the idea of imposing a "test" on candidates for election to parliament. Mahon had the impression that the Earl had been influenced by his brother, Thomas Grenville, who, as we have seen, had recently been running more closely with Fox and the Rockinghamites.

Mahon unfortunately had no time to spare. The Buckinghamshire Committee were due to consider the proposed Plan of Association that very day; and Mahon, realizing only at the last moment that now the vote would be bound to go against him, found it necessary to use every effort to secure a postponement of any decision. It is interesting to note that when it came to the point a supporter of the movement—in the very act of reversing his tactics—could use against its defects in procedure the very arguments which were so often employed by its enemies. Mahon secured the postponement "by perseverance and by stating the impropriety of coming to Resolutions of such Consequence . . . in so very thin a Committee [i.e. of fourteen or fifteen] without any kind of previous notice of the Object of the Meeting". The matter was deferred but Mahon and Shelburne were unhappy that even the renewed meeting of the Committee was to be held in London; for in this particular case it was difficult to raise a rebellion against Earl Temple unless the ordinary freeholders from the county could be called to the standard.

"Lord T[emple] will not fail to bring all his Friends, I imagine," wrote Mahon. "We must make a Point to do the same." Shelburne was to see that the "Wycombe Yeomen" came up to London. It was important to gain the Duke of Grafton, or to secure a line from him, as his opinion would influence other people's. Mahon interviewed this man and that. "I will do all I possibly can to carry this business down to the Committee," he wrote. Shelburne, replying to this letter, declared: "I cannot discover in the plan of the Yorkshire Association a single exceptionable principle." He confessed, however, that he saw no chance of inducing the yeomen of the district to go to London.

Even when he had been defeated on the Committee, Mahon declared his intention of proposing the Yorkshire Plan of Association to the general meeting of the county on his own behalf. That this produced great consternation amongst the Rockinghamites is shown by the fact that Edmund Burke wrote an address to the chairman of the meeting, moving tactfully, not declaring against parliamentary reform as such, but rather admitting the propriety of it if "a great and decided majority" were to desire it. Burke confessed that if the voice of the nation demanded it, and even if it were mistaken in desiring it, the country would be in a grievous condition supposing there existed any power sufficiently great to defeat its purpose. On the other hand he required "timely notice of meeting", and careful preparation in open Committees; and he pointed out[1] that when parts of the system of government are viewed in isolation they may seem to be self-evidently wrong, but

---

[1] *Works* (1812), IX, 316–22, Burke made a long speech against frequent elections in reply to Sawbridge's annual motion for shorter parliaments on 8 May. *Parliamentary History*, XXI, 603–15.

when the whole constitution is "viewed together" the self-same things may prove to be useful, if only as a remedy against a worse evil.

The more moderate party triumphed at the general county meeting on 13 April, when approval was secured for a Plan of Association which confined itself to the question of public economy, while professing "all confidence and earnest hope and expectation from the wisdom of Parliament". Mahon was still undaunted, however, and carried the campaign into a second meeting which was held on 27 May, and to which the Duke of Portland, in his turn, addressed a long letter on behalf of the Rockinghamites.[1] When Temple put the more moderate schemes to the meeting, Mahon made a great oration, saying that he would "not subscribe to any paper that contained such professions of confidence in Parliament"; and proposing a scheme similar to that of Yorkshire. By this time both Burke's economical reform and Dunning's parliamentary campaign had come to ruin, so that he was not without matter for his argument. According to the detailed report drawn up on behalf of his party:

The two Plans of Association were then separately proposed to the Meeting. That moved by Lord Mahon had a prodigious majority in its favour upon a show of hands; though the Chairman, who himself voted on Lord Temple's side, declined declaring which had the majority of hands for it.

The result was that in fact two Associations claimed to represent the county of Buckingham, one standing for public economy, while the other stood for parliamentary reform.[2]

In his own county of Kent Mahon met with similar difficulties. At a general meeting, which was not held until 31 July, resolutions in favour of parliamentary reform were actually carried; but the Committee on 22 April had only resolved to put the propositions to the meeting, and no Plan of Association was adopted.

[1] *Rockingham Memoirs*, II, 410–15.
[2] There is a long account of Mahon's speech and of the meeting of 27 May in the *York Chronicle*, 16 June. In the list of counties given, *ibid.*, 8 Dec. 1780, Buckinghamshire appears as having both kinds of Association.

APPENDIX B

The relations of Horace Walpole with the Yorkshire movement throw light not only on the man himself but on this whole chapter of English history. He was a whig of the old type, and in 1756 he had written,

> On each side my bed I have hung the *Magna Charta* and the warrant for King Charles's execution, on which I have written *Major Charta*; as I believe, without the latter, the former by this time would be of very little importance.

He had always lacked the force of personality which the turmoil of political life required; but if once he had seemed to find compensation in the writing of memoirs he was now beginning to make further capital out of a lifetime spent in political observation, and to pose as something of an elder statesman. He, who had so often declared that the scramble of politics was not to his taste, could now write to William Mason: "Oh, my dear Sir, allow me, who have never budged from the scene of action, to know, at least to think I know, more of these practices than you, who have been warbling in immaculate groves." His knowledge of the Yorkshire movement was usually accurate, if not complete, and he owed some of it to this old friend of his, William Mason, who had been collaborating with Wyvill almost from the very beginning.

As a whig, and now an enemy of George III, he had welcomed the Yorkshire movement from the very start. Since he had never forgiven the men who had overthrown his father—and hardly forgave even their successors, the Rockinghamites—he had rejoiced to see the way in which Wyvill had set out to avoid the patronage and escape from the predominance of the whig magnates.[1] We

---

[1] See, however, his *Last Journals*, 7 Jan. 1780: "The Lords at the head of the Opposition, I think, will find that by half-measures, and by waiting in hopes of favour with the King, that their influence will be wrenched out of their hands by lower and more popular demagogues, who will govern the Committees."

have seen, however, that he became perturbed when the local Committees proved to be so "ready to affect Parliamentary airs, and accordingly assumed cognizance of matters actually pending in Parliament". When they began to meddle with the constitution he was in dismay and presented the perfect picture of the older type of whiggism retreating from the semi-revolutionary ground in which at a moment of desperation it had been prepared to entrench itself.

"Bring them back, I beseech you, if you can, to some sobriety," he wrote to Mason on 22 March.

I lament the misapplication of the nation's returning sense; we shall be lost in controversy on speculative points, and the court will call itself defenders of the constitution . . .

The constitution "as it was at the end of the last reign" was his ideal; and he did not discern in his own time "the sublime legislators who can improve the system laid down at the revolution". On 13 April he wrote to Mason a letter which he refrained from sending because he afterwards came to think that in parts of it his language had been too strong. On this occasion he deplored the "speculative" and "experimental" proposals which had only divided the party.

I told you early that demagogues of districts would split us into petty factions and do the business of the court.

Seeing the resentment of Wyvill and his friends against the Rockinghamites he wrote in the same letter:

I, you well know, have not attachment to Lord Rockingham . . . yet I confess that I am shocked and disgusted that men, certainly honest and conscientious, and lovers of their country, should become unpopular, because they will not swallow implicitly novel nostrums . . . imposed arbitrarily and inquisitorially as articles of or as conditions of election.

Walpole in fact was turning against the Yorkshire movement altogether. Concerning Wyvill he had already written reproachfully to Mason: "You told me he was a sensible man." He later declared:

Any man who would dictate to a whole party ought to have given proofs of consummate abilities before he assumed so dictatorial a tone.

In his disillusionment we possess an epitome of his career and a pattern of his reactions to events; for in a curious way he would decide at such a point to withdraw into his shell again, and we can see the kind of treaty which, for his peace of mind, he made with destiny—the kind of face which he chose to show to the world. In the very letter in which he had written as from "the scene of action" to a Mason who had only been "warbling in immaculate groves", he could change his mood and deny even any wish to convert his friend; "you are an active man, and I only a speculative one". To the Rev. William Cole, who has already been quoted as an enemy of the petitioning movement in Cambridge, Walpole wrote:

I can as easily discern the faults on my own side, as on the other; nor would assist Whigs more than Tories in altering the constitution. . . . But a temperate man is not likely to be listened to in turbulent times; and when one has not youth and lungs, or ambition, to make oneself attended to, one can only be silent and lament, and preserve oneself blameless of any mischief that is done or attempted.

In this mood he could write to Mason: "I am not so convinced of the infallibility of my principles, of any modes of religion or government, as to risk the blood of a single being."

Whether he was too sympathetic in that he preferred friendships to politics, or too squeamish, so that he could argue: "Has Heaven authorized me to make this man happy at the expense of another man's life?"—whether he told himself that he was too old at sixty-two, or too much in love with his hobbies and his retirement, or too lacking in the force of personality which one must have "to make oneself attended to"—he found peace of mind in playing out his politics on paper, and was willing to watch the world slip into decay, taking refuge in the thought that he himself did not have the responsibility for it on his conscience. "As to this country, it is sunk perhaps never to rise again", he would write. "May not our globe be arrived at senility?"

My days are drawing to a conclusion and I wish to pass them with as little pain as I can and with as little vexation, consequently politics can but disturb them . . . I think we shall dwindle into an insignificant single island . . . we have neither wisdom nor virtue left.

To Mason he wrote in May:

The spirit you *raised* is evaporated or split into a thousand branches by mismanagement. . . . I can only lament that the sole chance we have had in so many years of recovering the vigour of this country has been thrown away.

INDEX

Absentees, Irish, 72, 76, 96, 98, 106, 142.

Acton: see Tyrone Ditches and Acton Volunteers.

Adam, William (1751–1839), speeches in House of Commons, 253, 330–31.

Addison, Joseph (1672–1719), 300.

"Alfred" (probably J. Jebb), 264 and n., 268.

Allan, Thomas, 175.

Almon, John (1737–1805), printer, 351–52.

American Colonies, Idea of Federal Union with the, 193, 261.

American Independence, War of, 16, 24, 27, 29–30, 68, 75,177–79, 83, 97, 138, 184, 212–13, 230–31, 248, 283, 319, 330, 358, 380–81; the opposition and the, 28, 41, 88, 166, 170, 172–73, 211, 213, 224, 226, 299, 352; Ireland and the, 72–73, 77, 84, 97, 157, 170, 354, 355; see also under Eden, W., Fox, C. J., and George III.

Amherst, Jeffrey Amherst (1717–97), 1st Baron, 54–56, 112, 125, 130, 380.

Annaly, John Gore (1718–84), 1st Baron, 145.

Armagh, county of, 108, 146, 363, 366.

Association, Idea of a National, 185, 191–93, 209 and n., 211, 248–49 260–63, 277, 297.

Other forms of, 257, 259–60, 264–66, 267 n., 345.

The Protestant, 310, 375–77.

The Yorkshire, v, 197, 209, 248–49, 252–68, 274–77, 282, 288–98, 311–12, 337–49, 382–91; the idea of restricting this to securing public economy, 278, 281, 290, 293, 387; see also under Wyvill, C.

Associations, in America, 209, 248, 263; In Ireland, 83–85, 115 n., 171–73, 208–09, 248, 263–65; see also under Volunteers.

Baker, William, representative for Hertfordshire at the General Meeting of Deputies, 277.

Barré, Isaac (1726–1807), 130, 196, 302, 314, 318.

Barrington, Admiral Hon. Samuel (1729–1800), 67–68.

Barrow, Dr., representative for Gloucestershire at the General Meeting of Deputies, 276.

Bathurst, Henry Bathurst (1714–94), 2nd Earl of, becomes President of the Council, 132.

Beauchamp, Francis Seymour-Conway (1743–1822), Lord (later 2nd Marquis of Hertford), 86, 174–75.

Bedford Whigs, 35, 44; and the militia bill, 46; and the reconstruction of the ministry, 69; attitude in October 1779, 121, 123, 133; plot to displace North, 124–28.

Bedfordshire and the Yorkshire movement, 337.

Belfast, 81–82, 364, 366.

Beresford, John (1738–1805), Commissioner of the Irish Revenue, and Robinson, 100–01, 108, 114, 148–50, 152, 154; on the Volunteer movement, 114; on the draft of Buckinghamshire's speech, 140; intrigues against Buckinghamshire, 150–52, 160, 356–58; candidate for the Chief Secretaryship, 357 n., 365.

Beverley and the Yorkshire petition, 207.